What Citizens Need to Know About World Affairs

SOCIAL ISSUES RESOURCES SERIES, INC.
P.O. BOX 2348
BOCA RATON, FLORIDA 33427-2348
TELEPHONE: (407) 994-0079

What Citizens Need to Know About World Affairs

Editor
Eleanor Goldstein

Educational Consultant
Jan L. Tucker, Ph.D.
Professor of Education and Director,
Global Awareness Program, Florida International University

Africa and the Americas Consultant
Harry A. Kersey, Jr., Ph.D., Florida Atlantic University

Editorial Staff
Kevin Farmer
Ann N. Gazourian

Revised Edition 1990
First printed in 1978, Revised in 1983
Copyright (c) 1990 by Social Issues Resources Series, Inc.

ISBN 0-89777-141-9 (What Citizens Need to Know About World Affairs)

Printed in the United States of America
CIP data is available. LC Card No. 90-411-69

Orders and inquiries:
Social Issues Resources Series, Inc. (SIRS)
P.O. Box 2348
Boca Raton, FL 33427-2348

Other books in this series:
What Citizens Need to Know About Government
What Citizens Need to Know About Economics
Teacher's Guides for each book are available.

What Citizens Need to Know About World Affairs

Contents

PART III Global Decision-Making

PART IV Global Issues

PART V Regions of the World: A Historical Sketch

Maps

Introduction

Rapid change characterizes our times, more than anything else. Today's technology enables us to learn about events happening anywhere in the world almost as soon as they happen. It's a far, far different world today than our ancestors inhabited, even in the recent past.

It's a world of danger now that weapons exist that can destroy civilization. It's a world of excitement now that each citizen can learn about and become involved in world events. It's a world of challenge now that knowledge and technology exist to stabilize world population, produce adequate food and improve material well-being.

Within the last few years, a structure has been developing for understanding the world with a global perspective; that is, a view of the world which looks at common problems that are shared by all nations, and ways of dealing with these problems.

To understand today, some background history is needed. Every event that happens has a history: a location where the occurrence took place and the circumstances which led up to it.

This book is divided into five major parts. Parts I, II and III — *Global Perspectives, Global Dynamics,* and *Global Decision-Making* — provide a basic structure for understanding the philosophies and concepts underlying world affairs. Part IV — *Global Issues* — contains information for understanding major world problems. Part V — *Regions of the World* — provides brief historical sketches as a background for understanding events as they happen in various parts of the world.

Every day's news adds to the continuing story of world events. This book has been written with the objective of providing a sound foundation for understanding world affairs with a global perspective.

PART I

Global Perspectives

Chapter 1

Space Perspectives

- **It has taken centuries of accumulated knowledge for humans to discover their place in the universe.**

- **Space exploration has created a new view of Earth.**

A new view

The first humans to walk on the moon were Neil Armstrong and Edwin Aldrin. The long journey to the moon took place on the spacecraft *Apollo 11.* On July 20, 1969, after orbiting the moon, a Lunar Lander separated from *Apollo 11* for the moon landing. Armstrong and Aldrin, in their special spacesuits, romped around in the low gravity. On the trip home, the astronauts were awed by the view of Earth. "It looked like a tiny pea," Armstrong said. "I put up my thumb and shut one eye, and my thumb blotted out the planet Earth. I didn't feel like a giant, I felt very, very small."

John Young, who served on two Apollo trips to the moon, referred to Earth when he wondered "how everyone is going to live on that small, crowded planet." Tom Stafford, who accompanied Young on *Apollo 10* remarked, "You don't look on the world as an American, but as a human being." Space exploration has provided "earthlings" with an entirely new view of our planet and universe.

Pioneer 10

On March 2, 1972, American scientists launched *Pioneer 10,* the first spacecraft to leave Earth's solar system. It continues on its endless journey traveling billions of miles through the Milky Way Galaxy. The spacecraft was built to last 21 months, but now it is expected to survive in interstellar space for 100 billion years.

The *National Aeronautics and Space Administration* (NASA) placed a plaque on *Pioneer 10.* Using symbols, the plaque showed when the ship was launched, where it came from and who built it. NASA scientists hope that intelligent beings, maybe trillions of miles away and, perhaps, millions of years from now, might find *Pioneer 10* and interpret the plaque. Those beings would learn that they are not alone in the universe.

Our place in the universe

Earth is one of nine planets rotating around a medium-sized star, the sun, located in a wheel-shaped galaxy called the Milky Way. A galaxy is composed of stars, planets, gas and dust. Within the known universe, there are hundreds of billions of galaxies, each with an average of 100 billion stars.

Voyager

Earth had its first, and perhaps only, family photograph taken on February 14, 1990. The spacecraft *Voyager 1,* traveling a million miles a day, looked back from about 4 billion miles and focused a camera on the solar system. Earth looks like an insignificant grain of sand. The stillness and emptiness are overwhelming. It is only on this little dot that life exists anywhere that we know of in the vastness of space. Astronomer Carl Sagan remarked: "This is where we live — on a blue dot. On that blue dot, that's where everyone you know, everyone you ever heard of, everyone who ever was, lived out their life."

Voyager will continue its journey forever. There is nothing to stop it. It carries messages if it should perhaps — sometime, somewhere — be found by intelligent beings. Greetings in 55 human languages and one whale language are recorded on a 12-inch gold-plated copper disk. Also on the disk is a 12-minute sound essay which includes a baby's cry and the sound of a kiss. There are 118 pictures, digitally encoded, about our civilization. Ninety

minutes of music of Earth's greatest hits is also on the disk, including a Pygmy girl's song of initiation, Mozart and a Navajo chant.

Carl Sagan, speculating on the possibility of the recordings being heard, wrote:

Perhaps the records will never be intercepted. Perhaps no one in 5 billion years will ever come upon them. Five billion years is a long time. In 5 billion years, everyone we know and love will be gone, all humans will have become extinct or evolved into other beings, no human artifacts will remain on Earth, the continents will have been unrecognizably altered or destroyed, and the Earth itself will have been reduced by the evolution of the Sun to a charred cinder. Far from home, untouched by these distant events, Voyager will fly on.

A Portrait of the Solar System

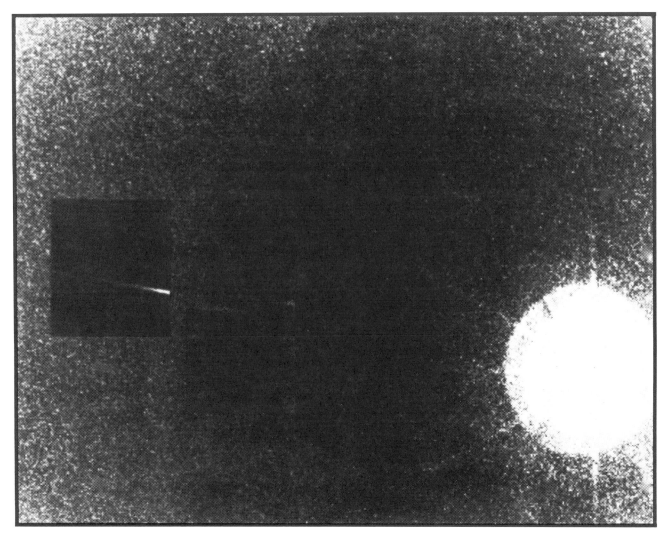

NASA

The cameras of *Voyager 1* took a series of pictures of the sun and the planets from a distance of about four billion miles. The above image is a portion of a wide-angle image containing the sun and the region of space where Earth and Venus were at the time. Photos of Earth (left) and Venus were taken with a narrow-angle lens to avoid the saturation of sunlight. Frames of Earth and Venus were digitally mosaicked into the wide-angle image at the appropriate scale. Earth appears as a tiny dot in the center of a ray of sunlight.

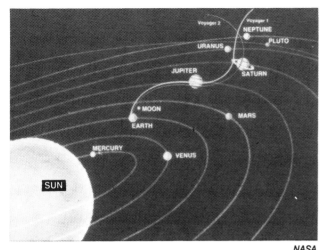

The paths of *Voyager 1* and *Voyager 2,* launched in 1977, on their journeys through the solar system.

Spaceship Earth

Buckminster Fuller, who wrote and lectured for many years on the implications of the revolutionary technology of the 20th century, urged people to look at our planet as Spaceship Earth. This tiny planet is self-contained and, like a space capsule, it has a limited amount of resources. Just as astronauts on a spaceship must cooperate and depend upon one another for survival, all of us are *interdependent* on Spaceship Earth. We share the same thin layers of soil and air and must learn that care and nurturing of the environment are vital to the survival of all living things.

Our place on Earth

It has taken centuries of travel and the development of the sciences of astronomy and geography for human beings to comprehend Earth's true size and shape and its relationship to other objects in the universe.

Earth is a sphere; therefore, no flat map can show true areas, true shapes, true distances and true directions. Only a globe can accurately indicate different features of Earth. Cartographers, those who measure Earth and map it, have developed several *map projections,* or ways to depict Earth on a flat surface, but each results in some distortion of distance or shape. When Earth is laid out like a flattened orange peel, shapes are accurate but the distances between them are not.

The *Mercator projection* is a type of map developed in Europe in 1569 for navigational purposes. The Mercator is still the flat map most widely used throughout the world. In order to be accurate for navigation, the map greatly exaggerates the size of areas north of the 40th parallel. These areas include most of North America and almost all of

Europe. On a Mercator map Greenland appears larger than Africa. India, Africa, South America, much of China and the Middle East generally appear smaller than they actually are. To correct this distortion, other maps have been developed including the *Robinson projection* and the *Peters projection.* The Robinson projection was recently adopted by the National Geographic Society for its general reference maps. The Mercator was designed to serve the Western world. The Peters projection, with its elongated distortions of Africa, India and South America, remains controversial in its attempt to highlight regions traditionally given little attention.

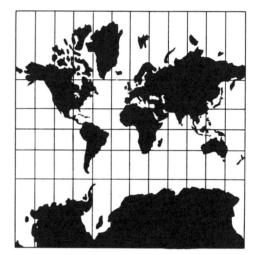

Mercator Projection

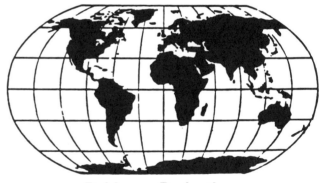

Robinson Projection

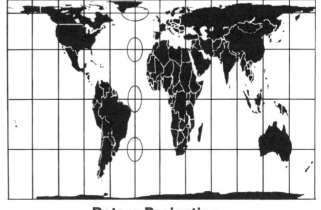

Peters Projection

Views of the world

Europe and England lie across the Greenwich meridian (its name taken from Greenwich, England), the starting point for global measurements, east and west. Therefore, Europe is placed in the center of many maps, a location that gives it a prominent position in the eyes of those viewing world affairs. Some maps used in the United States show the Americas in a more central location, even though the Asian continent is split in two. These views may give the impression that the West is the center of the world.

Many views of the world exist. Each reflects the culture and traditions of a region. A Chinese view is that the center of Earth is marked by the Temple of Heaven at the Emperor's palace in Beijing. The farther away a location is from this imperial center of authority, the less significant it is to civilization. Events in China, to the Chinese, are the focus of world history.

In India, Hindus believe that only where the sacred Ganges River flows can a person live the way of truth and holiness. The object is to live a good life now so that one can seek a higher station after rebirth. Time is infinite, space limitless, and the world a place to purify the soul by choosing good over evil.

In the Middle East, Moslems believe that the prophet Mohammed's birthplace, Mecca, is the center of Earth. The angels are thought to worship in the heavens above.

Early Jews and Christians drew maps showing Jerusalem as the center of the world. Ancient Romans believed that Rome was the focal point of civilization. In the 17th century, Galileo was excommunicated from his church for daring to suggest that Earth was not the center of the universe.

In modern times, people have access to verifiable scientific information about the world. However, differing views continue to exist. Some people still believe that their nation is the center of the planet, if not the universe.

A view of the world by an objective observer would show that no place is actually at the center. An arbitrary point can be selected but not everyone will accept it as Earth's center.

No longer isolated

Separated from the "old-world" nations by two mighty oceans, the United States has had its own vast spaces to explore, and Americans have spent several hundred years doing that. During those years a strong sense of independence and isolation developed. Nowadays, no area of the world is distant from any other area. Rapid transportation and new forms of communication have brought the nations of the world closer together.

Trade among nations increases every year and doubles in volume about every five years. The level of economic development and the natural resources of a country determine what goods a nation trades — exports and imports. The United States imports large quantities of oil and strategic minerals from many nations and exports manufactured goods and agricultural products to all corners of the globe. The standard of living of U.S. citizens depends largely on this trade. Four of every five new jobs in the U.S. depend directly upon international trade.

Regions: structuring the world

A *region* is any place in which there is internal similarity: something that distinguishes that place from the surrounding area. The major ways of looking at the world are through its physical, political and cultural characteristics.

Geographic regions

A *physical features* map or globe reveals that Earth is mostly water with some large land masses, or continents, and thousands of islands. The seven continents are: North America, South America, Africa, Antarctica, Australia, Asia and Europe (a peninsula of Asia). There are four oceans: the Atlantic, Pacific, Indian and Arctic. There are hundreds of thousands of islands on Earth. The largest is Greenland.

Major physical features of Earth's surface include: mountains, valleys, plains, deserts and rivers. Each has a significant impact on the way people live.

The simplest way to structure Earth is to divide it into quarters: the North and South, separated by the equator; and the East and West, separated by history. The distinctions among these four regions of the world have political, economic and cultural significance.

The North is generally considered to be the industrialized region of the world, the South an agricultural, developing region. While specific places in each region are exceptions to the generalization about it, for the most part the North is industrialized and the South is not.

The Eastern and Western worlds are divided by the ancient civilizations which influenced their development and cultures. The Western world draws its roots from the great ancient civilizations that flourished around the Mediterranean Sea at Babylon, Egypt, Greece and Rome. The Eastern world is characterized by the influence of two other great civilizations: the Chinese and the Hindu. The Eastern and Western worlds have interacted throughout

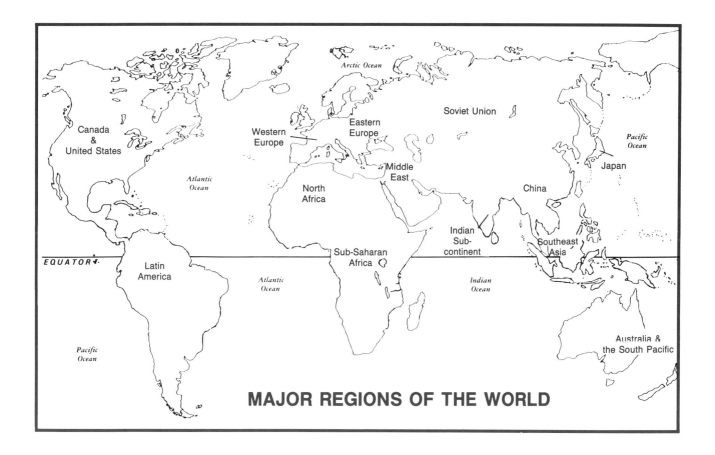

MAJOR REGIONS OF THE WORLD

recorded time. For example, the Roman Empire imported silk from central Asia. Islamic traditions are also usually associated with the East, although they share roots with the Babylonian civilization. Modern forms of transportation and communication have spread information about these civilizations all over the world, but for the most part, the East and West can still be distinguished by their historic and cultural differences.

The twelve major regions

Earth is commonly grouped into 12 major regions based on geographic similarities due to *proximity,* or nearness to one another, and socioeconomic similarities such as a shared history, culture, language or means of livelihood. Neighboring nations tend to have more similarities than nations distant from one another. They often trade with one another and have close cultural ties. Often, border disputes occur, because it may be difficult to determine where one nation ends and another begins.

United States and Canada. These nations share a common border, colonial history and language. Both are industrialized and have market-oriented economies. They have many economic and cultural ties. They are each other's best trading partners.

Western Europe. This area's economy is market-oriented and its industry is highly developed. Twelve of the nations are joined by the *European Communi-*

ty (EC). Most nations in the region are bordered by the Atlantic Ocean or have access to it through the Mediterranean Sea.

Eastern Europe. This is an inland region of planned, socialist economies that until recently were largely dominated by the Soviet Union. Many of these nations, less industrialized than their Western European counterparts, are attempting to develop market economies.

USSR. The Soviet Union is considered a region by virtue of its great size: It occupies one-sixth of the world's land area, stretching from Europe to the Pacific Ocean. The region is a multi-ethnic state made up of numerous republics, each roughly corresponding to a major ethnic region. Russia is the largest of these republics. The USSR is an industrial giant rich in energy and other resources.

Latin America. Consisting of Mexico, South America, Central America and the Caribbean islands, Latin America was colonized by Spain and Portugal in the 16th century. Spanish and Portuguese are still the dominant languages. Most of its land mass lies farther east than Miami, Florida. The population is concentrated in cities along the east and north coasts, and the urban growth rate is high.

The Middle East and North Africa. The region possesses the world's largest oil reserves and is in the midst of significant change. The Islamic religion gives the region a cultural unity. The Jewish state

5

of Israel is an exception, and the conflict between the Arab countries and Israel is a serious problem of the region.

Sub-Saharan Africa. The region shares a common historical experience as former colonies of European powers. Practically all became independent nations after World War II. This is a multi-ethnic region with population distributed along tribal lines with hundreds of different languages spoken.

Indian Subcontinent. This region, a former British colony, has a population in excess of 800 million, mostly Hindu. Pakistan and Bangladesh are independent Moslem states within the region.

China. This region is bordered by inland mountains and the Pacific Ocean along the coast. Nearly a quarter of the world's people live here. China is rich in natural resources. Despite having to feed the world's largest concentration of people, China has become a food exporter.

Southeast Asia. The coastal mainland and hundreds of islands in this region, including Indonesia and the Philippines, are populated by people of diverse languages and religions. Most share a history of cultural and economic influence from China and colonization by Western powers. Nearly 300 million people inhabit the region. Its economy is mainly agricultural, but it is a growing industrial center.

Japan. This is a unique region made up of four main islands, inhabited by over 120 million people of similar ethnic background. Japan is a highly urban society, with about 80 percent of the population living in cities. Japan must import much of its food and nearly all of its raw materials and energy. It is a mature industrial economy that exports many manufactured goods to world markets.

Australia and the South Pacific. The region exports wool, meat and wheat, but is somewhat hampered by the problem of great distances to world markets. Australia and New Zealand are former British colonies. Most of the "south sea" islands in the region are governed by various world powers, but there is a movement toward self-government. Hawaii, in the northern area of Polynesia, is one of the 50 United States.

Climate regions

The prevailing weather conditions in an area are determined by temperature and rainfall. Areas that are *contiguous* — next to one another, and have common climate conditions form a climate region.

Tropical — rainy, hot and steamy weather. Most tropical regions are near the equator and contain rain forests of lush vegetation. (Amazon and Congo river basins, Indochina)

Subtropical — rainy, long, humid summers, mild winters. Subtropical regions adjoin the tropics. (Southeastern U.S., South China, central Argentina)

Semiarid — hot summers, cold winters and little rain. Semiarid regions are often on inland plateaus. (North American Great Plains, southern Soviet Union)

Desert — hot with scarce rainfall. Desert regions are scattered in many parts of the world. (the Sahara in northern Africa, the Mojave in the United States)

Mediterranean — mild, moist winters; dry, sunny summers. Mediterranean regions are usually near the sea. (Italy, Southern California, central Chile)

Marine — rainy, moderate temperatures. Marine regions are usually on west coasts. (Pacific Northwest, British Isles)

Continental — hot summers, cold winters, varied rainfall. Continental regions are inland or on east coasts. (Northeastern U.S.)

High Latitudes — short summers, long, cold winters, humid. The high latitude areas are subarctic. (northern Canada, Alaska, Siberia)

Undifferentiated — varied weather patterns that are unpredictable, usually in mountain areas. (Andes, Alps, Rockies, Himalayas)

Many nations have a variety of climate regions within their borders.

Political regions

A *political region* is an area where all the people are ruled by the same government. There are several types of political regions: cities and states are political regions, but the most powerful political regions are countries or *nation-states*. Nation-states are the means by which the world is divided into political units. All nation-states have three basic characteristics: territory, population and government.

Nations have borders or boundaries that define an exact land area. The *territories* of different nations vary greatly in size and configuration. A nation's territory may be very large, as is the Soviet Union which covers nearly one-sixth of the world's land, or it may be small like Liechtenstein, a country in Europe, 61 square miles in area and no bigger than many cities in the United States. Nations vary in shape as well; some are fragmented and consist of two or more land areas separated by water. Japan, the United Kingdom, Indonesia and the Philippines are nations-states with such a territorial arrangement.

The people of a nation are citizens subject to the laws and regulations of the government. *Population density* is the number of people per unit of land area, usually square miles. *Distribution* describes population concentration, whether rural, urban or within a particular area of the territory. *Ethnicity* refers to characteristics that people have in common, including language, religion, race, as well as customs and values. Ethnicity binds people together.

Ethnicity is closely related to another element of nation-states known as *nationalism*. Nationalism is that feeling of loyalty and affection a person has toward his or her land and government.

Government, a third basic characteristic of nations, provides legitimacy and *sovereignty* — supreme control within its boundaries. Before 1700, the principal form of government was *monarchy* in which nations were controlled by kings whose claim to leadership was hereditary. Today there are several types of governments throughout the world: In addition to monarchies, there are *republics* where officials are elected by the people and *dictatorships* where power is in the hands of a strong leader or a small ruling class.

Economic regions

Economic regions are defined in various ways: Economic regions are distinguished according to the degree of industrialization or development. Nations of the world can be divided into so-called *developed* and *developing* countries.

Economic regions can be characterized by the way a large number of people in an area earn their livelihood, such as farming, fishing, manufacturing or mining. Farming regions are located in the great plains areas of the United States and Canada, Europe, the Soviet Union, central South America and in the rich fertile lands of eastern China. Major fishing regions extend along the coastal areas of the world's continents, while manufacturing regions are scattered, from north central and eastern United States to the heartland of Europe and the mainland of Japan.

Economic regions also can be defined by the way a country, or area of the world, solves the basic economic questions of the production and distribution of goods and services: what to produce and who will enjoy the benefits of production. In many countries the *market* decides: Goods and services are produced for profit and distributed according to demand — to those who have the money. In other countries, the basic economic decisions are made by *planning:* The production of goods and services, as well as the distribution of incomes, and, therefore, purchasing power, is determined through government planning.

The United States, Canada, Japan and most of Western Europe are largely market economic regions. The Soviet Union, Eastern Europe, China and Cuba are the world's major planned economies. However, the Soviet Union and many nations in Eastern Europe are moving toward market economies. With all market economies there is some government (and even business) planning, and in all planned economies some market forces also operate.

Most developing areas of the world lean toward either market or planned economies, but some are still *traditional* economic regions: Production and distribution decisions are based on tradition — what has been done for generations in families, tribes and communities.

Other economic regions are made up of countries that join together for trading and other commercial purposes. *The European Community* (EC) com-

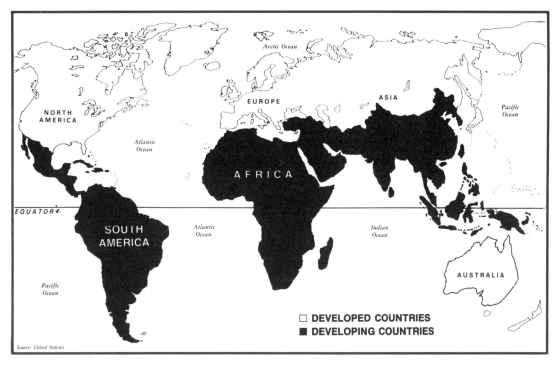

□ DEVELOPED COUNTRIES
■ DEVELOPING COUNTRIES

Source: United Nations

prises 12 Western European nations. The original six members, when the EC was established in 1958, were France, West Germany, Italy, Belgium, Luxembourg and the Netherlands. They were joined later by the United Kingdom, Ireland, Denmark, Greece, Spain and Portugal. Another economic trading region is the *Council for Mutual Economic Assistance* (COMECON), made up of the Soviet Union and its former Eastern European satellites. The EC is essentially an economic region of market economies, while COMECON is a region of planned economies. During the 1990s, the EC and COMECON will undergo many changes. For example, by 1992 the EC is slated to become a fully integrated economic union by eliminating trade barriers and allowing the free flow of money and labor among its members.

Religious regions

The world also can be divided according to the major religions of the world. *Christianity* is the religious belief of the majority of people in North America, much of South America and Europe. Christianity also is practiced in parts of Africa, particularly South Africa. *Islam* is the dominant religion of people in northern Africa and the Middle East, extending into the western part of Asia and Indonesia. Most people of Israel practice *Judaism*.

The eastern part of the world is influenced by three religions: *Hinduism, Buddhism* and *Shintoism.* Hinduism dominates in India and Nepal. Buddhism predominates in China, Japan and Southeast Asia. Many Japanese also follow the Shinto religion.

Large areas of the world are inhabited by people who hold various tribal religious beliefs. Regions of South America, Central Africa and remote parts of Australia are the major areas where tribal beliefs dominate.

Language regions

The language spoken by the largest number of people is *Mandarin Chinese,* spoken by almost 1 billion of the world's 5.3 billion people. Over 300 million Chinese speak other Chinese dialects.

Of the major world languages, the next most widely spoken is *English:* It is the main tongue of North America, Great Britain, Australia, New Zealand, Guyana in South America and parts of Africa. *French* is a widely spoken language used not only in France, but in French Guiana (South America), parts of Canada and in a large area of Africa. The next widely spoken languages are *Hindi* and *Urdu* on the Indian subcontinent; *Russian,* spoken in the U.S.S.R.; and *Spanish* which is spoken in Mexico, much of South America and Spain. In addition, sizable numbers of people speak *Arabic, Bengali, Portuguese, German, Japanese, Swahili* and *Indonesian.*

The 12 major languages are spoken by about 60 percent of the world's people. The rest of the world is split into smaller language blocks including *Italian, Tamil, Punjabi, Dutch, Flemish, Turkish* and *Greek.*

NASA

An American astronaut hovering above Earth during a NASA space test.

Chapter 2

Time Perspectives

- *Living creatures are dependent upon the past and upon other living creatures.*

- *Nations like to think they are independent, but in fact they are part of an inextricable web of interdependence.*

An incredibly complex network of events has occurred over the passage of billions of years to create the world as we know it. Only in the last few thousand years have human beings begun to unravel the mystery of our origins and the origins of the planet we inhabit.

Astronomy, geology, archaeology, biology, history and religion all contribute to understanding the past. The overriding theme of all of these disciplines is the concept of *dependency*. Every new discovery or invention is based upon a myriad of past knowledge. The present is dependent upon the past, just as the future depends on the present. Our ancestors have helped to forge our lives, just as we forge the lives of our descendants.

Astronomy

Astronomers study the origin of the sun and its planets. They believe that 10 or 20 billion years ago a titanic, cosmic explosion occurred in which the universe expanded, and still continues to expand. This cataclysmic event is known as the Big Bang. Why the Big Bang occurred is a mystery as yet unsolved. Perhaps the answer will be found as astronomers study the life and death of distant stars through the lenses of powerful telescopes. Scientists anticipate that the Hubble Space Telescope will provide data for accurate determination of the age, size and destiny of the universe.

Over the course of billions of years, changes occurred on Earth: volcanoes erupted, oceans formed, life began. Some changes took millions and millions of years; others occurred rapidly. Each change was the catalyst for more changes. If the Big Bang had not occurred, our sun and its planets would not have formed. That event shaped the course of all events to come.

Geology

Geology is the science that deals with the physical nature and history of Earth, including its structure, composition and forms of life found in fossils. Geologists say Earth is about 4.5 billion years old. They can determine the time and duration of the Ice Ages and thus determine when conditions were hospitable for life forms to flourish. Through fossils, they can date various strata of Earth and determine the likelihood of locating oil or minerals. Geology provides evidence that life is dependent on conditions in the environment. The age of Earth and the history of evolution is revealed in the strata studied by geologists.

Satellite photography and mapping, technological advances developed in the 1980s, now contribute tremendously to geological research. Satellites locate concentrated areas of mineral deposits and fossil fuels. Satellite technology is also helpful for monitoring environmental changes such as soil erosion,

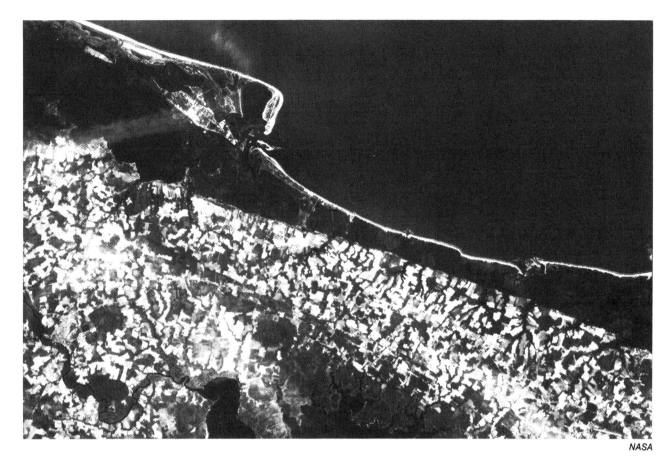

A satellite photo of part of the Eastern Shore of Virginia taken by NASA's Landsat-4 spacecraft from 441 miles above Earth. Satellite photographs can be used to help identify environmental problems.

the effects of acid rain, depleted rain forests and toxic waste dumps.

Archaeology

Archaeologists, who study human beings by examining fossils, look back millions of years to the ancestors of humans and trace the path to modern times by analyzing skeletal remains and cultural artifacts. They have accumulated evidence indicating that human ancestors, hominids, roamed the earth as long as 25 million years ago. These small, hairy, apelike creatures are considered humanlike because they used tools — sticks for digging roots and clubs for killing small animals. Although they are considered members of the human family, hominids were similar to wild animals in that they lived by the dictates of nature, foraging for food and following the good weather. They adjusted to nature, rather than adapting nature to their needs, and did not change much from generation to generation.

Biology

Charles Darwin developed what is considered the greatest general principle in biology, the *theory of evolution*. From 1832 to 1836, Darwin traveled as a naturalist on the ship *H.M.S. Beagle*. His observations and collections from this voyage were published on November 24, 1859, in an abstract entitled *Origin of the Species*. The findings in this book were met with controversy, especially from orthodox religious believers, for if the theory of evolution were true, it meant that the account of creation in the Book of Genesis in the Bible was not true, at least in a literal sense. The amount of evidence that Darwin had gathered on his voyage helped to convince many people that the theory of evolution had substantial merit. The theory holds that all species of plants and animals developed from earlier forms by hereditary transmissions. Slight variations may occur from generation to generation. This is known as *mutation*. The forms which survive are those that are best suited to the environment. This is known as *natural selection*.

Some 500 million species — existing and extinct — have evolved by mutation and natural selection. But human beings, who first evolved several million years ago, are unique. Only humans pass knowledge from generation to generation, not only genetically, as all species do, but by means of their culture. In the human species, cultural evolution is more significant than genetic evolution.

History

History is the story of the past — the people and

10

events that helped to create the present. The language we speak, the type of government we live under, the standard of living we enjoy all depend upon the actions and events of the past. Every culture looks to its origins. There are three basic ways to interpret history: *conservative, cyclical* and *progressive.*

In nonliterate cultures, history is transmitted orally from storyteller to storyteller to succeeding generations. New events are incorporated into the story as they happen. There is no distinct timeline of events. Everything, including recent events, happened "a long time ago." Each time the story is retold, it is changed somewhat by the teller. Eventually, stories about real events and people become myths about a golden time in the past. This perception of history is considered conservative, or regressive. Present events are measured and future events are shaped by past ideals.

History is sometimes interpreted as being cyclical. Often the statement is made that "history repeats itself." This view sees civilizations as going through periods of growth just as all living creatures do — birth, maturing, aging, dying.

In industrialized cultures, information about what happened in the past is gathered by the *scientific method.* Historians attempt to describe the past according to objective evidence: written records. The earliest surviving written record is about 6,000 years old. History is viewed as linear rather than cyclical. As much as possible, specific events are dated, and a chronology is developed. Interpretation of this chain of events leads to a *cause and effect* analysis — that one event caused or led to another. History is viewed as progressive, or evolutionary — moving from the simple to the complex.

Religion

Religions credit a divine or superhuman power or powers with the creation of the universe. Religions provide answers to many of the mysteries of life. Some religions believe that God created people in his own image and perceive God as humanlike or fatherlike. Others see God as a spirit governing all life in nature. Religions provide a *code of ethics* and a conscience for their followers.

Dependence — an idea in common

Each one of these disciplines provides a perspective of time. Astronomers view the cosmos in the time frame of billions of years, geologists view the Earth from a 4.5 billion-year perspective. Archaeologists view humans from about a 4 million-year perspective, historians view civilization in a time frame of about 6,000 years of written records.

Each religion views time within the context of its own doctrines.

One idea permeates every time perspective — the concept of *dependence.* Every living creature is dependent for its roots on the past and upon other living creatures for its present survival.

A global perspective in human affairs

For the major part of human existence, groups of people lived in relative isolation, developing civilizations on various parts of the globe unknown to one another. With the development of language and the written word, advances began to be recorded, and a rapid rate of change in human life occurred. Once technological advances were made, change accelerated. Each invention or discovery led to many other inventions, in what is known as the *trigger effect.* Change is felt in many places — often far removed in space and time from the origin of the initial discovery. Today's transportation and communication assure that no country is far from any other country, and the actions of one affect the others.

It's not surprising that until recently the world has been viewed as separate parts rather than a whole. Most nations were concerned with the struggle for *independence.* A spirit of *nationalism* flourished. Nations wanted to provide security from other countries and to resolve conflicts within their borders without outside interference.

In the 20th century, regional conflicts drew the world into two great wars. In the 1930s, an economic depression spread around the world. These events indicated the *interdependence* of nations. Nationalism is still strong, but an international world view is emerging because of circumstances beyond the control of any one nation.

A major factor in the development of a global perspective has been the rapid growth of world trade. For example, between 1913 and 1938 the volume of world trade increased by only 3 percent. But between 1948 and 1971 it increased by 500 percent. As nations come to depend more upon each other for goods and services, there is a greater need to know about the world — the languages, geography, history and culture of the world's people and nations.

Another factor in the development of a global perspective is the growth of tourism in the world. In 1985, 43 million people visited Spain; 37 million went to France; 28 million to Italy; and 21 million came to the United States. Travel is increasing in all parts of the world, including Asia, Africa and Latin America.

The problems of society are not confined by national borders. Global warming, acid rain, the uncontrolled use of pesticides, the explosion of nuclear weapons, the production of industrial pollutants, and the destruction of rain forests affects all nations. Interdependence demands an awareness that many activities of a country have a consequence far beyond its borders.

The century of the "J" curve

In the 20th century, we live beyond the bend of the "J" curve of human history. The "J" curve is a graphic representation of a pattern of change that grows by doubling. This is called *geometric change* and is sometimes referred to as exponential growth.

Many developments start slowly but, once the early stages take place, advances occur rapidly. World population growth presents a vivid example of the "J" curve, or geometric growth. Population rounded the bend of the curve near the year 1800, meaning it took thousands of years for the world population to reach one billion. It now takes about ten years to increase the world population by one billion.

Technological advances in transportation, communication and electronics lead to accelerated changes in lifestyle. While it took thousands of years for humans to develop basic tools, and less time to develop machinery, the array of sophisticated modern technology has virtually sprung up since approximately 1870. Fifty percent of all scientific knowledge acquired throughout history was created in the past generation (about 35 years). The technology of modern global civilization has also

rounded the bend of the "J" curve.

Global interdependence

In today's world, nations are mutually dependent upon one another — they are *interdependent*. A nation can no longer ignore events elsewhere in the world because it is affected by them. Henry Steele Commager, a renowned historian, wrote a statement on the eve of the United States' bicentennial in 1976. It was entitled *A Declaration of Interdependence:*

> When in the course of history the threat of extinction confronts mankind, it is necessary for the people of the United States to declare their interdependence with the people of all nations and to embrace those principles and build those institutions which will enable mankind to survive and civilization to flourish.

Professor Commager called for a new world order of compassion, peace, justice and security that would end national prejudices and acknowledge that all people are part of one global community.

The Declaration of Independence, written by Thomas Jefferson in 1776 to set forth ideals for a new nation, stated that all people are created equal, entitled to the blessings of life, liberty and the pursuit of happiness. Dr. Commager believes that people everywhere in the world have the inescapable moral obligation to preserve these rights for everyone and forever. He wrote, "The inequalities and injustices which afflict so much of the human race are the product of history and society, not of God or nature."

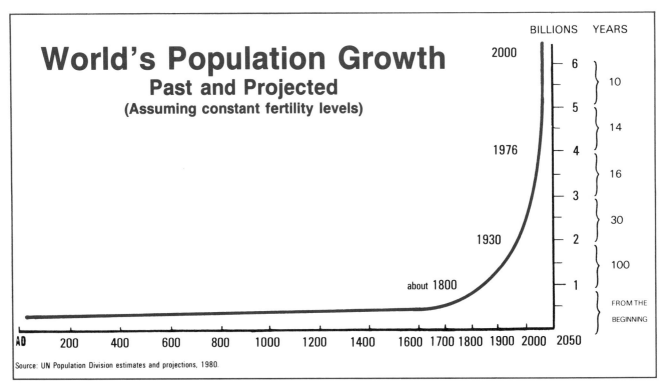

World's Population Growth
Past and Projected
(Assuming constant fertility levels)

BILLINGS YEARS

2000 — 6 } 10
— 5 } 14
1976 — 4 } 16
— 3 } 30
1930 — 2 } 100
about 1800 — 1 }
FROM THE BEGINNING

AD 200 400 600 800 1000 1200 1400 1600 1700 1800 1900 2000 2050

Source: UN Population Division estimates and projections, 1980.

Chapter 3

Cultural Perspectives

- *A trip around the world, which includes remote villages and modern cities, is like a trip through time.*

- *Although people vary greatly in customs and lifestyle, their similarities are greater than their differences.*

Today's world is a microcosm of the whole history of human existence. Some people live in skyscrapers, use microwave ovens, fly from city to city at speeds of hundreds of miles an hour, drive cars on great stretches of highway using technology of the 20th century. Others live much as their ancestors have lived for thousands of years before them, in shelters made of mud, cooking on open fires, seldom traveling more than a few miles from the places of their birth. People live such varied lifestyles on Earth that a trip around the world, including visits to remote villages and modern cities, is like a trip through time.

As different as people are, they also are similar. All humans are *gregarious:* They live in groups among others like themselves. A human baby is the most helpless of living creatures. It needs care and love, without which it could not survive. People, whether they live in an Amazon village or a European city, rely on other people to care for the young and teach them, to protect them from outside threats, and to make life enjoyable.

All people need food, clothing and shelter from the extremes of weather, and they need other people to interact with. People everywhere do essentially the same basic things: they eat, they create a place to live, and they seek pleasure and meaning in life. In different places, they may do these things differently. People learn things from one another, especially the young from the older people. Everything that people learn, including their language, knowledge, skills, and beliefs, is known as their *culture.*

Every society has a *government,* a set of rules for behavior; *religion,* an explanation for the meaning of life; *history,* a story of the past; *language,* a way to communicate; *family,* a kinship system and inheritance rules; *education,* a way to teach customs and skills to the young; and an *economic system,* a way to provide for the basic needs of food, shelter and clothing. The government, religion, history, language, family, education and economic system of a society combine to create its culture. Culture is that part of the environment created by humans.

Influences on culture

Culture is shaped, to a large degree, by *environment:* the total surroundings in which a group or person lives, including geographic location, climate, terrain and natural resources. In a society that has little contact with other tribes or nations, the food, clothing and materials for building shelters are derived from locally available resources. Most likely, the culture will change only slowly over time. When a society trades with outside groups, the resources available for these purposes begin to change and new ways of doing things are introduced. Interaction among cultures speeds up the change process.

Photo montage of people of the world created at the United Nations.

Culture is also dependent upon *technology:* the means employed to provide objects for human sustenance and comfort. Bushmen of the Kalahari Desert of southern Africa obtained meat for their families by hunting game with poisoned lances. Early settlers of the United States frontier hunted game with guns. Lances and guns are both examples of technology. Farming technologies differ greatly around the world. In some regions a simple stick is used to dig a hole for planting seeds. In others a tractor is used which automatically plants seeds in even rows.

Cultural diversity

People's *beliefs* and *values* also influence how the environment is used. Pueblo and Navaho Indians both occupy desert territory in the southwestern United States. Each group uses the environment in a different way. Pueblos live in village centers — clusters of dwellings that can accommodate up to 1,000 people. They farm the land and depend on religious ceremonies to provide a favorable climate and bountiful crops. The Navaho, on the other hand, live in small lodges, known as hogans, which are widely distributed over the territory they share. The main activity is raising sheep. Navaho religious rituals focus on the maintenance of personal health rather than on control of rainfall.

Traditions, the way things have been done in the past, play an important part in culture. The United

States is a relatively new nation, having celebrated its 200th birthday in 1976. Its population of approximately 250 million is made up of people from nearly every other nation on Earth. Therefore, the United States does not share as many common traditions as a nation like China with nearly 4,000 years of civilization and history.

While the basic needs for all people are universal, or common to all societies, the way in which these needs are met vary from place to place. The environment, technology, beliefs and traditions of the people are just a few factors that determine how people's needs are met. Cultural diversity tends to obscure the fact that similarities among people are greater than their differences. All people throughout the world feel pain, hunger, love, fear, joy. We all inhabit the same planet and we are all related in a web of cultural interdependence.

Communication

During the 20th century amazing developments in science and technology have created a situation different from ever before in the long history of human life. It is only in this century that all people, no matter where they are living, can see and hear events almost as soon as they occur by means of satellite television and radio.

What happens in one part of the world is rapidly reported all over the world. TV screens and newspapers show us victims of famines, war and earthquakes. We share happy and sad experiences with millions of people. The launching of a satellite, the wedding of a prince, the performance of a rock star, the funeral of a president are events recorded and broadcast throughout the world, increasing understanding and interdependence.

In the homes of many people around the globe, television sets are tuned to TV serials, movies and MTV produced in the United States. Television programs and feature films have become the United States' number one cultural export. In the ancient city of Jerusalem, which appears the same now as it has for centuries, along a dark winding alleyway one can find a disco where the Miami Sound Machine's latest record is heard blaring over the

stereo. Television, movies, radio, tapes and discs, computers and fax machines are powerful instruments of global communications.

The Global Village. Marshall McLuhan, author of many books, including *The Medium Is the Message,* wrote that people of the world will be united by a global television network. He stated that when television is in every adobe, chateau, hut and tent, nations of the world will become more aware and sympathetic to each other's cultures and beliefs. This view indicates that new communications technology is a major factor in easing world tensions.

Some people do not share this hopeful view. They believe that the international communications system is dominated by industrialized nations and multinational news agencies. They complain that the news presents developing nations in a negative light, focusing on events such as famine or riots which contribute to political instability and ignoring signs of progress. These people believe that access to satellites and other transmittal devices should be shared by all nations.

UN Photo 152.989/Laura Zito

Bedouin woman watching television in Dahab, Sinai.

Cultural pride

Patriotism, the love and devotion that one feels for his or her nation is an emotion that is developed in the citizens of most countries. National holidays honoring past heroes, parades, national flags and anthems, national athletic teams which compete in international athletics are all part of the efforts encouraged by governments to instill a sense of pride in one's own nation. This is known as patriotism.

Ethnocentrism is a belief in the superiority of one's own group or culture. All cultures and nations are ethnocentric to a degree. Unfortunately, ethnocentrism often means that other groups or cultures are considered inferior. Ethnocentrism is a result of seeing other people or cultures with limited vision. It is generally a result of a lack of knowledge. That which is unfamiliar is often considered strange or weird. An ethnocentric view often fails to perceive the variety and richness of other cultures. Under certain circumstances such as economic depression or political unrest, ethnocentrism can lead to *chauvinism* — blind and destructive intolerance of others.

Stereotyping. People often use devices to simplify the surrounding complex world. They skip over information that is complex. Stereotyping is a form of shorthand behavior.

Stereotypes are impressions or half-formed attitudes about people. They may be good or bad, favorable or unfavorable impressions. They may have a degree of truth or little relation to reality. While stereotypes may simplify things, they are often wrong.

Prejudice. When stereotyping results from forming an opinion based on little evidence, prejudice exists. Prejudice means to prejudge. To make a judgment before having sufficient evidence is a dangerous thing to do.

Cultural lag

Cultural lag refers to the idea that technology advances at a faster rate than the ability of humans to utilize the new technology to their advantage. Technology can be used to harm society rather than help it. The invention of dynamite by Alfred Nobel was intended to be used to build roads and quarry minerals. Instead, it is used in bombs with great destructive power.

Television can be used to educate people or enter-

Daniel James/SIRS Staff
The traditional culture of developing nations is often intermixed with Western culture.

tain them. It can also promote or provoke violence. The technology of dynamite or television is neutral — neither good nor bad. However, ways in which these technologies are used may be good or bad — constructive or destructive.

The technology exists for people to communicate across thousands of miles by phone, fax, computer, radio or TV. Yet, two people sitting next to one another often cannot understand each other because of cultural differences. Perhaps one speaks French and the other English. Even when speaking the same language, communication may be difficult because of cultural differences.

Cultural lag is increasing as some parts of the world continue using primitive technology and other parts of the world rapidly move into the computer age. In fact, cultural lag has never been greater than it is today. A growing concern is that technology will increase the differences between the rich and the poor, regardless of where they may live in the world.

PART II

Global Dynamics

Chapter 4

Ideologies

- *Ideologies, or belief systems, unify people who think and feel the same way.*

- *Often, ideologies conflict with one another and cause dissension among people.*

In order to survive on this planet, humans have had to solve many complex problems. Domesticating animals, planting seeds, taming fire were a few essential discoveries made after thousands of years of trial and error. Cooperation is essential for accomplishing most tasks. In fact, survival depends on people helping one another and working together for common objectives. However, while people often *cooperate* to accomplish necessary tasks, they are just as likely to *compete* for personal gain.

As society became increasingly complex, especially with the beginning of agriculture around 10,000 B.C., work tasks were specialized. The roles of men and women began to become more differentiated. Modern society is dependent upon thousands of intertwining tasks. If any of these tasks go unattended, life would be disorganized in a short time.

All human societies have basic decisions to make about the way they govern and the way resources are distributed. The study of *political science* addresses itself to government; the study of *economics* deals with the production, distribution and consumption of resources. Belief systems underlying political and economic systems are known as *ideologies*.

Ideologies attempt to create a "world view" or a way of perceiving reality. Ideologies affect the way people relate to nature and to one another. Society's relationship to nature has changed greatly since the scientific and industrial revolutions. Prior to that time, people had a view that was predominantly religious. The change or transition from a religious to a scientific view has been a major cause of conflict within societies as well as between them. Difficulties arise as people seek to maintain their cultural and religious traditions while incorporating scientific knowledge into their lives.

The idea of human progress is relatively new. As scientific knowledge grew, so did the idea of progress, that "tomorrow would be better than today." Progress involves change. Some societies welcome change. Others perceive it as a threat.

Ideologies give direction to one's life. Countries, also, are guided by ideologies. Ideologies are therefore very important in understanding what motivates people and why people or countries have disagreements and conflict.

Political systems

The basic role of government is to do things for the society that must get done, yet cannot be done on an individual basis. On a local level, governments provide such services as building roads, providing fire departments and police protection. On a national level, governments provide national defense, postal service and regulation of commerce. In every society the question to be determined is who has the *sovereignty,* the final authority, to determine what tasks to undertake and who will do them. It is a question of power. Who has the power or sovereignty? In a *democratic* society the sovereignty lies with the people. In an *autocratic* society the sovereignty is in the hands of one person. All forms of government fall into one of three categories: *custom,* where power is allocated according to tradition; *command,* where power belongs to one person or a small group of people; and *consent,* where power is shared by all the members of a society, generally by voting for people to represent them in government.

Custom

Government by *custom* or *tradition* is the earliest known form of government. Rule by custom generally has

Colour Library International

Queen Elizabeth II of England presides at the opening of Parliament. England's parliamentary democracy evolved over centuries of sharing power between the monarch and Parliament.

existed in small tribal communities and during earlier periods of history when most people lived in small, isolated villages, towns or feudal manors. Where custom prevails, everyone is familiar with the rules which are passed down from generation to generation and change slowly over time. Governments guided by tradition are relatively static.

For the most part, communities remote from global events and lacking a written language rule by custom. Some Indian tribes in the United States practice this form of government. *Common law,* or unwritten rules resulting from court decisions, is an example of political custom that has existed for centuries in nations such as England and the United States. Monarchies (headed by a king or queen) also are examples of government by custom. Although the few remaining monarchies have little power, they are symbols of traditional values and national unity.

Command

Command or *authoritarian* types of government have decision-making power in the hands of one person or a small elite group. Authoritarian governments flourished in early times and they exist in many political societies throughout the world today. The aim of such governments is to pursue clear-cut goals unhindered by public opinion, elections, a constitution and other measures of group will. Three

basic types of authoritarian governments can be identified: monarchy, oligarchy and dictatorship.

Monarchy, or "rule by one person," evolved from prehistoric times as growing tribes and communities looked to strong warriors or priests for leadership. The monarch (king or queen) has sovereign power over his or her subjects. Rule in a monarchy normally is based on birthright (heredity) or on authority from a supreme being (a god). Most monarchies today, such as in England, are mere symbols of government. The king of Saudi Arabia is an example of a modern-day monarch with considerable political power.

Oligarchy is "rule by the few." A small authoritarian group governs the society. Oligarchies often are headed by military leaders, as in some Latin American and African countries. Others are ruled by a group of wealthy business people who gain power and guide the political economy.

Dictatorships are governments in which absolute power is in the hands of one person or a single political party. Germany from 1933 to 1945 was ruled by Hitler and the Nazi Party. More recent examples include the late Nicolae Ceauşescu of Romania and Kim Il Sung of North Korea. Dictators, particularly military leaders, often come to power through a *coup d'etat* (a sudden overthrow of a government) with the support of the military. Having come to power through violence, dictatorships are likely to

Swiss National Tourist Office

The Swiss open-air parliament, a centuries-old tradition, is a rare example of direct democracy.

rule with the use of violence and be changed or overthrown in violent ways. Dictatorships are sometimes described as *totalitarian*. This means that every aspect of life in a society is totally controlled by the government, including what people read or see in the media, where they are permitted to travel and the types of jobs they hold.

Consent

In *consent* or *democratic* governments, power resides with the people. They have sovereignty. The underlying beliefs of a democracy are that governments are created by people, should govern with the consent of the governed, and that people have the right to change the government. Democracies have elections in which choices can be made, a political party system, constitutional and legal protection of rights and liberties, and government with limited power. All people are supposed to be treated equally under the law.

Direct democracy exists when citizens make decisions themselves on all matters concerning them such as taxes, zoning and schools. This practice still oc-

curs in some small New England towns as well as in certain Swiss cantons. Elements of direct democracy exist within the United States and other countries where citizens can propose legislation, recall public officials and vote in popular referendums on public questions.

In societies with a fairly large population, direct democracy is difficult if not impossible, but the test of people's freedom comes in the amount of opposition a society will tolerate. Human beings' great gift of the ability to think generally means that there are a variety of ideas. Invariably, if the opposition has not been expressed, it has been suppressed. Democracy flourishes when many opinions are allowed to be expressed, and there is a free press. When there is a great deal of conformity and little controversy, it is a good sign that an authoritarian government is in control.

Indirect or **representative democracy** is the more usual form of democratic government today. In this system elected representatives of the people make laws and decide public issues. In the United States there are 435 members of the House of Representatives. They represent the American people. A census is taken every 10 years to apportion these representatives equally according to the total population.

Indirect democracies have developed two forms of leadership — *presidential* and *parliamentary.* In the presidential system, a chief executive called a president or premier is elected for a definite term of office. Constitutions usually limit the chief executive to one or two terms and for a specified number of years. A president, for example, can hold office for no more than two four-year terms in the United States, one four-year term in Costa Rica and one six-year term in Mexico.

In parliamentary systems, of which the United Kingdom is an example, the nation's chief executive, called a *prime minister,* must be a member of the lawmaking body (in the United Kingdom, the House of Commons). The leader of the majority party automatically becomes the prime minister. Whenever the majority party loses a vote on a major issue, the prime minister is obliged to resign, and new national elections are called.

The Soviet Union, after 70 years of authoritarian government, is struggling to develop a system that is a mixture of the presidential and parliamentary systems. The office of Soviet president, created in 1990, has broad executive powers. Mikhail Gorbachev, the first Soviet president, was chosen by the Congress of People's Deputies, the Soviet equivalent of a parliament.

Economic systems

All societies, whether democratic or authoritarian, must solve two fundamental tasks: They must *produce* goods and services and they must *distribute* goods and services. Since there is not enough of everything for everyone, these are important tasks, and the ways to solve them are very controversial.

There are two basic ways to go about trying to solve the problems of production and distribution. One way would be for everyone to cooperate, then share the results of their labor. Another way would be for people to compete for the resources with the winners getting the benefits. In reality, no society depends solely upon one method or the other; generally there is a mix: Some tasks are accomplished by cooperating; other tasks are accomplished through competition.

Traditional economies

Traditional solutions to economic problems — production and distribution — are commonly found in agricultural or nonindustrial societies. Typically tasks are assigned according to a person's place in the family. Men perform certain types of work, and women

perform others. In an apprenticeship system the jobs and skills associated with them are handed down in the family from parent to child. In India, at least until recently, a person was born into a caste or class which determined the type of work he or she would perform.

The world view or ideology underlying many traditional economies perceives human beings as part of nature. The purpose of life is to meet basic needs from nature. It is inconceivable in a traditional economy that natural resources such as land, water or minerals could be owned by individuals or the government. The idea of the *"commons"* — grazing land jointly used by peasants in medieval England — expresses this traditional view of natural resources. No fences enclosed the commons or divided it up into private property. Although sheep and other grazing animals were individually owned by the peasants, all the animals had free access to the commons. The enclosure movement to fence in lands and keep peasants out ultimately destroyed the traditional economy of medieval England. It was replaced by the feudal system in which decisions about the economy were made by land owners.

Many traces of social custom and tradition remain in today's industrial economies. Tradition often allocates women to service jobs in modern industry and to a limited number of professional positions. Men have traditionally held managerial positions and most of the higher-income professional jobs. This has been changing as other work opens up to women — and men.

Tradition characterizes the economies in many developing nations, creating conflict as efforts are made to convert to modern economies.

Command economies

When economic decisions about production and distribution are placed in the hands of government through comprehensive planning, the system is considered to be authoritarian or command.

Communism is the ideology behind most modern command economies. The beliefs or doctrines underlying modern communism were developed by Karl Marx, a 19th century German philosopher and political economist who did most of his writing in London. Communists believe that the major means of production and distribution should be socialized — owned and controlled by the government rather than by individual members of the society. The ultimate goal of communism, as stated by Marx, is to create a classless society where property is owned collectively and each person will work according to his or her means and receive back from the society according to their needs.

Socialism is a system that features both government and private ownership of industry and property. In some socialist nations only a few basic industries, such as coal, steel, or the railway system are government-owned. In others, the nation's health care, airlines, welfare and school systems may also be operated by the government. Many nations in Western Europe, Scandinavia and the Third World have socialist features in their economies.

Economic command may be exercised within a democratic or an authoritarian political framework. Economic systems are the underlying frameworks for accomplishing the production and distribution tasks of a society. The political system deals with who has the decision-making power within the economic system.

Market economies

Tradition and command were the most common ways to get work done throughout most of history. But gradually, and through the course of hundreds of years, a new system of economic decision-making developed. This was a system in which each person looked after his or her own self-interest. Each would do as he or she wanted, whether it was farming the land, building furniture, tailoring clothing, or publishing a newspaper. This is known as the *market system.*

The United States has a market economy; decisions about what to produce are, for the most part, based on the "profit motive." What will people buy, rather than what is thought to be good for them is the theory behind the profit motive.

Capitalism is the ideology underlying the U.S. market economy — the *free-enterprise system.* Under capitalism, the means of production and distribution are privately owned. Ideally, government plays little more than a regulatory role in the society's economy.

It staggers the mind to understand how all the work in a society can get done if there are no customs or plans to follow. Who will do the hard tedious jobs and the dangerous work if no one is there to command others to do it, or if custom does not guide them? No master plan is developed. People tend to their own business, work as efficiently as possible to seek personal profit. If they are not efficient, competition will drive them out of business. Society as a whole will benefit from maximum productivity — assuming free competition prevails. Philosopher Adam Smith wrote a book, *Inquiry into the Nature and Causes of the*

Daniel James

Peruvian Indians gather to sell flowers at an outdoor marketplace.

21

Adam Smith

Karl Marx

Wealth of Nations in 1776. In this book he described the market system. Smith marveled at the way tasks were accomplished in the society he observed in England. It was as if an "invisible hand" were guiding the society, according to Smith.

The roots of market economics can be traced to traveling merchants who lived in Europe during the Middle Ages, from about 700 to 1500. These merchants traveled the rudimentary medieval roads, often in brightly-colored caravans, from town to town. They set up canopied stalls at fairs where the lords and ladies of the manors flocked to buy wares. From here the development of markets can be traced: from an assortment of craftspeople who molded, forged, wove, and in other ways constructed products for sale; to small shopkeepers who sold goods made in workshops and factories.

As production processes became more complex, markets began to lose the competitive interplay that Adam Smith and others argued assured a spirit of fairness or merit. As growing businesses came to operate on a national and then a global scale, power became centralized. Businesses planned production goals and altered the course of the market to their ad-

vantage. The intriguing "invisible hand" did not always function to benefit the larger society. *Monopolies* or *oligopolies* and *cartels* that formed created an "imperfect competition." Governments also altered the free play of the market mechanism — using the command method to produce goods. And labor unions worked to control the supply and price of labor.

Strict adherence to the traditional doctrines of command and market economies is no longer practiced by most nations. Command economies such as China allow some free enterprise to encourage economic growth. Many market economies are turning to stricter government control and long-term industrial planning to solve their economic problems. Global interdependence, competition for the world's resources, a rising population and other factors make economic matters the foremost issue as nations attempt to find the right balance to meet the demands of their people.

Both the market system and command system can operate under either a democratic or authoritarian government. Free enterprise does not guarantee democracy, just as socialism does not mean that the government will be a dictatorship.

Chapter 5

Balance of Power

- *Nations, like people, form relationships. Often those relationships pose real or imagined threats to outsiders.*

- *Superpowers come and go. Who can predict the superpowers of the future?*

Throughout history, using military, political or economic means, one or more nations often garnered enough power to become a real or perceived threat to other nations. When this happened, other nations joined together to gain strength that offset the power of the strong nation or nations. These alliances and partnerships created a *balance of power*.

In the 17th and 18th centuries, Europe was informally aligned in a balance of power system. Its purpose was to try to ensure the independence of newly established countries and to maintain peace in Europe.

Under this informal alliance each nation was considered a sovereign unit — not subject to conquest or to external political control. When a strong nation threatened war, the other nations would align themselves with the weaker nation to maintain the balance. Alignments were based on mutual interest in keeping another nation from becoming too powerful rather than on ideological or political lines. The method of restoring the balance of power, should one country get too strong, was for the others to wage war against it. The balance of power system collapsed in the years before World War I as Europe split into two hostile blocs, or groups, of countries: *The Triple Alliance,* composed of Germany, the Austro-Hungarian Empire and Italy; and the *Triple Entente,* of Russia, France and Great Britain.

The grouping of various nations into defense agreements created what became known as *entan-gling alliances*. The major powers in Europe were committed to fight in defense of weaker nations. When Austria-Hungary invaded tiny Serbia, Russia mobilized to defend the Serbs. France honored its commitment to fight with Russia, and Germany backed Austria-Hungary. To invade France, German troops marched through Belgium. The British had a mutual defense treaty with the Belgians, and thus they were drawn into the conflict. This conflict grew into what is called World War 1.

The First World War nearly destroyed European civilization. The countryside of France was devastated. So many men were killed that it was said that Europe had ''lost a generation.'' After the war, the *League of Nations* was formed to prevent any repeat of these horrors. The League was not successful in preventing war. Just 20 years after the end of the First World War, a second and even more terrifying and costly conflict erupted — World War II.

One of the reasons Germany could become so strong only two decades after defeat in the First World War was that the balance of power in the Western World had been disrupted. England and France had been weakened. Russia was undergoing a revolution and did not take an active role in European affairs. The United States refused to join the League of Nations. There was a desire in America to remain aloof from the affairs of Europe, to be *neutral*.

Emergence of superpowers

The tremendous drain of waging war and the development of nuclear weapons changed the nature of balance of power after World War II. Power was no longer distributed nearly equally among European countries. Germany, France, Italy, the United Kingdom and Japan had been devastated by war. Two strong nations with differing ideologies emerged to fill the power vacuum: the Soviet Union and the United States.

Both the United States and the Soviet Union developed a capacity to destroy each other with nuclear arms. This led to a *mutual deterrence,* or a stalemate in which neither country can attack the other for fear of massive retaliation. This is also called a *balance of terror.* The critical factor in a successful deterrence is that the threat must be credible. Each side must be convinced that the other has sufficient power, and a willingness to act. Both sides usually ''exchange'' information through spying on one another.

Regional alliances

The growth of just two major world powers changed the nature of military alliances. For over 40 years following World War II, most agreements for common defense among nations were based on alignment with the United States or the Soviet Union.

The *North Atlantic Treaty Organization* (NATO) was an alliance established by 12 West European countries, Greece, Turkey, Canada and the United States. The *Warsaw Treaty Organization* (WTO), also called the Warsaw Pact, was an alliance formed by six East European countries and the Soviet Union. The countries of each alliance pledged to regard an attack on one of their respective members as an attack on all.

Since World War II, many local wars have occurred, but these conflicts remained limited in scope. Some observers saw these smaller conflicts, such as those in the Middle East between Israel and the Arab states, as substitutes for a larger war. Each superpower supported a combative nation that, in effect, represented the superpower's political interests. In turn, these conflicts remained limited because of potential participation by the two superpowers — the United States and the Soviet Union — and their allies.

Arms build-up

Each superpower responded to a new build-up by the other side with even more sophisticated and lethal weapons. Military expenditures supported large industries and employed millions of workers. These outlays, however, were a tremendous drain on the resources and finances of both nations. Both economies have enormous deficits due to the military build-up.

In 1990, events occurred in the Soviet Union and other Eastern European nations which led to changes in the Warsaw Pact. The Soviet Union wants to keep the Warsaw Pact as a political union. If the Warsaw Pact disintegrated, the question of NATO's future also becomes a significant issue.

New power blocs

The cold war atmosphere of superpower confrontation which had maintained the balance of power for over 40 years has given way to a new spirit of negotiation and arms reduction. As the predominance of American and Soviet influence in the global balance of power diminishes, other nations are assuming leadership roles.

Department of Defense

Multiple warhead nuclear missiles are the product of the superpower arms race. Photo shows the U.S. Intercontinental Ballistic Missile (ICBM) called Peacekeeper, with a range of over 4,000 miles.

Paul Kennedy, professor of history at Yale University, described the shift from a bipolar to a multipolar world this way:

Militarily, the United States and the Soviet Union stayed in the forefront as the 1960s gave way to the 1970s and 1980s.... Over the same few decades, however, the global productive balances have been altering faster than ever before. The Third World's share of total manufacturing output and GNP, depressed to an all-time low in the decade after 1945, has steadily expanded since that time. Europe has recovered from its wartime batterings and, in the form of the European Economic Community, has become the world's largest trading unit. The People's Republic of China is leaping forward at an impressive rate. Japan's postwar economic growth has been so phenomenal that, according to some measures, it recently overtook Russia in total GNP. By contrast, both the American and Russian growth rates have become more sluggish, and their shares of global production and wealth have shrunk dramatically since the 1960s. Leaving aside all the smaller nations, therefore, it is plain that there already exists a multipolar world once more.

The global power centers of the 1990s include: China, Japan, the European Community, the Soviet Union and the United States. It is expected that national power in the 1990s will be determined more and more by economic strength and trade and less and less by the acquisition of territory through military might.

Terrorism

On November 4, 1979, 52 American embassy employees in Iran were seized as hostages by supporters of the new Iranian regime headed by the Muslim religious leader, or Ayatollah, Ruhollah Khomeini. The hostages were held for 444 days in the capital city, Teheran. Khomeini's followers claimed it was the only way to express their anger at the American government. They were angry because the U.S. government, despite warnings from the Ayatollah, allowed the Shah of Iran to seek medical treatment for cancer in the United States after he had been deposed by Khomeini's soldiers. These terrorists, who drew worldwide attention, demanded the return of billions of dollars taken by the Shah when he fled the country.

Terrorism is often a calculated act designed to serve specific goals by instilling fear in a population or specific group. Terrorism is goal-oriented action, usually political and often involving extraordinary violence. Terrorists aim for world attention so they will have a forum from which to express their ideas. They depend upon the media to air their viewpoints.

Terrorist organizations can be divided into various categories. For some groups, the conflict is over territory. Long-time residents, often the majority in a given area, may desire independence or self-rule.

AP Photo

Standing guard: This armed and masked young woman was one of the Iranian terrorists who held the 52 American hostages in the U.S. embassy in Iran in 1979.

The Irish Republican Army, which opposes British control of Northern Ireland, falls into this category. Also in this group are the Basque separatists (ETA) in Spain who seek independence for their "homeland," and the Palestinians (PLO) who desire the establishment of an Arab Palestine.

Other terrorists represent political factions of the left or the right. Their violence is directed against the established power-holders of a society in general and incumbent governments in particular. These organizations either represent or are self-appointed representatives of the powerless in societies where economic and other grievances of the people go unheeded. The Red Brigades of Italy, for example, directed their terror at public officials and politicians as a protest against economic conditions that left millions of Italians jobless.

Right-wing death squads in Latin America, often supported by the government, have been responsible for the murder of thousands of people in Guatemala, El Salvador and Argentina. Their targets are people who express a point of view considered threatening to the regime.

Terrorist groups operate throughout the world. There are religious fanatics, hate groups, death squads, drug smugglers and political revolutionaries who use terrorism to further their causes. The problem of eliminating terrorism is as complex as the reasons for the existence of so many terrorist groups.

Terrorist or patriot

Terrorists use a variety of methods: bombing, kidnapping, assassination, hijacking and armed attacks. Terrorists generally consider themselves patriots, committing what they believe to be heroic acts.

Hostage or political prisoner

Muslim fundamentalists have taken hostages to publicize their struggle against Western influence in the Middle East. They have seized Americans and Europeans working in Beirut, Lebanon, and held them in secret hideaways for years. It had been suggested that the kidnappers would trade the American hostages for Muslim fundamentalist prisoners held by Israel. Israel viewed the Muslims as prisoners of war who had committed violent acts against the state of Israel. The Muslim groups claimed that their compatriots held by Israel were hostages. Prisoners of war can be distinguished from hostages. A hostage is often an innocent bystander, sometimes women or children or professors or journalists who have not been involved in decision-making that the terrorist opposes. Terrorism is random and is used to create fear. Political prisoners are generally involved directly in an activity sponsored by a government.

Narco-terrorism

International drug dealers based in Medellín, Colombia depend on terrorist acts to maintain their profitable operations. High government officials, judges, newspaper publishers and police are often murdered by members of drug cartels who control the production and distribution of cocaine worldwide.

In August 1989, presidential candidate Luis Carlos Galan was assassinated by Colombian drug lords. Galan was an outspoken critic of the drug barons. He was extremely popular among the Colombian people. His assassination prompted a nationwide crackdown on the drug cartels by the Colombian government. The drug lords reacted with even more violence and murder.

Anti-Americanism

Although less terrorism occurs within U.S. borders than in many other countries, American influence and presence abroad has long been a target for terrorist attacks.

Attacks aimed at U.S. military bases have been persistent in recent years. In October 1983, a fanatic terrorist on a suicide mission drove a truck loaded with explosives into U.S. Marine headquarters in Beirut, Lebanon. The truck exploded and 239 Marines were killed.

In May 1990, communist *guerillas* — members of an irregular army who operate in small, mobile groups — in the Philippines claimed responsibility for killing two U.S. servicemen. They said the killings would continue until all American troops were withdrawn from the Philippines.

Other acts of terrorism are designed to create fear among the general public — the feeling that anyone could become the victim of a terrorist attack. Air travelers are sometimes the targets of terrorists. The ill-fated Pan American flight 103 was bombed out of the sky over Lockerbie, Scotland, in December 1988. All 259 passengers and crew and 11 people on the ground were killed.

SSgt. Charles M. Reger — U.S. Air Force

Manuel Noriega, formerly Commander in Chief of Panama, accused of drug-trafficking and money-laundering, was arrested by U.S. officials in Panama and taken to the U.S. for trial. It appeared that he had close ties with the Colombian drug terrorists.

Chapter 6
Technology

- *Technology is rapidly transforming our lives; will we be its masters or its servants?*

- *The United States has become an "information society;" adjustments are required in the way we think, work and govern ourselves.*

Instant satellite television communications carry live the coronation of a new pope in Rome or a world heavyweight championship boxing match to all parts of the globe. Global communications and transportation have become commonplace and are changing our lives. A world-wide culture of music has been developed through the new technologies. Michael Jackson is as popular in Japan and Europe as he is in the United States. Computer technology enables students in Japan to communicate with students in Saudi Arabia and researchers in France to share ideas with colleagues around the world right from their homes and laboratories. Goods made in one country are shipped by sea and air to many regions of the world.

These and many other changes are the result of *technology.* Technology is a complex concept: it consists of machines — advanced machinery for the most part — and production processes. Technology also includes less tangible things such as workers' skills, and the stock of knowledge either retained in human minds or retrieved from journals, books and computers.

The information society

The development of the computer has created a technological revolution. It has made an information explosion possible by providing a way to store and retrieve tremendous amounts of information

almost instantaneously. Developed nations of the world are becoming what analysts call information societies.

What is *information?* Simply stated, it is data arranged in a useful form. Data are observations and measurements. Information is data put in different forms so that it is meaningful. Numbers translated into percentages and ratios or arranged in chart or graphic form; generalizations or conclusions drawn from observations — are examples of data transformed to information.

The sources of data are almost endless; anyone who keeps records provides data for individuals, schools, government, businesses and other organizations.

When information leads to new ways of doing a task and new understanding so that it can be used by others, *knowledge* is created. The computer and other technological devices store, produce and transmit information, but they do not create knowledge. Knowledge is shaped by research, analysis and experience. Information in itself has limited value; knowledge is doing something with information. It is "know-how." It can be used to solve problems.

High technology

Tremendous advances in computer know-how

27

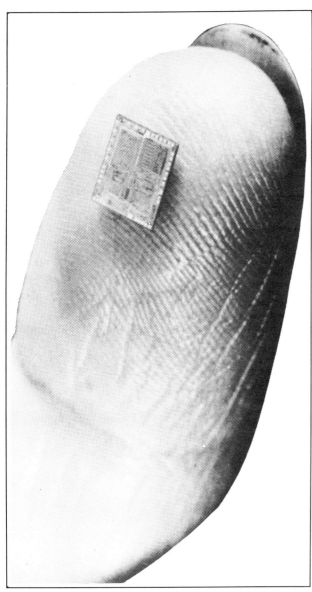

A computer chip is smaller than a human fingertip yet performs the work of thousands of electronic circuits.

have led to the development of the fast growing *high-technology* industry — computers and related electronic technology such as microprocessors and telematics.

Technically a computer is an electronic device that can be programmed to store, retrieve, and process data and information. It can add, subtract, multiply and divide at fantastic speeds.

A *microprocessor* is a tiny silicon chip that contains the electronic circuits needed for a computer. Engineers call the chips "integrated circuits;" one of them replaces thousands of electronic circuits. Advances in computer technology have been tremendous: A computer system that not long ago would have filled an entire room can now be placed, like a typewriter, on a desktop or on one's lap.

The cost of producing computers was reduced significantly in the 1980s. With the advent of pocket calculators, digital watches and video games, peo-

ple were seeing just the beginning of what *microelectronics* would bring. Electronic encyclopedias and other reference books, computerized kitchens, automated classrooms, household robots and computerized medical parts are no longer items of the future.

Telematics, the blending of computers and communications, has changed the transmission of information and knowledge. People from all areas of the globe are brought closer together by the standard language of computer networks. As a result, related economic activities, such as banking and international trade, can be performed in different geographic areas and coordinated through the medium of computerized communications. An insurance company in Boston can send all of its claims via computer to an office in Ireland to be processed for less than it would cost to do it at home. Some call it the global office. The computer is also making it convenient for many people to work from their own homes rather than travel to an office five days a week.

Robotics

A *robot* is a mechanical or electronic metal arm, complete with "shoulder," "elbow" and "wrist," which is programmed by computer to perform certain tasks.

Robots can pick, place, stack, pack, feel, find, search, inspect, assemble and even make decisions. Japan is a leader in pioneering robots for industrial use. Other nations, particularly in Western Europe, are outfitting factories with robots. Robots are used to assemble cars and other types of equipment. Robots can do jobs that humans find dangerous or tedious, such as applying polyvinyl chloride (PVC) to the underbodies of cars or assembling heavy sacks on pallets. Robots are used in nuclear research to protect humans from exposure to harmful radiation. Some robots have "eyes," or television cameras, and other sensing powers to perform more sophisticated jobs such as welding.

Biotechnology

Biotechnology is the application of science and technology to the development of new forms of plant, animal and human life. *Genetic engineering* — the transfer of genes from one life form to another — is the best-known line of research in biotechnology. We can now mass produce genetically altered bacteria that will, in turn, produce hormones to speed up and increase the weight of beef cattle and increase the milk production of dairy cows. Since it deals with life itself, biotechnology is very controversial.

Research and development

Throughout history many major discoveries were accidental. The usefulness of fire was probably discovered when lightning struck, and the resulting heat was recognized as valuable. Early humans learned to hunt, fish and farm from trial, error and inventiveness. Modern technology, by contrast, is the product of systematic *research and development.*

Research and development is costly. Research involves a high risk of failure. The results of most experiments do not meet projected expectations, and many discoveries have little industrial application. Research also requires technically trained people and costly scientific equipment.

Advances in technology are based on *science* — the search for knowledge through the logic of observation, inference, deduction and experimentation. Scientific work is not always aimed at applying results to practical technological uses. Scientists must be free to experiment and discover, or invent.

Many technological advances result as a byproduct of scientific research. Technology is the application of knowledge gained from research or experience. Today, most advances in food production are not due to the struggles and inventiveness of farmers, but, in large part, to efforts in the agricultural sciences.

In order to use technology, money and human effort must be invested. Sometimes governments make this investment, such as when they use technology to develop military systems. U.S. Government-supported research and development in aeronautical engineering for military purposes was made available to private aircraft companies. This enabled them to become world leaders in the field of commercial aviation. Transforming knowledge into technology requires a large commitment of resources.

Developing nations

Research and development is best conducted in countries that have a technologically advanced *infrastructure* — experienced technical personnel, established research facilities, a wide range of manufacturing capability, and access to recent scientific knowledge. A nation's infrastructure also includes advanced education, transportation and communications systems. Accordingly, most of the world's research and development — over 90 percent — takes place in and benefits industrialized, or developed countries. Developing countries would like to have more access to high technology. Many see technology as the key to their development.

Developing nations look to industrial nations for this technology. When it is supplied by communist or socialist nations, the government of the supplying nation plans and provides the new technology. When it is supplied by capitalist nations, large corporations often provide the technology. Large international companies are called *multinational corporations.*

Department of Energy

The Nova Laser Facility at Lawrence Livermore National Laboratory contributes significantly to the U.S. Department of Energy's inertial confinement fusion program.

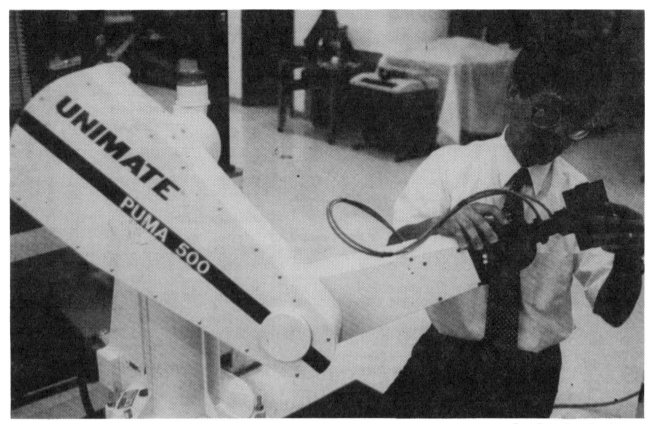

A professor at a Florida university is preparing a robot for a demonstration. *Boca Raton News/Janet Jarman*

Many multinational corporations have production plants in the developing nations, but most of their research and development facilities are located in the companies' home country. Many developing nations are becoming impatient with the slow pace of technological development in their homelands. These countries are very dependent on decisions made in the industrialized nations. Technology can be transferred from an industrialized nation to a developing one, but without the infrastructure and base of experience, it is not easily applied.

Emerging nations look for ways in which they can develop the scientific base and needed technology. One idea is to start "international centers of learning" where scientists from developing countries can work with counterparts from the more scientifically advanced nations. Ultimately, to be of greatest benefit to the developing nation, plants must be constructed and equipment provided in that nation.

The "brain-drain" phenomenon is an example of how difficult it can be to transfer technology as knowledge. When students from developing nations are educated in the different branches of science, usually in other countries, they often do not find satisfying jobs upon returning home. They sometimes shift to administrative or other jobs where their training is not as well used. The availability of facilities and the level of pay often lure them back to where they were trained. Out of frustration, developing nations are beginning to require that students trained abroad must return to the homeland to serve a minimum number of years.

Appropriate technology

High technology alone is not the answer to the needs of developing nations. The technology also needs to be appropriate for a particular country. Until recently, most developing countries wanted the best and most modern technology available, often ignoring the appropriate use of the technology for their needs.

Much new technology in the developed countries is capital-intensive and labor-saving. Most production is accomplished by sophisticated equipment operated or programmed by a few technicians. In most developing countries, where there is a surplus of unemployed people and a lack of funds for capital investments, expensive, laborsaving technology can make matters worse, by increasing unemployment.

Appropriate technology makes the best use of a country's natural resources, workers and their skills. In most developing nations, appropriate technology should create the need for more workers, not fewer, and be simple to run and repair. For example, many Third World villages use small-horsepower pumps rather than large power plants to generate electricity. Also, using locally-produced raw materials is preferable to spending scarce foreign exchange to import materials.

Chapter 7
Manufacturing

- *Most of the components of the clothes we wear and the products we use have traveled around the world, having been manufactured by workers of a "global factory."*
- *Large corporations often operate in many nations, creating increasing interdependence.*

Automobiles made in Japan, Germany and Korea; clothes from Hong Kong, Taiwan and Malaysia; shoes from Italy and Brazil; bicycles made in France and the United Kingdom; computers developed in the United States; and a myriad of other manufactured goods are commonplace in today's international marketplace. Large-scale production and trade did not just spring up. Manufactured goods result from sophisticated production processes.

Manufacturing is the process of producing something — of making products from raw materials using machinery or mechanical power. A manufacturing company may have been built close to raw material sources, where abundant labor was available, or near product markets. If a new company is successful, it is likely to expand from its first facility to a larger plant. In time, with the growth of sales, a single manufacturing plant may no longer be adequate, so the company builds additional facilities. The new plant or plants may be located to take advantage of promising markets or cheap labor.

Growth leads to international trade

To expand operations further, the company begins to *export* its products, entering into international trade. It establishes branch offices to handle distribution abroad. When a company exports its products to a foreign nation, it must often compete with the same type of product manufactured in that nation. A Japanese company which exports cars to the United States is in direct competition with U.S. automakers. A car exported from Japan becomes an *import* in the United States. Foreign imports are often discouraged because sales of domestic-made products might decrease.

A *tariff* is a tax or duty placed upon imports to raise the price of an imported product in relation to the price of the domestic product. High tariffs tend to reduce imports. The *quota* is a limit on the amount of a particular product that can be imported. This reduces competition from foreign producers, helping manufacturers at home protect their share of the market.

The multinational corporation

An exporting company can try to overcome high tariffs or low quotas by producing items in the country where it sells the product. Such items are not considered imports. In the process, a new type of business is established: a *multinational corporation* (MNC).

Many companies are expanding operations to overseas plants. It helps them avoid tariffs and quotas. Other reasons to expand operations may be to place the company nearer to resources, including skilled and less expensive workers.

International investments. Foreign manufacturing is the natural outgrowth of an expanding domestic enterprise. When a corporation expands outside of the nation, the capital it spends is considered *direct international investment.* These companies build or buy existing manufacturing facilities abroad and maintain control over business operations. Direct investments make up the major part of American investments abroad. The other category is *international portfolio investments.* Here, private individuals or companies buy shares in foreign business enterprises but have no control over operations.

Expanding global production. Multinational corporations increase their operations in two basic ways: by *integration* or by *diversification.* Integration is the combining of manufacturing activities to form a larger production system. The integration is horizontal if the company expands by acquiring or building similar production facilities: for example, a bottling company buying another bottling company.

The integration is vertical if the company expands into activities that directly support production. When a steel company expands by acquiring iron ore fields it is known as backward, or downward, vertical integration because it is an earlier step in production. If a steel company expands by purchasing a tool manufacturing company, it is known as forward vertical integration because it is a step advanced in production.

Diversification is expansion by the purchase of related but not supporting companies: for example, if a soup company purchases a bakery. Diversification into unrelated companies is known as *conglomeration.* If a soup company purchased a tire manufacturing plant, it would be an example of a conglomerate.

The growth of multinationals

By the end of the 1950s, when MNCs became a major source of industrial production, American companies were the most powerful. American companies then controlled about 70 percent of the more than 150 MNCs that dominated the 13 major industries — aerospace, automotive, chemicals, electrical equipment, food products, general machinery, iron and steel, metal products, paper, petroleum, pharmaceuticals, textiles, and commercial banking. By 1980, U.S. multinationals accounted for less than 40 percent of these powerful businesses.

In 1945, at the end of World War II, the United States, with 5 percent of the world's population, produced 50 percent of the world's industrial output. By 1990, that share had dropped to 25 percent with

USAID Photo

A worker for Coca Cola — one of the world's largest multinational corporations — in Somalia, Africa.

the same 5 percent of people. The per capita share of global manufacturing by the United States decreased by one-half during this period.

The rest of the world began catching up to the United States after 1960 for several reasons: Latecomers in marketing products have the advantage over pioneers in not having to duplicate the pioneer's development costs. The technology is there to be copied or adapted, and productivity in the early stages is higher than it is for pioneer producers. Western Europe and Japan also have a more modern industrial base than the United States. Most of their industry had been destroyed by bombing raids during World War II. After rebuilding, these countries had modern plants and equipment. Additionally, the developing nations of the world increased their manufacturing output, increasing the global output and reducing the overall contribution of the United States.

The superior quality of many goods manufactured in other nations was a very important factor in the relative decline of the U.S. share in global output. This quality gap was most obvious in electronics and automobiles. Multinational corporations in other nations successfully gained a global market share by manufacturing a high-quality product and keeping the price down. Auto manufacturers in the United States were slow to respond to the consumer's desire for small, reliable, fuel-efficient cars. By the time that General Motors, Ford and Chrysler had developed a better, more desirable product, Japanese and German car manufacturers had developed a reputation for quality that has made it difficult for American-made cars to compete. In 1990, research demonstrated that the buying public in the United States was more likely to purchase a car with a Japanese name than the exact same car with an English-type name. Similar consumer attitudes are held toward video cassette recorders, cameras, stereo sound equipment and watches, especially those made in Germany and Japan.

The United States also uses a tremendous amount of resources for the military and space industries. As a result, the rate of innovation and the amount of production in civilian industries has declined significantly. About 6 percent of the United States' gross national product (GNP) — the total dollar value of the nation's output of goods and services — goes for military spending. In comparison, France and West Germany spend about 3 percent of their GNP, Canada 2 percent, and Japan 1 percent.

The global factory

More and more manufacturing of finished products is being carried out on a global scale and managed by multinational corporations. The mining, refining, sewing, soldering and mixing of resources for a single product is likely to be carried out in different countries. With different parts of the production process on different continents, a planetary division of labor has been formed. The once local factory system, that was replaced by integrated domestic production, has evolved into a *global factory*.

The production process for many goods today is broken down into small components, each performed in a far-flung place to take advantage of the unique features of a country. Silicon chips, which are the heart of *microcomputers,* typically are made in Japan and the United States. They are likely to be sent to Korea or Singapore where gold threads are soldered to the terminals, then flown back to the United States for further processing.

This development of global products has been made possible by new technology such as jet air-cargo carriers, containerized shipping and telecommunications. Much manufacturing takes place in the developing countries of the world, where there are natural resources and inexpensive labor. A number of multinational corporations in developing nations

now are emerging as significant manufacturing centers.

Corporations have found that not only is labor cheaper in the developing countries, but it is often more productive. Global manufacturing in the developing nations is concentrated heavily in industries where unskilled or semi-skilled labor is required, such as fabrics, garments, toys, metal products and electronics. Work tasks include sewing, soldering and assembling. Women and children are often hired for the tasks and the wages are low.

Production in the developing countries takes place mostly in "free production zones." These are areas designed by the developing countries to attract foreign capital. The host governments offer a variety of incentives including: exemption from duties and taxes on machinery and raw materials, a five-to-ten year income tax "holiday," freedom from foreign exchange controls, and sometimes furnishing of office and factory buildings by the local government.

Multinationals in the developing nations

Many MNCs in developing nations are oil producers. South Korea has MNCs in shipbuilding, electronics, textiles and transportation. Multinationals in Zambia and Chile are based on copper mining and metal refining.

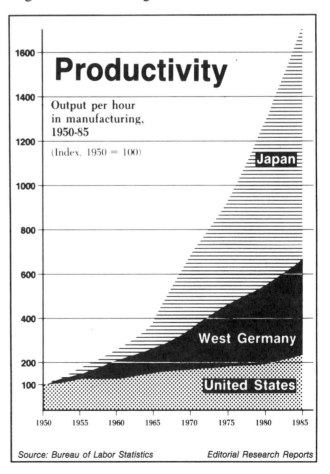

Productivity

Output per hour in manufacturing, 1950-85

(Index, 1950 = 100)

Japan

West Germany

United States

1950 1955 1960 1965 1970 1975 1980 1985

Source: Bureau of Labor Statistics   *Editorial Research Reports*

The developing countries are finding that industrial development can bring problems. Some countries rushed into heavy industrialization and neglected agriculture. No real development is possible without a solid agricultural foundation. After concentrating on industry for years, many developing nations neglected to maintain farm-to-market roads, storage facilities, processing plants, irrigation systems and farm equipment. These nations have allowed their infrastructure to deteriorate. Consequently, food shortages, hunger and malnutrition have occurred in some areas.

World unemployment

South Korea is an example of a country that rushed into industrialization. During the 1980s, South Korea had a high economic growth rate. It competed with Japan in electronics and textiles as well as in heavy industries such as auto manufacturing, shipbuilding and steel production. Development in heavy industry tends to be *capital-intensive* — using much capital equipment compared to labor. Hard times hit South Korea: High unemployment and a slowdown in economic growth occurred. An emphasis on steel production and machinery has resulted in high wages

for some people, but poverty for those who are unemployed. South Korea wants to revitalize the light industries which are more *labor-intensive* and energy-saving.

Steel, automotive, shipbuilding and machinery are industries that depend more on capital equipment than labor. Heavy industrial development does not create the new jobs that more *appropriate technology* would. New factories can create increased unemployment in some areas. Something called "island labor migration" typically happens when the announcement of a new plant is made. Many more potential workers than can be hired migrate from the countryside to the city seeking employment. Those who don't get a job often stay in the urban area looking for other employment, often unsuccessfully.

Nearly all countries are troubled by unemployment, but the situation is especially acute for those in the South, or developing part of the world. In India alone it is estimated that 8 million jobs must be created each year. With 850 million people and growing, India has a GNP only 40 percent the size of the United Kingdom which has 57 million people. Only economic growth that creates many new jobs will help overcome the world unemployment problem.

AP Photo

Heavy industries, such as this South Korean steel company, help contribute to national development, but do not create as many jobs as smaller industries do.

Chapter 8

Trade

> ● *A steady increase in trade is creating a "global village."*
>
> ● *In a recessionary economy, demands for protectionism grow as nations compete for markets.*

No modern nation is self-sufficient when it comes to providing all the material resources needed to meet its needs. Nations trade to obtain necessary resources for production. Nations also trade to acquire goods that they otherwise could not produce, or produce as efficiently as another country. Nations also trade in order to sell what they have produced.

In a country such as the United States, whose economy is built on private enterprise, business corporations generally initiate trade. When companies need resources that they are unable to obtain at home, they buy *(import)* them from other countries. Companies in search of new markets sell *(export)* products to other nations.

In many countries, international trade decisions are made by the national government. In nations with socialist economic systems, government planning committees decide what goods are traded. In Japan and France, both capitalist economies, the government still makes some trade decisions — such as how much food to import. Even the U.S. government organizes trade when it arranges to sell grain to other countries or buy oil from the Mideast.

In the process of exporting goods to other countries, nations obtain foreign currency which in turn is used to import other items from abroad. Virtually all of this money is carried on the books of major banks which handle the financial transactions. Still, it represents shifts in the international purchas-

ing power of corporations, governments and nations.

Nations tend to specialize in certain goods or services on the world market. *Specialized production* is efficient: more goods and services of a higher quality can be produced with a given amount of resources or inputs. A country specializes in the items it can best produce relative to the production capabilities of other countries. What a country specializes in depends on the resources — availability of raw materials and labor, or the quality of technology and capital — that it can devote to production. Even if a country such as the United States is an efficient producer of many items, it is best for it to concentrate on producing some goods and services while importing others. Nations want to use their resources to the best *comparative advantage* in producing for both domestic and foreign markets.

Trading patterns

Nations of the world fall into three broad economic classes: *developed, newly-industrialized countries* (NICs) and *developing*. In the developed nations, manufacturing and advanced technological production are the primary economic activities. Newly-industrialized countries like Hong Kong, South Korea, Singapore and Taiwan depend upon specialty products and finding a niche to sell them in the global market. Developing nations are in various stages toward reaching the goal of economic development,

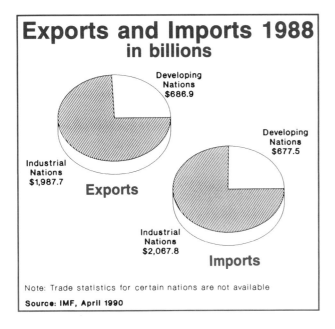

Exports and Imports 1988
in billions

Developing Nations $686.9

Developing Nations $677.5

Industrial Nations $1,987.7

Exports

Industrial Nations $2,067.8

Imports

Note: Trade statistics for certain nations are not available

Source: IMF, April 1990

and most of the work force is employed in agriculture.

Most world trade takes place among governments and businesses in the developed or industrialized countries; Western Europe and the United States alone account for 70 percent of this trade. Seven of the world's 10 leading trading nations are located in Western Europe. The United States and Japan, in that order, are the leaders in international trade.

Canada is the largest trading partner of the United States. More than 20 percent of U.S. exports go to Canada, while 60 percent of Canada's exports are sent to the United States. On December 30, 1988, the Canadian Parliament ratified a free-trade agreement that eliminated all tariffs on goods traded between the two nations. There are indications that Mexico would like to join to make it a three-nation agreement.

Developing nations comprise a very important part of world trade also. About 40 percent of exports from the United States go to developing nations mostly in Latin America, Africa and Asia; about 35 percent of our imports come from nations in these areas of the world.

International business is very important to the economy of the United States.

• Thirty-three percent of U.S. corporate profits are generated by international trade.

• The 23 largest U.S. banks derive almost half their total earnings overseas.

• Four of every five new jobs in the U.S. are generated as a direct result of international trade.

• Current U.S. investments abroad are valued at more than $300 billion.

• Some 350,000 international students attend colleges and universities in the United States.

• Individuals and corporations from other nations are estimated to have invested $1.5 trillion in the U.S., most of it since 1975.

• The United States exports twice as much food and other agricultural commodities as it imports.

The United States is the world's largest economy, the largest consumer market, the largest importer and second largest exporter — after West Germany. For the United States, however, it has been increasingly difficult to maintain this edge in the global economy. In 1987, some 70 percent of U.S. manufactured products had to compete with a foreign product, as compared with 25 percent in 1960. Of the goods manufactured in the U.S., 88 percent require imported parts and materials. The United States must depend entirely upon imports to acquire scarce metals needed to produce strong and dependable products for space technology and national defense. In 1985, the U.S. became the world's largest debtor nation, meaning that it owed more money to other nations than anyone else. In 1990, the U.S. *trade deficit* (the dollar value of exports subtracted from imports) was calculated at $110 billion.

In order to remain economically competitive with other nations, many U.S. leaders are urging that America's education system be improved. The educational reform movement in the United States during the 1980s and '90s is predicated on the belief that the nation is "at risk." It is argued that all American students need to be literate; to improve achievement in science and mathematics; to acquire a second language; to know the history, geography and culture of other nations and peoples; and to be aware of global issues such as environmental deterioration, human rights violations and the impact of technology on daily life.

The international marketplace

Items exchanged in *foreign markets* fall into six general categories:

1) foodstuffs — grains, meat and processed foods;

2) raw materials — renewable and nonrenewable resources including ores, metals, fossil fuels and lumber;

3) technology — knowledge, methods and skills used to improve production;

4) manufactured goods — from machinery to toys;

5) arms — the materials of war and defense;

6) currency — foreign money with which to pay for exports.

Food. Food is traded largely among developed

Worldwide Exports and Imports, 1988
in billions

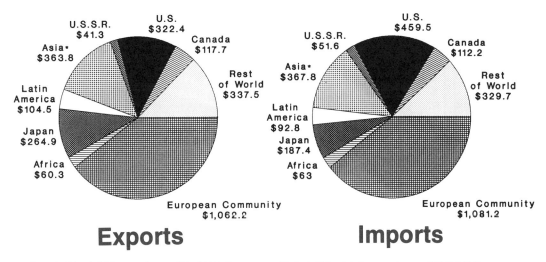

Exports

U.S.S.R. $41.3
Asia* $363.8
Latin America $104.5
Japan $264.9
Africa $60.3
U.S. $322.4
Canada $117.7
Rest of World $337.5
European Community $1,062.2

Total World Exports – $2,674.6

Imports

U.S.S.R. $51.6
Asia* $367.8
Latin America $92.8
Japan $187.4
Africa $63
U.S. $459.5
Canada $112.2
Rest of World $329.7
European Community $1,081.2

Total World Imports – $2,745.2

• Excluding Japan

Source: IMF, April 1990   Note: Trade statistics for certain nations are not available

countries. The United States is the world's largest producer of grain and meats. In turn, the Soviet Union is the largest grain purchaser, importing roughly 20 million tons annually to feed its population. Japan is not far behind the Soviet Union, importing over half of its total grain consumption.

The developing countries usually export one special crop. In Brazil and Colombia this crop is coffee, while in Cuba the crop is sugar. Argentina exports two main crops: meats and grain. Much of the trade of former colonies is still with their former colonizers. There is little trade between developing countries because their markets are too small, and it is more advantageous to exchange their foodstuffs and other resources for goods that can only be obtained from developed nations.

Raw materials. A major part of the raw materials traded is exported from the developing countries to the developed industrial nations. The developed nations use metals, ores and fossil fuel produced at home and purchase even more from other countries. The United States would be in a critical condition without the zinc, oil, chromium, manganese and other raw materials it imports. In turn, many developing countries do not have the technology to put the natural mineral resources in their lands to use. They depend upon these exports for needed foreign currency.

Technology and manufacturing. Most of the world's trade today is among the developed nations. Most of this trade involves technology and manufactured goods.

Much technology developed today, except in socialist nations, is the property of multinational corporations. A major part of this technology is a product of new knowledge and new manufactured goods. Governments are involved in research and development, but most of the production of manufactured goods for industry and the military is carried out by private business corporations.

Because of the high cost involved, corporations and nations tend to *specialize* in what they produce for world markets. American corporations specialize in such items as computers, aircraft, tractors and trucks. Japanese manufacturers specialize in televisions, radios, camera equipment and automobiles. English and French companies produce aircraft, while Germany has large international markets for automobiles.

Nations also specialize in making component parts

North High School
Salem, Oregon

of manufactured goods. A country or multinational corporation may produce transistors, airplane engines, tires, semiconductors or other components of a computer system. There is often a great deal of competition among nations for their share of the world market for the products they produce. Specialties tend to change over time.

Military goods. Weapons are exported by developed countries and purchased by a wide variety of nations. The two major producers are the United States and the Soviet Union who account for about 70 percent of arms exports.

DURING DEPRESSION PIGS WERE BARTERED FOR WOOD

In the early 1930s, when normal means of payment broke down, many countries resorted to barter arrangements. For example:

• 29,000 Hungarian pigs were paid for with 20,000 wagonloads of Czechoslovakian firewood.

• Hungarian eggs were paid for with Czechoslovakian facilities for Hungarian tourists.

• The Brazilian government and a private U.S. company exchanged 1.3 million sacks of coffee for 25 million bushels of wheat.

• Turkish and Greek tobacco were exchanged for Austrian and Swedish merchandise.

Currency. Nations exchange international currencies, not only in payment for goods and services traded, but also to obtain money that can be used later to purchase items in international markets. Large amounts of dollars, yen, pounds, francs and other currencies are not shipped among trading nations. Most transactions are bookkeeping entries handled through the *International Monetary Fund* in Washington, D.C.

Some effects of trade on economies

International trade — both exports and imports — generally benefits a nation's economy. But like households and businesses, the outflows and inflows of goods or money need to balance out sooner or later.

If countries import more then they export in money value, they acquire a *balance of payments* or *trade* deficit. Other items help balance off a trade deficit or surplus — loans, interest on loans, aid grants, military expenditures, investments — but trade in goods and services is the most important entry. The

United States pays for imports with American dollars; more U.S. imports result in a greater amount of dollars on the world market. As the supply of dollars increases in comparison to the demand for dollars by foreign buyers, each dollar is worth less. It takes less of another currency to trade for the dollar, and more dollars to get other currencies.

If a country exports more than it imports, less of its currency will be in world circulation, and each unit will be worth more. If the United States exported more than it imported, the value of the U.S. dollar would increase in relation to other currencies. Fewer of the dollars could then be exchanged for a given amount of another currency. Said differently, foreign goods would become cheaper for Americans to buy.

Nations attempt to restrict trade

Countries may want to restrict international trade — particularly imports — in order to affect payment balances with other countries. Business interests also pressure their government to erect barriers against certain goods imported from abroad to protect home industries from competition.

The *quota* — setting limits on the amount of certain products that may be imported from abroad — is one widely used measure for restricting foreign trade. Reducing imports has the effect of decreasing the flow of currency out of the home country.

Another effective trade restriction device is the *tariff* — imposing a tax on items purchased from other nations. The effect of a tariff is to raise the price of imported goods like French wines, Japanese stereos, German automobiles, thus reducing the number of these items sold in home markets.

Quotas and tariffs may be of immediate benefit to a home industry or a nation's payments deficit, but other nations may retaliate by erecting barriers against goods they import.

Nations sometimes will agree upon a *voluntary restriction* of exports by a country, usually at the request of the importing nation. This has the effect of a mutual decision, reducing bad feelings created by unilateral restrictions. Sometimes in return for such a favor, the requesting nation will offer technological assistance, military support or the reduction of other trade barriers.

The *cartel* is a formal agreement among nations who export the same product to control the sale of this item on international markets. This is done by restricting the supply on the market and dividing, or sharing, the market. The effect is to maintain high prices. The most successful cartel has been the *Organization of Petroleum Exporting Countries,* commonly known as OPEC. OPEC has been able to control the supply of petroleum to world markets and keep the price far above what it would be with free competition.

Nations may impose a trade restriction for political rather than economic reasons. The *trade embargo* is most commonly used for this purpose. An embargo is a refusal by one nation to trade with a specific country. A limited embargo means that trade in certain vital items — war goods or energy products — is curtailed. A total embargo prohibits any exchange whatsoever. The United States has imposed an almost total embargo on trade and travel with Cuba.

International organizations, such as the **European Community** (EC) and the **General Agreement on Tariffs and Trade** (GATT), attempt to regulate trade. The EC maintains a general tariff for all of its member nations. There are no trade restrictions within this economic union of European states. GATT is a commercial treaty among a number of nations — really a series of bilateral agreements to systematically reduce tariffs and promote free trade.

The trade debate

In 1824, a time of fierce economic nationalism, the English historian Thomas Macaulay wrote,

"Free trade, one of the greatest blessings a government can confer on a people, is in almost every country unpopular." Although world trade has grown by leaps and bounds since World War II through the lowering of international trade barriers, debate continues between supporters of *protectionist* and *free trade* policies.

Free traders believe that the competitive forces of supply and demand should determine the flow of international trade, rather than artificial restrictions by nations and organizations. The benefits of free trade include: lower producer costs for raw materials, improved productivity, lower consumer prices and reduced world tensions.

Protectionists favor the right of a nation to regulate imports in order to protect its domestic jobs and industries, its national security and balance of payments. Protectionists believe that the differing economic systems and levels of development throughout the world compel every nation to defend its economy from free competition with others.

The arguments for protective tariffs and quotas can be persuasive. Proponents say that low wages in foreign countries endanger the jobs of workers in similar industries in their own country. And sometimes they do. A multinational company in the

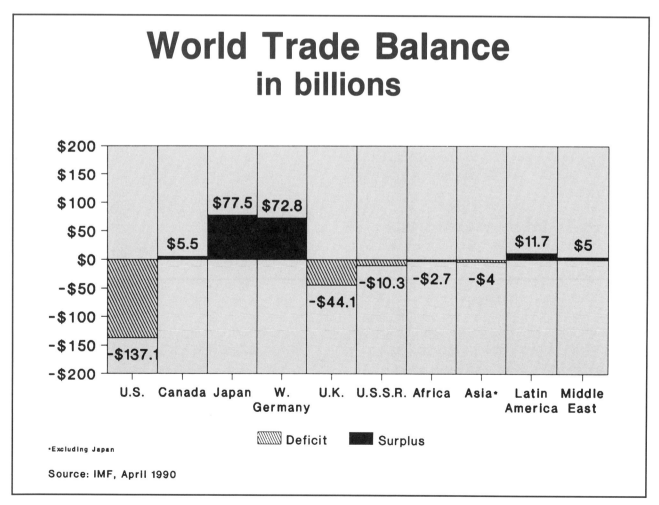

World Trade Balance
in billions

*Excluding Japan

Source: IMF, April 1990

39

United States may ship cloth to its plant in East Asia, where labor is cheap, to be tailored into clothing. The finished product is then returned to the U.S. for merchandising. But factors other than the cost of labor also determine whether a nation can compete for trade. The cost of raw materials, quality of machinery, management skills and workers' skills are just as important.

Productivity — how efficiently resources including labor are used — is the key to how well a company or industry can compete with others. Some countries, such as South Korea, have low labor costs and can compete with other nations, like the United States, that rely on modern machinery. The clothing industry is one area where there is strong competition between these two nations.

Importing goods provides industries with the critical raw materials they need. Importing also provides consumers with a greater variety of products at lower prices. Importing also means that a nation can concentrate production in those areas in which it is most efficient, buying from other nations either what it cannot make or make as efficiently.

It is considered wise to restrict trade that threatens the existence or well-being of a strategic or "infant" (new developing) industry. The United States uses both tariffs and quotas to protect American steel producers from Japanese and Korean competitors. However, the case for steel protection is not overwhelming. While the U.S. steel industry is critical to the economy and national security, it could compete successfully if steps were taken to modernize equipment and increase productivity.

In addition to economic considerations, trade among nations has political benefits. U.S. foreign relations with Western Europe, Japan and Latin America would be hurt by an increase of protectionist barriers.

Leaders in international trade

The United States enjoyed economic supremacy in the period following World War II. However, the U.S. faced increased trade competition as the nations devastated by the war rapidly recovered. Japan and West Germany, the losers of World War II, experienced high rates of economic growth. These three nations — the United States, West Germany and Japan — are the leading exporting nations in the world. Both Japan and West Germany, in addition to the major industrial nations of Western Europe, rebuilt their industries largely with American aid.

During the 1970s and 1980s, Japanese industrial production grew remarkably. Japan's economic strength is based on its ability to efficiently manufacture and export quality consumer products. With a considerable share of the world automobile and electronics market, Japan's economic success since World War II has been phenomenal.

The 12-nation European Community is committed to a unified, integrated economy, eliminating all trade and travel barriers and establishing unified standards within the member nations. Except for Germany, any of the individual nations of the EC could not expect to be an economic power such as Japan or the United States. By cooperating, the European Community has established the largest single market in the world.

The United States, in spite of Japanese and European strength, is still the wealthiest nation in the world. With its abundance and diversity of natural and human resources, America possesses immense potential for economic growth. Yet, the United States is presently faced with a large balance of trade deficit and a deteriorating infrastructure while Japan and Germany have substantial balance of trade surplus.

The United States and Japan have been involved in a serious trade dispute for several years. Japanese trade policy prevents the import of many American-made products. U.S. manufacturers find it difficult to compete with the flood of Japanese products in America. Japanese cars became very popular because of their high quality, low price and fuel efficiency. Japan also produces quality, low-cost televisions, video cassette recorders and cameras. Many Japanese products cost less in the United States than in Japan. Some members of the U.S. Congress have argued that the United States should impose tariffs on certain goods imported from Japan in retaliation for the refusal of Japan to open up its markets to the United States.

With the Japanese economy booming, many wealthy people emerged with the ability to purchase major American companies, including Rockefeller Center in New York City and Columbia Pictures. There is controversy surrounding Japanese purchases of U.S. properties. In 1990, to help the U.S. reduce its trade deficit, Japan promised to buy more U.S. products such as satellites, wood products and super computers.

In the book *Megatrends 2000,* John Naisbitt and Patricia Auberdene write that in the 1990s the world will reap increased benefits from the global economy. According to these authors: "The new global economy cannot be understood if it is thought to be merely more and more trade among 160 nations; it must be viewed as the world moving from trade among countries to a single economy. One economy. One marketplace." Although not all observers are so optimistic, there is nearly unanimous agreement that international world trade is an important fact of our future.

Chapter 9

Development

> - *The GNP per capita of developing nations is less than $2,000 a year.*
>
> - *Developing nations spend almost twice as much on armies and armaments as for health and education.*

The amount and quality of products available to people determine their *standard of living.* Never before this century has there been such a great diversity in standard of living. Millions of people on Earth live much as their ancestors have for centuries before them, tilling the soil with wooden plows and growing barely enough food for survival. They live at a *subsistence level,* having just enough to sustain life. The technology of the last few centuries, particularly the last 100 years, has hurtled many other people into the industrial, scientific and computer age, providing luxuries undreamed of in the past. The degree to which nations utilize technology for the improvement of the standard of living is known as *development.* Throughout the world, nations are in many different stages of development.

Many factors are involved in describing development. They include: (1) the standard of living, (2) use of modern technology, (3) the shift of production from agricultural to industrial activities and (4) the level of productivity. Specific indicators of development include the following variables:

- Gross national product per capita
- Gross national product annual growth rate
- Exports
- Annual export growth
- Manufacturing production
- Industrial production
- Life expectancy in years

- Infant mortality rate (number of infants who die before reaching one year of age per 1000 live births every year)
- Literacy rate (percent of adult population able to read at 6th grade level or higher)

Developing nations

Developing nations are said to be the "have not" countries; they do not have the abundance of material goods, such as modern housing, packaged foods, televisions and other manufactured products, that developed nations have. Developing nations are sometimes referred to as Third World nations. The terminology for poor nations is controversial and many scholars debate what they should be called. It is important to have some way to classify them because they have unique characteristics and problems that need to be addressed.

The term Third World came to be used in order to distinguish those nations that were not as developed industrially as either the First World (capitalist nations such as those in Western Europe, the United States and Japan) or the Second World (communist nations in Eastern and Central Europe). However, in the early 1990s significant changes in the economies of the Second World nations made the term Third World less meaningful. Eastern and Central European communist nations seem to be headed in the direction of allowing more free market activities in their economies.

On the other hand, the term "developing nations" does not really define the status of these nations because developing usually means improving. As bad as the standard of living has been in the past, it appears to be getting worse, due to increasing population pressures, large debt and world-wide economic inflation followed by recession.

The World Bank lends money to governments that have low income GNP per capita mostly for development projects. The Bank divides developing countries into two groups: *low-income developing countries* and *middle-income developing countries.* These countries are so poor that the basic needs of the majority of their people are not met. The goal of the World Bank for economic development is to "raise standards of living in developing countries,

so that people can live healthier, fuller lives."

A few developing nations, such as Saudi Arabia and Kuwait, have a great deal of wealth due to their oil resources. Wealth and income are often unevenly distributed within a developing nation. A small percentage of the population usually owns most of the land and resources. Business activity often is concentrated in a few hands, and export production — goods produced for sale to other countries — is usually foreign-owned. Industrialization is underway in many developing nations, and their growth rate as a whole actually exceeds that of industrial nations. A former president of Brazil summed up the irony of development in these countries when he remarked, "Brazil is doing well, but the people are not."

Developing nations have other general characteristics in common: Their basic economic activity is agricultural rather than industrial. Most of the population resides in rural areas and is employed in subsistence production. Rapid population growth rates are generally the rule with an important exception being the People's Republic of China.

Government spending in developing nations is usually financed with export revenues instead of with income and sales taxes. Since most industry is in the early stages of development, or used for items to be exported and consumed by wealthier nations, most manufactured products for internal use must be *imported* — bought from other countries. The products *exported* — sold to other countries — are usually raw materials such as rubber, petroleum, zinc, manganese, and other minerals or agricultural cash crops like coffee, sugar, cacao and bananas.

Most developing nations are traditional societies, which means that the vast majority of people live in small agricultural communities and rely on the past for ways to do things. Farm production is mainly for local consumption. Much of the population is illiterate. Government control is in the hands of the better-educated, upper-class. Young adults from rural families continue to live with parents after marriage and contribute their earnings to a family pool. The family provides support and security for the elderly out of current production. Since most of these people live at a subsistence level, there is little chance to acquire financial assets, or *capital*. This tends to inhibit development, because capital is necessary for production.

Traditional societies have other obstacles to development. A son has the duty to remain in his father's house; he cannot move easily from the country to the city and from agriculture to industry. Even after his father's death, the son is tied to the farm to support dependent family members. Development, when it comes, breaks down family traditions.

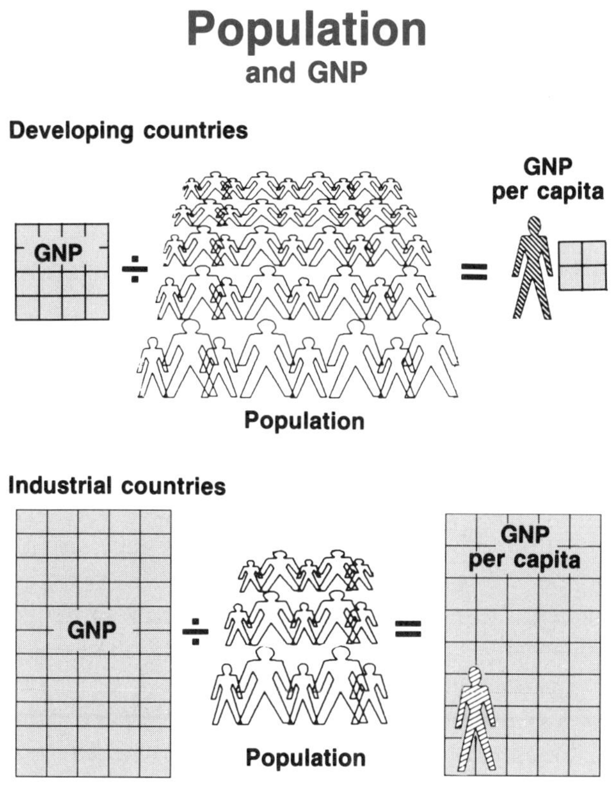

Population
and GNP

Developing countries

GNP ÷ Population = GNP per capita

Industrial countries

GNP ÷ Population = GNP per capita

GNP per capita is low in developing countries. They produce only a fifth as many goods and services as industrial countries but have five times as many people. The chart shows — for both groups of countries in 1986 — GNP and total population. It also shows GNP per capita, the part of GNP each person would have *if* GNP were divided equally. GNP per capita helps measure the material standards and well-being of a country, but it does not show whether all people share equally in the wealth of a country or whether they lead fulfilling lives.

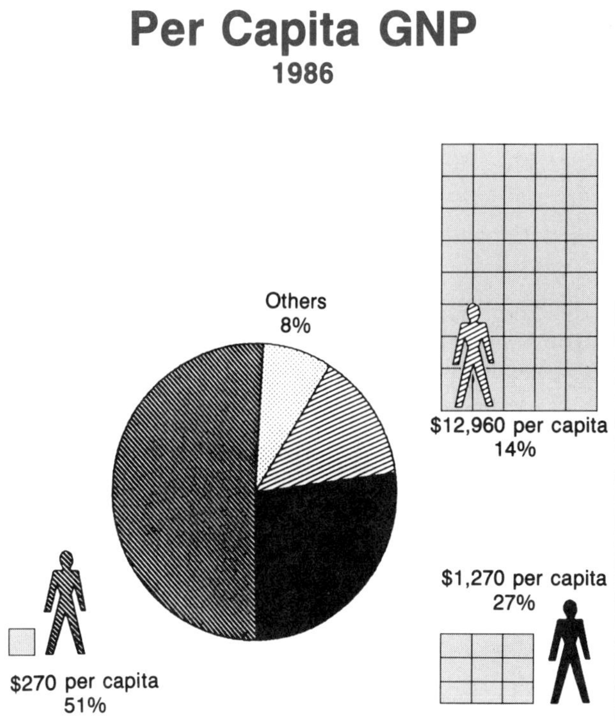

Per Capita GNP
1986

Others 8%

$12,960 per capita 14%

$1,270 per capita 27%

$270 per capita 51%

Half the world's population lives in low-income developing countries, where the average GNP per capita is $270. The chart shows population and the average GNP per capita in low-income and middle-income developing countries and in industrial countries in 1986. "Others" includes high-income oil-exporting countries, countries with population of less than a million, and countries for which no World Bank data are available.

Source: World Bank

SIRS Staff/Michelle McCulloch

The North-South split

Developing nations are typically found in the southern lower-income half of the world. Much of the turbulence around the globe exists in the developing nations — the "have not" nations of Latin America, Africa and Southeast Asia. In 1980, the Independent Commission on International Development Issues, chaired by former West German Chancellor Willy Brandt, published a report *North-South, A Program for Survival*. This report concluded that for the rest of the century North-South relations are the "great social challenge of our time. Peace, stability, and human justice around the globe depend on how well nations cooperate to help people in all lands share in the earth's resources and wealth."

The most needy nations

About 45 developing countries, those having a yearly output per person of less than $300, have been placed in a separate category called the "least developed nations." Other developing nations have an annual per capita output of up to $2,000. Among the least developed nations are: Afghanistan, Bangladesh, Chad, Sierra Leone, Haiti, Western Samoa and Niger. Botswana is the "richest" of these least developed nations with a gross national product (GNP) per capita in 1987 of $1,030.

As a North-South split illustrates the division between the industrialized and developing world, a West-East division, within the Southern hemisphere, separates the developing and the poorest nations. Virtually all the nations of Latin America and the Caribbean are developing. Most nations in Africa, many in Southeast Asia and the Indian sub-continent, still struggle to house, clothe, and feed their people at a bare subsistence level.

A revolution of rising expectations

Until the advent of radio, global travel and television, many inhabitants of developing nations were unaware of how they compared with the rest of the world.

The rapid spread of knowledge by means of television is causing far-reaching consequences. The more people hear and see, the more they know, the more they want. *Dallas* or *Miami Vice,* when televised around the world are not just entertainment. They demonstrate the conspicuous consumption of fast cars, expensive homes and furnishings, and plentiful, rich food. People who see these things want them. All over the world, for people who live in poverty and lack material goods, there is a *revolution of rising expectations.* These people want a share of the advantages and opportunities provided by 20th century technology, for themselves and for their children.

Measures of development

No single measure can be used to gauge development in absolute terms. *Gross national product (GNP) per capita* and *national income* (NI) per capita are conventional indicators of development. GNP is the sum of all the goods and services a country produces in a given period; NI is the sum of all the incomes earned — wages, rent, interest, and profit.

These measures are not always accurate indicators of development. Resource-rich countries such as Kuwait have a high NI per capita but have all the other characteristics of a developing nation. Data on population size is seldom accurate; many countries have never conducted a systematic population census. In addition, most poor countries have overvalued exchange rates: The price of their money is set at a higher rate than it is worth. Converting the NI or GNP data of these countries to U.S. dollars (the standard of measure) overstates their value.

Factors in development

Land is a non-reproducible resource: It cannot be created by the process of production nor can it be transported from place to place. The quality of a country's land affects its development. The agricultural productivity of land varies greatly because soils differ widely in fertility. Temperature, rainfall, and erosion also limit crops and yields.

Agricultural activities produce not only food but also raw materials for industrial use. Cotton, flax and hemp are a few examples.

Technology affects the productivity of land. Technological advances have increased the capacity of land to support larger numbers of people at higher standards of living. New farming methods, hybrid crops, irrigation and chemical fertilizers have tremendously increased food production. New production techniques and modern technology also have created new resources. A raw material is not considered a resource until it can be used in the production process. For example, uranium ore was not a resource until nuclear technology was developed.

Communication and transportation are basic to economic development and are often affected by the topography of a region. Mountains are a barrier to transport, while rivers promote both trade and communication. Flat land presents little obstacle either to communication or transportation. Access to the sea speeds development since most of the world's goods and resources move by water transport. As a consequence, the world's largest urban concentrations are located in coastal areas at the mouths of large river systems.

Urbanization — the movement of people from farm to city — results from several causes. The pro-

The contrast between the rich and poor that is all too common in developing nations is evident in two types of urban housing: modern high-rise apartments for the wealthy and dilapidated shantytowns for the poor.

portion of people employed in agriculture declines as the country develops. Improved labor productivity, a result of development, means that fewer farm workers are needed; people are forced to move to cities to find work. Often poor economic conditions in rural areas force people off the land and they crowd into already overburdened cities. Mexico City is the most rapidly growing city and will become the world's largest city in the early 21st century if its current growth rate continues.

The movement of people to cities speeds the process of industrialization. New industry tends to locate in centers that offer an available labor force. Supportive industry grows alongside. Service industries develop to take care of the growing population, attracting still more people to the city. Congestion and pollution are by-products of rapid urbanization.

International trade is essential to a country's development, since few nations have all the necessary natural resources or manufacturing capability to develop on their own. Some items necessary for development are only available from other nations. To acquire these items, a country has three choices: (1) increase exports — to sell more goods abroad so that they will have money with which to buy needed imports; (2) import substitution — to substitute homemade goods for items currently imported. (The money saved can then be used to purchase materials needed for development.);

(3) international transfers — to obtain foreign assistance to pay for necessary imports.

A country which derives its income primarily from exports is dependent upon a stable world market for development. Stability depends on the *inelasticity of demand,* a continuing need for an item. Oil, fertilizers and iron ore, inelastic products, enjoy a stable demand. Textiles, grain and coffee are elastic; their demand goes down when prices go up. Even with stable exports, supply may exceed demand for the item if the price is too high.

Developing nations which import mainly manufactured products and export largely raw materials suffer a *balance of trade* deficit. The price of raw materials does not increase as fast as the price of manufactured goods. If they import more than export, buy more than sell, they will have a deficit.

Foreign investment brings technology and development. Although most of the profits from such investments go to the foreign investor, the developing nation may benefit from the improved technology brought into its country, employment may increase and there is usually an increase in export production.

The development loan is another form of foreign investment frequently used to help a nation develop its economy. A country's ability to repay such a loan depends on the loan's contribution to increased productivity. The country must increase exports or decrease imports in order to raise the necessary funds for both development and repayment of the loan. When the loan does not result in greater productivity, the country may not be able to meet debt payments. In such a case the debt is usually rescheduled. The debt may be rescheduled many times and the interest payments grow each time. A debt service problem exists when a country's repayment of principal and interest takes up a large amount of its export revenues; little is left for development.

Debt emerges as a problem

In the late 1970s oil prices increased greatly. Developing countries struggled to meet rising fuel bills and maintain payments on their international debts. Major banks in world centers, such as New York, London and Tokyo, extended new loans to these financially strapped countries. When oil prices eased, the burden of debt lightened for some, but many developing nations find that they must constantly borrow to industrialize their economies.

Some of the more developed countries — Mexico, Brazil, South Korea and Argentina — have the largest debt. Some countries may default on their loans. The impact from a series of defaults could threaten the stability of the international money system.

The debt problem is growing worse. In 1982, Argentina owed $43.6 billion and in 1988 owed $59.6 billion and had a per capita debt of $1,863. Brazil has the largest debt — $120.1 billion — up from $91.9 billion in 1982. The picture is the same in Mexico, Poland, Hungary, Ivory Coast, Nigeria and the Philippines. Just paying the annual interest on the debt is a greater burden than many of the nations can bear. Venezuela, in an attempt to cut expenses, reduced some government subsidized services such as urban transportation. As a consequence, riots broke out in Caracas and hundreds lost their lives. More money is now flowing from the developing nations to the developed nations because of the effort by the developing nations to pay their loans. So the rich nations are getting richer at the expense of the poorest. Several plans have been put forth to help solve the problem. Canada went so far as to forgive the debts that some African nations owed them. But the problem still exists and is becoming more serious with each year.

Joint ventures

Joint ventures are becoming increasingly popular in developing countries. Multinational corporations (MNCs) often enter into partnerships with the host country government to extract a resource. The conditions of investment are negotiated and a contract signed. The host country benefits from this arrange-

People in Poverty
1989 (estimated)

Region	Number of People	Share of Total Population
	(million)	(percent)
Asia	675	25
Sub-Saharan Africa	325	62
Latin America	150	35
North Africa and Middle East	75	28
Total	1,225	23

Estimates are midpoints of ranges that extend 10 percent above and 10 percent below listed figures.

SOURCE: Worldwatch Institute

ment in two ways: A larger share of profits remain at home, and the contract may be terminated if the MNC performance is not satisfactory.

Joint ventures may create problems for the MNC in that they lack the flexibility of operations available with complete ownership. The host country may impose restrictions on MNC activities. For example, it might grant the MNC permission to sell in some countries but not in others. This usually occurs for political or other nonbusiness reasons.

Prospects for development

Countries remain underdeveloped when they can not make efficient use of their physical and human resources. Illiteracy, rapid population growth, and lack of capital generally impede development and industrial takeoff.

Seventy percent of the world's population accounts for less than 15 percent of the world's economic production. Eighty percent of the world's trade and investment, over 90 percent of its industry and nearly 100 percent of the research is controlled by the industrialized nations.

Developing nations realize that they are dominated by world institutions of production and trade — banks, government and big businesses. These countries are working to change this situation. Most of the world's "have nots" have formed a federation,

The by-product of industrial growth — chemical pollution.

U.S. Dept. of Interior

called the *Group of 77,* to further their position. The group is so named for the number that joined when the federation was originally formed in the 1960s. Today, about 120 nations are members.

The developing nations may presently be in a weak position, but they are potentially powerful. Many of these countries are important to the more developed nations because they supply natural resources and provide markets. These resources are vital to the production of many industrial goods. Developing countries also purchase large quantities of foodstuffs and finished products. Almost 40 percent of U.S. exports go to developing countries.

Pollution: a by-product of economic development

The Coatzacoalcos River is a sluggish muddy waterway that winds through Minatitlan, an industrial region in Mexico that is home for over 300,000 people. Women carefully descend the river's banks, which are coated with sticky black *chapo* (oil tar), and splash openings in the oily surface of the river to dip water buckets for drinking and cooking. Fishermen drop crab traps and lines into the murky water for catch to sell in the market and serve at the family meal.

The air, rivers, lagoons, creeks and marshes of Minatitlan are contaminated with mercury, lead, ammonia, sulfuric acid, hydrochloric acid, oil, lubricants, chemical soaps, fertilizers and many other pollutants. Residents of the area are told not to eat the fish, but that is their main food source.

When confronted with a choice between food poisoning and malnutrition, they choose to eat the contaminated fish.

In the rich farmlands of the Magdalena Valley of Colombia, birds are only visitors. Those that linger too long soon die from pesticides that permeate the atmosphere. In the Magdalena Valley and elsewhere, people are increasing the use of pesticides to kill insects and rodents, which normally destroy a large share of the crops. The *World Health Organization* estimates that 500,000 people annually around the world get sick from exposure to pesticides, resulting in 5,000 deaths.

In the early 1970s when Brazil, Mexico and Argentina were beginning development programs, their leaders were not too concerned about pollution and environmental issues. They were eager to attract capital and industry into their country — not discourage it. Warnings from environmentalists to plan development and control pollutants were not taken seriously. Many thought that concern about the environment was a luxury they could not afford; industrialization had top priority. Multinational corporations, unrestrained by environmental regulations, were very willing to locate plants and produce goods or extract resources in the developing world. The costs of production were much lower without environment-quality laws.

In a few years, policy makers saw the damage that industrial wastes, pesticides, soil erosion, deforestation could do to their environment. Most countries now recognize the importance of taking an ecological perspective. They are still energetically working to build a strong economic base, but they are now attempting to control industrial development and bear the cost of protecting natural resources.

Development and arms production

Many developing nations, when part of the colonial world, were deliberately disarmed by more powerful nations in Europe and North America. After World War II, these former colonies were drawn into regional defense pacts and treaties. Thereupon, they built large armies and arsenals.

Many developing countries built their military sectors in part with assistance from the United States, the Soviet Union and other industrial countries with strong military programs. Most programs were developed by diverting a big part of their national resources from non-defense uses. Iran, Jordan, Oman, Argentina and Saudi Arabia, among others, spend 15 percent to 20 percent of their gross national product (GNP) on military items. Egypt devotes 35 percent to the military. In contrast, such well-armed industrial nations as Canada, West Germany, France, Poland and Great Britain spend less than 5 percent of their GNP on defense. The United States spends about 6 percent and the Soviet Union about 10 percent. Military expenditures in many developing countries are double their combined education and health spending.

Willy Brandt in the *Report of the Independent Commission on International Development Issues* points out that for the price of one jet fighter ($20 million) 40,000 village pharmacies could be set up. The world military expenditures of only half a day would finance the whole malaria eradication program of the World Health Organization.

The annual world military bill is approximately $700 billion. The developing nations' share of this spending, excluding the People's Republic of China, is about $90 billion. The most significant transfer of technology from the rich countries to the poor has been for armaments. Money spent for jet fighters, armored tanks, advanced weapons and soldiers are funds that cannot be used to build factories and equipment nor to train workers.

General Dynamics

The Stinger anti-aircraft missile launcher is a popular selling item in developing nations.

48

PART III

Global Decision Making

Chapter 10

International Relations

- *Each nation in the world has sovereignty – authority over its people.*

- *Ways for nations to relate to one another have evolved throughout the long history of civilization.*

International relations is the interaction between and among nations. It is based on the notion of *sovereignty:* that a nation has absolute authority over the territory within its borders and should be free from external control.

A code of behavior for nations to interact with one another has developed over hundreds of years. The emergence of the United States as a nation is an illustration of how the code works.

Months before the United States became a nation by signing the Declaration of Independence in 1776, the Continental Congress saw the need for contacts with other nations. Some leaders realized that without the aid of a major European power, the colonies could not hope for military success against Great Britain, the most powerful nation in the world. The Congress therefore set up a secret committee to seek military supplies and credit in Europe.

Secret agents dispatched by the committee soon received assurances that France and Spain would provide aid to the colonies, but not openly. In September 1776, the Congress voted to send the most widely known and respected American of the time, Benjamin Franklin, to Paris. His mission was to secure official French recognition of the United States as an independent nation, more loans, and later, an alliance. The first recognition of the flag of the Continental Congress occurred when Dutch guns on the island of St. Eustatius in the West In-

dies fired a salute to the American vessel, the *Andrew Doria,* as it entered the harbor on November 16, 1776.

Official recognition was granted by France with the signing of a treaty of alliance and a treaty of friendship and commerce on February 6, 1778. The fledgling United States had achieved its first major foreign policy objective.

Foreign policy

The goals and guidelines that shape the conduct of a nation's relations with other nations are called *foreign policy.* It consists of a wide range of actions, procedures and instruments a nation can use to protect its interests in the world.

The level of participation in international relations depends upon a nation's perception of its best interests. All nations have a fundamental interest in protecting their territorial borders from attack or *aggression* by others. A nation's economic interests frequently require that it negotiate favorable trade agreements with other nations. Such concepts as freedom of the seas, world peace, or human rights can prompt a nation to interact with others and participate in international relations.

A nation's foreign policy choices range from *isolationism* (detachment from world affairs) to *neutrality* or *nonalignment* (refusing to take sides on an international issue or dispute) to active *in-*

volvement or *intervention* in the affairs of other nations.

A nation can pursue a foreign policy of *expansionism:* the outright *annexation* or incorporation of another nation into its territorial boundaries. This generally involves military action. Some nations try to develop a *sphere of influence* over strategic regions of the world. Regions such as the Middle East, the Caribbean or the Indian Ocean are considered strategic because they contain important natural resources or are gateways to travel in international waters. Nations develop a sphere of influence in a region by negotiating agreements and treaties and through foreign aid programs.

Recognition

Before a nation can conduct foreign policy, it must be formally *recognized* as a nation by other nations. During a revolution or civil war, a country may have no government or have two or more disputed governments. The government that succeeds in being recognized as the country's legitimate government gains the right to conduct foreign policy.

Embassies

Recognition of one nation by another occurs through the exchange of ambassadors, or representatives of the two nations. *Embassies,* consisting of an ambassador and a staff, are stationed in the capital city of the host nation. As a nation's official representatives, ambassadors have *diplomatic immunity* in the host nation. They are not subject to its laws. They cannot be arrested or hindered from performing their jobs. The land and buildings occupied by an embassy are considered their home territory. Attacks on embassies are viewed as seriously as an attack on the nations they represent. Citizens of a host nation wishing to leave or *defect* from their country can find *asylum* from arrest by fleeing to an embassy if it will accept them.

The function of an embassy is to gather and report information about the host nation, and to represent its own government. Embassies maintain official communication between nations and perform public relations tasks. If a nation is displeased with another, it can *recall* its ambassador or reduce the ranking of its representative to *charge d'affaires* whose authority is limited to maintenance of day-to-day operations. It can also request that a nation withdraw its ambassador. In the world of international relations, nations cannot easily communicate with one another without exchanging embassies. Nations which do not exchange embassies do not recognize each other's existence. Communication between

them must be conducted by the embassy of a third nation which recognizes them both.

Consulates

Many nations also post *consulates* in major cities of the world to promote their commerce and trade. Consuls and their staff assist citizens of the home nation who are visiting abroad, enforce customs laws, and help potential visitors or immigrants to the home nation obtain visa applications.

Negotiations

Diplomacy — the art of international consultation and negotiation — defines how foreign policy is conducted among nations. A great deal of formality and ritual is associated with diplomacy. *Protocols,* codes of ceremonial forms and courtesies in official dealings, determine where representatives of nations should sit at meetings and banquets, and the order of their introduction to heads of state. Many of the procedures and terms of diplomacy originated in France. The original language of diplomacy was French.

Through diplomacy nations reach understandings with each other and negotiate agreements for their mutual benefit.

Treaties

Written documents describing the terms of an agreement between or among nations are called *treaties*. They may be negotiated by heads of state, ambassadors, or appointed representatives from each of the participating nations. These representatives are usually called *envoys*. Treaties go into force when signed by each nation's head of state, or other official representative. Nations have varying ways to approve a treaty. In the United States, it must be approved by a two-thirds vote of the Senate in addition to being signed by the President.

Treaties serve many purposes. They can describe the terms for ending a war — a *peace treaty;* settle border disputes; or pledge friendship between two nations. The *most-favored-nation treaty* is a frequent statement of trade friendship. It obligates the signing nations to grant each other the most favorable trade benefits they might individually negotiate with a third nation.

Treaties can be signed by groups of more than two nations. Generally, the more parties to a treaty, the more complicated it is to negotiate.

Alliances

When two or more nations agree to support a common goal, such as to come to the aid of each other if a war occurs or jointly to develop the economy or defense system of a region, the agreements are

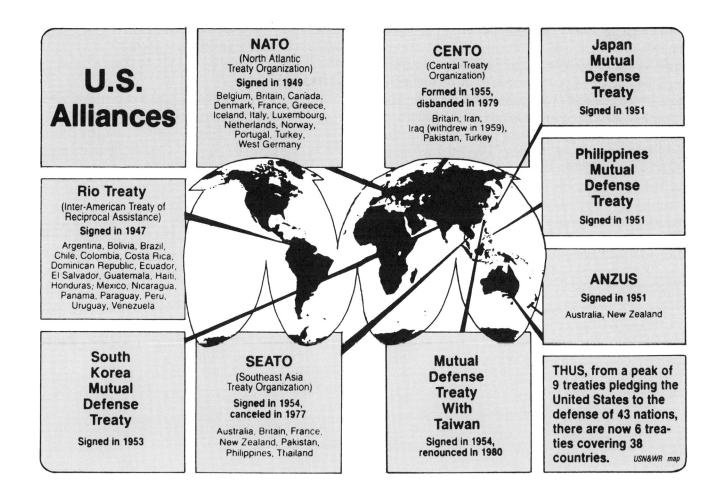

U.S. Alliances

NATO
(North Atlantic Treaty Organization)
Signed in 1949
Belgium, Britain, Canada, Denmark, France, Greece, Iceland, Italy, Luxembourg, Netherlands, Norway, Portugal, Turkey, West Germany

CENTO
(Central Treaty Organization)
Formed in 1955, disbanded in 1979
Britain, Iran, Iraq (withdrew in 1959), Pakistan, Turkey

Japan Mutual Defense Treaty
Signed in 1951

Rio Treaty
(Inter-American Treaty of Reciprocal Assistance)
Signed in 1947
Argentina, Bolivia, Brazil, Chile, Colombia, Costa Rica, Dominican Republic, Ecuador, El Salvador, Guatemala, Haiti, Honduras, Mexico, Nicaragua, Panama, Paraguay, Peru, Uruguay, Venezuela

Philippines Mutual Defense Treaty
Signed in 1951

ANZUS
Signed in 1951
Australia, New Zealand

South Korea Mutual Defense Treaty
Signed in 1953

SEATO
(Southeast Asia Treaty Organization)
Signed in 1954, canceled in 1977
Australia, Britain, France, New Zealand, Pakistan, Philippines, Thailand

Mutual Defense Treaty With Taiwan
Signed in 1954, renounced in 1980

THUS, from a peak of 9 treaties pledging the United States to the defense of 43 nations, there are now 6 treaties covering 38 countries. USN&WR map

called *alliances*. Other terms for an alliance include: *pact, accord, league, union* or *organization*. The terms of an alliance are usually sealed by the signing of a formal treaty.

Some agreements between nations are less formally concluded. The French word *détente* has been used to describe the relationship between the United States and the Soviet Union during the 1970s and '80s. Détente means a relaxation of tension between two nations — a willingness to overlook perceived threats. *Peaceful coexistence* is another term used to describe detente.

World opinion. Nations also interact with one another through a "war of words" aimed at influencing *world opinion*. Most nations conduct public relations campaigns to assure that their actions are seen abroad in the best light. The two *superpowers* — the United States and the Soviet Union — have developed sophisticated public relations campaigns. Both nations regularly broadcast news about their policies to each other's citizens as well as to neutral nations they wish to influence.

Covert activities

Nations often rely on indirect methods of getting information about each other. Elaborate networks of

security systems and spies have been devised by nations to keep their own activities secret from the world and to find out other nation's secrets. In the United States the **Central Intelligence Agency** (CIA) is responsible for this task. The **Commission of State Security** (KGB) has similar duties in the Soviet Union.

Summit meetings

Heads of state of friendly nations sometimes meet at *summit meetings*. Every U.S. president since Franklin Roosevelt in World War II has met with his Soviet counterpart in attempts to work out mutual agreements between the superpowers. Occasionally, U.S. presidents arrange journeys that hopscotch across the globe with stops in major political centers for short summit meetings on particular issues.

Foreign aid

Foreign aid is the international transfer of money, goods or services for the mutual benefit of countries and their people.

Bilateral aid. Most foreign aid consists of financial transactions between two countries — that is, one country (the creditor) provides assistance to another country (the debtor). This is known as bilateral aid.

Bilateral aid may be in the form of *grants,* which the recipient country does not have to repay, or low-interest long-term *loans.* Grants constitute only a small proportion of foreign aid and are used primarily to provide emergency assistance, or relief, and to finance specific projects such as the construction of a school or hospital. Loans are used to finance development programs for key sectors of the recipient country's economy.

Tied aid. Many foreign aid loans have conditions placed on them. This is known as *tied aid.* Sometimes recipient countries must use the funds to buy goods made in the donor country or transport them in its ships. Tied aid creates special problems for the countries receiving assistance. The creditor's goods may be priced higher than world market prices. Some creditor countries make their high-priced goods more attractive by offering easy-credit terms. Many developing countries consider tied aid a scheme to sell surplus goods at inflated prices. Creditor countries see it as a chance to get some return for the money they spend helping other countries.

Other conditions of tied aid include requiring performance criteria by the recipient country. In return for aid, the recipient is required to enact specified policies on such matters as exchange rate practices, import regulations, bank credit, foreign investment or human rights.

Multilateral aid. When foreign aid is supported by many donor countries and is generally distributed by an international organization, it is considered *multilateral aid.* The major agency distributing multilateral aid today is the ***International Bank for Reconstruction and Development*** — referred to as the ***World Bank*** — which began operations in 1946 as an independent, specialized agency of the United Nations. It makes low-interest, long-term development loans which are financed by contributions from member countries. The ***International Monetary Fund,*** the ***World Health Organization,*** the ***World Food Program*** and the ***African Development Bank*** are other international organizations that provide multilateral aid.

Types of aid

Reconstruction aid is a good example of the mutual benefit to be derived from foreign aid. The United States developed the ***Marshall Plan*** to help rebuild Europe after World War II. American assistance focused on the relief of war victims and on the economic reconstruction of Europe. The Marshall Plan provided Europe with $13.6 billion for reconstruction. Most of this money was spent on American technology and products and helped stimu-

USDA Photo

Food and milk being distributed by CARE to victims of a devastating flood in the Punjab region of India.

late the American economy. An economically strong Europe provided markets for American products.

Military aid is the practice of providing military personnel, training and equipment to other countries. Considered part of a donor nation's defense and security system, military aid usually goes to friendly countries in areas considered strategic to the donor's national interest. The United States and the Soviet Union are the largest donors of military aid.

Development aid is loans and grants designed to improve the economy of a debtor nation. Aid includes technical assistance, training, materials and equipment to help a nation industrialize its economy. The hope is that the project will create jobs and raise the national income of the recipient country so it can compete in the world economy. Development aid is seen as an investment in trade and economic expansion by the creditor nation.

Development aid is not always effective. Recipient countries may lack money and skilled technicians to operate sophisticated machinery and equipment. In 1973, the U.S. shifted its development aid away from dams, reservoirs and capital projects with high maintenance costs and toward farming and other projects that help the poor directly. One successful approach in many countries has been to build feeder roads into relatively isolated areas to permit farmers to get their goods to market.

Some nations render development aid indirectly through liberal trade policies with a recipient nation or by accepting goods as repayment of development loans. This form of aid comes mainly from East European nations.

Food aid is the gift or sale of surplus food to nations which do not produce enough to feed their people. It also includes technical assistance to improve food output.

A U.S. program, *Food for Peace,* typifies how food aid works. Some food is sold to recipient countries on long-term credit, repayable in dollars. The country then sells the food to its people, with the requirement that the proceeds must be used for economic development.

Some food is donated to countries for special projects such as a child health program to meet basic nutritional needs. Other food is donated to private organizations such as *CARE, Catholic Relief Services* and the *YMCA* for distribution to the hungry. Donated food also goes to international organizations such as the *World Food Program* or the *International Red Cross.*

A feature of the U.S. program is *Food for Work.* People in rural communities of a recipient nation may be partially paid in food for working on small-scale development projects such as building roads or irrigation systems.

Critics of food aid have pointed out that programs sometimes backfire. Corrupt government officials in recipient countries have been known to keep the food or sell it at inflated prices, pocketing the profit. On the other hand, if the recipient government sells the food too cheaply to its people or gives it away, local farmers may be discouraged from producing. Cheap food hurts farmers by depressing prices for their crops.

Disaster aid is the emergency relief of human suffering in the wake of floods, earthquakes, epidemics, famines and drought. It is distributed by voluntary organizations such as the Red Cross and CARE, as well as by nations. Disaster aid includes airlifts of food and medical supplies, as well as grants designed to promote disaster preparedness and prediction capabilities in regions vulnerable to disasters.

U.S. foreign aid

In 1961, Congress authorized the *Agency for International Development* (AID) to administer most of the various foreign assistance activities. Military aid is not included; that remains under the direction of the Defense Department. Funds for AID are appropriated by Congress.

As a percentage of the nation's gross national product, U.S. foreign aid has declined from .7 percent in 1970 to under .3 percent in the 1980s. U.S. aid to multilateral organizations has declined, while bilateral tied aid has almost doubled, mainly to countries which have military relationships with the U.S. Approximately 40 percent of U.S. foreign aid goes to two nations, Egypt and Israel. With the democratic election of a new government in Nicaragua, the invasion of Panama and the toppling of the government of Manuel Noriega, and the democratization of governments in Poland, Hungary, Czechoslovakia, Bulgaria, Romania and East Germany,

NATO

Leaders of the seven main industrialized nations, with the President of the European Commission, stand against the background of the Louvre pyramid in Paris following their meeting in July, 1989.

there will be pressure for the United States to allocate a higher proportion of its foreign aid dollars to these nations.

Among the top 17 industrialized nations, the United States ranked next to last in 1987 in the dollar value of foreign aid as a percent of GNP. Only Austria was lower. Norway, ranking first, provided 1.09 percent of its GNP for foreign aid while the United States contributed .20 percent, or less than 1/5th of the Norwegian aid. Because it has the world's largest GNP, the United States was the single largest contributor of foreign aid with nearly $9 billion being distributed.

Foreign debt accumulation

Loans must eventually be repaid, but many countries cannot afford to repay on schedule. Interest is then charged on the unpaid loan and a new schedule for payment is determined. These countries become increasingly reliant on foreign aid. Some countries use current aid to repay debts incurred by previous loans.

World debt surfaced as a major financial issue in the 1980s. In the early 1970s, total outstanding international debt was less than $100 billion; a decade later it had climbed to over $600 billion and was rising. In 1989, the figure stood at $1.3 trillion. Many nations in the Third World and Eastern Europe took out huge loans from banks in the industrialized nations — mainly those in the financial centers of the United States, Japan and Western Europe. Most of these loans were to pay for purchases of Western technology and to stay ahead of skyrocketing oil prices.

Some of the nations attempting to develop most rapidly were incurring the largest debts: Brazil, Mexico, South Korea and Poland. As their outstanding IOUs became larger and interest rates rose, the funds required to make principal and interest payments increased at an alarming rate. A worldwide recession hit in the early 1980s, and prices of raw materials on global markets declined. Many countries were hard pressed for foreign currencies to repay the loans. When the price of oil declined, Mexico, which produces oil, became economically depressed and its foreign debts ballooned. Economic woes increased the borrowing needs of countries determined to sustain development.

Financial institutions in the creditor nations became vulnerable to loan defaults by developing nations. The situation was more alarming than expected: Major banks in one country, such as the United States, would make sizable loans to a foreign borrower not realizing the amount of indebtedness incurred by the debtor with banks in other nations. If the borrower was unable to pay back the loan, the U.S. bank suffered serious losses.

Reforming international development aid

The threat of a worldwide recession has called into question the quantity and quality of international development aid. *North South: The Brandt Report,* which analyzed international development issues in 1980, found gaps in both areas. The authors believe that, if the gaps are closed, the world economy will improve for both developed and developing sectors. They recommended that the amount of development aid should be increased and that it should involve all nations of the world. They wrote: ''The attack on world poverty should involve all countries in a truly universal joint enterprise.'' The report recommended that developed countries should raise their level of foreign aid from the current average of .35 percent to at least .7 percent of GNP, with a goal of 1 percent by 2000. Other countries should give according to their ability. Only the poorest nations should be exempt from giving.

The Brandt Report also argued for increased participation by developing nations in World Bank and IMF aid allocation decisions. It stressed the need for more aid to the poorest countries. Supplements to foreign aid revenues were also discussed, such as levying a development tax on all international trade. The report suggested that development financing should be expanded and stabilized. It recommended that creditor nations recycle payments on loans from debtor nations back into new loan programs.

Chapter 11

International Organizations

- *The United Nations has a far-reaching impact throughout the world.*

- *Few nations are willing to give up their sovereignty to international governing bodies.*

Nations often join together to achieve certain objectives. These objectives can be political, as when the *Organization of African Unity* (OAU) was formed to improve relations among African nations and strengthen Africa's voice in world concerns. Organizations also are formed for economic reasons: the *European Community* (EC) allows nations to trade goods and services among themselves without tariffs. Some pacts are designed to ensure a common defense. These include the *North Atlantic Treaty Organization* (NATO) and the *Warsaw Pact.* These agreements stipulate that, if any member nation is attacked, the other nations will join in its defense.

International organizations have existed for many years. The *Concert of Europe* in 1815 was an organization which brought together the leaders of European nation-states. They did not confer on a regular schedule, only when pressing issues required settlement. War or impending war was the most common reason to convene. The concept of ''great powers'' came into being during this time. These conferences were regional rather than global in that they involved only European states. The great powers dominated proceedings and established themselves as the self-appointed guardians of Europe. No permanent institutions or organizations developed from these conferences.

The *Hague System* was an attempt to organize the world into a collective security organization. The first Hague conference was held in 1899; a second met in 1907. The Hague conferences did not settle any specific disputes, but they did establish the principle of universality of representation and the acceptance of the idea that each participating nation, large or small, should have equal voting power. In addition, a committee was formed to collect and study items of interest and to prepare an agenda for the next meeting. This was the first international meeting of its kind.

The League of Nations

The first formal attempt to create a permanent global organization came at the end of World War I. The high cost of the war, in dollars and in lives, pointed to the need to try to avoid wars as a way of settling disputes. To ensure peace a world organization was proposed and established in 1920. Designated the *League of Nations,* the organization was pledged to promote collective security.

For collective security to work, the following conditions must be met:

- Universality of membership: An attack on any member country is regarded as an attack on all countries.

- Nonalignment: There can be no alignment except against the aggressor country.

- Consensus on aggression: All countries must

agree on what is an act of aggression and respond as one when it occurs.

• Diffusion of power: No outside single country should be powerful enough to resist collective action.

The League of Nations failed on all counts. At first its membership was limited to countries which had been on the winning side in World War 1. Russia and China were excluded. The United States declined to join; even though President Woodrow Wilson wanted to, the Congress did not. In 1926, Germany was admitted, but with only a limited membership, since it had been the adversary of the other member nations during the war.

The League was unable to check the aggressions of its more powerful members. It merely condemned Japan for attacking China in 1933. Sanctions imposed on Italy for invading Abyssinia in 1935 were ineffective. Nor was the League able to protect Austria, Spain and Poland from aggression. By 1935, 17 of its member states had withdrawn. The world was on the threshold of World War II.

After World War II, the *United Nations* (UN) was formed. Its purposes (stated in Article I of the charter) are political, economic, cultural and humanitarian. Mainly it was designed to be a forum for the peaceful resolution of conflict.

The United Nations

In 1989, there were 159 member countries in the United Nations.

The foundations of the United Nations were laid at the Dumbarton Oaks Conference in Washington, D.C. Representatives from the United States, the Soviet Union, Great Britain and China met from August to October of 1944 to work on a plan to establish an organization of nations for the maintenance of world peace. This work led to the United Nations Conference on International Organization held at San Francisco in 1945 where the Charter of the United Nations was drawn up. Fifty nations signed it on June 26, 1945. (A fifty-first, Poland, signed on October 15, 1945.) The Charter went into effect on October 24, 1945.

The United Nations was established in part in response to the horrors of the just-ended Second World War and to the failure of the League of Nations. Its purpose is outlined in its charter:

• to maintain international peace and security;

• to develop friendly relations among nations;

• to cooperate internationally in solving international economic, social, cultural and humanitarian problems and in promoting respect for human rights and fundamental freedoms;

U.N. Rules Affect Life Almost Everywhere in World

Rules in Force. . .

Commercial aviation. Worldwide uniformity assured for pilot licensing, runway lighting, fuel dumping, engine noise and air-traffic language—English.

Shipping. Cooperation mandated between nations on collisions at sea, oil spills, safety of passengers, luggage liability and rules of the road.

Energy. Most nuclear power plants inspected regularly, and shipments of radioactive materials monitored to contain danger of nuclear proliferation.

Broadcasting. Space assigned on all radio-TV bands and interference monitored; sanctions against unwanted transmission of television and shortwave signals into other countries.

Telephones. All international telephone rates and tariffs regulated.

Postal. International postal charges regulated, and rules set for agreements on insured letters and money orders.

Food. Standards set on quality and hygiene of over 130 foods such as canned tomatoes, applesauce and mushrooms. Infant formulas prohibited from being advertised or sold directly to nursing mothers. (Only 10 countries so far have accepted the marketing code.)

Drugs. Lower cost and less duplication of drugs in Third World nations facilitated through list of generic drugs available on international market.

Disease. Travelers in certain parts of the world required to show proof of vaccination against epidemic diseases.

Labor. International guidelines set for wages, hours worked, minimum ages and industrial safety. No U.N. enforcement mechanism exists.

Business. Exporters of technology barred from imposing restrictions that limit importers' freedom to exploit the technology.

Deep-sea mining. Companies engaged in seabed mining required to sell their technology to an international monopoly that will license all such undersea mining.

These soldiers from Nepal were part of the United Nation Interim Force sent to Lebanon in 1978. *United Nations*

• to be a center for harmonizing the actions of nations in attaining these common goals.

Although the United Nations has had varied degrees of success in achieving its aims, it is also true that the United Nations is unparalleled in both size and scope. Its membership has grown from 51 nations to nearly 160. Any subject of international concern may be discussed in one or more of its organs.

The "United Nations System" is made up of six major organs and 16 autonomous organizations and specialized agencies.

Security Council. Of all the organs of the UN, the Security Council has drawn the most attention. This is the branch of the UN responsible for maintaining international peace and security, the UN's most ambitious goal. However, it is the most highly political organ of the system, a fact which has often prevented it from taking action. The Security Council is made up of five permanent members (China, France, the United Kingdom, the Soviet Union and the United States) and 10 nonpermanent members elected by the General Assembly to serve on the Council for two-year terms.

The Security Council is the only major organ of

the UN that does not proceed on the principle of equal voting for all members. Decisions of the Council (except for those regarding procedure) require the affirmative votes of nine members including the "concurring votes" of the permanent members. Thus, if a permanent member casts a "no" vote, the motion will fail; if, however, the permanent members abstain from voting or are absent, this is not considered a "veto."

Allowing vetoes in the Security Council has hampered its ability to take action in some situations. But the reasons for having such a provision reflect the political realities of modern international relations. First, the major powers were unwilling to submit to a simple majority in the Security Council. Whereas the other organs of the UN may "recommend" action to governments and organizations, members are obligated, under the UN Charter, to carry out the decisions of the Security Council. The Council may investigate disputes, recommend methods of adjusting such disputes, call for economic or diplomatic sanctions, and take military action against an aggressor. It is also empowered to direct peace-keeping forces. Second, it was felt that, in light of the functions of the Security Coun-

🇺🇳 THE UNITED NATIONS SYSTEM

● Principal organs of the United Nations

● Other United Nations organs

○ Specialized agencies and other autonomous organizations within the system

TRUSTEESHIP COUNCIL

SECURITY COUNCIL

GENERAL ASSEMBLY

INTERNATIONAL COURT OF JUSTICE

SECRETARIAT

ECONOMIC AND SOCIAL COUNCIL

Main Committees

Standing and procedural committees

Other subsidiary organs of the General Assembly

UNDOF United Nations Disengagement Observer Force

UNFICYP United Nations Peace-keeping Force in Cyprus

UNIFIL United Nations Interim Force in Lebanon

UNMOGIP United Nations Military Observer Group in India and Pakistan

UNTSO United Nations Truce Supervision Organization in Palestine

Military Staff Committee

Regional commissions

Functional commissions

Sessional standing and ad hoc committees

United Nations Relief and Works Agency for Palestine Refugees in the Near East **UNRWA**

United Nations Conference on Trade and Development **UNCTAD**

United Nations Children's Fund **UNICEF**

Office of the United Nations High Commissioner to Refugees **UNHCR**

World Food Programme **WFP**

United Nations Institute for Training and Research **UNITAR**

United Nations Development Programme **UNDP**

United Nations Industrial Development Organization **UNIDO**

United Nations Environment Programme **UNEP**

United Nations University **UNU**

United Nations Special Fund

World Food Council

United Nations Centre for Human Settlements (Habitat) **UNCHS**

United Nations Fund for Population Activities **UNFPA**

IAEA International Atomic Energy Agency

GATT General Agreement on Tariffs and Trade

ILO International Labour Organisation

FAO Food and Agriculture Organization of the United Nations

UNESCO United Nations Educational Scientific and Cultural Organization

WHO World Health Organization

IDA International Development Association

IBRD International Bank for Reconstruction and Development

IFC International Finance Corporation

IMF International Monetary Fund

ICAO International Civil Aviation Organization

UPU Universal Postal Union

ITU International Telecommunication Union

WMO World Meteorological Organization

IMO International Maritime Organization

WIPO World Intellectual Property Organization

IFAD International Fund for Agricultural Development

United States Department of State, Bureau of Public Affairs, *Washington, D.C.*

cil, its decisions would be meaningless or severely weakened without the support of the permanent members. In 1945, the permanent members of the Security Council were the major economic and military powers; they also included the major colonial powers. (One of the UN's first concerns was the independence of colonial peoples.) Although the Security Council could have made decisions without the agreement of the permanent members, it would have had a hard time implementing them.

General Assembly. The other crucial organ of the UN is the General Assembly. It is made up of all the members of the UN and is charged with making recommendations on all matters coming within the scope of the organization, especially international peace and security, disarmament, initiating studies, considering reports from the other organs of the UN and generally supervising the work of the organization. The General Assembly operates under the principle of "one nation, one vote" in recognition of the sovereign rights of nation states. All members' votes carry equal weight, and all but a few specific kinds of decisions are determined by simple majority.

The point of the General Assembly is to serve as a forum for discussion of international issues in order to foster cooperation. Often the General Assembly becomes more the site of excessive rhetoric than cooperation, but even the function of "letting off steam" has a place in diplomacy. Better to insult your enemies in an international arena, it is said, than on the battlefield.

The General Assembly may establish subsidiary organs. These have included the UN Conference on Trade and Development, which tries to help developing countries expand their trade, and the UN Industrial Development Organization, which assists developing countries to establish an industrial base.

With the sharp increase in the number of countries in the world since World War II — many are former African colonies which gained independence in the 1960s — the complexion and tone of the United Nations have changed a great deal. This change has been most pronounced in the General Assembly, but it has been reflected in all the organs and agencies of the UN system. Whereas most of the UN's original members were industrialized, long-established nations, the present majority is made up of developing, recently independent states. The friction between the two groups, growing out of a feeling of exploitation and conflict in political and economic beliefs, has also led to efforts at cooperation. Developed nations are recognizing more that they have certain obligations to improve the lot of developing nations. This focus of the UN

reflects the new awareness of the needs of developing nations. Most UN activities are geared toward development of the Third World. In the General Assembly, this is reflected in what is known as the "North-South Dialogue," with the "North" representing the industrialized nations and the "South" representing the developing nations.

Secretariat. The secretariat functions as the administrative heart of the UN system. Headed by the Secretary-General, who is appointed to a five-year term, the secretariat carries out decisions of the Security Council, the General Assembly and other UN agencies, but plays no role in policymaking. A major duty of the Secretary-General is to alert the Security Council to any situation considered a threat to world peace. The Secretary-General also attempts to end international disputes and provide administrative support for peace-keeping operations.

Trusteeship Council. One of the organs of the United Nations has almost worked itself out of business. That is the Trusteeship Council whose purpose was to supervise the administration of Trust Territories (mostly former colonies) until they gained independence. There were originally eleven Trust Territories; now there is only one left, the Republic of Palau, which is administered by the United States.

Economic and Social Council (ECOSOC). This body is charged with planning the promotion of economic, social and humanitarian activities of the organization. It has a membership of 54, elected on a rotating basis.

ECOSOC has called numerous international conferences, such as those on human settlements, on the human environment, the World Food Conference, and World Population Conference. Among its subsidiary bodies are Committees on Negotiations with Intergovernmental Agencies, Natural Resources, and Science and Technology for Development. Its commissions include those on population, human rights and the status of women.

Specialized Agencies. An important function of the United Nations is that of coordinating the work of the specialized agencies through consultations and recommendations. These agencies are separate, autonomous organizations with their own charters, constitutions, members and purposes. They are linked to the UN system by special agreements.

Most of the agencies are primarily concerned with development in their particular fields. All of them are aware of the needs of developing countries. For instance, nuclear energy is most widely used in developed countries, but the *International Atomic Energy Agency* (IAEA) participates in the search for natural resources in developing countries. It also promotes improved safety measures for nuclear materials and peaceful uses of nuclear energy. If nuclear energy should be established in the developing countries, IAEA undoubtedly will be involved.

Other agencies such as the *Food and Agriculture Organization* (FAO), the *World Health Organization* (WHO), and the *UN Educational, Scientific and Cultural Organization* (UNESCO) gear most of their activities toward the needs of the developing world. They provide technical assistance, training programs, and field services and call international conferences. In 1985, the United States withdrew from UNESCO on the grounds that the organization was being mismanaged. The United Kingdom left soon after. Neither nation has asked to reenter, although discussion was taking place in 1990. The *World Bank* provides funding for major projects in developing countries. This has now become the major source of multilateral development finance.

The development activities of the specialized agencies are complemented by semiautonomous "voluntary programs" that are established by the General Assembly but have their own governing bodies and are financed through contributions from their members. The largest voluntary program is the *UN Development Program* which concentrates on direct field service activities. It works with 24 international agencies in 150 countries to foster economic growth and improve the standard of living. UNDP usually does not carry out projects itself. Instead, it funds projects which are then carried out by other agencies. Sometimes UNDP projects involve two or more agencies working together, coordinated by UNDP.

World Court

The *International Court of Justice* — or World Court, as it is commonly called — resides in the Palace of Peace in the Hague, the capital city of the Netherlands. The court is presided over by 15 judges from 15 different countries. Funded by the United Nations, the Court is responsible for ruling on international disputes brought before it by member nations.

Many cases considered by the World Court involve operations conducted by nations in ocean areas where no clear national jurisdiction has prevailed. Greece, for example, went to the Court to keep Turkish oil ships from exploring in the Aegean Sea; Nicaragua protested U.S. mining of its harbors.

The World Court, like its parent the United Nations, only has as much power as member nations are willing to grant. All the members of the UN have pledged to support the Court, but only a few nations, none of them major powers, have agreed to accept the Court's jurisdiction without reservations. Neither

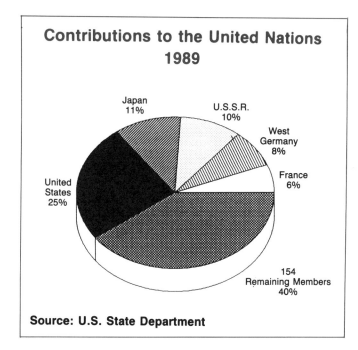

Contributions to the United Nations 1989

Japan 11%
U.S.S.R. 10%
West Germany 8%
France 6%
154 Remaining Members 40%
United States 25%

Source: U.S. State Department

the United States nor the Soviet Union has taken any major dispute to the Court.

Several nations, including the United States, have ignored court decisions without being reprimanded. Within any law-enforcing government, courts need police or military power to see that their rulings are enforced. The World Court does not have such power. Without the cooperation of members to both observe and support judicial decisions, the World Court has not become a strong organization.

The United Nations is involved in the areas of human rights, self-determination, international law, settlement of disputes, and other matters. No member has ever withdrawn from the organization, and newly independent countries apply for membership. This indicates that, in spite of some flaws and inadequacies, the United Nations serves a useful purpose in relations between nations.

With the shift from a bipolar to a multilateral global political structure, the role of the United Nations is likely to become a much more important and effective organization. It is to the United Nations that the world turns for leadership in seeking solutions to global problems such as environmental deterioration, widespread illiteracy, human rights violations and poverty.

The United States is the largest single contributor to the United Nations. But often the United States fails to make its payments on schedule due to domestic political pressure. As global problems magnify, the United States and other leading industrial nations will probably view the United Nations as an increasingly important part of foreign policy.

PART IV

Global Issues

Chapter 12

Population

> - *Earth's population is expected to reach 10 billion by 2025, presenting a monumental challenge to sustain life-supporting systems.*
>
> - *Increasing population will create a far different world than we know now.*

Now that the world is viewed as a spaceship with limited resources, uncontrolled, limitless population growth is seen as a serious threat to civilized life.

Two thousand years ago, the world's population was only 250 million — about the same as the population of the United States in 1990. It took millions of years for the world's population to reach this level. By 1850, there were 1 billion people in the world — a four-fold increase. Eighty years later, there were two billion; 30 years after that, three billion. It took only 15 years for the world's population to grow from 3 billion in 1960 to 4 billion in 1975 and over 5 billion in 1990. The world's population is growing geometrically. Charted on a graph it looks like the letter "J" and is sometimes called a "J-curve."

By the year 2000, according to United Nations projections, over 6 billion people will be competing for the planet's food, water, fuel and other limited resources. By 2025, the world's population will reach 10 billion. This is a best-case scenario. According to Nafis Sadik, Executive Director of the United Nations Population Fund, "If we fail (to control population growth), there could be 14 billion people on Earth in the year 2100."

The United Nations is convening a high-level international meeting in 1994 to assess the successes and failures of population planning programs initiated in 1984. On the agenda will be some familiar issues: the momentum of world population growth, population and sustainable growth, population and the status of women, family planning needs, urbanization, and internal and international migration. New issues to be considered include regionalization of persistent high-growth rates as in Africa and Latin America; the possible demographic impact of the acquired immune deficiency syndrome (AIDS); aging of the population; and the "demographic collapse" of many industrial nations, especially in Europe.

Demography

Demography is the study of human populations with respect to size, distribution and vital statistics — sex, age, race. The growth of any population is dependent on the relationship between births and deaths. If births are greater than deaths, then the population grows. If the reverse is true, the population declines.

In 1980, for example, the populations of El Salvador (4.75 million) and Finland (4.8 million) were nearly the same. Between 1980 and 1990, El Salvador gained almost 2,000,000 people. In contrast, Finland grew by only 100,000 people in the same decade. By 1990, the population of El Salvador had increased to 6.5 million, while that of Finland was only 4.9 million. A close look at the *crude birth rate* (CBR) and *crude death rate* (CDR) reveals why.

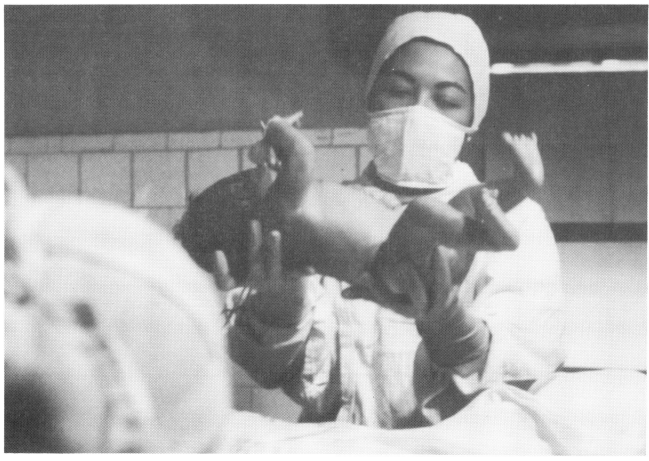

United Nations

New babies are born every second of the day around the world. How many can the world support?

(A rate is any statistical measurement which compares two numbers or quantities.)

CBR is calculated by dividing the number of births by the population and multiplying the result by 1,000. This gives the crude birth rate for every 1,000 people in the population. The CBR for Finland in 1980 was 13.1; for El Salvador, it was 34.7. Population gain is the result of CBR minus CDR (crude death rate). CDR, like the CBR, is expressed in persons per thousand. In El Salvador the CDR was 7.9, while in Finland the rate was 9.4. Using simple arithmetic, the population of El Salvador increased at a rate of almost 27 people per 1,000 population; the population of Finland increased less than four people per 1,000.

Factors of population increase

Before the 1700s, both *fertility* (CBR) and *mortality* (CDR) were at high levels. The principal determining factor of population increase was mortality. Fertility, or birth rate, needed to be high to offset a high mortality, or death rate. In the 1700s, mortality began to fall, but fertility remained high. The revolution in agriculture resulted in a larger and more stable food output. Crops from the New World, improved farming methods, and better transportation and distribution of food diminished the effects of famine, which at that time was the primary killer. In the 1800s, public health and sanitation measures — sewers, garbage collection, purification of drinking water further reduced mortality. By the 1900s, advances in medical technology and in the distribution of medical services had reduced mortality throughout the world.

The result was a *population explosion*. Mortality no longer balanced fertility.

Geometric population growth

The more births, the more people; the more people, the more births. Even at a "low" rate of population growth — 2 percent — a greater number of people will inhabit Earth each year than the year before. As long as the population continues to grow, it will eventually double in size: It will grow at a *geometric rate* (1, 2, 4, 8, 16, 32, 64 . . .). The length of time it will take to double depends on the *annual rate* of growth: A population growing annually by 3.5 percent doubles in 20 years; by 2.5 percent — 28 years; by 2 percent — 35 years; by 1 percent — 70 years.

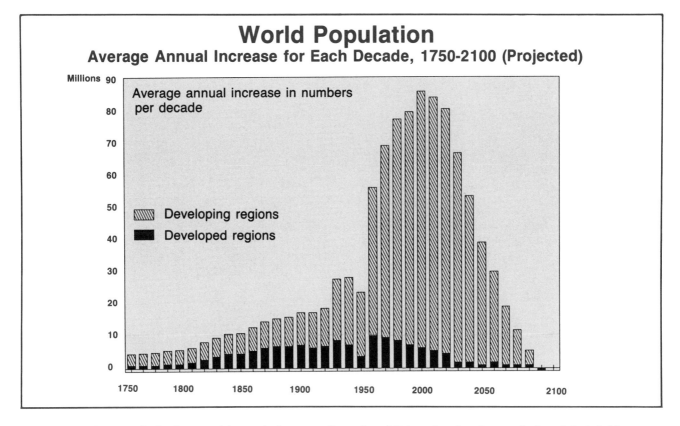

World Population
Average Annual Increase for Each Decade, 1750-2100 (Projected)

Millions

Average annual increase in numbers per decade

///// Developing regions

■ Developed regions

1750 1800 1850 1900 1950 2000 2050 2100

The above bar graph depicts world population growth past and future by showing each decade's total increase (expressed as the average annual increase over that decade). As can be seen, the 1990s are projected to be the historic peak decade of population growth in terms of absolute numbers.

Source: "World Population in Transition," *Population Bulletin,* by Thomas W. Merrick and PRB staff.

Demographic transition

Demographic transition describes the changes in a population group as it becomes industrialized. The normal path is from (1) a condition of high fertility (CBR) and high mortality (CDR) — a small rate of population growth — through (2) a condition of high fertility and low mortality — a population explosion — to (3) a condition of low fertility and low mortality — a stable population increase.

Europe has almost completed this demographic transition and reached a level of *zero population growth.* United Nations experts foresee that Europe will achieve a stable population in about the year 2030; North America will stabilize about 30 years later, around 2060. East Asia is expected to level out next, in 2090, and the Soviet Union, Latin America and Southern Asia all are expected to stabilize around 2100. Africa will be the last to stabilize its population by the year 2110.

Lester Brown, president of the Worldwatch Institute, cautions that the model of demographic transition patterned after the history of Europe may not apply in all other cases. He writes:

The demographic transition has been widely used by demographers to explain differential rates of growth and to project national and global populations. But as we approach the end of the twentieth century, a gap has emerged in the analysis. The theorists did not say what happens when developing countries get trapped in the second stage, unable to achieve the economic and social gains that are counted upon to reduce births. Nor does the theory explain what happens when second-stage population growth rates of 3 percent per year — which means a twenty-fold increase per century — continue indefinitely and begin to overwhelm local life-support systems.

It is desirable for nations to achieve a stable population growth in the long run. Unless this occurs, solving the world's hunger and employment problems will remain illusive goals.

Declining populations. Switzerland, Germany, Austria and the United Kingdom have experienced declining population in recent years. While the CDR is low as expected, the CBR is even lower. As fewer children are born and people on the average live longer, a nation's population grows older. This creates some problems:

• There are fewer workers to support greater numbers of older, retired people.

• Businesses and industries producing children's items lose markets.

• Declining school enrollments provide fewer jobs for teachers.

• Some countries find it difficult to maintain a strong military force.

Developing nations. People in many lands will continue to suffer as world population climbs to 6 billion, 7 billion and beyond. Developing nations are growing at a fast pace, and they will be hard-pressed to provide employment and decent living conditions for their people. A United Nations study notes that, by the year 2000, the cities of many developing nations will become centers of concentrated urban poverty because of the flood of migration from rural areas. Mexico City is projected to be the world's largest city by the year 2000 with 24.4 million people. The bulging centers, mainly in Asia and Latin America, will be ripe for social unrest. Millions of residents of the urban clusters will be unemployed — yet hopeful for a better life.

Fertility decline

The decision to have smaller families is a personal one based on social and economic considerations. *Industrialization,* or the change from an agrarian to an industrial economy, contributes to fertility decline. In agriculture, children provide labor; in industry, children do not serve such an important economic function. Most countries have laws prohibiting or limiting child labor. Industrialization reduces the economic utility of children and they become a liability. They must be fed, clothed, housed and educated even though they contribute little to the economic well-being of the family unit.

Urbanization, or the movement of people from rural to urban residence, also affects fertility. In the city, housing space is costly and in some places not readily available. The prospect of crowding tends to convince people to have fewer children.

Along with industrialization and urbanization comes a change in the *status of women.* Industrial society provides the opportunity and actually requires women to break away from the traditional roles of mother and wife. Working women employed outside the household are likely to have fewer children than homemakers.

Improved *education* for women has an impact on fertility. The more educated women are, the fewer children they tend to have. Both education and employment outside the home affect childbearing decisions. Education of men and women improves their ability to understand and use family-planning methods. The better educated parents are, the more education and opportunities they want for their children. This generally means that they decide to have only the number of children they can afford to support.

Rising *affluence* also influences fertility. There is an inverse relationship between income and fertility: The more affluent a family, the more likely it is

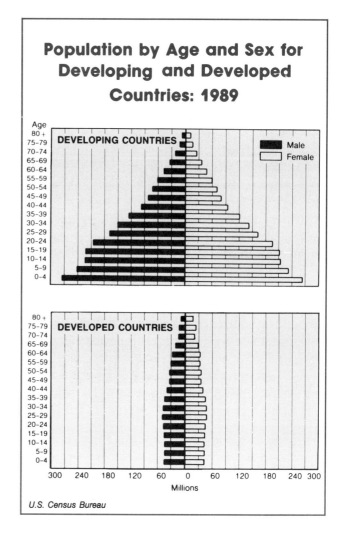

Population by Age and Sex for Developing and Developed Countries: 1989

U.S. Census Bureau

to have fewer children. With more money, families are able to take part in activities — travel and recreation — that are not centered around children. By contrast, in less-developed areas with lower standards of living where most families are engaged in agriculture, children are considered an economic asset. They perform farm chores and household work. They also serve as security for parents when they reach old age. Developing countries do not usually provide social security or old-age benefits. Economic development creates the social conditions that reduce fertility. As countries develop, a downward trend in the rate of population growth occurs.

Family planning

Family planning is an *antinatalist* policy: It aims to prevent births by introducing methods of contraception to a population. A pronatalist policy promotes population growth by encouraging people to have children.

The demographic transition to low fertility has occurred in most developed countries. Less-developed countries are still in transition. Their birth rates are characterized by a gradual decline as development proceeds.

The *World Fertility Survey,* a major study of birth rates around the world, reports that a larger number of women want fewer children than in past years. Family-planning information in the vast majority of nations studied is effective. Millions of couples are having smaller families. Others may desire small families, but contraceptives are either unavailable or unaffordable.

The introduction of contraceptive devices alone to countries of low development and high fertility does not reduce the birth rate. A developing society usually must experience the economic and social changes that promote fertility decline.

Population and development. High birth rates result in a high percentage of dependent children per adult. This makes it difficult for families to save what is needed for investment in economic development. Investment can barely keep up with the growing number of workers, much less improve their working conditions and their productivity. Population growth also results in the decrease of arable land per person. Money that could be invested in development and increased productivity must then be used to import food.

Migration

One solution for people living in nations of the world trapped, as Lester Brown says, in the second stage of the demographic transition is to migrate to an industrial nation that has completed the transition. As the population in the wealthy nations of the world levels off, the poorer nations will expand to 80 percent of the world's population by the year 2000. As a result, the migration of people from the southern countries to the northern countries will increase dramatically.

Migration is the geographic movement of people. It involves a permanent change of residence. The motivation to migrate can be explained in terms of "push" and "pull." Migrants are pushed to relocate by conditions in their region of origin: Famine, resource depletion, overpopulation, persecution and war are typical causes of movement. Migrants are pulled by conditions in the region of their destination: The prospect of employment, the promise of a better life, are examples of migrant attraction. Although most migration is the result of both push and pull factors, in some instances — such as persecution, famine or war — push alone may be enough. Communication is important to the pull factor; people must know something about their potential destination before they migrate.

Voluntary migration. People migrate voluntarily when they choose to move from one area to another. Since most people relocate for economic

reasons — that is, to find better jobs or living conditions — voluntary migration is usually an individual or family endeavor. Young adults make up a large percentage of voluntary migrants, since the likelihood of finding improved conditions is greater for them than for older people who have long been established in jobs and neighborhoods.

Between 1820 and 1970, about 36 million people migrated to the United States from Europe. Most were voluntary migrants. During the first 50 years of this migration, settlers came primarily from Ireland and Great Britain. Irish farmers fled from hunger; British migrants had been thrown out of work by industrialization. Both groups were attracted by the hope of economic prosperity in the United States. During the next 50 years, thousands of immigrants from Germany, Russia, Italy and Poland made their way across the Atlantic. In 1920, the United States imposed restrictions on incoming immigrant groups, establishing a *quota system.*

Forced migration. People involuntarily moved by a government or some other group that holds power over them are forced to migrate. Examples of forced migration include deportation — the expulsion of an individual from a country and compulsory exchange, or transfer, of ethnic minorities. During and after World War II, many Eastern Europeans were forced to migrate for reasons of ethnic uniformity. Hungary, for example, sent approximately 30,000 Slovaks to Czechoslovakia in return for nearly the same number of Magyars.

Refugees

People who have been forced out of their homelands and deprived of citizenship are known as *refugees.* They may be victims of war, territorial change, economic or political oppression, or victims of environmental disasters. Ethnic, religious and political minorities also have long been objects of persecution by governments desiring to enforce conformity on their citizens.

Religious persecution. Religious discrimination is one of the oldest forms of intolerance. For many centuries, governments exiled or deported entire religious groups in order to enforce religious conformity. In some cases, an uncaring world permitted attempts to exterminate entire ethnic groups.

As Nazi armies marched through Europe during World War II, they rounded up Jews for execution or export to concentration camps where millions were tortured and murdered. Approximately 67 percent of Europe's pre-war Jewish population of 8,851,800 died during the *holocaust* — almost 6,000,000 Jews were exterminated in this terrifying example of genocide. Only two European coun-

Vietnamese refugees rescued at sea.

UNHCR/P. DeLoche

tries, of more than 20 under the influence of Nazi Germany, refused to cooperate with the round-up of Jews: Finland and Denmark.

Before the war, Jews attempting to escape Nazi oppression were turned away by almost every country. Only three small countries — the Netherlands, Denmark and the Dominican Republic — agreed to accept Jewish refugees.

Territory disputes. Some of the largest refugee movements have been triggered by changes in territorial boundaries. The partition of colonial India in 1947 into the countries of India and Pakistan resulted in the migration of nearly 14 million Muslims who left Hindu India for Muslim Pakistan. The partition of Palestine to establish Israel in 1949 triggered a military confrontation between Israel and five Arab countries; an estimated 500,000 to 1,000,000 Arab refugees fled Israeli territory. Most of them have never been resettled, and a new generation is living in refugee camps.

Refugees may wait long periods of time before they are resettled. Usually they are housed in refugee camps during their wait. European refugees displaced by World War II were housed in several camps. Their number totaled about 1.1 million in 1946.

War and political oppression. Political persecution and war account for several million refugees worldwide. Hundreds of thousands fled Vietnam, Cambodia, Ethiopia, Afghanistan, El Salvador, Haiti and many other nations due to civil war, foreign invasion and fear of political oppression. Most nations, fearing social and economic problems, refuse to accept refugees.

Many refugees are relocated to relief camps or settlements where conditions are extremely poor. Despite aid from the United Nations and over 300 voluntary agencies, the problem is getting worse.

Economic opportunity. The United States has historically provided an opportunity for immigrants who sought a better quality of life. Millions of European and Asian immigrants came to America when employment opportunities were plentiful during the 19th and early 20th centuries. Tight restrictions presently prohibit mass immigration to industrialized nations for those in search of better jobs and housing. Thousands of Latin Americans continue to cross the U.S. border illegally to escape poverty and despair. Many of these unfortunate refugees end up in detention centers and are eventually deported.

66

UN Photo 153599/John Isaac

Drought and famine periodically devastate parts of Africa. Members of the Tuarag nomadic tribe in search of water in Mali.

The global community has made little effort to solve the problem of refugee resettlement. Most countries are reluctant to admit large numbers of refugees. The Office of the United Nations High Commissioner for Refugees (UNHCR) offers refugees legal and political protection during the resettlement process and prevents their being sent back to the country of origin against their will. But resettlement can only take place with the consent of individual governments. Less than half of the members of the United Nations support the UNHCR financially.

Since refugees are not citizens of any country, they have no legal rights or status in the country of refuge. In 1951, a UN convention granted refugees a minimum legal status and certain basic rights. Sixty-two countries, excluding the United States, have ratified the convention.

The resettlement process does not usually restore refugees to their former economic and social positions. While some adapt to their new homes rapidly and successfully, many resettled refugees can only find work in poorly paid jobs. They also face the problems of adapting to unfamiliar lifestyles and alien languages.

Environmental refugees

Millions of people have been forced to leave their homes because the land has become uninhabitable. Some people flee temporarily due to natural disasters such as earthquakes and floods. Most *environmental refugees* are forced from their homes because of land degradation — the result of desertification, soil erosion, deforestation and the depletion of the water supply. The problem is most severe in Africa where most of the population farms small tracts of land. Due to overpopulation, much arid land has become useless.

Other environmental refugees are the victims of "unnatural" disasters. The explosion at Chernobyl's nuclear power plant forced the evacuation of thousands from that region. The dumping of toxic wastes has created more refugees, especially in developing nations — where it is cheaper for industrialized nations to dispose of toxic chemicals.

Environmental refugees are not recognized by the UNHCR because they do not fit the traditional definition of refugees. There are an estimated 10 million environmental refugees — almost as many as the number of "official" refugees recognized by the United Nations. Environmental refugees often relocate to large cities, adding to the congestion and poverty.

Poverty

The world's poor became poorer and more numerous during the 1980s. Grinding poverty is a fact of life for millions — and hope for the future is bleak. More than 40 developing nations probably finished the decade of the '80s poorer, in per-capita terms, than they started it. The 14 nations most affected — including Zambia, Bolivia, and Nigeria — saw per-capita income plummet as drastically as did the United States during the Great Depression. In fact, according to Alan Durning of Worldwatch, "the term 'developing nation' has become a cruel misnomer; many countries are no longer so much developing as disintegrating." Much of this poverty is found in nations of Africa and Latin America. In Latin America the per-capita income of the

UN Photo 154269/John Isaac
Poverty is often seen in the faces of children.

average citizen is 9 percent lower than it was in 1980. In some countries the standard of living has slipped back to what it was 20 years ago.

Poverty's greatest toll is in the lives of children. As income declines, family size increases. Fifty-five to 80 percent of poor families in developing nations have eight or more members. It is estimated that two-thirds of the world's people living in poverty are under the age of 15. Under these conditions, infant mortality rates sharply increase. Many of the children who survive infancy are chronically hungry, physically stunted, and mentally impaired.

AIDS: a worldwide epidemic

Epidemics have sometimes occurred which have considerably destroyed populations. In Europe, in the 1300s, half the population died from the plague.

AIDS may now threaten populations as it spreads throughout the world. Millions of people may now carry the AIDS virus. By 1990, there was no known cure for AIDS. Central and eastern Africa have been hit very hard. Blood testing in Africa indicated that from 20 percent to 30 percent of the sexually active adults in the urban centers of the Congo, Rwanda, Tanzania, Uganda, Zaire and Zambia are already infected. Female prostitutes in some urban areas showed infection rates higher than 50 percent. Officials fear that the scope of the AIDS tragedy in Africa may well overwhelm local health facilities and set back economic development efforts.

A global perspective on AIDS shows different patterns of transmission. In the United States, Europe and most other industrialized nations, AIDS has spread mostly among male homosexuals and intravenous-drug abusers. In Africa and in some parts of the Caribbean, however, heterosexual sex is mainly responsible for the spread of the AIDS virus.

The United States has a high incidence of AIDS cases with about nine cases per 100,000 population. The rate is expected to increase rapidly. The U.S. General Accounting Office (GAO) has predicted that 300,000 to 480,000 cases of AIDS would be diagnosed in the United States by the end of 1991. AIDS has become a global issue of major proportions, and the search for its prevention and cure requires rising public expenditures for education and health care.

Chapter 13

Food

> ● *Enough food is grown to properly feed every man, woman and child on Earth.*
>
> ● *Hunger in the world is more a result of unequal distribution than insufficient production of food.*

Most people of the world are *malnourished;* they do not have the proper diet for maximum good health. About half of the world's people are *undernourished;* they have too few calories to sustain bodily functions properly. Another proportion of people are *overnourished;* they have too many calories to be efficiently used by the body.

According to estimates by the *Food and Agricultural Organization* (FAO) of the *United Nations* (UN), over 300 million people in the developing nations are living at a *subsistence level;* they have just enough food to barely stay alive. They are starving to death. Another 700 million people are at a level just a little higher. Their caloric intake is enough so they are not in life-threatening situations, but they are hungry all of the time.

Most of the world's undernourished live in Asia, Africa and Latin America. Approximately 5 percent of the hungry are scattered throughout the developed world. Most of the overnourished live in affluent nations such as the United States, Switzerland, the United Kingdom, France and other Western nations.

Malnutrition and starvation are avoidable. People go hungry not so much because too little food is produced, but because the food is not distributed to where it is needed. It is estimated that hunger could be eliminated with only a 5-percent increase in world food production if better distribution systems were developed.

It has been estimated that almost half the world's food is destroyed by pests each year. Insects, birds, rodents, bats, as well as microbial pests are responsible for this damage. Pesticides and herbicides to fight pests and plant diseases are available. However, many pests and plant diseases have developed immunities.

Food distribution

Since the beginning of agriculture in the river-valley civilizations of the Nile, Tigris/Euphrates, Indus and Hwang Ho some 12,000 years ago, food has been eaten near the place where it was produced. Most members of the society were engaged in producing it. The people lived and worked close to their food sources. In modern, industrialized societies like the United States, less than 5 percent of the population works in agriculture. The problems of distributing food today are enormous.

Transporting food quickly and safely to distant markets where people can buy it is a food distribution problem. Roads, railways and other forms of transportation must be available to move the food to market efficiently.

Food consumption

What people eat depends primarily on where they live. Traditionally, food has been consumed in the area in which it is produced. As more and more food

World Bank Photo by Yosef Hadar

A farmer threshing rice in Kunming, China, just as hundreds of generations have done before him.

is grown for export (bananas, for example), this situation is changing. Some of the poorest countries in the world devote more acres to *cash crops* to sell to richer nations than to fruits and vegetables to feed their own people. Hunger today depends as much on who grows food and where it is marketed, as on how much food is grown.

What people eat also depends on how prosperous they are. Among other things, food serves as a guide to the economic status of a country. At the base of the food hierarchy are roots and coarse grains. Root staples such as yams and cassavas, high in starch, are basic to the Central and West African diet. The coarse grains, millet and sorghum, also are consumed in the poorer or "food-deficit" countries. The people of these areas eat little that is not grown locally.

Much of the land for growing root crops is subject to drought and uncertain yields. Some of the best land in these regions is used to produce cash crops — vegetables and grains that can be sold to other countries. Twenty-five to 30 percent of the children in most developing nations die before their fifth birthday. The cause is protein deficiency — eating too little food or foods low in nutritional value. The survival of many people in the developing world depends on the abundance of wild berries and fruits.

Staples

While there are about 250,000 identified plants, only about 300 are used for food. The majority of

the human race relies on seven plant species for their basic diet. These *staple* foods are: wheat, rice, maize, barley, soybeans, the common bean and potatoes. Many biologists believe this base can be greatly enlarged. In one supposedly barren stretch of desert in the Southwestern United States, scientists identified 375 species of consumable vegetation.

Rice is the staple in Asia, the world's most populous region. Rice is eaten throughout the world, but the demand for rice in Asia is four times the demand in other areas. China, which produces over one-third of the world's rice, is able to grow enough food for its more than a billion people. The Chinese also consume wheat, corn, soybeans, fish, pork and chicken, but rice remains the basic food. In Japan, consumer preference for rice has declined. Wheat products, including wheat-fed beef, are growing in popularity.

Corn (maize) originated in Latin America and is the major food of people on this continent. Corn is the largest commercial crop in the United States. Much of it is exported, but most is either fed to animals or used to make such processed foods as oils and margarine. Some corn is fermented to create methane, an ingredient of gasohol.

Soybeans originated in China and have been an important supplement to rice, especially in Japan, Indonesia and China. In recent years, soybeans have been a bumper crop for U.S. agriculture. The United States grows over half of all the soybeans produced in the world. Some of the U.S. soybean crop, high in protein and fat, is used to make margarine. Huge quantities are exported. Most of the U.S. beef feedstock is soybean. Soybeans also are increasingly used as protein substitutes for meat in processed foods such as bologna and hot dogs.

Wheat is grown in temperate climates in the industrialized, developed nations. People in these more prosperous countries have larger and more varied diets than those who live in developing nations. Almost two-thirds of the world's wheat is consumed in North America, Europe, Japan, Australia, the Soviet Union and China.

Animals, particularly beef cattle, are another major source of food in developed nations. North Americans derive almost three-fourths of their protein from animals. The United States and Canada use much of their grain to feed animals: dairy cows, chickens and, mostly, beef cattle. The diet of Soviet citizens in the past 30 years has shifted from mainly bread and potatoes to one with meat and other animal products.

Until the 1970s, increases in the demand for food resulted primarily from population growth. In recent years, increases in per-capita income have begun to influence the rate and amount of food consumption. In developing countries each person consumes about 400 pounds of grain annually, most of it in the form of bread or some type of cereal. In developed countries, by contrast, the yearly per capita consumption of grain totals about 2,000 pounds. Bread and cereal account for only 200 pounds of this amount; the rest is fed to livestock and indirectly consumed by people in the form of meat, milk and eggs.

The people of Japan and Western Europe have recently joined Americans, Canadians, Australians and Russians in using large amounts of grain to satisfy their appetites for hamburgers and steaks. The increase in livestock production that accompanies rising affluence threatens global grain reserves. As more of the world's corn, wheat and soybeans goes to feed cattle, the ability to feed the malnourished people of the developing world and to prevent famine in time of poor harvests is being diminished.

Food production and population growth

In 1798, the English economist Thomas Robert Malthus wrote that population grows faster than food supplies and that famine thus would balance the rate of population increase.

Malthus' prediction has not come to pass, mainly because of the revolution in agricultural production. A dramatic 2.6-fold increase in grain production between 1950 and 1984 raised per-capita consumption by nearly 40 percent. Modern farm technologies, new types of crops, and an increase in arable land have brought about a tremendous rise in the production of food. But in the late 1980s, this growth stopped, and the original problems identified by Malthus have surfaced again. Although the problem today, in large part, is one of inequitable food distribution, there is increasing concern that the Earth's ability to produce enough food to keep up with population growth may have reached its limit.

The outlook for future food production is mixed. Even with a more equal distribution of food, the problem is not easily solved. Over the past 30 years, global food production has been leveling off, while population gains have not diminished correspondingly. A recent trend, however, is encouraging. Birth rates in some developing nations, especially in China, have begun to decline.

Population growth in modern times follows a pattern, called *demographic transition*. The introduction of public-health measures and better nutrition reduces the death rate while birth rates remain constant. When a country develops and becomes more

United Nations/Photo by B.P. Wolff

An Egyptian woman living in a garbage dump looks for morsels to eat. Millions of people live this way now.

prosperous, the birth rate declines. Parents want fewer children as their standard of living increases; additional children become a burden rather than an asset. Many developing nations are still in the first phase of the pattern: The death rate has been reduced. But to the poor, marginal farmers in developing nations, children are their major asset — to work the fields or be hired out to big landowners. As the level of prosperity increases for a country, birth rates decline.

Factors affecting food production

Land. Two basic factors contribute to growth in food production: increases in the total amount of land under cultivation and increases in food yield per cultivated acre. As world population continues to grow and land is put to non-agricultural uses, the amount of cultivated land per capita has declined.

A key to increased productivity will be to bring

An abandoned village in Mauritania where drought often occurs.

under cultivation potentially arable land. About 80 percent of the growth in world food output since 1950 has come from this source. In some areas, this will mean spending money to prepare the land, such as that in Africa infested with the tsetse fly. Less than one-third of the agricultural land in the developing world is presently in use. It is estimated that about 25 percent of the world's ice-free land could grow food. This is more than twice the land that has been cultivated during the last few decades. However, important tradeoffs are involved. Much of the world's unused agricultural land is marginal due to the climate, soil composition and accessibility. In addition, the soil currently under cultivation is suffering very serious degradation from salinization of irrigated areas and soil erosion. Worldwide, an estimated 25 billion tons of topsoil is being lost from cropland each year, roughly the amount that covers Australia's wheat fields.

Increases in yield per acre of land are beginning to level off: fertilizers, pesticides and irrigation — primary contributions to improved productivity — are nearing their limit of influence. Plant physiology places the ultimate constraint on growth and yield. Plants grow through the process of photosynthesis, using solar energy to convert water and soil nutrients into edible material. It takes a certain amount of time

from seed planting to harvest time. Scientists have not yet found a way for plants to grow faster. Genetic engineering offers great promise for the future. Scientists have successfully developed strains of grain and seeds with increased crop yields and improved growing efficiency.

The expansion of human and animal populations past the basic sustaining capacity of the land causes environmental damage. *Overgrazing* of livestock and *deforestation* have resulted in the erosion of topsoil and the spread of desert areas. The Sahara Desert is moving southward along a 3,500-mile-wide strip east to west across Africa at a rate of approximately 6 miles annually.

The unused arable land in the developing world is unevenly distributed. Over 80 percent of the unused land is in South America and parts of Africa; only 9 percent is in Asia. If cultivation cannot increase yields enough in those areas where land is scarce, the only way to increase the food supply will be through trade.

Climate. An area's climate — its temperature, rainfall and winds — has the single greatest influence on its agriculture. A long, warm growing season, combined with plentiful rainfall, creates ideal conditions for food production.

Temperature is a result of *insolation* — incoming

solar radiation. The further an area lies from the equator, the less heat it receives from the sun. The equator receives three times more heat energy than the poles.

The distance of a place from a large body of water — known as *continentality* — is another factor that affects temperature range. Large bodies of water, such as oceans, heat up and cool down less quickly than land areas. The farther inland a place is, the more extreme its temperature range is. Seattle, Washington, and Duluth, Minnesota, are both located at 47 degrees latitude. While their summer temperature ranges are similar, coastal Seattle is much warmer during the winter months than inland Duluth.

The southern region of the United States, both for reasons of insolation and continentality, has a warmer climate year round and a longer growing season than the upper Midwest. Continentality affects rainfall as well. The closer a place is to an ocean body, the greater the chance that it will receive abundant rainfall. Eighty percent of the moisture carried by air has been evaporated from the oceans.

Topography — the terrain, or land form, of a place — also affects rainfall. For example, mountain ranges are barriers to the inland movement of moisture-laden air. As winds carry wet air up the sides of mountains, the air cools, releasing moisture as rainfall. Meteorologists call this phenomenon *"orographic precipitation."* Because hot dry air comes down the other side of the mountain, little moisture falls in the lee of the mountain range — the *rain shadow effect*. Seattle, on the windward side of the mountain, will receive about five times as much rain, for a given period of time, as Yakima, Washington, on the leeside. In the Northern Hemisphere the prevailing winds are from the west; the reverse is true in the Southern Hemisphere. Thus, the dry areas in the nations south of the equator lie west of the mountains.

Irrigation. Since rainfall is distributed unevenly over the world's land masses, people long ago developed the means of artificially supplying land with water — a process known as irrigation. Irrigated agriculture provided the surplus food to support ancient cities. Increases in the demand for food were followed by increases in the amount of land under irrigation. Today, China and India account for nearly half of the world's irrigated land, while Egypt has almost all of its cropland under irrigation. Rice oc-

In the Sahel, when water is available, crops can be grown.

cupies more irrigated land than all other grain crops combined. Irrigation contributes to higher yields; it facilitates the application of chemical fertilizers; and it relieves the dependence on seasonal rainfall, thereby minimizing the risk of drought.

Energy. Modern agriculture is *energy-intensive.* Modern technologies use large energy inputs to increase the productivity of land and labor. The amount of energy used to produce food compared to the energy food contains is increasing constantly. In the 19th century, the energy contained in food grown in the United States was higher than the energy used to grow, process and distribute it. Currently, it takes eight times more energy to produce a unit of food than what can be obtained from it.   The processing, transportation and marketing of food accounts for three-quarters of the energy input. Canning food for preservation uses moderate amounts of energy; freezing food uses large amounts, not only in the freezing process but also in the storage of the final product. Urbanization increases the distance between farm and consumer, thereby increasing the amount of energy used for transportation. The remainder of the energy input takes place on the farm in the form of machine power, pesticides and chemical fertilizers. The latter contain more energy than any other input.

Fertilizer. Modern agriculture requires the extensive use of fertilizer. Since the 1970s, worldwide fertilizer shortages have developed. These shortages result from a failure to meet increased demand with increased production. If the use of fertilizer were reduced, productivity in countries practicing intensive agriculture would drop by half or more. An unlimited supply of fertilizer, however, would not result in food without limit. This is due to the *law*

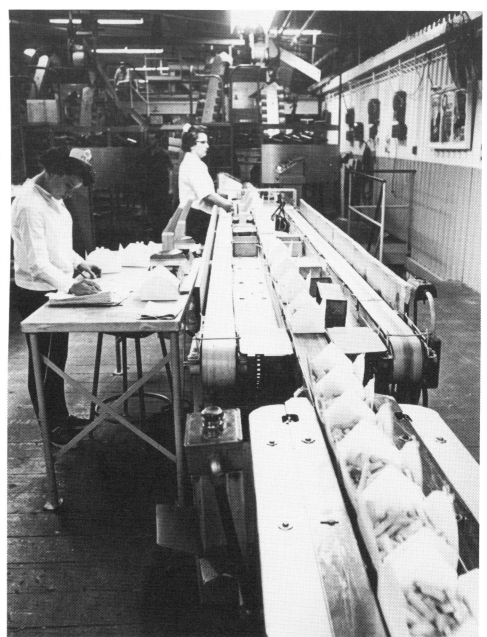

USDA

Energy use is high in fast-food production.

of diminishing returns. As more fertilizer is applied to an acre of corn or other crop, the yield increases at first; then after a time, with equal applications of fertilizer, the yield begins to decrease. For the first 40 pounds of fertilizer, a corn farmer might receive an additional 27 pounds of corn. For the second 40 pounds applied, the yield is only 14 more pounds of corn. A third application accounts for only nine additional pounds of corn; and for a fourth application of 40 pounds of fertilizer, the farmer would get only four extra pounds of corn. Also, enormous amounts of fresh water, scarce in many areas of the world, are required to make the maximum use of commercial fertilizers.

Developing countries use very little commercial fertilizer. More yield per fertilizer input is potentially available in countries which have not yet used fertilizers in large amounts.

Eighty percent of the world's chemical fertilizer is produced in the developed countries. The most widely used manufacturing processes use natural gas as a raw material. Unlike natural or mineral fertilizers, chemical fertilizer that is unused by plants does not remain in the soil. It is washed out and must be fully replenished each growing period. A shortage in chemical fertilizer is felt immediately as a drop in food production.

Food from the sea

The world fish catch accounts for a major portion of the world's annual protein consumption — well above the beef intake. Two-thirds of the fish caught are consumed directly by humans; the remaining third is turned into fishmeal and fed to livestock. The consumption of fish varies from country to country: Japan consumes over 70 pounds of fish per capita each year; the Soviet Union consumes about 25 pounds; and France, 18 pounds. The United States consumes only 15 pounds of fish per person annually, compared to 200 pounds of meat.

Food production and distribution is big business

More food is being produced than ever before. Many people are eating better, namely the middle class and rich, in both the developed and developing nations. But hunger also is increasing. More food is being produced, but fewer people are producing it. The production of food has become a big business. Worldwide food production and distribution are coming under the control of a relatively small number of multinational corporations.

Five multinational grain companies control the production and distribution of corn, wheat, barley and soybean. These originally were family operations, dating to the early 19th century, in Europe, Argentina and the United States. Today, these corporations are far-reaching. Grain companies control the entire process of buying, transporting, milling and selling. As a result, they effectively set grain prices. Farm machinery and the world feed market also are in the hands of a few omnipotent multinational corporations.

With the increase in technology — sophisticated farm machinery, petrochemical pesticides and hybrid seeds — small farms have given way to large, mechanized operations. Food growing has become an *agribusiness*. These businesses want to maximize profits.

The production of food for export generates income

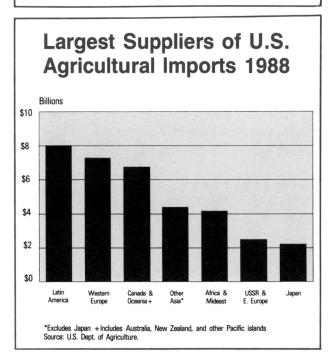

in the developing countries. Potentially, this money could be used to feed, clothe and house the people. Multinational corporations are inclined to use the money to further develop company operations.

As small farms give way to large agribusiness, people either seek work with the large farms or migrate to urban areas. Extensive use of technology, in both agribusiness and urban industry, reduces jobs, and unemployment rises. In most countries where people are hungry, large landowners control most of the land. Seventy percent of the children are undernourished in Central America and the Caribbean, and the best land tends to be used to produce crops and cattle for export. Where small farms exist, hunger is less of a problem. Though family incomes are low, the people at least can eat what they grow, and the remainder is sold in local markets.

Large populations in a country are not necessarily the basic cause of hunger. China, with the most number of people for each acre of cropland, has virtually eliminated undernourishment in recent years. In contrast, Mexico, Brazil and Bolivia have large amounts of arable land per person, but the number of undernourished people is great.

Many countries are becoming increasingly dependent on a few other nations for food supplies. Only the United States, Canada, France and Australia have major wheat surpluses. The United States produces about one-fifth of the world's grain and exports almost 40 percent of all wheat in international trade. The United States also dominates in the production of soybeans, corn and sorghum for export. U.S. power over the world food economy is much greater than Saudi Arabia's role in the oil industry. Many countries, industrialized and developing, depend on food imports, mostly from the United States, to supply needed calories and proteins.

Many nations are reluctant to become overly dependent upon external sources of food. Japan, for example, has a great surplus of rice, yet the farmers are heavily subsidized. Many Japanese remember the difficult days after World War II when rice was scarce, and hunger and starvation racked the nation.

Food reserves

Grain reserves are measured in terms of the amount in storage at the beginning of a new harvest. Reserves are concentrated in the United States, Canada, Argentina and Australia.

When *food reserves* are low, the global ability to respond to food emergencies is not very great. It is not only a case of too little food to distribute; high prices also prevent poor countries from purchasing needed food from available supplies. During the late 1980s, the prospects for world food security diminished. Writing in 1989, Lester Brown described this decline:

> As the eighties draw to a close, climate change is being added to an already long list of environmental stresses and resource scarcities that are undermining global food security. Soil erosion, desertification, the salting of irrigated lands, and a scarcity of new cropland and fresh water are combining to lower the growth in food output below that of population in dozens of developing countries. Partly as a result, the world now has far more hungry people than it did when the eighties began.
>
> At the start of the 1987 harvest, world grain stocks totaled a record 459 million tons, enough to feed the world for 101 days. When the 1989 harvest begins, the ''carryover'' stock will likely drop to 54 days of consumption, lower even than the 57 days at the beginning of 1973, when grain prices doubled. During a brief two years, world reserves of grain — which account for half of all human caloric intake when consumed directly and part of the remainder in the form of meat, milk, butter and eggs — will have plummeted from the highest level ever to the lowest since the years immediately following World War II.

UN Photo 153495/Peter Magubane

People in Ethiopia are headed toward a relief plane carrying supplies from the UN and other international organizations. Frequent drought creates disaster for the people.

Chapter 14

Resources

- *Population growth and improvement in the standard of living create increasing demands on scarce resources.*

- *More natural resources have been used in the decades of the '70s and '80s than were consumed in the prior 100 years.*

Any element that is included in production is a resource. A resource is determined by the needs and means of people. *Needs* are what people — consumers and producers — demand, those items they must have. *Means* are the processes of resource extraction.

Both needs and means vary with a society's development and from region to region. Resources also change over time and from place to place. When needs and means change, there is a change in resource utilization. For example, the properties of uranium have been known for some time. One of these properties — high-weight per volume — prompted the use of uranium ore as ballast in the holds of sailing ships. A smaller volume of ballast meant more room for cargo. When nuclear technology was developed, uranium became an energy resource used to fuel reactors.

There are large deposits of oil shale, petroleum-laden rock, in the United States. The means of extracting oil from shale exist, but the process is too costly at today's prices to warrant production. Processing shale also involves enormous indirect costs when whole landscapes are chewed up and vast quantities of water are needed. As the price of other oil increases, as the supply of oil declines, and as the cost of extracting oil from shale decreases, oil shale may become a usable resource.

A society's production capabilities depend on its resources.

Types of resources

Natural resources are physical in nature. They include climate, arable land, water supply, mineral deposits and forests.

Human resources are the people of a region. The quality of human resources varies with the size and distribution of the population, the level of education and the development of productive skills. A country's human resources depend in part upon its natural resources. People living in a region with few mineral deposits are not likely to develop any mining skills.

Capital resources include machines, tools, buildings, money and anything else that can be used in production.

Scarcity and distribution

Complex technology has produced a wide assortment and an increasing supply of products. Industries based on the extraction of resources and the manufacture of goods have expanded greatly. As population grows, resources are used to feed, shelter, transport and equip an increasing number of people. As economic development expands in more countries, the demands on the world's resources grow at an increasing rate.

Rising demand has consumed large quantities of the earth's natural resources. Within the last 20 years, far more resources were consumed than during the previous 100 years.

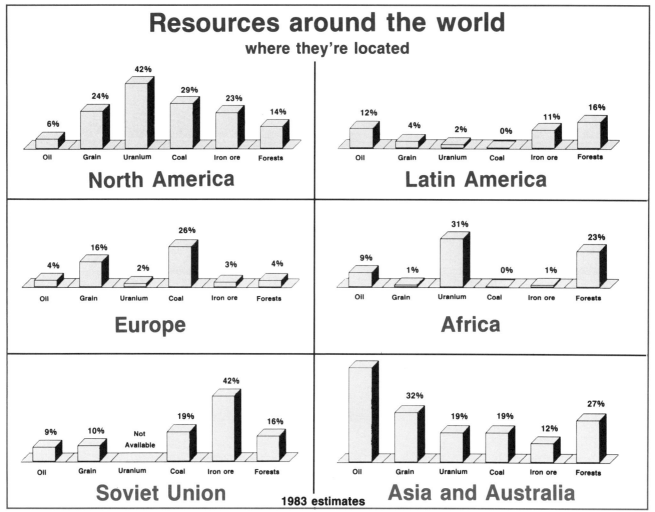

Resources around the world
where they're located

North America
Oil 6% · Grain 24% · Uranium 42% · Coal 29% · Iron ore 23% · Forests 14%

Latin America
Oil 12% · Grain 4% · Uranium 2% · Coal 0% · Iron ore 11% · Forests 16%

Europe
Oil 4% · Grain 16% · Uranium 2% · Coal 26% · Iron ore 3% · Forests 4%

Africa
Oil 9% · Grain 1% · Uranium 31% · Coal 0% · Iron ore 1% · Forests 23%

Soviet Union
Oil 9% · Grain 10% · Uranium Not Available · Coal 19% · Iron ore 42% · Forests 16%

Asia and Australia
Oil · Grain 32% · Uranium 19% · Coal 19% · Iron ore 12% · Forests 27%

1983 estimates

Basic Data: *Oil & Gas Journal.* U.S. Depts. of Agriculture, Interior and Energy.
Organization for Economic Cooperation and Development, Global 2000 Study

SIRS Staff/Michelle McCulloch

The United States imports 80 percent of its mineral requirements and consumes about half of the world's *nonrenewable resources.* Nonrenewable resources do not replenish themselves.

An industrial economy requires a large quantity and a great variety of natural resources to sustain itself. The underlying geological structure of a country determines the types of nonrenewable resources to be found. The topography, or terrain, determines what *renewable resources* are available. Large countries are more likely to have an adequate quantity and variety of resources than small countries. However, no single industrial country is totally self-sufficient in raw materials, which include petroleum, iron ore, copper, bauxite (aluminum ore) and coal.

Resources and industry

Industrial production consists of four phases: (1) extraction of raw materials — mining and agriculture; (2) assembly of raw materials — stockpiling; (3) transformation of raw materials — refining and manufacture; (4) distribution — sales and marketing of a product. Assembly and distribution both involve transportation. The greater the distance, the greater the cost incurred. Handling costs remain the same. Thus, the geographic location of raw materials influences where industry develops.

The iron and steel industry is the most important part of an industrial economy. This industry is raw-material intensive — that is, it uses large amounts of iron ore and coal. Deposits of coal and iron ore are not located near each other for geological reasons. Most coal and petroleum resources are found in sedimentary rock — the layered rock of river or ocean bottoms — while metal ores are found in metamorphic rock — rock that has been changed by tremendous heat and pressure. Some ores also are found in igneous rock, which is volcanic in origin.

It takes more coal than iron ore in combination to produce a given quantity of metal. To overcome excessive transportation costs, industry originally developed adjacent to the source of the raw material most used by weight — namely, coal.

In Europe the iron and steel industry developed in

the Ruhr valley of Germany next to large deposits of high-quality coal, and in the Midlands of the United Kingdom for the same reason. In the United States, industry first developed in Pittsburgh, near the northern edge of the Appalachian coal deposit. Similarly, Soviet industry initially established itself in the Donbas (eastern Ukraine) near the country's largest coal-producing area. These regions are the most important areas of heavy industry in the world.

Modern technology has changed the effect of resource location on industry. The ratio of coal to iron ore is no longer three-to-one: Equal portions of each are now used to produce a given amount of iron. Moreover, most industrial countries import some coal and iron. Since water transport is the cheapest method of moving heavy materials, most industrial development takes place in coastal regions. In the United States, heavy industry is located on the east coast, Baltimore and Philadelphia, and in the Great Lakes region which has deep water ports.

Resources are distributed unevenly around the globe. Also, resource utilization changes as nations undergo economic transformation. As people's wants change and the availability of resources fluctuates, relationships among regions of the world are affected.

Oil and natural gas

People in industrial countries live in an age of oil. Petroleum has shaped life in modern societies. The world uses about 2.6 billion gallons of oil a day, or 60 million barrels. This figure has remained fairly constant during the 1980s. While the number of automobiles has increased during this time, they have also become much more fuel-efficient. One barrel, the standard measurement for oil, equals 42 gallons. About one-third of the oil produced is consumed in the United States.

Oil has put Americans on wheels and made the U.S. society a mobile one. The development of the automobile went hand in hand with the use of petroleum. Over 50 percent of America's oil is used for motion of some sort — cars, trucks, airplanes and other modes of transportation. In comparison, Europeans devote just over 25 percent of their oil resources to transportation.

The oil age began in 1859 in Pennsylvania with the drilling of the first oil well. It wasn't until almost 100 years later, during the 1950s, that oil emerged as the dominant fuel. From 1950 to 1980, world oil production increased 7 percent annually but held steady during the '80s. World population grew at a steady pace over much of those 30 years, but at nowhere near the rate of oil production. Industrial growth among mostly the rich nations — not population growth — explains the tremendous increase in oil consumption. The United States, with 5 percent of the world's population, uses 30 percent of all the petroleum. Combined, the United States and the Soviet Union, with 10 percent of the world's population, produce and consume about 44 percent of the world's energy.

The Department of Energy (DOE) provides funds for research to improve oil recovery from an old oil well.

Department of Energy

There are trillions of barrels of oil under the earth's surface. Whether and when it is retrieved and made ready for travel, heating and air conditioning depends on many factors: market prices, production costs, advances in technology and many political issues.

Oil has dramatically changed the lives of many people since 1950. These people will have consumed in one generation the readily accessible reserves that took hundreds of millions of years to form. Oil can be found in many parts of the world, and North America has been a major source. However, the United States has used most of its easily accessible oil sources and today relies on imports for almost half of its needs. The largest remaining world oil reserves exist in Saudi Arabia, other Middle East nations, northern areas of Africa, Mexico, Ecuador, Venezuela and Indonesia.

Thirteen oil-producing nations combined to form the *Organization of Petroleum Exporting Countries* (OPEC) in 1960. In addition to Saudi Arabia, there are five other members in the Middle East (Iran, Iraq, Kuwait, Qatar and the United Arab Emirates), four in Africa (Algeria, Libya, Gabon and Nigeria), two in Latin America (Venezuela and Ecuador) and one in Asia (Indonesia). OPEC is an international cartel set up to control the supply, hence the price, of oil on world markets. OPEC has had mixed success. From a low of $1.30 a barrel in 1970, the price climbed to over $30 a barrel in the early 1980s, only to fall precipitously later in the decade. OPEC nations that depended almost entirely upon petroleum exports to support their economic development suffered greatly. Nigeria and Venezuela were especially hard hit. Non-OPEC nations such as Mexico and the United Kingdom also felt the pinch, as did the "oil patch" states in the United States such as Alaska, Colorado, Louisiana, Oklahoma, Texas and Wyoming.

Minerals

Energy and industrial development have been the central reasons for change in the lives of people in many nations. The world's non-fuel minerals — iron, bauxite, copper, nickel and manganese — have provided the framework for building industries.

The world's supply of most minerals seems inexhaustible, but no one knows for sure. Our planet is 4,000 miles deep to the core, and the deepest mines reach only five miles. We probably have only scratched Earth's surface. How abundant different precious metals are, or how difficult it will be to retrieve them, is unknown.

While mineral deposits apparently are abundant, they are far from evenly distributed throughout Earth. Some countries, such as Brazil and the United States (upper Great Lakes region) have huge deposits

of iron, but most nations have little or none. Chile is endowed with generous copper deposits; Canada with zinc and nickel; Malaysia with tin; and South Africa and Zimbabwe with most of the world's chromite.

Consumption of minerals by nations is even more unequal than the natural distribution of the resources. Poor nations such as Bolivia and Ethiopia use very few minerals, but each man, woman and child in the United States is supported by 20 tons of minerals a year. The U.S. auto industry and highway system account for a large share of this consumption. Americans consume about 25 percent of the world's production of minerals, down from over 40 percent in 1940. The industrialization of the Soviet Union, China, Japan and some other nations and the *reindustrialization* of Europe after World War II, decreased the United States' percentage of world consumption.

Because of their wide distribution, large quantities of minerals are traded among countries. Approximately 30 percent of all iron ore, for example, crosses national borders. Leading exporters include France, Canada and the Soviet Union. Increasingly, the United States is importing iron ore since its deposits of high-grade ore have been exhausted.

Despite large mineral deposits of iron, copper, phosphates, zinc and other minerals, the United States has become very dependent on imports from countries such as Canada, Zaire, Indonesia, Zimbabwe, and South Africa. The industrial world as a whole is even more dependent upon imported resources than is the United States, because they are less well-endowed. Japan must import nearly all its tin, copper, bauxite, lead and nickel. Western Europe is nearly as dependent.

The need for precious metals has in some cases entangled industrial countries in the politics of less-developed countries. South Africa, for example, has become a powerful custodian of valuable mineral deposits, particularly manganese, chromium and platinum. Manganese and chromium are essential for the production of steel and iron, and the United States is dependent upon South Africa for significant amounts of these minerals. South Africa alone has over 80 percent of the world's chromium and platinum reserves. The United States finds itself in the difficult position of having close economic relations with this controversial state ruled by a white minority.

Mineral markets can be risky, particularly for the less-developed economies who depend on the sale of a resource. Jamaica, along with several other Caribbean nations, had been a major supplier of bauxite ores rich in aluminum. In the Caribbean, bauxite mines have been controlled by international aluminum companies, such as Alcoa, Kaiser and Reynolds. A vast majority of revenues generated in making aluminum products accrue to companies outside the Caribbean; a host country benefits primarily from low-value activities involving the actual mining of the ore. When the Jamaican government tried to raise higher taxes from U.S. aluminum companies, the companies were able to shift their businesses elsewhere. As a result, the Jamaican economy suffered considerably.

Valuable mineral deposits scattered through the earth's crust and ocean bed have created both cooperation and conflict among suppliers and users. The extraction of minerals has been a helter-skelter process laced with economic exploitation and political intrigue.

Water

The most essential resource of all for sustaining life is water. A healthy adult can go without food for weeks, but people can only survive a few days without water. Humans need less than a quart of drinking water a day. However, we use a lot more indirectly to grow food, to mine metals, to produce energy and to manufacture anything.

Water is virtually everywhere. About two-thirds of the earth is water. Even though less than 3 percent is fresh water, this is more than enough for every person in the world. The problem lies in its distribution: Global maldistribution of water is even greater than that of energy or food. While some areas of the world literally drown in water, the arid and semiarid regions thirst. Within the United States water distribution is a serious issue. The Midwest and Northeast generally have plenty of water, subject to periodic droughts. But the dry Southwest is chronically plagued with water shortages.

As with other resources, the developed industrial countries are by far the heaviest users of water. Population increases account for some of the heavy demand on water around the world, but the greatest use is due to modern plumbing, large-scale agricultural irrigation and industrial cooling.

The average household in the United States uses 293 gallons of water each day. It takes six gallons to flush a toilet, 25-30 gallons to take a shower, and 20 gallons to wash dishes by hand. As mining becomes more difficult, the consumption of water to produce oil, coal and non-fuel minerals rises. The biggest user of water

UN Photo 156276/Doranne Jacobson

Water, once an abundant resource, is now considered scarce in many places. Navajo Indian girls in New Mexico drinking from a stream.

The Grand Coulee Dam, one of the largest concrete structures in the world, is open for power production, irrigation and flood control.

is agriculture where more than 80 percent of the U.S. water supply goes for irrigation.

Daily water consumption in the United States is about 400 billion gallons but, thanks to modern technology, most household water is reused. Still, the United States loses over a fourth of its clean water to contamination, inefficient industrial and agricultural use, and leakage in transportation.

Water shortage, or famine, is a serious problem in many parts of the world, particularly developing nations. About one fourth of the world's population lives with inadequate or unsafe water supplies. A majority of people without sanitary drinking water live in rural areas of Asia. According to the *World Health Organization* (WHO), a safe and ample water supply is the key measure for improving the health of people living in rural areas. The quality of a country's water system often determines who will live and who will die. Diarrhea, malaria, worms, sleeping sickness transmitted by the tsetse fly, and other parasitic diseases — all caused by bad water — are the worst killers of children in poor countries.

Water supplies can be increased and improved by several means: building dams, restructuring rivers, collecting and storing rainfall, *desalination* of seawater and harvesting icebergs. Harvesting icebergs is a fascinating possibility involving enormously complex technology. At least for the present, the challenge to engineers is staggering. Desalination plants have been built to supply much water for the Middle East and parts of Africa, areas desperate for water. Desalination plants, once very

popular in the United States, have proven to be too costly in comparison to alternative sources.

Dams, reservoirs, rerouting streams and other engineering feats have transformed the landscape of many places, particularly the southwestern United States. The great dams on the Colorado River led to the tremendous growth of Southern California, particularly its agricultural development.

The 1,450-mile Colorado River originates in the snow fields of the Rocky Mountains and empties into the Gulf of California in Mexico. Seven states: Colorado, New Mexico, Utah, Wyoming, California, Arizona and Nevada, take water from the river for their needs and empty sewage into it. By the time it reaches Mexico, the Colorado River is a salty trickle. One of the major points of disagreement between the U.S. and Mexico is over the use — or misuse — of the Colorado River.

Conflict over the distribution of water constantly affects many countries. Major rivers, shared by India and Pakistan, have been a steady source of conflict between these neighboring nations. In 1975, Iraq deployed tanks and infantry units on Syria's border, demanding that more water be released from the Euphrates River. Of the 200 largest river basins in the world, 148 are shared by two or more countries.

Coal

Coal was the world's leading fuel source from the early 1800s, at the beginning of the industrial revolution, until the 1960s. Since then, coal production has not dwindled; rather, oil production has increased tremendously. Coal is dirty, hard to mine and clumsy to transport. Yet coal has become a standby as a fuel source. When the supply of convenient sources is threatened, coal comes to the energy rescue. In 1987, coal accounted for 28.2 percent of the world's primary energy production. Its production and use in the United States has climbed slowly but steadily to the point where its tonnage had nearly doubled between 1950 and 1988.

Bituminous coal is the most widely used of the different types. Because its quality is not consistent, its potential for heat energy also varies. There are two other types of coal: Anthracite is the hardest and burns without smoke; lignite is the softest and dirtiest.

The United States sits on a virtual coal mine. About three-quarters of all fossil fuel reserves in the United States are coal. U.S. reserves make up almost one-fourth of the total world supply. In the United States 80 percent of the coal produced comes from the Appalachian Field, which extends from northwestern Pennsylvania to Alabama. It is the most productive coal-mining region on Earth.

More than 3 billion metric tons of coal are produced annually in the world. China is the major producer with the United States and the Soviet Union ranking a close second and third. Australia is also a large producer of coal.

In Europe, coal is found in a belt extending from England and Wales through northern France, Belgium, Germany and Poland. Poland is Europe's largest producer. Most coal is consumed in the general area where it is mined. Yet, many areas do not have sufficient quantities. The United States, Poland, Australia and Germany are the leading exporters. France, Canada, Italy and Japan are among the major importers. Germany supplies France and the Netherlands. Poland ships coal to East European countries.

Coal is used throughout the world to generate electricity and produce steel. Nearly four-fifths of the coal consumed in the United States is used for electricity. Virtually all of the remainder goes to industry. Little coal is now used for residential and commercial heating or transportation. In contrast, China, India and the Soviet Union have railway systems fueled by coal. In China, coal is still widely used for heating homes and buildings.

As oil prices remain high, coal is likely to fill the gap — at least temporarily until a suitable substitute is developed. Many oil importing countries, such as Japan, are converting some industrial plants to coal use rather than oil. Coal is particularly suited to generating electricity and the production of *synthetic fuels.*

Energy decisions

Industrialization and technology. The increasing use of energy resources has been due in large part to *industrialization* and the growth of *technology.* From 1880 to the present, the population of the world increased four-fold, while energy consumption increased more than 13 times. Production in both agriculture and manufacturing made use of new technology. In order to supply the power for technology, natural resources as a source of energy were substituted for human energy.

Mechanized farm production meant fewer people needed to be employed in agriculture. The displaced farm workers migrated to cities. To accommodate this growth, urban centers grew in physical size. Cities mushroomed with expanding suburbs. In urban areas many people live great distances from their places of employment and even greater distances from areas of food production. Transportation use has increased accordingly.

Affluence. The rise in productivity through technology has also meant an increase in general affluence. Not only are there more people, but they have more money to spend. Even if the world were to achieve zero population growth, the steady rise in standards of living would lead to increasing energy demands.

The developed countries, with only 20 percent of the total population, use 85 percent of the world's annual energy production. These countries enjoy a material well-being far in excess of what exists in the less-developed world. To bring all countries to this level of development would tax the global environment beyond its capacity to provide the necessary energy — and to absorb the resulting pollutants.

Exploring alternatives. The United States consumes oil at a rate of 30 barrels per person per year. If the entire world were to consume oil at this rate, the world's *proven reserves* would be exhausted within five years.

Higher prices and greater fuel efficiency for automobiles have slightly decreased the world demand for oil. But the fear of depleting oil reserves has influenced oil-rich nations to withhold the production of oil. World oil production per capita has been decreasing since 1980 and is projected to decrease steadily the rest of this century.

Beyond the proven, readily *recoverable reserves,* lie about 2,000 billion (2 trillion) barrels of reserves that are more difficult to recover. Tapping these sources will involve new technologies and higher costs. The outlook is for oil to become continuously more scarce and expensive. From a world output of five barrels per person annually in 1980 (the U.S. is consuming 30 barrels per person), production will fall to about three barrels per person by the year 2000. As nations develop industrially, the struggle among countries for dwindling oil supplies will intensify.

The world will be living with less oil to meet increased energy needs. The big question concerns what alternative sources will fill the void.

Oil is a fossil resource. Other fossil resources — oil shale, tar sands, and coal — can provide energy reserves. However, it is very costly to extract petroleum from these sources. In addition, shale and tar sand must be processed at a higher temperature requiring the availability of large amounts of fresh water, which becomes contaminated with by-products.

Coal is the most likely resource to see nations through any immediate energy crisis. There is enough coal in the United States to last this nation 300 years, even if output is expanded tremendously. But coal has problems. The processing of coal (gasification) releases carbon-dioxide and sulphur-dioxide gases and leaves an ash residue. Coal production will almost certainly be expanded by using strip mining. The damage to the environment is great. Coal mining is also a dangerous occupation and the industry has a poor safety record.

Nuclear energy is a controversial solution to energy needs. The nuclear power plant disasters at Three-Mile Island (USA) and Chernobyl (USSR) have caused people to be very concerned about the further development of nuclear energy. France has forged ahead with nuclear technology; its domestic nuclear power plants provided 70 percent of its electricity in 1989, as compared with 20 percent in the United States.

There are many problems with nuclear energy production, including the comparatively short life-span of a nuclear plant. The expense of building a nuclear plant is enormous. Also, there is a serious question about the disposal of spent nuclear fuel. This waste is dangerously radioactive. The waste must be sealed in containers and stored underground where it creates heat and may leak radiation for thousands of years. It cannot be destroyed or deactivated. These problems must be weighed against the increasing needs for energy sources and our overdependence upon fossil fuels that are becoming more scarce, expensive and environmentally destructive.

Solar energy is a rapidly developing form of renewable energy. Using solar collectors, sunlight can be tapped directly to heat homes or water. It can also be trapped indirectly in photovoltaic cells and converted to electricity. Invented in 1954,

Department of Energy

Three Mile Island site of a nuclear power plant accident.

photovoltaic cells were first used by the *National Aeronautics and Space Administration* (NASA) to power satellites in space. The most widely used and efficient materials for making solar cells is silicon. As light strikes the silicon, electrons are set in motion, creating electricity.

Cost is the major factor preventing conversion to solar energy use. When the cost becomes competitive with conventional sources of energy, solar energy will become more widely used.

Other forms of renewable energy such as *wind, wave* and *geothermal power* are still prohibitively expensive for general use. *Biomass,* crops grown by solar energy and then used as fuel, is also in the developmental stage. It must compete for land that is now used for growing food. Solar and other renewable forms of energy hold great promise for the future, but further technology is needed for their development.

Meanwhile, extending to the year 2000 and perhaps beyond, people can practice the simplest energy alternative — *conservation.* Conservation means using energy more efficiently. If oil supplies are cut off or reserves dwindle to dangerously low levels, conservation will be forced on people. A more desired alternative is for nations, particularly the industrialized, to use energy more economically. Higher gasoline mileage standards for automobiles, home insulation, using industrial heat to produce local energy, and expanding public transportation systems are major measures.

Chapter 15

Environment

- *The biosphere is shared by all living creatures on Earth.*

- *Twentieth century technology can irreparably damage the biosphere.*

The concept of interdependence is well-illustrated when the environment is considered. The *biosphere* is the layer of air, water and land on our planet Earth where life exists.

For much of history, the destruction or pollution of an area was a local matter, affecting a single neighborhood or country. Until the industrial era, pollution was *biodegradable* waste made by humans from natural substances. Biodegradable waste eventually disintegrates and returns to the soil.

Natural pollution of air and water occurs periodically. When volcanoes erupt, cinders and gases are carried by winds and may affect weather conditions even thousands of miles from the volcano. Flooding can divert silt and other materials into the ocean, adversely affecting fish and other sea life.

With the coming of the industrial revolution, the burning of fossil fuels on a large scale and the development of chemicals, a new type of pollution occurred. *Industrial* and *chemical pollution* is long-lasting. It does not break down by natural processes and return harmlessly to the sea or soil. And not only that, when it enters the atmosphere or the oceans, it travels from nation to nation. Industrial air pollution from the northeastern U.S. falls as acid rain in Canada. Oil spills from Mexican wells cover beaches in Texas. Radiation from nuclear explosions in China lands on American soil. Banned U.S.

pesticides are sold to developing nations and returned to us on sprayed, exported produce. Earth has a capacity to recover from some pollution. One theory called *Gaia* (the Greek name for Earth goddess) argues that Earth itself is a coherent system of life, self-regulating, self-changing, a sort of immense organism. Even though Earth will survive environmental degradation, there is a *threshold,* a point beyond which recovery is not possible if human life on Earth is to be sustained.

The food chain

Food sustains life. In a process called *photosynthesis,* plants convert matter into food which is then eaten by fish and animals, who are in turn eaten by humans. The passage of food from one species to the next is known as the *food chain.* Toxic materials, which are not easily decomposed by natural processes, enter the food chain and travel with the food as it is consumed by different species. The toxin accumulates in the bodies of those who are in the food chain.

Air pollution

Serious problems result from air pollution. When combined with water in the atmosphere, pollutants form acid rains. Pollutants can destroy the *ozone —* an outer atmospheric layer which protects the earth from harmful ultraviolet rays in sunlight. Pollutants

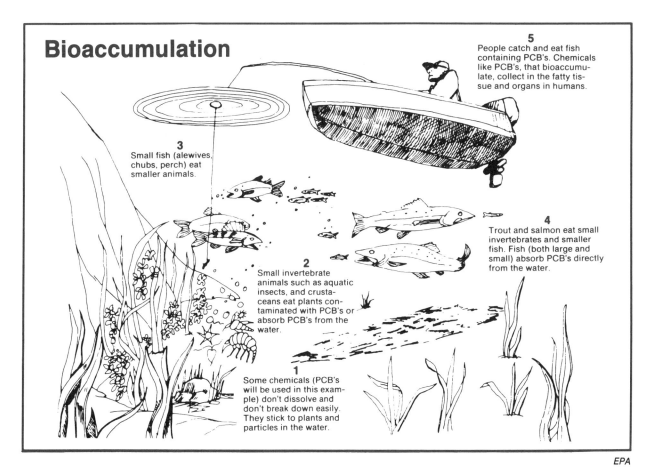

Bioaccumulation

5 People catch and eat fish containing PCB's. Chemicals like PCB's, that bioaccumulate, collect in the fatty tissue and organs in humans.

3 Small fish (alewives, chubs, perch) eat smaller animals.

4 Trout and salmon eat small invertebrates and smaller fish. Fish (both large and small) absorb PCB's directly from the water.

2 Small invertebrate animals such as aquatic insects, and crustaceans eat plants contaminated with PCB's or absorb PCB's from the water.

1 Some chemicals (PCB's will be used in this example) don't dissolve and don't break down easily. They stick to plants and particles in the water.

EPA

Bioaccumulation — the process by which dangerous chemicals work their way up through the food chain and become more concentrated in the tissues of fish and humans — is explained in the diagram above.

may affect climate patterns by changing the chemical composition and temperatures of the atmosphere.

Acid rain. Each year the burning of coal, oil and other fossil fuels releases more than 130 million tons of sulfur dioxide pollution into the atmosphere. The United States accounts for almost one-fourth of this. Nitrogen oxides are also emitted with the burning of industrial fuels. When sulfur dioxide and nitrogen oxides combine with moisture in the atmosphere, they produce sulfuric acid and nitric acid. These compounds form on raindrops and snowflakes and fall to Earth as acid rain. Traveling on winds, acid compounds cross state lines and international boundaries.

Acid rain kills life forms in lakes, corrodes metal and stone and causes billions of dollars worth of damage to building materials each year. Some scientists believe that acid rain has contributed to declines in crop productivity and forest yields in many parts of the world.

Acid rain generated in England and Europe is responsible for the death of fish in about one-fifth of Sweden's 90,000 lakes and most of the lakes in southern Norway. Scandinavian fishing and lumber industries, as well as farming, are also in danger from acid rain.

Hundreds of lakes and rivers in eastern Canada and the United States have died from acid rain. The primary source of the pollution is power plants in the Ohio River Valley.

Tall smokestacks, originally installed in factories to prevent local fossil fuel pollution, release the pollutants to the higher atmosphere where prevailing winds carry them great distances. Scrubbers to remove pollutants can be installed in smokestacks. This is expensive. No international authority exists to enforce laws regulating such pollution.

Scrubbers will not remove heavy metal pollutants, such as zinc and cadmium, which eventually fall in lakes and streams, contaminating the food chain. The metals lodge in plankton (water plants) which are eaten by fish, causing them to be harmful for humans to eat.

Acid rain, according to some scientists, has become the most immediate peril to Earth's environment. The only problem considered more serious in the long run is the greenhouse effect from carbon dioxide pollution.

Greenhouse effect. Carbon dioxide, among Earth's most common gases, is a by-product of all fires and a primary part of air exhaled in breathing. Carbon dioxide is 25 percent higher in the atmosphere than in pre-industrial times. Other complex gases are building steadily. They include:

nitrous oxide, methane and *chloroflourocarbons* (CFCs). Chloroflourocarbons are a class of synthetic chemicals not normally found in the atmosphere. Combined, these gases are creating a blanket of gases that allow sunlight in but trap the resulting heat.

By burning large amounts of coal and oil, industrialized nations gradually put more carbon dioxide into the air. Large concentrations of this gas create a *greenhouse effect* around the globe. Like the glass of a greenhouse roof, the molecules of carbon dioxide allow sunlight to reach the ground, but block the escape of heat radiating off Earth's surface. This increases the temperature of Earth's atmosphere. Coal is the largest fossil fuel resource left on Earth. For every ton of coal burned, three tons of carbon dioxide are emitted into the atmosphere.

Researchers found that levels of carbon dioxide started to rise in the early 1900s, as the industrial revolution, with its massive use of fossil fuels, was getting into full swing. Global average temperatures are now about 0.6 degrees Celsius warmer than they were 100 years ago. Scientists are more concerned about the future. Computer models have projected that Earth's average temperature will increase 2.5-5.5 degrees Celsius (4.5-9.9 degrees Fahrenheit) by late in the next century.

The high rate at which the world's great forests have been harvested also is probably contributing to the rising levels of this gas. All plants depend on carbon dioxide for life in the same way animals and people rely on oxygen. Trees consume more carbon dioxide than other plants and are essential to Earth's carbon dioxide-oxygen exchange. Without enough trees to consume carbon dioxide, the gas rises into the atmosphere. Earth's forests, especially the rain forests, serve as a giant holding tank for the increasing amounts of carbon dioxide being spewed into the air through fossil fuel burning.

Researchers believe that a temperature increase of as little as two or three degrees could have a significant impact on the environment over the next few decades. Fertile areas in the United States could become arid. Desert regions in Africa could be transformed by increased rainfall. The polar ice caps could melt over the next 300 years, raising sea levels 15 to 20 feet. The impact of these changes on political and economic systems and their relationships would be catastrophic.

Thermal air pollution. In addition to the indirect greenhouse effect of fossil fuel consumption on the

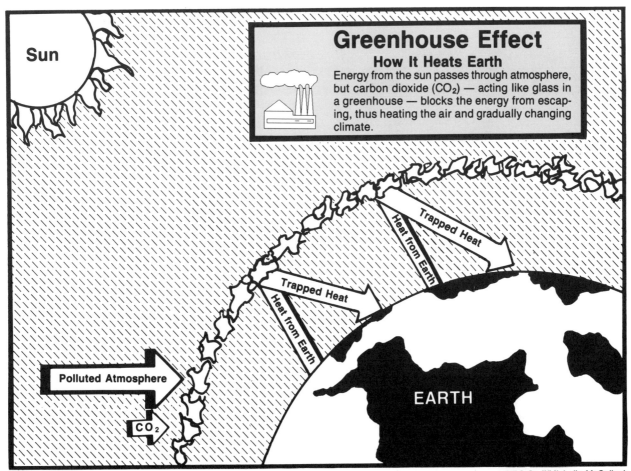

SIRS Staff/Michelle McCulloch

atmosphere's temperature, there is also a direct effect. The consumption of fossil fuels requires combustion. Oil or coal is burned to generate heat energy which is used to create steam and in turn to produce electricity. The thermal efficiency of this process is at best about 30 percent; 70 percent of the heat energy escapes into the atmosphere. This heat raises Earth's atmospheric temperature.

Radioactive pollution. Above-ground nuclear explosions emit radioactive particles into the atmosphere that can be carried by winds to distant places. While a certain amount of radioactivity is naturally present in the environment, excess amounts of it are known to cause cancer and may trigger mutations in organisms. Mutations in small, short-lived organisms such as insects can transform an entire species in a short time with unpredictable effects on the environment. During the 1950s, several nations tested atomic weapons above ground. Particles containing radioactive strontium-90 were emitted into the atmosphere and carried by winds thousands of miles from the bomb sites. The radio-

Igor Kostin

This mutant foal, the victim of radiation contamination from Chernobyl, was born three years after the nuclear disaster.

active particles fell on grazing land and entered the food chain when they were eaten by cows. Strontium-90 soon began appearing in milk. Nuclear power plants also emit radioactive elements into the environment. Nuclear accidents at Three Mile Island in Pennsylvania and Chernobyl in the Ukraine (Soviet Union) have created great concern about the peaceful uses of nuclear power.

Ozone and pollution. About 25 miles above Earth's surface is a layer of the atmosphere called *ozone*. Its chemical structure blocks out ultraviolet

rays from the sun which are deadly to humans, plants and animals. Chloroflourocarbons, which are used as refrigerants and insulators, rise in the atmosphere and destroy the fragile ozone layer. Scientists have discovered a huge hole in the ozone layer over Antarctica. Without the ozone layer, deadly ultraviolet rays from the sun will reach Earth causing skin cancer.

Meanwhile, too much ground-level ozone (commonly referred to as smog) is being created near Earth's surface by hydrocarbon pollutants released by auto exhausts, fertilizers and power plants. This ozone damages crops. One study estimated the annual cost of ozone damage to U.S. agriculture to be about $10 billion. More research on the relationship between ozone and pollution is required.

Water pollution

Seventy percent of Earth is covered by water. The oceans and interconnecting systems of lakes, rivers and streams which flow into the oceans constitute a precious and vital environmental resource. In an everlasting process, water on Earth's surface evaporates into the atmosphere, condenses and then returns to Earth as rainfall. All living things in the biosphere require a regular supply of clean water in order to survive. The world's wetlands also serve as the habitat for fish and other life forms which are an important source of food.

The immense size of the world's water supply has led many people to believe that it is indestructible and unlimited. Every year, millions of tons of toxic wastes are dumped into the world's waterways and carried by ocean currents to distant places on the globe. In 1983, the United Nations announced an International Drinking Water Decade to focus attention on water pollution. About 15 million children under five die every year due to contamination of the world's water supply.

Garbage pollution. Waterways are a tempting place to dump unwanted wastes. Human sewage is an organic waste. Microscopic plants feed on it, contributing to its decomposition. But when there is a lot of it, the plants multiply and use more than their share of available oxygen in the water. This disruption of the delicate balance of life in the water can lead to *eutrophication*. Plants multiply, oxygen-starved fish die, and lakes and harbors can become clogged with plants. Sewage dumped off-shore can be swept by currents out to sea where, one researcher has suggested, it can become a growing medium for dangerous viruses.

Inorganic industrial wastes, such as mercury, pesticides or PBCs have been dumped in oceans and poisoned the fish. Other fish are contaminated by

Tony Amos/Courtesy of the Center for Marine Conservation

Plastic debris discarded in the ocean becomes a serious threat to marine life.

the wastes which are then passed along to the people who eat the fish. Mercury can cause a deforming and fatal disease in humans called Minimata's disease.

Inorganic wastes also destroy or deform plankton, the tiny floating plants in the ocean which are Earth's major source of oxygen. Plankton also begin the food chain because they are eaten by fish.

Oil pollution. Oil spills on the ocean from tankers and off-shore oil drilling are a threat to the environment. It takes a long time for the ocean to dilute oil floating on its surface. The oil can wash up on beaches and coat the feathers of floating birds. Laboratory tests have demonstrated that oil can deform the larval development of fish and interferes with photosynthesis. Once dissipated from the ocean's surface, toxic materials in the oil fall to the ocean floor affecting life forms which breed there. Scientists have been working to develop a microorganism which consumes oil in order to remove oil spills before they damage the ocean.

The largest oil spill in U.S. history occurred in Alaska's Prince William Sound on March 24, 1989. The Exxon Corporation's tanker *Valdez*, off its course, struck a reef and spilled 240,000 barrels of oil into the surrounding water and beaches. An environmental and economic crisis of major proportions followed. One year later, workers were still struggling to clean up the Sound so that the life cycle of fish and wildlife in the area would not suffer permanent damage.

Nuclear pollution. All nuclear power plants emit radioactive elements into the environment. Disposing of radioactive wastes from nuclear energy production is a serious concern because the dangerous radioactivity in the waste does not dissipate for thousands of years. Some nuclear wastes have been placed in concrete containers and dumped into the ocean. Scientists fear that the containers may leak

or break, contaminating the surrounding sea. The effect of radioactivity on the life of the ocean is considered to be harmful.

Thermal water pollution. Many power plants locate near large bodies of water that are used for cooling equipment or to produce energy. When returned to the lake or river, the water may be warmer than before. When the temperature of a lake rises only a few degrees, more oxygen escapes into the atmosphere, upsetting the balance of oxygen and carbon dioxide in the water. As the supply of oxygen diminishes, fish weaken and die.

Higher temperatures also prevent the normal development of fish eggs and cause some fish to migrate and spawn at the wrong time of year.

Land pollution

As cities expand and land is cleared for housing developments, shopping centers and roads, valuable soil is pushed aside or covered up. The world loses an estimated 24 billion tons of topsoil each year. By the end of the 1980s, the effect was being felt in some of the world's major food-producing regions through lower crop yields.

Food production depends on the vitality of topsoil — the carpet of living dirt on Earth's land surfaces. Topsoil is home to trillions of microscopic life forms. This organic matter provides nutrients for plants to grow. Topsoil is only inches thick, usually less than a foot. In relation to Earth's size it is tissue-thin. By contrast, the skin on an apple is miles deep.

Soil erosion is a natural process, but so is soil formation if the fertile organic mixture is given enough time to re-create. These processes occur slowly in nature. When land is cultivated intensively, soil erosion increases. The topsoil thins and eventually disappears, leaving much less productive subsoil or rock. Farming that does not permit areas of land to lay uncultivated and to regenerate for periods of time risks depleting the topsoil. Since 1950, the world has lost nearly 20 percent of the topsoil from its farmland. Water and wind erosion of soil occur naturally, but farming practices can reduce the effects of nature's erosion and virtually eliminate man-made causes.

The American landscape is rich with fertile soil, but much of it is being eroded. The strain on American soil results from many causes: overuse of chemical fertilizers and pesticides, monocultures (growing one crop over a large area of land) which makes the crop more vulnerable to pests and requires more mechanization. Enough soil to fill a five-ton truck every second of every day is lost in Iowa alone. *Conservation* practices are costly to individual

Daniel James

Recently cleared section of the rain forest in South East Peru.

farmers. The immediate benefits of conserving soil do not match the expense. Without government support, many farmers choose to wrench added returns from the land at the cost of less productivity in future years.

The strain of agricultural production on the soil exists in many countries. Soviet Union farm productivity lags today, in part due to damaged soil that has been neglected for years. In Australia, a major exporter of grains, nearly one half of the farmland needs some sort of conservation efforts to prevent erosion and restore productivity. Land, no longer capable of growing crops, is being abandoned in Pakistan, Indonesia, Ethiopia and other developing nations due to erosion and overuse. In these nations, seasonal crop yields not only determine how much food is available and at what prices, but who will live and who will die. Brazil is the only nation in the world today that can claim significant new land for agriculture. But part of the tradeoff is reduction in the size of the Amazon rain forest, needed by the world to consume poisonous carbon dioxide and produce life-giving oxygen.

Desertification. In semiarid regions, once useful land is turning into desert or desertlike terrain — a process called desertification. The world's major deserts are growing larger due to human abuses: overgrazing, deforestation and overplowing. Northern Africa, the Middle East and India are areas most affected. Tens of millions of people subsist on lands

that are almost useless. The lands have been eroded and encrusted with salt.

Overgrazing. Agricultural land that is not suitable for cultivation is often used to feed livestock. Nearly one-fourth of the earth's land surface supports about three billion domesticated *ruminants:* beef and dairy cattle, sheep, goats, water buffalo and an assortment of other animals. Ruminants play an important role in the world economy. These animals, unlike people, have digestive systems capable of processing roughage (cellulose). They can live on grasses, shrubs and trees. The livestock, in turn, are a source of meat, milk, cheese and butter as well as fertilizer, leather, wool and other materials.

Many African nations have more cattle than people, and these cattle compete for precious land that could be used for growing food. A family's wealth, however, is typically counted in the number of cattle owned, and it would not be an easy matter to change the economy.

As the number of livestock worldwide increases, pressures on some grasslands become serious. In areas of the Middle East, where the number of sheep and other grazing animals exceeds what can be supported, the land has deteriorated to desertlike conditions. Parts of the southwestern United States and Chile in South America also have suffered from overgrazing. Eventually land use and food production planning must take into account the limits of grasslands.

Deforestation. Forest products are an important part of the lives of people throughout the globe. In developed countries, wood is used to construct houses; make furniture; and manufacture paper, plywood, fiberwood and many more products. In many developing countries, wood is the major source of energy. An estimated 40 percent of the world's population uses firewood as a primary fuel source.

In 1950, one-quarter of Earth's land surface was covered by forests. By 1980, it was less than one-fifth; Earth's forests are shrinking. Deforestation claims about 36,000 square miles of land a year, an area roughly the size of Hungary. Latin America and the Soviet Union contain over one-half of the world's forests; most of the rest are in North America and Asia.

Of particular concern is Brazil's rain forest, comprising 2 million square miles in the Amazon River basin. At least 5 percent — maybe as much as 12 percent — has been lost to ranchers, farmers and developers. The pace of destruction has accelerated in recent years. In 1987, an area of rain forest nearly two-thirds the size of Florida was cut, burned and destroyed.

The rain forest of Brazil is an enormous global resource and its destruction could permanently alter the world's ecology. As many as 50 percent of the 5 million to 10 million of the world's plant and animal species live in the rain forest. Twenty percent of Earth's fresh water flows through the forest. Thousands of different species of birds and fish and millions of different insects dwell in the rain forest. People who earn a living from the rain forest — families who tap natural latex from rubber trees, gatherers of Brazil nuts and roughly 100,000 Indians — have also been threatened with a loss of habitat.

The ecological function of forests is just as important as their economic role. Among other functions, forests catch rainwater and permit it to percolate downward, seeping slowly into the ground. This permits water tables underground to be replenished and streams or rivers to flow more evenly. When land is stripped of its forest, the water runs off the land, quickly leading to soil erosion, reduced water tables, heavy sediment in streams, and flooding rivers. Deforestation in the Himalaya

Mountains has caused more frequent and severe floods in India, Pakistan and Bangladesh.

Forest lands are shrinking at different rates around the world. The forest areas of much of Europe, North America and Japan have stabilized, but they are shrinking in many developing nations. Much of the world's forest products are being produced in the tropical developing countries and exported to the industrialized nations.

It is difficult to ask developing nations to conserve their forests if they must export to live — especially since most of the forest products are in demand in industrial nations. Costa Rica has led the way with a "Debt for Nature" plan. Costa Rica has agreed to save its remaining rain forest in exchange for a reduction of its external debt owed to other nations. In this way, nearly 6 percent of Costa Rica's external debt has been waived in return for placing part of its rain forest into a permanent conservation area. Other nations with forests and external debts are studying this creative plan to save the forests and to pay off their debt at the same time.

Pesticides and herbicides. Insects have existed on Earth for about 400 million years. Among the more than five million species, some are so small that about a hundred could sit on the average thumbnail. The largest insect is the Indian atlas moth which has a 12-inch wingspan. Insects consume or spoil enough food every year to feed about 500 million people.

Locusts, the strongest living creatures on Earth for their size, devour their weight in food every day. Periodically, swarms of locusts, some weighing collectively about 50,000 tons, gather and sweep through about 40 countries from West Africa to cen-

WHO

A plane spraying pesticides to improve food production

tral Asia. They devour vegetation on about a fifth of the globe's land surface. Other crop-destroying insects include the granary weevil, Indian-meal moth, rice weevil, Khapra beetle and corn borer. In Kenya, insects have destroyed about 75 percent of the nation's crops.

Pests such as the fire ant and tsetse fly kill livestock and other animals. Cattle bitten by tsetse flies become ill and lose weight. Many eventually die. The tsetse fly inhabits more than one-fourth of the African continent.

Throughout India there are about three times as many rats as people. These rodents devour or spoil about 10 million tons of grain a year. A train 3,000 miles long would be needed to haul all the grain eaten by Indian rats in a single year. In some countries rodents destroy more than 50 percent of the food crops. In Australia, mice are more destructive than rats. Thousands of common field mice descend into grain pits where crops are stored and multiply faster than they can be eradicated.

The African quelea bird, or weaver finch, is reputed to be the most destructive fowl on Earth. Every year dense flocks of quelea descend on grain fields and feed on crops. Farmers have abandoned fields because of the destructive birds. In Mexico and Latin America, birds migrating from the North feast on corn, rice, sorghum, fruits and soybeans.

A *pesticide* is a general term for any substance or mixture of substances used to prevent, destroy or repel any pest, including insects, rodents, fungi or weeds. For 40 years, the agricultural industry has waged all-out war on insects, worms, weeds and other pests. More than four billion pounds of pesticides are used by farmers every year. This amounts to about a pound of pesticide for every man, woman and child on Earth.

A *herbicide* performs the same function against weeds and other plant forms that interfere with the food-growing process. An example of a herbicide is Agent Orange — used to defoliate the jungle in the Vietnam War to expose camouflaged roads and supply depots. Vietnam War veterans back in the United States claimed that the indiscriminate use of Agent Orange had caused many severe illnesses and deaths due to its lingering effects.

Despite the widespread use of pesticides, pests destroy at least one-third of the food crops each year. Many pests are developing an immunity to pesticides. Heavier doses of pesticides are used to combat the immunized pests. The battle between humans and pests goes on. Unfortunately, pests are not the only ones to die in this struggle. Workers in many countries are exposed to unsafe dosages of pesticides that are applied in fields and villages. The World Health Organization estimates that about 500,000 people are poisoned from direct exposure to pesticides every year and that about 5,000 die.

Americans first became aware of the hazards of widespread pesticide use when Rachel Carson wrote **Silent Spring** in 1962. Carson argued that pesticides have unknown and cumulative toxic effects and that their use should be curtailed. Many pesticides are unsafe because they are not biodegradable and may remain in the environment as pollutants for a long time. In addition to their toll on pests, poisonous pesticides damage or destroy plants and animals. Pesticides and herbicides interfere with the reproductive systems of some animals. In many cases, the natural predators of destructive animal and plant pests are killed by pesticides and herbicides.

Toxic wastes. Poisonous chemicals and nuclear wastes from the production and use of energy, paints, plastics, fertilizers, herbicides and pesticides have piled up to crisis proportion in industrialized nations. As nations produce chemical technologies in their quest for affluence and modernization, toxins are left behind and contaminate the environment. For many years, toxic wastes were disposed of carelessly: poured into untreated sewers, stored in leaky barrels, or spilled into unlined pits. Much of this poison seeped into streams and lakes.

The environment and the global economy

Environmental degradation is beginning to slow the increase in food production created in the 1960s and 1970s with the "Green Revolution." Air pollution is damaging crops in both the industrial nations of the West with their auto emissions and in the coal-burning economies of the East. Hotter summers and drought-reduced harvests of the 1980s may be early indications of the greenhouse effect. From 1950 to 1983 there was a 2.6-fold gain in world food output. Since then, there has been very little increase. The population has increased during this time; therefore, the world grain output per person is down 7 percent since 1984.

Lester Brown, founder of the Worldwatch Institute located in Washington, D.C., says that protection of the environment is necessary to our economic well-being and to the development of a sustainable society. He writes:

> Throughout our lifetimes, economic trends have shaped environmental trends, often altering Earth's natural resources and systems in ways not obvious at the time. Now, as we enter the nineties, the reverse is also beginning to happen: environmental trends are beginning to shape economic trends.

Chapter 16
Defense

> • *The world's present nuclear arsenal can destroy civilization.*
>
> • *Today's major question regarding armaments is "How much is enough?"*

When atomic bombs were dropped on the Japanese cities of Hiroshima and Nagasaki in 1945, people were made shockingly aware of the destructive power of military weapons. In Hiroshima alone, 78,000 people were killed immediately, 84,000 were injured and 62,000 buildings were demolished. Until then, the most destructive weapon that could be dropped from the air was the blockbuster, a bomb equal to the power of about 10 tons of dynamite. The first atomic bomb had a destructive capacity equal to about 2,000 blockbusters.

Since 1945, the amount, sophistication and destructive power of weapons have increased many times. Today's nuclear bomb is to the atomic bomb what the atomic bomb was to the blockbuster. Nations of the world have about 20,000 megatons of nuclear warheads, and the United States possesses half of these. The world's nuclear stockpile is the equivalent of two million atomic bombs like those dropped on Hiroshima and Nagasaki.

The global arms race

The major concept fueling the arms race since World War II was *deterrence* — a belief that "the best defense is a good offense." The philosophy behind deterrence was that if one nation could build a superior military force, other nations would be discouraged or prevented from attacking it.

One of the measures of military superiority in the nuclear age was *first-strike capability*. The major objective of a first strike is to destroy an enemy's nuclear forces before they can be launched. The Soviet Union and the United States both developed a strategic system for launching missiles. The system is a nuclear triad made up of three parts: missiles launched from "silos" on land, submarines at sea and bombers in the air. If one part of the triad is destroyed, the remaining parts can retaliate.

By 1970, the Soviet Union and the United States had reached a point in the arms race where they could simultaneously deliver first strikes. This condition is known as MAD — *mutually assured destruction.*

The stand-off created by MAD led to the development of a new concept, *limited first-strike capability*. Recognizing that no nation would risk total nuclear war because it would mean suicide, nations began to see themselves vulnerable to smaller attacks. *Conventional,* non-nuclear, *warfare* was seen as a possibility, as well as a *limited nuclear war.*

The term *window of vulnerability* first emerged during the late 1970s. The United States, which had been devoting its efforts to massive first-strike weapons was now seen by some analysts as unprepared for small or limited wars.

By 1990, the global arms budget had peaked at an estimated $1 trillion ($1,000 billion) per year, after having doubled several times during the

Hiroshima — one month after it was destroyed by an atomic bomb in 1945.

previous 30 years. The United States and the Soviet Union are the largest producers of weapons. In 1990, each nation accounted for almost 30 percent of the world's total military expenditures, representing nearly $300 billion annually for each nation. The nations belonging to the ***North Atlantic Treaty Organization*** (NATO) and the ***Warsaw Pact*** represent more than 80 percent of the world's arms budget.

Between 1960 and 1987, global expenditures for the military totaled $17 trillion and exceeded spending on education ($15 trillion) and health ($10 trillion). Since 1960, military expenditures have risen faster than other parts of the world's per-capita economies. The military spending deprived people of receiving the benefits of an expanding economy in terms of education, health and a clean environment.

Arms trade

The United States and the Soviet Union account for over 70 percent of all arms trade. The United States exports about 45 percent of all arms sold abroad; the Soviet Union, 30 percent. France and Great Britain account for roughly one-half of the balance, or nearly 15 percent. Japan and China are

emerging as important worldwide suppliers. Japan builds aircraft, tanks and electronic guidance systems for export. China builds missiles and nuclear warheads.

Military budgets are beginning to level off around the world with the United States and the Soviet Union leading the way. The arms trade declined from a peak of about $57 billion in 1984 to $47 billion in 1987, due mainly to the faltering economies in many developing nations. With the rapid decline of the Cold War many regional conflicts also are tapering off, including Afghanistan, Central America, Angola and Southeast Asia. Arms trafficking, however, is shifting to the drug trade as cartels around the world attempt to expand and protect their empires.

Attempting to control arms

In strict, clear language, *arms control* is any measure that alters the quantity or quality of weapons produced. There are three basic characteristics of arms control: (1) restrictions on the production and sales of arms, (2) total disarmament by nations of the world or the reduction of arms inventories, and (3) requirements governing the way arms may be used or deployed.

The argument for arms control

The reason for controlling the production and use of military weapons is clear. Modern warfare is potentially catastrophic. Not only would millions of people be killed, but life on this planet could be virtually destroyed. If the amount and destructive power of modern weaponry are reduced, the tendency to resort to warfare will also be less likely, or so it is reasoned.

Finally, there are heavy economic burdens to the ongoing arms race. Military goods production uses much of a nation's capital, human capabilities and natural resources. These are productive factors that could be put to valuable use, supplying the medical, educational and basic material needs of nations.

Impediments to disarmament

With such persuasive arguments in favor of disarmament or some form of arms control, why the slow process? First, it appears that if disarmament is to take place, it will have to be across the board, rather than unilaterally. Yet one or even a few nations must take the lead and disarm. The nations who take the chance and disarm first will be vulnerable; others may be inclined to take advantage of their weakness. This is known as "the other-guy" argument. That is, "We wouldn't take advantage of a nation that disarmed, but we can't afford to be the first to disarm because the other guy would attack us."

There are practical considerations inhibiting the process of arms control. The most realistic way for disarmament to proceed is in stages with periodic observations. *Inspections* to ensure that nations are abiding by an agreement require access, not only to physical facilities, but also the observation of decision-making processes and the research work of both government and private in-

dustry. This is a tedious, complex task. Few nations want outside observers monitoring their activities.

There also is the problem of *measuring* the military might of existing weapons. This not only means counting the number of weapons and launchers, but also determining the accuracy of delivery systems and the size of warheads. The weapons of the United States, for example, tend to be more accurate than those of the Soviet Union, but the latter's arms are more powerful.

The issue of *parity,* having equality, has plagued disarmament talks since the end of World War II. At that time, the U.S. was the only nation in the world capable of producing a nuclear bomb. The

The dot in the center represents all the firepower of World War II — three megatons. The other dots represent the world's nuclear weaponry in the 1980s, an arsenal that equals about 6,000 World War II's (18,000 megatons). The U.S. and the Soviets share this firepower with approximately equal destructive capability.

The top left-hand circle, enclosing nine megatons, represents the weapons on one Poseidon submarine — equal to three World War II's, enough to destroy more than 200 large cities. The circle in the lower left-hand square (24 megatons, eight World War II's) represents one new Trident sub with the power to destroy every major city in the northern hemisphere.

Just two squares (300 megatons) represent enough firepower to destroy all the large- and medium-sized cities in the world.

This chart, which was reviewed for accuracy by U.S. Senate staff members, appeared in the *The Trimtab Factor: How Business Executives Can Help Solve the Nuclear Weapons Crisis,* by Harold Willins, published in 1984 by William Morrow and Company, Inc.

The B-2 or Stealth bomber (being refueled) was designed to avoid detection by enemy radar. The cost is over $500 million per plane.

U.S. was more than willing to sign an agreement with the Soviet Union halting the build-up of nuclear arsenals. But the Soviet Union was unwilling to sign until it too had a nuclear arsenal on par with, or comparable to, that of the United States.

In order to assure parity, many arms agreements actually temporarily feed the arms race by setting arms production limits that haven't yet been met. Comparing and equating the nuclear power of different nations is a difficult task. While attempts to negotiate take place, both sides continue to expand and improve existing arsenals.

Enforcing disarmament

Assuming disarmament is accomplished, the following question arises: How does the world deal with a potentially warlike country? There are two standard answers. One is for each nation to keep some arms. This in turn raises other questions: How many arms are enough to ensure peace, and how will this be decided?

The second answer is for all nations to support an international peace-keeping force. Again, serious questions surround this solution: How large a police force is necessary, and how will it be set up and controlled?

Arms agreements

Arms negotiations between the United States and the Soviet Union go back many years. In 1959, the two powers agreed to ban all military activities in Antarctica. In 1963, they were among 103 nations to sign the limited-test ban treaty that prohibited testing nuclear weapons in the atmosphere, outer space and underwater. Such testing released dangerous radioactive elements. Several other treaties were signed by the two nations in the late 1960s and 1970s that, among other things, prevented the installation of nuclear weapons in outer space and limited the yield of warheads used in underground testing.

SALT I

In 1972, after several years of negotiating, the United States and the Soviet Union concluded the *Strategic Arms Limitation Talks* (SALT) that were hoped to be the key to halting the arms race. SALT I failed to stop the escalation of nuclear arms, but it was an all-important step in that direction. SALT I placed a ceiling on the number of Soviet and American intercontinental ballistic missiles, submarine-launched ballistic missile launchers and missile submarines produced. Although the agreement officially expired in 1977, the two nations have continued to observe the provisions of SALT I.

The Soviet SS-X-24 rail mobile ICBM

Responsibility of the superpowers

In the aftermath of the UN special conference on disarmament in 1978, diplomatic observers believed that negotiations to bring the global arms race under control depended on the United States and the Soviet Union. Since the late 1970s, the two superpowers have engaged in wide-ranging arms-control negotiations on a half-dozen fronts. These include a comprehensive nuclear-test ban, an arrangement to stabilize and reduce Soviet and American military forces in the Indian Ocean, a prohibition against chemical and biological weapons, a limitation on antisatellite weapons, and restraints on arms sales. The most significant of agreements would have been SALT II if it had been ratified by the U.S. Congress.

SALT II

SALT II was designed to go beyond SALT I and establish equality of numbers of strategic missiles and bombers that the two countries could have. The agreement also would have restricted the production of multiple warheads. The treaty was not ratified by the United States. Although SALT II was approved by the U.S. Senate's Foreign Reations Committee, it never reached the Senate floor because President Carter withdrew his support for the treaty following the Soviet invasion of Afghanistan in December 1979. The arms race spiraled.

New rounds of arms-control talks, labeled *Strategic Arms Reduction Talks* (START), were begun in 1982. The aim of START is not just to restrain nuclear arms production but to reduce the number of missiles, bombers and warheads. START provided the framework for the continuation of discussions about arms reduction during the 1980s. In 1987, President Reagan and Chairman Gorbachev signed the *Intermediate-Range Nuclear Forces* (INF) *Treaty* that eliminated all medium and short-range nuclear missiles. The INF Treaty was ratified by the U.S. Senate in May 1988.

The agenda for arms reduction is long and very complicated. But the United States and the Soviet Union appear to be headed in a direction that will result in significant arms-control agreements. The goals include: a 50 percent reduction in strategic (long-range) nuclear weapons; making deep cuts in armies deployed by NATO and the Warsaw Pact; reducing stockpiles of chemical weapons to about 20 percent of the current U.S. capability; and providing verification of the 1974 and 1976 treaties that limited the size of underground nuclear tests to 150 kilotons.

Anti-nuclear rally in New York City in the 1980s.

The decade of the '90s

From the end of World War II until the beginning of 1990, the Cold War dominated the world economy. People lived under the threat of nuclear destruction. Suddenly, it all changed. One after another, Communist governments changed in Eastern Europe, and free elections were held in nation after nation. It no longer seemed appropriate to speak of a "cold war." But for the years the war lasted, the costs were enormous. While the 1990s start out as a decade of promise for the largest nations to achieve peaceful solutions to their conflicts, regional wars continue and the amount of armaments stockpiled and in production is overwhelming.

The arms race became so expensive for the major powers that the United States and the Soviet Union seem to have concluded that they cannot have "guns and butter." The economies of both nations began the 90s with crisis. The U.S. had a huge debt that threatens its stability and the Soviet Union faced a crisis of consumer shortages that led to mass demonstrations. The 1990s may see an armament "build down" because the major powers can no longer afford the "build up."

In June 1990, Presidents George Bush of the United States and Mikail Gorbachev of the Soviet Union met in Washington, D.C., to sign historic agreements on arms limitations. These agreements on strategic arms, chemical weapons, nuclear testing and conventional armies marked a major turnaround of the armaments buildup by the major world powers that began with World War II.

Although many conflicts remain in the world, there is a growing sense that the world is at an historic turning point, and reliance on force and arms will be increasingly counterproductive. Michael Renner points to the challenge:

> In an age of weapons of mass destruction and delivery systems of global reach, arms no longer provide the security we expect; more important, the pursuit of military prowess is undermining our economic health. Yet few governments, communities, or military contractors have the expertise and the institutions to reverse the armament process without social and economic upheaval. Accomplishing this difficult task will require a careful program of economic conversion — releasing resources now tied up in the military sector and planning for their use in health and education programs, environmental protection, and other areas of need.

As the Cold War appeared to come to an end in the 90s, the questions may be asked: Did it end because the policy of MAD was successful? Did it end because the peace demonstrations were successful? Did it end because the major nations were learning that their economies were being destroyed by the high cost of preparing for war?

Chapter 17

Human Rights

- *Many nations advocate human rights, but few nations protect the rights of all of their citizens equitably.*

- *Lack of educational opportunity is considered a denial of an important human right.*

No one is "free" in the absolute sense. Freedom is often sacrificed voluntarily for comfort or security. As soon as a person interacts with other people, absolute freedom must be given up in the name of compromise. As social structures develop, more freedom is sacrificed. Perhaps the most important consideration in discussing freedom centers on who will decide which freedoms will be relinquished. A person voluntarily gives up some freedom when he or she joins a club, or a religious group, or gets married. When an outside force arbitrarily takes away freedom, it is a violation of *human rights*.

Seventeenth-century English philosopher John Locke and 18th-century French philosopher Jean Jacques Rousseau concluded that individuals are born with certain rights, and such rights are not conferred by society or government, nor can they be taken away. They are freedom of speech, conscience, religion, dissent: rights that in large part are embodied in France's *Declaration of the Rights of Man and of the Citizen* (1789), and in the United States' *Declaration of Independence*.

The League of Nations was an international organization formed early in this century to promote harmony and interrelations among countries. In 1919, the League admitted Ethiopia on condition that it abolish slavery. This was the first official statement by a world organization on the rights of human beings. Until that time, the treatment of national citizens was considered solely the business of individual countries.

Before and during World War II, a systematic plan of genocide — a program to exterminate an entire ethnic group — was carried out in Nazi Germany and resulted in the deaths of 6 million Jews and millions of others who were considered unworthy to coexist with the master German race. Murder, of course, is the ultimate abridgment of human rights, but the world outside of the German Third Reich was slow to react to the Nazi atrocities.

International human rights

At the close of World War II, in 1945, representatives of 50 nations with diverse political and economic systems founded the *United Nations*. In ratifying the UN Charter, member nations made it clear that human dignity and worth of the individual are to be cherished. The Charter encourages respect for human beings without distinction as to race, religion, language or sex. The Charter, however, does not define human rights. Later conferences addressed this issue.

In direct response to the massacre of Jewish people by Nazi Germany, the UN General Assembly in 1948 adopted the *Genocide Convention*. *Genocide* was defined in this document as the intention to destroy a national, ethnic, racial or religious group; to cause social conditions which would destroy a group; or to actually kill members of a group. Genocide, the Assembly states, is a crime in peace and war.

On December 10, 1948, the General Assembly of the United Nations adopted and proclaimed the *Universal Declaration of Human Rights.* This document is a detailed list of civil, political, economic, social and cultural rights — the first international statement defining human dignity and rights.

Among the basic *civil* and *political rights* are the following: liberty, security of person, prohibition of slavery and torture, freedom from arbitrary arrest, a free trial, and freedom of speech, religion and assembly.

The basic *economic, social* and *cultural rights* include: opportunity to develop one's personality and talents, social security and protection against unemployment, equal pay for equal work, an existence worthy of human dignity, and rest and leisure.

The UN document on human rights is not legally binding on nations. The United Nations' only real force is that of moral persuasion.

In 1966, the UN General Assembly adopted a *Covenant on Economic, Social and Cultural Rights* and a *Covenant on Political and Civil Rights.* These Covenants were designed to transform the statements of the Universal Declaration into binding treaty obligations, as well as to establish machinery to supervise and enforce the application of these rights. Both covenants also proclaimed that ''all peoples have the right of self-determination.'' That is, citizens should be free to choose the type of government they wish. It took 10 years to achieve ratification of the covenants by 35 countries. The U.S. is not among them.

There were complicated reasons why the United States did not ratify the covenants, which would give strength to a Universal Declaration that was predicated on many American ideals. In 1953, when it was time to vote on the Declaration, the conservatives in Congress and the Republican party feared that the United Nations would ''infect'' the U.S. with ''socialistic'' ideas, and they would not support any proposition the UN favored. There was also a foreign-policy reason for non-ratification. John Foster Dulles, Secretary of State under President Eisenhower at the time and a proponent of the Cold War, was concerned that those on the political left or right might use such treaties as legalistic instruments for military action.

Helsinki Accords

A new chapter unfolded in the drama of human rights on August 1, 1975, with the signing of the *Helsinki (Finland) Accords on European Security and Cooperation.* The United States, Canada, the Soviet Union and 32 other nations of Western and Eastern Europe signed this agreement. Embodied in the accord is a section calling for freer movement of people, ideas and information between East and West.

Within a short time, the two major superpowers — the United States and the Soviet Union — became embroiled over the human rights aspect of the Helsinki agreement. President Carter, in 1977, made human rights a cornerstone of his administration's foreign policy and proceeded to criticize the Soviet Union for restricting the ''movement of people and information.'' Specifically, President Carter criticized the Soviet treatment of dissident citizens (particularly writers and scholars who expressed dis-

Helsinki Accords
Key Provisions

The Final Act of the 1975 Conference on Security and Cooperation in Europe, held in Helsinki, calls on the 35 signatory nations to:

• Respect the inviolability of existing borders.

• Refrain from the threat or use of force against any state.

• Refrain from any intervention, direct or indirect, in the internal or external affairs of other states.

• Respect human rights and individual freedoms.

• Grant exit visas to permit the reunification of families.

• Support confidence-building measures such as advance notification of military maneuvers and exchange of observers for maneuvers.

• Facilitate freer exchange of people, publications and information.

Eleanor Roosevelt was chairperson of the United Nations Commission on Human Rights in 1948. She was mainly responsible for writing the Universal Declaration of Human Rights. Despite opposition to the Declaration by some U.N. members, she guided it to successful adoption by the General Assembly.

Where, after all, do universal rights begin? In small places, close to home — so close and so small that they cannot be seen on any maps of the world. Yet they are the world of the individual persons; the neighborhood he lives in; the school or college he attends; the factory, farm, or office where he works. Such are the places where every man, woman and child seeks equal justice, equal opportunity, equal dignity without discrimination. Unless these rights have meaning there, they have little meaning anywhere. Without concerned citizen action to uphold them close to home, we shall look in vain for progress in the larger world. — Eleanor Roosevelt

agreement with government policies) and Soviet policies hindering the emigration of citizens to other lands.

In response, Soviet representatives claimed that President Carter had no right to meddle in the internal affairs of another country. This principle, they pointed out, was established in a diplomatic agreement between the two nations in 1933. The United States, they countered, is not above reproach in regard to violating the civil rights of radical groups, African Americans, Native Americans, and in its support of dictatorships in some countries in Latin America, Asia and Africa.

The Helsinki Accords have been a major influence in the democracy movement in Eastern Europe in the late 1980s and early 1990s. Poland and Czechoslovakia, in particular, looked to the Helsinki Accords to support the development of democratic institutions such as freedom of movement, freedom of the press, and the establishment of a multi-party political system.

Amnesty International

A worldwide movement called *Amnesty International* was founded in London in 1961 to work on behalf of *prisoners of conscience* — hundreds of thousands of people who have been persecuted, imprisoned and tortured solely because of their race, religion or ideas. The organization works to gain the freedom of people who have been arbitrarily imprisoned and seeks humane treatment for all prisoners and detainees. Each year, Amnesty International has published reports on the state of human rights in most of the nations of the world, including the United States.

Freedom as a human right

Agreements and good intentions notwithstanding, there is still much deprivation of human rights. In 1988, there were nearly 14.5 million refugees throughout the world, people deprived of basic human rights. Six million of these are Afghanis who fled into Iran and Pakistan to escape the violence of the 1979 Soviet invasion of their nation. The second largest group is the Palestinians, over 2 million of whom live in Lebanon, Syria, Jordan and Israel.

Most of the world's refugees were displaced when they fled from war or famine. Just a few other examples of abuse:

• Between 1898 and 1918, a million Armenians, an ethnic minority in Turkey, were killed. Despite appeals by the victims' descendants, the United Nations has not recognized the killings as genocide because of Turkish opposition.

• Thousands of babies, from places as far-flung as Latin America and Sri Lanka, are being sold for $15 to $50 and smuggled to Western Europe and the United States. Many of them, it is hoped, go to decent homes, but some are raised to be servants. Some are exploited sexually.

• In South Africa, 20 million blacks, 4 million whites, and 3 million "coloreds" and Asians live in a segregated society where the whites dominate the nation, and the others barely exist as "second-class" citizens. In 1989, the system of *apartheid,* under heavy pressure from other nations and open struggle from inside the country, began to break down in South Africa. Nelson Mandela, leader for human rights imprisoned by the government for many years, was released and reassumed a strong leadership role. Many public services were opened for the first time to the non-white population.

• From 1975 to 1979, the Khmer Rouge under Pol Pot slaughtered 1 to 3 million Cambodians.

Indian peasants in a Guatemala City garbage dump. Poverty has forced some 45,000 Guatemalans to flee across the border to Mexico where refugee camps have been built with help from the U.N. High Commissioner for Refugees.

Thousands of others fled their country seeking refuge in Thailand. In 1978 the Vietnamese toppled the Khmer Rouge regime, and hundreds of thousands more became displaced persons, escaping to refugee camps just outside the Cambodian border. In 1990, half the population of Cambodia was 15 years of age or under; of those over 15, most were women.

• In Argentina during the 1970s, between 6,000 and 30,000 dissidents were rounded up by the government's security police and never seen again. Fear for the safety of the disappeared and their families prevented a public outcry. Meanwhile, thousands of mutilated bodies appeared in rivers, ditches and garbage heaps. A full accounting of Argentina's disappeared has not been made by the government.

• People in El Salvador, Guatemala and other countries in Latin America, live in terror of persecution from government troops and guerrilla fighters in their troubled countries.

• Thousands of Haitians have risked their lives on leaky boats to leave their homeland where secret police arbitrarily arrest dissenters to the regime.

Education as a human right

Without the ability to read and write, almost a billion of the world's adults are unable to participate effectively in the societies to which they belong. These men and women have little to say about their own destinies. In a world becoming increasingly complex, an illiterate person suffers a serious handicap. To deny education is to deny a basic human right. Article 26 of the Universal Declaration of Human Rights states: "Education shall be free at least in the elementary and fundamental stages. Elementary education shall be compulsory . . . Education shall be directed to the full development of the human personality and to the strengthening of respect for human rights and fundamental freedom."

Poverty and illiteracy go hand in hand. According to a UNESCO analysis, three in ten adults in the world are illiterate. Nearly three-quarters of these people live in Asia, approximately 20 percent in Africa and 5 percent in Latin America. Twenty-three countries have an illiteracy rate higher than 70 percent. The proportion of illiterate women is increasing. In 1960, 58 percent of the illiterates were women; by 1980, the number had increased to 60 percent. In some communities almost every woman

UN Photo 155034/Milton Grant
Child at a UN-sponsored day care center, Bogota, Colombia.

is unable to read or write.

Illiteracy is not just a developing-world problem. A conservative estimate is that between 10 and 15 million residents of 10 European Common Market nations are illiterate.

Assessments in the United States indicate that it too has a serious literacy problem. It is estimated that well over 20 million Americans, approximately one in five adults, lack reading and writing skills to handle minimal demands of everyday life, such as reading maps, numbers on buses, job applications or instructions for simple tasks.

Almost 30 percent of 9th-graders fail to complete high school. Even graduation from high school does not guarantee an adequate level of literacy. A report published in 1983, *A Nation at Risk: The Imperative for Educational Reform,* states that, ''the educational foundations of our society are presently being eroded by a rising tide of mediocrity that

Some American Presidents' Views on Human Rights

Woodrow Wilson

''The world must be made safe for democracy. . . . We shall fight for the things which we have always carried nearest our hearts—for democracy, for the right of those who submit to authority to have a voice in their own governments, for the rights and liberties of small nations, for a universal dominion of right by such a concert of free peoples as shall bring peace and safety and make the world itself at last free.''

Address to Congress, April 2, 1917, requesting declaration of war against Germany

Franklin D. Roosevelt

''We are committed to full support of all those resolute peoples, everywhere, who are resisting aggression and are thereby keeping war away from our Hemisphere. . . . In the future days, which we seek to make secure, we look forward to a world founded upon four essential human freedoms. . . . Freedom of speech and expression . . . . freedom of every person to worship God in his own way . . . . freedom from want . . . freedom from fear.''

Annual message to Congress, Jan. 6, 1941

Harry S. Truman

''I believe that it must be the policy of the United States to support free peoples who are resisting attempted subjugation by armed minorities or by outside pressure. . . .

''The free peoples of the world look to us for support in maintaining their freedoms. If we falter in our leadership, we may endanger the peace of the world — and we shall surely endanger the welfare of this nation.''

Special message to Congress on Greece and Turkey, March 12, 1947

Dwight D. Eisenhower

''We shall always hold that there can be no true peace which involves acceptance of a *status quo* in which we find injustice to many nations, repressions of human beings on a gigantic scale, and with constructive effort paralyzed in many areas by fear. . . . The domination of captive countries cannot longer be justified by any claim that this is needed for purposes of security.''

Address to American Bar Association, Aug. 24, 1955

John F. Kennedy

''Let every nation know, whether it wish us well or ill, that we shall pay any price, bear any burden, meet any hardship, support any friend or oppose any foe in order to assure the survival and success of liberty.''

Inaugural address, Jan. 20, 1961

Jimmy Carter

''The world itself is now dominated by a new spirit. Peoples more numerous and more politically aware are craving and now demanding their place in the sun — not just for the benefit of their own physical condition, but for basic human rights. The passion for freedom is on the rise. Tapping this new spirit, there can be no nobler nor more ambitious task for America to undertake . . . than to help shape a just and peaceful world that is truly humane.''

Inaugural address, Jan. 20, 1977

Refugees are encouraged to participate in income-generating activities.

threatens our very future as a nation and a people.''

Employment as a human right

Unemployment has surfaced as a major issue throughout the world in both developed and developing nations. It is estimated that in developing nations, 1 billion new jobs must be created for the work force by 2000, if famine and political upheaval are to be averted. Citizens of the newly-democratic nations of Eastern Europe are concerned that unemployment will increase rapidly as they shift from a command to a free-market economy.

As the world market globalizes, competition for marketplaces becomes fierce. A worker in Taiwan or Korea works more cheaply than one in New York, thus, production of clothing or electronics, for example, is often moved from the U.S. to other countries. Germany, Japan, France and the U.S. all produce cars. Foreign cars, perceived as having higher quality, are competing successfully with American-made cars and idling many American auto workers.

An important factor in creating unemployment in the 1990s is technology. Computers and robots are doing many jobs once done by people. The technological society requires sophisticated job skills.

Jobs are considered one of the most basic of human rights because poverty and hunger stem largely from a lack of productive employment. Article 23 of the Universal Declaration of Human Rights states: ''Everyone has the right to work, to free choice of employment, to just and favourable conditions of work and to protection against unemployment.'' The article lists other employment rights: to equal pay for equal work, to just wages, and to form and join trade unions.

Robert Reich, political economist at Harvard University, has pointed out that workers at the low end of the wage scale in the United States are now competing with workers all over the world. As a consequence, the cheap labor available in the transnational economy is reducing the share of domestic wealth of the lowest 20 percent of wage earners in the United States. Reich concludes that this global competition for cheap labor is a major factor in the finding that the rich in the United States are getting richer, and the poor are getting poorer. Reich argues that the United States needs to place a higher priority on providing a better education for all its citizens, especially minorities, so they can participate fully in the global economy.

PART V

Regions of the World: An Historical Sketch

SOVIET UNION *

The United States Government has not recognized the incorporation of Estonia, Latvia, and Lithuania into the Soviet Union. Other boundary representation is not necessarily authoritative.

Scale 1:19,000,000

0   500 Kilometers

0   500 Nautical Miles

The World Factbook, 1989

*The map of the Soviet Union appears in Chapter 21, p. 150.

Chapter 18

Europe

At the end of World War II, Europe lay in ruins. The dream of Adolph Hitler, Chancellor of Germany, of creating a fascist empire that would last 1,000 years turned into the worst nightmare the world had ever known. Over 45 million people were killed in the war, mostly European civilians. Science and technology applied to killing and destruction accounted for the large number of civilian deaths. Unlike previous wars, women, children and other non-combatants faced the same dangers as uniformed soldiers. There was no distinction between neighborhoods and battlefields. Governments, economies, families, industries, cities, farmland, historical and cultural relics were destroyed throughout Europe. After the war, Europe no longer dominated and influenced the rest of the world as it had for centuries.

World War II involved almost every major nation in the world. The political, economic and social problems caused by the war still affect today's world. The war created a climate of fear and suspicion that brought the human race to the verge of extinction. To understand Europe's position in the world today, it is necessary to take a brief look at its past — a turbulent history of nations competing for power, wealth and territory.

Europe — many nations on a small continent

Europe, the second smallest of the seven continents, has had the greatest influence of all on the rest of the world. The European continent, about the same size as the United States, is made up of many independent countries, each with its own language, customs and characteristics. With a long history of cultural achievement, Europe was the birthplace of Western civilization. The many nationalities of Europe provided the foundation for advancements in Western philosophy, science, art, music, education and literature. Many European cities have been centers of culture for hundreds of years.

The terms Western and Eastern Europe are commonly used and are related to the political and economic makeup of the continent. Some nations, however, do not easily fit into either category. Since World War II, Western European countries are generally considered to be the nations with free-market economies and multi-party political systems. Western Europe, more industrialized and prosperous because of its access to major waterways, includes the United Kingdom, France, Germany, Italy, Spain, Portugal, Austria, Switzerland, the Netherlands, Belgium, Luxembourg, Denmark, Norway, Sweden and several smaller countries. Eastern Europe, mostly landlocked, remained largely agricultural until after World War II. Eastern Europe is the general term referring to nations with command economies that came under Soviet control following World War II. These nations include Poland, Czechoslovakia, Hungary, Romania and Bulgaria.

The eastern border of the European continent is not easily defined, Europe being an extension of Asia, but the Ural Mountains are generally considered the eastern boundary line. The Soviet Union lies in both Europe and Asia and has historically played an important role in European affairs, especially during the 20th century.

A history of warfare

Warfare always disrupted European society. Various countries often sought to expand their territory at the expense of a weaker neighbor. Violent revolutions and civil wars have also been a major part of European history. There have been several attempts by a nation or a ruler to conquer the entire continent and establish an empire. The greatest European empire of all, the Roman Empire, collapsed over 1,500 years ago. During the height of their power, the Romans controlled the entire Mediterranean world including most of Western Europe, North Africa and the Middle East.

Reasons for empire-building

The idea of creating an empire to make one nation dominant remained alive in Europe since the fall of Rome. Nations often desire to establish an empire and dominate other nations in order to keep from being dominated themselves. The fruits of empire are tempting for ambitious leaders. Territorial expansion, control of trade, enslavement of conquered people, the acquisition of precious resources, expanded revenue through taxation — are incentives some rulers have considered to be more important

than international cooperation. As a consequence, many European nations developed strong military forces to defend against invasion and conquest.

Maintaining the balance of power

England, never a threat to dominate Europe, used its military power and resources to maintain the balance of power in Europe, that is, to prevent other nations from expanding their borders and power. France expanded its borders and threatened to control Europe under Louis XIV in the 17th and 18th centuries. One hundred years later, Napoleon became the most successful empire builder since the Romans, having conquered all of continental Europe in the early 19th century. This French dominance of Europe and the spread of its revolutionary ideals was short-lived.

After Napoleon, warfare changed drastically with the beginning of the Industrial Revolution. Machine guns, submarines, heavy artillery, mass-produced armaments, later tanks, bomber planes and aircraft carriers made warfare a most deadly gamble.

European imperialism

Germany, Britain and the United States were the leading industrialized nations during the 19th century. The British established a worldwide empire which once included North America. By the late 19th century, Western European countries, following Britain's example, had gained strongholds in Asia, Africa and the Middle East. Pre-industrial societies throughout the world were exploited by the industrialized nations for profit. Timber was cut down and precious metals were mined and sent back to Europe. The native people were often conquered and used as laborers.

World War I

Fierce nationalism and global competition for control of markets and raw materials for industry were factors that caused governments to enlarge their military forces. The European nations were divided into two entangling alliances which led to World War I. This war cost Europe an entire generation of men. It was supposed to end war for all time but actually set the stage for another war only 20 years later.

World War II

Adolph Hitler came to power in the 1930s. Germany's economy at that time was suffering from uncontrolled inflation. Hitler was able to build his party by claiming that the *Treaty of Versailles,* which ended World War I, was injust. The treaty required Ger-

SIRS Staff

About 1,000,000 soldiers died at the Battle of Verdun in France during World War I. Most were buried on the battlefield where they died. The cross marks the grave where a soldier who fell in battle was buried.

many to pay reparations and accept full blame for World War I. Hitler appealed to German nationalism and promised to make Germany the strongest nation in Europe. His ambitions led to the most destructive of all wars.

The destruction of World War II

The Soviet Union suffered the most destruction of any nation during World War II (1939-1945). Over 20 million Soviet people were killed in the war; 15 million of these were civilians. Among the soldiers who returned from battle, millions were injured or weakened by malnutrition. Farmland was ruined, and homes and factories were destroyed. Every family in the Soviet Union was affected by the war with 28 million people left homeless. Nearly an entire generation of women were never able to establish families of their own because there were so few men to marry.

At least 4.5 million Germans, including 1 million civilians, were killed in the war. Six million European Jews were systematically killed, by orders of Adolph Hitler and other Nazi officials, in ghettos and death camps throughout Nazi-occupied Europe.

Many German cities suffered major losses, especially from Allied bombing. German industrial capacity was severely damaged. By 1945, Germany's economy and its industrial output were in a state of ruin, and the people's morale was crushed by the defeat and destruction.

Britain suffered about 400,000 military deaths and 65,000 civilian deaths from German bombing.

France lost approximately 200,000 soldiers and 400,000 civilians. Its material losses were greater than any European nation except the Soviet Union and Germany. French industry and agriculture were either under German control or destroyed in battle. The last great offensive of the war devastated large areas of France, destroying roads, communications, public monuments, businesses and farmland.

Many areas of Italy were destroyed during the Allied invasion of 1943-45. Lost lives were about 400,000.

About 300,000 Americans lost their lives in World War II, including 6,000 civilians living abroad. Many soldiers returned home badly wounded.

The two superpowers

Two military superpowers — the Soviet Union and

SIRS Staff

World War II cemetery at Normandy where thousands of American soldiers are buried.

109

the United States — emerged from the rubble of World War II. Both nations had effectively mobilized their entire populations for the war effort. With little time to prepare for war, both the United States and the Soviet Union built enormous military forces. The United States, although fighting the Pacific war as well as the war in Europe, enjoyed the advantage of not being threatened by invasion of its home territory.

The Soviet army was initially no match for the well-trained German army and suffered extreme losses from 1941-43 as the Germans advanced quickly to the outskirts of Moscow. The tide turned in late 1943 as the Germans were defeated on the Russian front and in North Africa. In April 1945, Soviet tanks and troops entered Berlin. The Soviet Union emerged from the war determined never again to be caught unprepared against foreign invaders.

The United States had converted its factories from civilian to military production and had the most powerful armed forces in the world at the end of World War II. The United States secretly developed the atomic bomb, a powerful new weapon with a potential for destruction that would forever change the course of warfare. The nuclear age began with the dropping of atom bombs on Hiroshima and Nagasaki in Japan.

The superpowers' global competition for economic supremacy and political influence produced an arms race which threatened the destruction of the entire planet. For over 40 years, tension resulting from mutual distrust between the Soviet Union and the United States, allies during World War II, created an atmosphere where the threat of nuclear war loomed over everyone. This was called the *Cold War* and began shortly after the end of World War II. The Cold War divided Europe. Most of Western Europe formed a military alliance with the United States. Most of Eastern Europe joined an alliance with the Soviet Union.

Origins of the Cold War

Soviet suspicion of the West, particularly of Germany, Britain and the United States, had a long history.

In 1918, during the Russian Revolution, Russia negotiated with Germany to withdraw from participation in World War I. *The Treaty of Brest-Litovsk* required Russia to give Germany a great amount of territory. During the civil war following the Russian Revolution, Britain, the United States and Japan sent troops to Russia to fight against the communist Red Army. The United States did not give diplomatic recognition to the Soviet Union until 1933, shortly after Franklin Roosevelt became president.

During the Spanish Civil War in 1938, the Soviet Union attempted to counter German and Italian military aid to General Franco's fascist forces by supporting the Spanish Loyalists. Both the United States and Britain refused to send aid to the Loyalists — but did allow volunteers from their nations to fight for the Loyalist cause. The Soviet leaders believed that the United States and Britain preferred a fascist government in Spain to the freely elected, left-wing Loyalist government.

During World War II, the United States provided the Soviet Union with massive military assistance to fight the Germans. The Soviets were suspicious of the U.S. because they felt the United States was helping them so they could continue to bear the brunt of the German attack. Eighty-five percent of all German casualties in World War II were inflicted by the Soviet Union on the eastern battlefront.

Stalin repeatedly called on Churchill and Roosevelt to open a western front; their reluctance to do so reinforced Soviet suspicions of Western motives. Stalin believed the delays were to conserve the lives of British and American soldiers — at the expense of the Russians. He felt that Churchill and Roosevelt were hoping Germany and the Soviet Union would battle one another into exhaustion, and that the longer the western front was delayed, the more likely it was that this would happen. The Allies' reason for the long delay was that until June 1944, British and American forces were not prepared to invade Western Europe.

When Germany surrendered in May 1945, ending World War II in Europe, the primary Allied objective was to clear away the destruction left by the war. This was a complex operation which involved determining boundaries, rebuilding wrecked cities and industries, and resettling millions of people displaced from their homes. The delicate balance of power was shifted because the Soviet Union had emerged from the struggle as a strong power.

The Big Three

Once victory in Europe was in sight, the wartime alliance which worked so well to defeat Germany began to fall apart over decisions concerning postwar Europe. The Big Three — Roosevelt, Churchill and Stalin — met at Teheran in 1943 and Yalta in 1945 to discuss the political shape of Europe following the war. Each had different ambitions: Winston Churchill, the staunch anti-communist British prime minister; Joseph Stalin, the Soviet leader and enemy of western imperialism which, to him, the British Empire personified; Franklin Roosevelt, the U.S. president and mediator between the two. Issues concerning political spheres of influence, the occupa-

British Prime Minister Winston Churchill, U.S. President Franklin D. Roosevelt and Soviet Premier Joseph Stalin met at Yalta in the Crimea in February 1945 to plan the final Allied attacks on Germany and Japan.

UPI

Truman at Potsdam

By the time of the post-war Potsdam conference (July 1945), Roosevelt had died and was succeeded by Harry Truman. Truman was less willing than Roosevelt to compromise with Stalin. He was waiting for the result of the atomic bomb test which, if successful, would give the U.S. military superiority. Truman's confrontational style of dealing with Stalin was an early sign that U.S.-Soviet cooperation on many post-war European decisions would be unlikely.

Soviet policy for Eastern Europe

Stalin's main concern was the establishment of friendly neighbors on its western frontier. All of the Eastern European countries which eventually came under Soviet control, except Czechoslovakia, had authoritarian governments before World War II. Stalin initially discouraged communist revolutions in Eastern Europe in order to maintain favorable relations with the Western Allies. Until 1947, Stalin's policy was to support ''popular- front'' governments — that is, a ruling coalition of all anti-fascist groups and political parties.

Western allies and anti-communism

The United States and Britain had already set the precedent for a hard-line anti-communist policy in Italy, Germany's wartime ally, by denying communists, many of whom were active in the anti-fascist resistance movement, a voice in the new post-war government. Because American and British troops occupied Italy after the war, they were able to deny the Soviet Union a voice in the political situation there. Thereafter, the Soviets denied the U.S. and Britain input in the governments established in the Eastern European nations under Soviet occupation. Soviet intentions in Eastern Europe to install friendly governments was interpreted by the West as an attempt to establish a worldwide communist empire. This helped to create an atmosphere of antagonism between the U.S. and Great Britain against the Soviet Union that steadily worsened and lasted for about four decades.

tion of post-war Germany, boundary changes, Soviet involvement in the Pacific war, were all discussed; but decisions were postponed, for the priority was still the ongoing military strategy of the war.

The Big Three disagreed on a plan for the division of Europe after the war. This stemmed from a wide divergence of goals, with Britain and the United States on one side and the Soviet Union on the other. Before Germany's defeat, it was assumed that there would eventually be a peace treaty, similar to the *Versailles Treaty* which settled World War I. This did not happen after World War II. No peace treaty was signed between Germany and the Allies. No official post-war European boundaries were established.

Following World War I, the Treaty of Versailles gave a considerable amount of Russian territory to newly established nations. Stalin was determined to regain as much of this land as possible. The Soviet Union had signed a non-aggresssion pact with Germany in 1939 that enabled the Soviet Union to occupy a large part of Poland; annex Estonia, Latvia and Lithuania on the Baltic, Bessarabia in Romania, and part of Finland.

Germany's purpose in making the Soviet Union an ally was to assure non-interference when Germany invaded Poland in 1939. In June 1941, Germany ignored the non-aggression pact and attacked the Soviet Union. The Soviet Union then joined forces with the Allies.

111

United States policy in post-war Europe

The attitude developed that capitalism and communism could not survive in the same world. It was thought that one would dominate the other. Communism would mean that markets would be closed to U.S. goods. U.S. policymakers feared the *domino effect* — country after country falling, like dominoes, under communist control. The U.S post-war European policy was to stop the spread of communism.

A divided Germany

In 1945, most German cities were a pile of rubble from almost continuous Allied bombing in the final year of the war. Over 60 million Germans were desperate for food and shelter. Another 10 million non-Germans, mostly survivors of concentration camps and labor camps, had to be provided for.

Germany was divided into four zones of occupation with the United States, the Soviet Union, Great Britain and France each occupying a zone. The U.S. decided on a policy to rebuild Germany's industry and economy. A strong U.S. military presence to direct the reconstruction of the German economy and government was a vital part of the U.S. policy.

The Soviet Union demanded *reparations* (compensation for war damages) from East Germany and seized industrial facilities and resources for their own use. A communist government under Soviet control was established in East Germany.

Disagreement between the U.S. and the Soviet Union over post-war German policy was one of the primary reasons for the division of Europe during the Cold War. The U.S. and Britain believed that a strong industrial German economy and a military force allied with Western Europe was essential for overall European economic growth and security. The Soviet Union, having fought two recent wars with Germany, feared another German invasion. The Soviets preferred a weakened, and neutral, demilitarized Germany which could never threaten European stability. The failure to compromise on German policy eventually resulted in the establishment of two separate German nations.

Britain weakened in the Eastern Mediterranean

A faltering economy meant that Britain could no longer sustain its military presence in post-war Greece where a communist movement, independent of the Soviet Union, threatened to seize political control from the unpopular British-supported monarch. A communist government in Greece would endanger British colonial interests in the eastern Mediterranean, so Britain requested military assistance from the United States to fight the communists. When the Soviets put demands on Turkey for joint control of the Dardanelles, which would give the Soviets a base on the Mediterranean Sea, the U.S. dispatched a naval force to the area, and the Soviets backed down.

The Truman Doctrine

When the British withdrew from Greece and Turkey, Truman asked Congress to approve military aid to the two countries and any other country fighting against the threat of communist domination. By putting these local political conflicts in the context of a worldwide ideological struggle between the forces of good and evil, the nature of U.S.-Soviet relations was decidedly altered. Known as the *Truman Doctrine,* U.S. determination to stop the spread of communism with military force ended the possibility for U.S.-Soviet cooperation in Europe and the rest of the world.

The containment policy

America's determination to fight communist expansion was called the *containment policy.* This policy required a strong military presence in Europe in addition to the promise to provide military and economic assistance to any nations resisting communist takeovers. Thus, the United States adopted a long-term foreign policy that proclaimed itself the champion of freedom and democracy around the globe.

The Marshall Plan

In June 1947, shortly after the Truman Doctrine was proposed, Secretary of State George Marshall announced that the United States was willing to provide the money to rebuild Europe's ruined economy. Economic assistance was offered to all European nations including the Soviet Union and Eastern Europe. The *Marshall Plan,* later called the *European Recovery Program,* insisted on economic cooperation among European nations as a condition for U.S. aid. The Soviet Union considered the Marshall Plan an American plot to control the European economy. They refused to participate and pressured Eastern Europe to follow the same policy.

The Marshall Plan ultimately provided over $13 billion to Western Europe, Greece and Turkey. This program was enormously successful not only in rebuilding the damaged economies of Western Europe, but also for providing a foundation for further European cooperation. The United States also felt that a strong European economy would further strengthen the American economy and help prevent communism from spreading to Western Europe.

A thermonuclear detonation in the Pacific Test Area on February 28, 1954.

Toward Western European unity — the post-war years

Despite traditional antagonism, the industrialized nations of Western Europe soon realized that economic cooperation would be necessary to rebuild Europe's shattered economy. New domestic and foreign policies took root in Western Europe as leaders accepted their weakened role in the world economy. Long-term economic planning became essential for European recovery. Most Western European governments established production goals and investment incentives. They regulated wages and prices because citizens were expected to cooperate in peacetime as they had done so well during the war. Public ownership of large industries and the provision of social welfare for all citizens were consequential changes in Western Europe, permanently altering the traditional social structure.

Britain provided the post-war model of parliamentary democracy and the establishment of the welfare state, that is, providing all citizens with insurance against sickness, unemployment and old age. Britain's two-party parliamentary political system meant a stable, efficient government.

While Britain's political stability facilitated economic growth, weak multi-party parliamentary governments in France and Italy suffered one political crisis after another, and these economies faltered following World War II. Both France and Italy required the cooperation of various political parties in order to form a ruling coalition to run the government. Both nations had strong Communist Parties which normally received 20 percent of the vote and strong parliamentary representation. After 1948, no other French or Italian parties were willing to include the Communists in a ruling coalition, leaving them virtually no voice in determining national policy despite their widespread support. This weakened the ability of the ruling coalition to effectively run the government and direct economic policy.

The French government was eventually strength-

113

ened in the late 1950s under the leadership of Charles de Gaulle, France's World War II military leader. Faced with a military coup and civil war because of events in the French colony of Algeria, de Gaulle was offered unlimited power for a temporary period to solve the Algerian crisis and to write a new constitution for France. De Gaulle's new government, the Fifth Republic, gave most governmental power to the president rather than Parliament. De Gaulle, enjoying widespread popular support, served as France's president from 1958 to 1969. He modernized the French economy and attempted to restore the power and prestige of France by defining a leading European role for France.

Despite a long tradition of German authoritarian governments, West Germany successfully created an efficient two-party parliamentary system and was granted full independence in 1955. With Konrad Adenauer providing strong post-war leadership, West Germany rebuilt its industrial economy at an astonishing pace and, by the late 1950s, had one of the strongest economies in Western Europe.

The European Community — the goal of a "common market"

Soon after World War II ended, ideas of a united Europe were discussed. Idealists dreamed of a United States of Europe where European interests held priority over nationalist aims. Many hoped for economic and political unity to replace the balance-of-power policy which traditionally kept ambitious nations in check.

With U.S. insistence on European economic cooperation for the disbursement of Marshall Plan funds, 16 nations formed the *Organization for European Economic Cooperation* (OEEC). This cooperative spirit among Western European nations, accustomed to rival alliances, led to greater international unity. The success of the *European Coal and Steel Community* (ECSC), which included France, West Germany, Italy and the Benelux countries, in placing common European interests above national interests meant economic growth for all members. The *Treaty of Rome* signed in 1957 by these same six nations established the *European Economic Community,* presently known as the *European Community* (EC). The goal was to create a common European market by abolishing trade restrictions and tariffs, instituting common financial policies and allowing the free movement of capital and labor. A European Parliament set up to administer the policies of the European Community meant that each member nation must be willing to give up a part of its national sovereignty. Quarreling among nations and an unwillingness to forego national interests for the good of the Community produced obstacles to the realization of the EC's goals for the first 30 years. Another problem was that the United Kingdom did not join the EC because commitments to its non-European Commonwealth clashed with EC regulations. The United Kingdom was finally admitted in 1973 along with Ireland and Denmark. Europe suffered an economic recession during the 1970s and early 1980s. Nationalist bickering continued as EC agricultural policies favored some nations and hurt others. Greece was admitted to the EC in 1981, and Spain and Portugal joined in 1986.

Soviet control of Eastern Europe

Just as the United States feared Russian expansion and the threat of communism, the Soviet Union viewed the growing American involvement in European affairs as an imperialist attempt at world domination. To the Soviets, the Truman Doctrine and the Marshall Plan marked a departure point for any possible future cooperation or negotiation with its former wartime allies. Churchill's statement in 1946 that "an Iron Curtain has descended across the continent," would soon be realized.

Thereafter, Stalinism was established in Eastern Europe. Stalinism meant that all communist regimes would be controlled by the Soviet Union. In Poland all non-communists were purged from the government, and opposition parties were outlawed. Soon after, Stalin enforced the same policy in Hungary, Czechoslovakia, Romania, Bulgaria and East Germany. As in the Soviet Union, all of these countries were characterized by the establishment of a secret police, forced labor camps, strict government control of culture, forced industrialization, elimination of private ownership of land and Soviet military occupation. Yugoslavia, because of its strong resistance movement during the war, was able to maintain an independent communist regime.

The Berlin blockade and airlift

The pre-war German capital, Berlin, although located in the Soviet-occupied zone, was also divided into four Allied zones. In June 1948, the Soviets, reacting to Western economic policy, blocked passage into West Berlin from the surrounding Soviet zone. It was an attempt by the USSR to cut off West Berlin from food and supplies and take over the city without force. The United States responded by flying in supplies daily from West German cities to provide the residents of West Berlin with the necessities for survival. The airlift was a huge success, and after nearly a year the Soviets called off the blockade, but the city remained divided — a continuing source of friction between the

U.S. and the Soviet Union for over four decades.

A divided Europe — NATO and the Warsaw Pact

As the Soviets strengthened their control of Eastern Europe, U.S. influence in Western Europe increased. Both nations maintained large armies in Europe, especially in Germany. Eventually, each of the superpowers formed military alliances with their European allies. In 1949, the *North Atlantic Treaty Organization* (NATO) was formed. The treaty stated ''that an armed attack against one or more of (the members) in Europe or North America shall be considered an attack against them all . . .'' The original NATO members included the United States, Britain, France, Italy, Belgium, the Netherlands, Luxembourg, Denmark, Norway, Portugal, Iceland and Canada. They were later joined by Greece and Turkcy (1952), West Germany (1954) and Spain (1986). In 1955, the Soviet Union arranged a similar treaty, called the *Warsaw Pact,* with the Eastern European countries under its control. Sweden, Finland, Ireland, Switzerland, Austria and Yugoslavia remained neutral.

NATO countries
Warsaw Pact Countries

Nuclear arms race

The United States lost its monopoly on nuclear weapons when the Soviet Union exploded its first atomic bomb in September 1949. Both countries have continued to expand their nuclear arsenals since then. In the early 1950s, both countries developed hydrogen bombs (thermonuclear weapons), hundreds of times more destructive than the atom bombs dropped on Japan during World War II.

Technological competition moved to outer space after the Soviet Union launched *Sputnik,* the first satellite to orbit Earth. This caused great concern that the Soviets possessed more advanced technology than the U.S. The success of Sputnik also meant that the Soviets possessed the technology to launch nuclear missiles from Russia that could reach the United States in a matter of minutes. This frightening realization led to increased attempts by the U.S. to surpass Soviet technology through the development of the space program, a new education policy which emphasized science and mathematics, and the development of new nuclear weapons.

The Korean War

Korea, previously under Japanese control, was divided into two separate nations after World War II. The Soviet Union supported the communist regime in North Korea and the United States supported the South Korean republic. When a war between the two nations began in 1950, President Truman quickly proclaimed the need to turn back the communist assault. The United Nations condemned the aggressive action of the North Korean army and sent an international force (90 percent American) which fought the North Koreans, who were aided by communist China, to a stalemate after three years.

The Korean War made many Europeans fear the possibility of

U.S. Defense Dept.

Berliners watch U.S. plane bringing supplies to Allied garrisons and 2.5 million citizens of West Berlin. The eleven-month airlift of 1948-49 kept the city alive and thwarted Stalin's attempt to bring all of Berlin under communist control.

a similar conflict in Germany, both countries being similarly divided. Western European military forces were too weak to provide security against a potential Soviet invasion — a reason the NATO alliance was strengthened. Besides a stronger U.S. commitment, West Germany was permitted to establish a military force which could only be used as part of the NATO alliance for the mutual defense of Western Europe.

Khrushchev's new policies

Stalin's death in March 1953, created a power struggle for Soviet leadership. By 1956, Nikita Khrushchev had outwitted his political rivals and assumed the leadership of the Soviet Union. Khrushchev denounced Stalin for his brutal crimes, incompetent leadership, elimination of political enemies and cruel repression of innocent citizens. It has been estimated that 25 million Soviet citizens were killed on Stalin's orders. Khrushchev introduced changes in Soviet domestic and foreign policy. Censorship in the arts was substantially eased, spawning an era of Soviet cultural achievement. He spoke of *peaceful coexistence* as an alternative to confrontation, hoping to lessen tensions with the West. Still, maintaining Soviet military strength and control of Eastern Europe remained his priority in foreign policy.

Eisenhower and Dulles — new cold warriors

Dwight Eisenhower, who had been a popular World War II general in charge of U.S. forces in Europe, was swept into office just before Stalin's death during an atmosphere of intense anticommunist sentiment. He appointed John Foster Dulles as Secretary of State who established a new, even more hard-line, policy against the "menace of communism." With the fear of communism spreading throughout Asia, Dulles spoke of a policy which would liberate those nations under communist control. The new U.S. policy was announced when the Soviets were expressing an interest in some form of *détente*. In 1955, the Soviet Union agreed to withdraw its troops from Austria if neutrality was maintained there. Pressure from Western Europe for a policy which would relax U.S.-Soviet tensions led to a summit meeting in Geneva in 1955, although nothing substantive was accomplished.

The Hungarian revolt

Khrushchev initiated a less-repressive policy in Eastern Europe which led to growing criticism of the totalitarian regimes there. This new taste of freedom

following Stalin's death led to open demonstrations and worker strikes first in East Berlin in 1953, which was quickly repressed, and in Poland and Hungary in 1956. While the situation in Poland was kept under control, an attempted revolution in Hungary caused much concern in Moscow. Growing opposition to the Communist party and Hungary's subservient role in the Warsaw Pact resulted in a multi-party coalition government under a popular prime minister, Imre Nagy. When Nagy demanded the withdrawal of Soviet troops and promised to hold free elections, the Soviet army attacked the country's capital, Budapest. Over 25,000 Hungarians were killed as the Soviets restored order with military force. Nagy and other leaders were executed.

The 1956 Hungarian revolt indicated that the United States recognized Soviet control of Eastern Europe. Despite previous radio broadcasts promising to help liberate Eastern European countries from communist control, the United States made no attempt to assist the Hungarian revolutionaries.

The Russian invasion of Hungary also indicated that allowing the people of Eastern Europe a taste of freedom would lead to further demands for reform and ultimately the desire for independence from Soviet control.

Superpower tensions grow

With both the United States and the Soviet Union taking a hard-line approach during the late 1950s, the Cold War intensified, and the arms race escalated. Although neither side was willing to compromise, a *summit meeting* was arranged for May 1960. The most pressing issue was the German problem. Thousands of East German professionals and skilled workers were fleeing to West Berlin where economic conditions were better than in East Germany.

However, a crisis occurred. Kruschchev announced that the USSR had shot down an American U-2 spy plane over Soviet territory. He expressed indignation and demanded an apology. At first, the U.S. denied that a spy plane had flown over the USSR. The U.S. claimed that the U-2 was a weather plane that had gone off course. But the pilot was captured, and photos were released.

The pilot, Francis Gary Powers, confessed to being a spy.

The U.S. still refused to apologize, and the summit, involving Eisenhower's visit to the Soviet Union, was cancelled.

Powers was later released in exchange for a Soviet spy held in the U.S. But any opportunity for improving relations between the two superpowers was lost at this time.

Children peek over the formidable Berlin Wall, built in mid-city by the East Germans in 1961 to prevent refugees from fleeing to West Germany. At that time, refugees were pouring into West Berlin at the rate of 2,000 a day.

The Berlin Wall

John Kennedy succeeded Eisenhower as president in January 1961. In June 1961, Kennedy met with Khrushchev in Vienna to attempt to solve the German dispute. Both leaders refused to compromise, even at the threat of war. During the night of August 13, 1961, the Soviet and East German armies blocked off all passage into West Berlin and constructed a wall, eventually 26 miles long, that prevented East Germans from entering West Berlin. The *Berlin Wall* was a somber monument to the Cold War.

Détente

Shortly after Khrushchev was removed from power in 1964, American policy toward the Soviet Union changed to one of peaceful coexistence. China, communist since 1949, and the Soviet Union had a long history of tense relations which they failed to mend despite their common political ideology. As Chinese-Soviet relations deteriorated in the 1970s, the United States courted China as a potential ally, indicating that nationalist motives can predominate over ideology.

By the early 1970s, tension between the United States and the Soviet Union and between Eastern and Western Europe had eased considerably. *Détente,* or a relaxation of tensions, was the term which defined the cold-war situation during most of Leonid Brezhnev's term as Soviet leader (1964-1982). Both superpowers possessed enough nuclear weapons to ensure the destruction of the planet in case of a full-scale war. The huge military build-up continued and sapped the economies of both countries.

Economic cooperation between the superpowers grew during the 1970s as the United States became a major supplier of grain to the Soviet Union. The

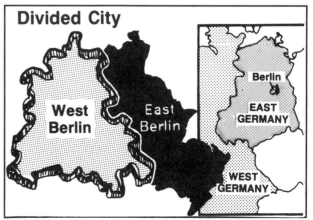

U.S. also favored economic collaboration between Eastern and Western Europe; a growing interdependence between East and West favored all nations and helped lessen Cold War tensions.

In 1975, 35 heads of state, including those of the Soviet Union and the United States, signed the *Helsinki Accord* at the Conference on Security and Cooperation in Europe. Although non-binding, it furthered peaceful prospects by agreeing to establish European boundaries for the first time since World War II, encouraging economic cooperation and pledging to respect human rights. It did not, however, lead to a reduction in military forces.

Several arms control agreements were negotiated during the 1970s and 1980s, demonstrating little more than a mutual concern for the enormous cost of maintaining military parity. Ideological warfare remained a priority for both sides, and both superpowers were involved in military conflicts, but not with each other, during the 1970s and 1980s.

The Brezhnev Doctrine

A group of reformers within the Czechoslovakian Communist party gained control of the government in 1968. During a six-month period, the new government abolished censorship and police repression, allowed intellectual and religious freedom, and introduced economic and political reforms. Responding to pressure from Soviet hard-liners who opposed detente, Brezhnev ordered Russian troops to Prague to quash the peaceful revolution and replaced the reformers with leaders loyal to Moscow.

The Soviet invasion of Czechoslovakia, during the height of U.S. involvement in Vietnam, established the *Brezhnev Doctrine.* This proclaimed that the Soviet Union would intervene in nations in the communist community when hostile forces, whether internal or external, threatened to establish a capitalist regime. Throughout the 1970s and 1980s, the Brezhnev Doctrine and political control by communist party leaders faithful to the Soviet Union effectively prevented any situations in Eastern Europe which demanded Soviet military intervention.

The Reagan era

The early 1980s brought several international crises which damaged U.S.-Soviet relations as both superpower leaders returned to a hard-line policy. Terrorist attacks against Americans in the Middle East, violent revolutionary movements in Central America and the Soviet invasion of Afghanistan created an atmosphere of renewed nationalism and anticommunism among the American public. Ronald Reagan, responding to a new conservatism in American politics, enjoyed enormous public support during his two presidential terms. Reagan's reference to the Soviet Union as the "evil empire" and his massive military build-up appeared to be a return to a 1950s-style cold-war policy. Many Americans and Europeans feared the possibility of nuclear war for the first time in almost 20 years, and movements for *nuclear disarmament,* especially in Europe, gained much attention and support.

Growing European independence from U.S. and Soviet influence

In the two decades following World War II, Western Europe prospered. As Western Europe became less dependent on American economic aid, certain nations sought a more independent stand in the Cold War. France especially opposed the Americanization of Europe and the influx of American popular culture and consumer products. France took a leading role in European affairs and under Charles de Gaulle demanded that the United States share its control of nuclear weapons with the rest of the NATO nations. When the U.S. disagreed, de Gaulle refused to allow nuclear missiles on French soil. France eventually developed its own nuclear arsenal.

Britain was America's closest ally in Europe throughout the Cold War, especially during the Reagan era — coinciding with the rule of Prime Minister Margaret Thatcher, who shared Reagan's conservative philosophy.

West Germany had the most to fear during the Cold War; military operations were expected to originate there if war broke out. In the late 1960s, West Germany established a new Eastern policy, *ostpolitik,* and initiated friendly relations with East Germany and other Soviet satellites. Despite the renewed U.S.-Soviet tensions of the 1980s, economic cooperation favoring both Eastern and Western Europe continued.

Eastern Europe under Soviet domination

The communist countries of Eastern Europe, mostly agricultural societies before World War II, experienced major changes during the cold-war domination of the Soviet Union. The economic policies of the Warsaw-Pact nations, politically controlled by the Communist Party whose leaders took their orders from Moscow, were intended to serve the needs of the Soviet Union. Rapid industrialization following World War II resulted in a more urban society and the accompanying congestion, pollution and housing shortages. Production of consumer goods was a low priority, and East Europeans, although guaranteed housing and jobs, had little access to consumer items.

Soviet control of Eastern Europe counted on a visible military presence and the threat of force. Public demonstrations, intellectual freedom, opposition political parties and labor unions were prohibited. In 1980, Polish workers, outraged by low wages and high prices, defied the Communist Party and created the labor union *Solidarity.* Led by Lech Walesa and strongly supported by the Catholic Church, Solidarity's long courageous struggle to attain political legitimacy was finally achieved in 1989.

New Soviet leadership

In 1982, Yuri Andropov assumed the Soviet leadership and continued the traditional policies of the aging old-guard Soviet politicians. Renewed superpower tensions called for a greater role for the military and a tightening of control over Eastern Europe. After 15 months, Andropov died and was replaced by Konstantin Chernenko (1984), at 72 the oldest man to become Soviet leader. The following year, Chernenko's death symbolized the end of a generation of Soviet leadership from the Stalin era.

Mikhail Gorbachev, at 54 the youngest General Secretary of the Communist Party since Stalin took over the Soviet leadership in 1924, personified not only a new generation coming to power in the Soviet Union but also a radical departure from traditional Soviet policy.

The declining Soviet economy, a result of spending trillions for weapons without providing for basic consumer needs, required serious reform. Gorbachev proclaimed a new economic policy to combat serious problems such as declining industrial output, bureaucratic corruption and inefficiency, alcoholism and lack of worker incentive which plagued the entire Soviet system. Gorbachev called his plan to restructure the economy *perestroika.*

Gorbachev recognized the need for reductions in military spending for *perestroika* to be successful. Several superpower summit meetings between Gorbachev and Presidents Reagan and Bush resulted in limited arms-reduction agreements.

Glasnost

Gorbachev also recognized that political and social changes in the Soviet Union were necessary. Gorbachev continued to identify and expose the failures of the Soviet system. He brought attention to corruption at high levels of government and industry and called for an end to the special privileges enjoyed by Communist Party officials. He loosened censorship of the media and allowed intellectual freedom and criticism of the government. He received the support of dissidents, including the late Andrei Sakharov who was released by Gorbachev after over six years in exile. Gorbachev encouraged an end to the lies that were official Russian history bringing a new policy of openness, or *glasnost,* to Soviet society.

In 1989, Gorbachev allowed nationwide elections to the new 2,250-member Congress of People's Deputies. The people overwhelmingly voted against the traditional hard-line Communist-party candidates. Gorbachev called for the creation of a new office of president to replace the Communist-party's political control. In March 1990, Gorbachev was elected the first Soviet president for a five-year term. He was granted unprecedented power as Soviet ruler. To strengthen the economy, he announced his plan to institute free-market reforms but remained committed to socialism.

Yet, after five years of Gorbachev's leadership, the economy continued to decline. Shortages of food, soap and other basic necessities created inflation and pessimism. Gorbachev was criticized by both aging hard-liners including high military officials who oppose his radical reforms and those who insist his program is too conservative.

Europe enters the 1990s

The 1990s began with important changes in both Western and Eastern Europe. In Western Europe, the nations of the European Community were planning for complete economic union by 1992. During the closing months of 1989, the people of Eastern Europe revolted against one-party rule and the economic failures of communism. The Soviet Union continued their plans for economic reform and encouraged the same in Eastern Europe.

A new relationship between East and West became a reality in light of the dramatic changes in Eastern Europe. With the end of the cold-war atmosphere, the future of the Warsaw Pact and NATO alliances remained uncertain.

The reunification of Germany, long feared by most Europeans, occurred in 1990. The changing political climate and the restructuring of economies made the distinctions between East and West Europe less pronounced. The need for large armies appeared to diminish.

Nations of the European Community

As economic conditions improved slightly during the mid-1980s, the 12 member nations of the European Community expressed a new desire to eliminate all barriers and create the largest single market in the industrialized world. In 1987, the EC set 1992 as a deadline for the end all trade barriers. All EC nations will have the same unified standards, testing, certification, labeling and value-added tax and will enact over 300 economic proposals. All citizens of EC member nations will have a single European passport and may freely seek employment in any EC nation. Europeans hope the ambitious 1992 program will create new jobs, cut consumer prices and establish Europe as a first-rate economic competitor with the United States and Japan. The key to the success of the European Community is cooperation among nations who have a history of deep-seated fear and hatred for one another. As Europe enters the 1990s, many other factors complicate the traditional obstacles to European unity, especially German reunification.

The cultural accomplishments and past glories of nations usually earn them a certain prestige among other nations. Leaders of certain nations are considered important international figures, while the rulers of small countries remain virtually unknown outside their own countries. Member nations of the European Community include the former great powers of Europe as well as smaller, less powerful nations. All benefit from their membership in the European Community.

The **United Kingdom** includes the island of Britain (England, Scotland and Wales) and Northern Ireland. Beset by social and economic problems throughout the 1970s and 1980s, the U.K. experienced a few years of economic growth under the leadership of Margaret Thatcher. Britain's first woman prime minister, Thatcher has been in power since 1979 — longer than any other British leader since World War II. Thatcher has enjoyed periods of immense popularity as well as times of intense scorn. Her political career has been helped by a weak opposition party.

The United Kingdom has been more closely aligned with the United States since World War II than any other European nation. A late joiner of the EC, the U.K. has not always been an enthusiastic supporter of many European Community policies.

In 1981, François Mitterand became the first popularly-elected Socialist president of **France.** Under Mitterand, France has continued to modernize its economy and is a leader in high technology. France has held an important position in the European Community since it was established.

French relations with **West Germany** improved during the 1950s with Charles de Gaulle and Konrad Adenauer as respective heads of state. Chancellor Helmut Kohl of West Germany and French President Mitterand are close allies, and the cooperation of these two nations, the backbone of the EC, is essential to the future success of European unity.

West Germany has one of the strongest economies in the world; its exports nearly equal that of the United States. The reunification of East and West Germany means that West Germany will have to direct much of its assets to the reconstruction of a struggling East German economy.

Faced with a serious economic recession and escalating political terrorism throughout the 1970s, **Italy** has rebounded and now has the fifth largest economy in the world. Economic growth during the 1980s mostly benefited the industrial north. Southern Italy, mostly agricultural, remains a stark contrast to the modern cities of northern Italy. Much of Italy's economic success is credited to its membership in the European Community. Because of Italy's unstable, inefficient political system, the regulations of the EC provide a certain degree of order that is lacking from the government.

The Low Countries — **the Netherlands, Belgium** and **Luxembourg** — are small, prosperous nations in northwest Europe. Shipping and trucking industries in the Netherlands expect to benefit when customs controls are eliminated under the EC's 1992 plan. Brussels, the capital of Belgium, is where the EC Commission meets, and the Belgian economy benefits from the presence of thousands of "Eurocrats." Luxembourg, the EC's smallest member, hopes to prosper as a financial center as the nations of the EC move toward economic integration.

Denmark, with one of the highest standards of living in the world, has a favorable coastal location and is a bridge between northern Europe and the other Scandinavian countries. One of the seven original members of the *European Free Trade Association* (EFTA), Denmark joined the EC in 1973 during a period of economic recession and high unemployment. Danes are still split on the question of remaining in the EC or aligning with their fellow Scandinavians in the EFTA.

The four poorest nations of the European Community — **Spain, Portugal, Greece** and **Ireland** — are to receive tens of billions of dollars in economic adjustment aid from the wealthier members. Membership for Spain and Portugal will not only stimulate their economies but help integrate these two nations culturally and politically with the rest of Europe. Both Portugal and Spain were ruled by repressive dictators from the 1930s until the 1970s. Both nations presently have parliamentary governments led by socialist parties.

Political instability as well as a lack of resources and poor soil in **Greece** has hindered economic

The European Community at a Glance

	Area (Square Miles)	Population (millions)	Per capita GDP* (US $)
West Germany	154,505	61.64	10,633
France	342,808	54.22	9,538
United Kingdom	151,608	56.34	8,072
Italy	187,176	56.64	6,208
Netherlands	21,083	14.31	9,190
Belgium	18,991	9.86	8,126
Luxembourg	1,609	0.37	8,721
Denmark	26,716	5.12	11,020
Greece	82,403	9.79	3,505
Ireland	42,811	3.48	5,120
Spain	313,838	37.94	4,237
Portugal	58,583	10.00	2,055

*GDP, gross domestic product, is the total market value of goods and services produced by a country's domestic businesses.
Sources: Statistical Office of the European Communities (Eurostat), Organization for Economic Cooperation and Development (OECD).

growth. Despite these obstacles, the Greeks have made some gains, especially in shipping and commerce. Greece is optimistic about the contributions it can make to the EC and the benefits it expects to receive as a member nation.

Ireland, long controlled by Britain, was established as a republic in 1949. Traditionally an agricultural nation, Ireland began a period of industrial development during the 1960s. A very high unemployment rate has forced many Irish to leave the country to seek work. Under the EC's 1992 plan, a person from any EC member nation can freely seek employment in any other member nation.

The independent Republic of Ireland does not include the northern six counties. Northern Ireland, with a Protestant majority, remains part of the United Kingdom. Political violence linked to a long history of religious and social differences is widespread in Northern Ireland. The Protestants in Northern Ireland are mostly descendants of 17th- and 18th-century Scottish settlers who, supported by Britain, seized control of land owned by the Catholic Church. These transplanted Protestants have long been a powerful force in a country that has a long tradition of fervent Catholicism. The *Irish Republican Army (IRA),* a terrorist group, uses terror and violence against British troops in Northern Ireland and random acts of violence, mostly bombings, throughout Europe. The goal of the IRA is to include the northern six counties in a unified Irish Republic.

Some nations who do not belong to the EC belong to the *European Free Trade Association* (EFTA), which was established in 1959. The original members included Austria, Denmark, Norway, Portugal, Sweden, Switzerland and the United Kingdom. For various reasons, these Western European nations were opposed to joining the EC. Three of these nations — Denmark, Portugal and the United Kingdom eventually became members of the EC. The EFTA presently has six members with the addition of Iceland and Finland.

Upheaval in Eastern Europe

Dramatic events inspired and influenced by a number of factors occurred throughout Eastern Europe during 1989. Gorbachev's program for domestic reform in the Soviet Union brought popular demands for similar changes in other nations in Eastern Europe. The images from modern mass media and the influence of Western popular culture encouraged a desire for some of the material comforts and human rights enjoyed in the West. As protests against the old authoritarian regimes grew, Gorbachev made it clear that the Soviet military would not intervene as in 1956 and 1968.

The governments in Czechoslovakia, East Germany, Bulgaria and Romania were oppressive regimes with powerful Communist-party leaders opposed to reforms Gorbachev was introducing in the Soviet Union. Hungary and Poland were firmly under Communist-party rule, but were adapting to new economic and popular demands as opposition

AP/Wide World

East and West Berliners gather at the Brandenburg Gate to celebrate the opening of the Berlin Wall.

groups and dissidents gradually gained political influence. As Hungary and Poland slowly allowed more individual freedom, the hard-line regimes tightened their control over the people.

In January 1989, while Hungary was granting human rights, Czechoslovakia was arresting those protesting for human rights. In February, Solidarity was officially recognized and began negotiations with the Polish government; Hungary legalized independent political parties; and Václav Haval, Czechoslovakia's dissident playwright, was sentenced to prison. In June, while Romanians continued to suffer under the ruthless tyrant Nicolae Ceauşescu, Solidarity candidates were overwhelmingly victorious in Poland's first free elections since World War II. In August, Solidarity's Tadeusz Mazowiecki became Poland's prime minister in a peaceful and democratic transfer of power; Czechoslovakian police arrested hundreds of protesters recognizing the 21st anniversary of the 1968 Soviet invasion. In September, Hungary allowed free passage across its border with Austria to thousands of East Germans escaping to the West. In October, over 100,000 East Germans in Leipzig protested for freedom; the harsh rule of East German leader Erich Honecker came to an end; Hungary was proclaimed a free republic; police still battled demonstrators in Czechoslovakia.

On November 9, the concrete symbol of the Cold War which separated Germans for almost 30 years, the Berlin Wall, was knocked down as thousands of East Germans streamed into West Berlin where they were jubilantly welcomed by the West Germans. Many Berliners celebrated by using sledgehammers to attack the wall. The next day, Todor Zhivkov, Bulgaria's oppressive ruler for 35

years, was ousted. In late November, over 200,000 demonstrators in Prague demanded and received the resignations of Czechoslovakia's hard-line Communist-party leaders. One month later Václav Haval, the country's leading dissident, became president of Czechoslovakia.

In December, thousands of Romanian protesters were murdered by the *Securitate,* Ceauşescu's feared secret police. The Romanian military joined forces with the demonstrators and overthrew the government. Ceausescu and his wife were captured while attempting to flee the country. On Christmas Day, the Ceausescus were executed by the provisional government.

At year's end, Communist-party rule was over in Eastern Europe. The people of Eastern Europe prepared for free elections and a multi-party political system. The Iron Curtain was lifting. The Cold War was ending.

German reunification

With the collapse of the East German authoritarian government and the opening of the border between East and West Germany, the question of German reunification arose. Germany had been divided for 45 years, and both East and West Germany were excited about the prospect of a reunited German nation. East Germans flocked to the West and were amazed at the material wealth and availability of consumer items. Thousands of East Germans, lured by lucrative job offers and a high standard of living, immediately planned to settle permanently in West Germany. Most, however, expressed a cautious optimism for a better future where they lived and preferred to remain in East Germany. An overwhelming majority of East and West Germans looked forward to reunification.

In March 1990, East Germans voted for the first time in a multi-party election for representatives to a national parliament. The main issue was the direction to be taken toward unification. The vote would decide if East Germans desired the cautious approach to unity preferred by the Social Democrats or immediate currency union and a speedy process of full unification by 1991, as promised by the Christian

Democrats and West Germany's Christian Democrat chancellor, Helmut Kohl. With promises that they could cash in almost worthless *ostmarks* for the highly valued West German *deutschemarks,* the East Germans voiced their preference for a speedy conversion to a market economy and unification with economically powerful West Germany.

The end of the Cold War

Following a June 1990 summit meeting in Washington, D.C., with President Bush, Soviet President Mikhail Gorbachev addressed an audience of college students in San Francisco:

> In our cooperation to build a better future, I would take as a point of departure the fact that the Cold War is now behind us. And let us not wrangle over who won the Cold War. There can be no winners in the Cold War, just like in a nuclear war.

Earlier in the week, Presidents Bush and Gorbachev signed arms control and trade agreements that set the stage for further disarmament and better relations between the two countries. But the superpower leaders could not agree on important issues concerning the future of Europe.

The United States insisted that a reunified Germany must be part of the NATO alliance, with the Soviet Union allowed to maintain military forces in East Germany. Gorbachev declared that the cold-war alliance system in Europe is outdated, and European cooperation must replace confrontation. He said that an alliance encompassing all of Europe which relies on international accord rather than tanks and missiles is necessary to keep the peace in Europe. Gorbachev also stated that in the post-cold-war world, the principle of alliance-building "should mean unity to create conditions for a life worthy of a human being — protect the environment, combat hunger, diseases, drug addiction and ignorance."

People in various Soviet republics, especially the Baltic states — Estonia, Latvia and Lithuania — demonstrated for independence from the Soviet Union and to form their own nations. Ethnic groups in other Soviet republics turned to violence. In addition to ethnic unrest, the Soviet Union also faces another serious problem: a shortage of consumer goods.

Gorbachev spoke of new priorities for the world. He said it was the universal problems of hunger, disease, ignorance, pollution and drug abuse that need to be addressed. He expressed his belief in the necessity to dismantle the massive military forces built up during the Cold War. The cost of the Cold War was high. The two "superpower" nations neglected many of the needs of their people in order to allocate resources to building armies and constructing weapons. At the end of the Cold War, both the United States and the Soviet Union had enormous debts.

The environment of many nations in the world has been polluted. In the 1990s, the environment became a major issue.

U.S.-Soviet summit meetings have resulted in better relations between the two nations.

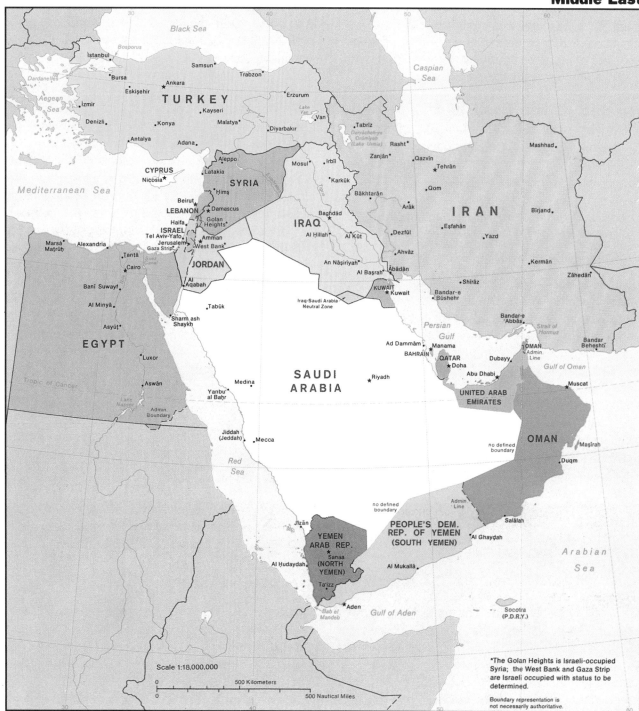

The World Factbook, 1989

Chapter 19

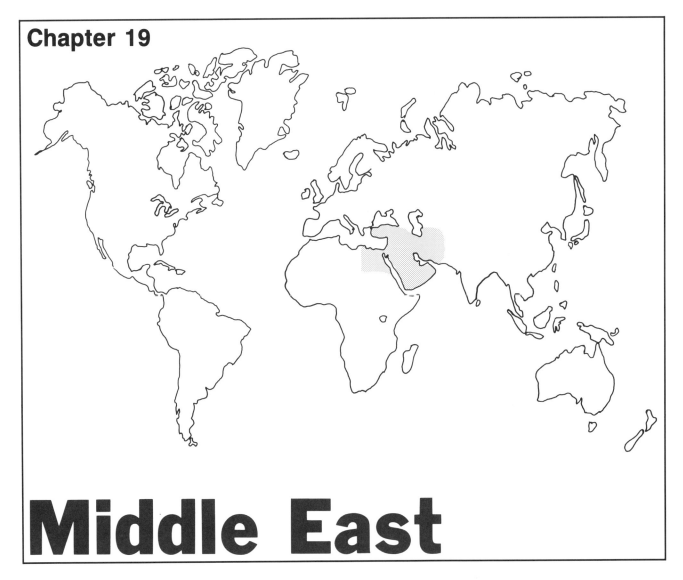

Middle East

The Middle East is a bridge between Europe, Africa and Asia. It lies between the Mediterranean Sea and the Persian Gulf. The major countries of the Middle East are Egypt, Saudi Arabia, Israel, Jordan, Lebanon, Syria, Iraq, Iran, Oman, Yemen, Kuwait and Turkey. The countries of the Middle East, with over two-thirds of the world's petroleum reserves, have close trade connections with Europe, Japan and the United States. Since its lands are intimately associated with three of the world's great religions — Judaism, Christianity and Islam — these countries are holy territories to millions of people.

World War I resulted in the breakup of the Turkish Ottoman Empire, whose sovereignty had once extended over the whole eastern and southern Mediterranean shore. The lands east of the Mediterranean — Lebanon, Palestine and Syria — were lost by Turkey as a result of the war. Britain and France held mandates from the League of Nations to establish governments throughout the Middle East. Egypt was a British protectorate for 40 years (until 1922) and was strongly influenced by British policy after that, since the British had bases on Egyptian territory (most of them near the Suez Canal).

The British had permitted Iraq to become an independent kingdom in 1932 but retained a mandate over the territory comprising Palestine and Jordan. The two were divided, with greater autonomy given to what was then called Transjordan, while Palestine remained the only region in the Middle East whose status was uncertain.

Partitioning of Palestine

The movement for a Jewish homeland in Palestine is known as *Zionism*. This movement was founded in 1897 by Theodor Herzl, a journalist. On November 2, 1917, during World War I, Arthur Balfour, the British foreign secretary, pledged British aid to establish a ''homeland'' for Jews in Palestine. This became known as the *Balfour Declaration*.

Israel Government Tourist Office

Jerusalem — a holy land for three major religions: Islam (above), Christianity (below) and Judaism (opposite page).

Jews had lived in Palestine since biblical times. Arabs, Christians and other ethnic groups also lived there. Small numbers of Jews began immigrating to Palestine from other nations in the last part of the 19th century. The flow of Jewish immigrants increased during the early 1900s when Jewish persecution in eastern Europe, particularly in Russia, increased in frequency and severity. By 1938, over 500,000 Jews had migrated to Palestine. This immigration was resisted by the non-Jewish population in Palestine.

The horrors of World War II and the Holocaust in which six million European Jews were systematically and ruthlessly murdered in concentration camps, vividly dramatized the need for Jews to have a homeland. Jews had suffered prejudice and persecution, but never before had there been an attempt to completely eradicate them. European Jews who survived the Holocaust were convinced that, in order to survive as a people, they had to have a Jewish state. The homeless Jewish refugees were not readily welcomed to other countries.

Soon after World War II ended, fighting broke out between Arabs and Jews in Palestine. The British, who lost men as well as prestige in their attempts to maintain order, referred the problem to the United Nations in February 1947.

It was a difficult issue. There was strong support for a plan to enable Jews to migrate to their biblical homeland. On the other hand, Palestine's sizable population of non-Jews strongly objected to the influx of large numbers of immigrants. The Arabs wanted a unified Palestine which they would control, but it was proposed in the UN that Palestine be partitioned into Jewish and Arab areas.

U.S. government officials were divided on the issue. Many did not want to alienate the oil-rich Arab states, but President Truman backed partition.

The Soviet Union also supported partition, although it had initially sided with the Arabs. With this backing, the UN General Assembly voted on November 29, 1947, to recommend the division of Palestine.

The founding of Israel

Britain announced its withdrawal from Palestine on May 14, 1948, and the state of Israel was proclaimed on that same day, receiving immediate recognition from the United States and the Soviet Union. The United States also promised aid to the new nation.

Meanwhile, the neighboring Arab states — Egypt, Lebanon, Iraq, Saudi Arabia, Syria, Jordan and Yemen — had formed an *Arab League* and were determined to occupy all of what had been Palestine. Five of the Arab countries invaded Israel a few hours after the proclamation of its independence. Jordan occupied Old Jerusalem and the West Bank of the Jordan River, and Egypt took a strip leading to the city of Gaza. Israeli troops were able to turn back

Israel Government Tourist Office

the Arab invaders and, when the war ended, the Israelis were in possession of a territory almost 50 percent larger than had been provided by the original UN grant.

Armistice agreements between Israel and the neighboring Arab states (Jordan, Lebanon, Syria and Egypt) were signed in 1949, but the dispute continued. The Arab states did not want to recognize any Jewish nation in Palestine; they were, in effect, fighting the UN decision to partition. They also refused to accept an independent Arab government outside of Israel — that is, in the Arab sector of what had been Palestine. Some 600,000 non-Jewish Palestinians had fled to Arab territories. These Palestinians mingled to some degree in the economies and societies of the Arab states, but many remained in camps, supported largely by the UN. The refugees' fate became a key issue in the ensuing conflicts between Israel and the Arab states.

Israel established a stable and workable democracy headed by a moderate labor party, while most of the Arab countries remained kingdoms. As Israel began to grow in population and industrial strength, the Arab people, largely dependent on either traditional pastoral economies or on newer, inequitably distributed oil-produced wealth, became restless under their conservative governments.

Egypt under Nasser

Egypt was the first Arab country to develop a modern style of government. The Egyptian government that took shape was a combination of authoritarianism, Islam and socialism. Egypt's government changed in 1952, when a group of army officers, still chafing at their defeat by the Israelis, ousted King Farouk and put General Mohammed Naguib in power. The real force behind the Egyptian revolt, however, was Colonel Gamal Abdel Nasser who became president in 1954 and soon became the dominant figure in the Arab League.

A primary goal of the new Egyptian government was to acquire the Suez Canal, built in the 1860s across an Egyptian isthmus. Construction of the canal had been backed by a French corporation which eventually was taken over by the British. The canal provided Britain a major link with its Asian empire. In effect, Britain ruled Egypt throughout the two world wars, fighting to keep the canal open to its ships.

After World War II, the Egyptians demanded a British military withdrawl. The United States supported the Egyptian position, but stipulated that the British were to have access to the canal when strategically necessary. This compromise was ac-

cepted by Britain and Egypt in 1954, and the United States gave a grant of $40 million to Egypt. This was followed by a promise of U.S. support for a loan of $200 million from the World Bank to build the Aswan Dam — a project intended to increase Egyptian farmlands through irrigation of the desert.

Soon after, Nasser announced he was obtaining arms from Czechoslovakia. The United States abruptly canceled its offer of financial assistance, claiming that the Aswan Dam project was not economically sound. It was generally believed, however, that Secretary of State Dulles feared a growing communist influence in Cairo.

Israel Government Tourist Office
The Wailing Wall, a place of reverence for Jews, is believed to be a remnant of the temple of Solomon.

Dispute over the Suez Canal

During the years from 1949 to 1956, the Arab nations enforced an economic boycott of Israel and did not allow Israeli ships to pass through the Suez Canal. Egypt allowed Arab guerrillas to operate from Egyptian land to attack Israel. In 1955, Egypt negotiated to buy arms from communist nations. In 1956, fearing the military build-up in Egypt, Israel invaded and quickly defeated Nasser's armies and overran the Sinai peninsula. Britain and France, in order to control the Suez Canal, also attacked Egypt.

The United Nations condemned the actions of Israel, England and France and stationed a peace-keeping force in Egypt on the Israeli border.

Closed for eight years due to the Arab-Israeli wars of 1967 and 1973, the Suez Canal was reopened in 1975. Today, traffic through the 103-mile-long canal is brisk as it is used by more than 20,000 vessels a year. The canal is a boost to Egypt's economy, but other countries benefit as well. The United States, Western Europe, the Soviet Union, Israel, and the oil-rich states of the Persian Gulf all use the canal. Ships from over 100 nations pass through this waterway every year, travelling between the Mediterranean Sea and the Indian Ocean.

Revolution in Iraq

In the wake of Nasser's seizure of power, revolutionary impulses spread throughout the Arab world. Iraq, although a strong supporter of the Arab cause against Israel, pursued a conservative policy under King Faisal II. This included membership in the *Baghdad Pact*, an anti-Soviet group that became known as the **Central Treaty Organization**, one of many defense treaties around the world which is backed by the United States. In July, 1958, King Faisal and his prime minister were killed in a military uprising. There were several subsequent outbreaks of violence in Iraqi politics, but a military government prevailed.

Although the Arab states have generally taken the same position on the issue of Israel, they have differed in many other ways. Attempts at closer association among Arab-League members never lasted long.

Nevertheless, the resolution of the Israeli question has persisted as a common Arab goal. After the Suez crisis, the Palestinians began to take a more active role in events, using propaganda and terrorist tactics and forming organizations to pursue their national aims. *Al Fatah* is the largest of the many Palestinian guerrilla groups; its leader, Yassir Arafat, has long been head of its umbrella organization, the **Palestine Liberation Organization** (PLO). The PLO, founded in 1964, has been officially recognized by the United Nations and the Arab states.

The Six-Day War

In 1967, hostilities between Israel and the Arab states again came to a head. Nasser closed the Suez Canal to Israeli trade, blocked the Tiran Straits (the only direct water route from the Red Sea to Israel), and ordered the UN peace-keeping force out of the area, removing the barrier between the Israeli and Arab armed forces. Threatened by these events, Israel attacked.

It took the Israeli army and air force only six days to defeat the surrounding Arab armies. They took Egypt's Sinai Peninsula, from the Red Sea to the Suez canal, Jordan's West Bank (including the old city of Jerusalem) and Syrian land along the Golan Heights.

The Israeli army astonished the world with its speed and efficiency during the *Six-Day War*. But the war was followed by a long period of stalemate. Although a truce was arranged, it merely served to reinforce the existing fighting fronts. There were acts of terror and reprisal for years to come.

UN Resolution 242

The United Nations Security Council made an effort to settle the problem when, on November 22, 1967, it unanimously adopted a resolution setting up principles for a Middle-East peace. *UN Resolution 242* demanded Israeli withdrawal from occupied territory; called for the acknowledgment of the sovereignty, territorial integrity and political independence of all states within the region; asserted the right of all of its people to live at peace "within secure and recognized boundaries." Calls for free navigation of regional waterways and a just settlement of the refugee problem were included as well.

As is true of most statements of principle, Resolution 242 was open to contradictory interpretations. What are "secure" boundaries, when planes and missiles can fly over strategic topographical lines (such as mountains and rivers)? Many Arabs persisted in their belief that Israel should be incorporated into a Palestinian state. What would be a "just" solution of the refugee question? By this time, there had been, in effect, a population exchange in the Middle East: Palestinians had left Palestine to live in surrounding countries (many more fled during the Six-Day War), while Jews from nearly all of the Arab states had migrated — generally under pressure — to Israel. Would it simply be a question of restoring the exiled Palestinians to their homes in Israel or as the partition plan intended — creating a separate Palestinian state?

The PLO wanted all of the territory originally mandated to Palestine. Its warlike efforts to achieve this aim, launched from neighboring nations, brought Israeli reprisals.

The Yom Kippur War

The United States made efforts to start negotiations for a settlement on the basis of Resolution 242, but there was a prolonged stalemate, interspersed with sporadic violence. Nasser died in 1970, and his successor, Anwar Sadat, seemed at first to be carrying out Nasser's policies. Egypt joined with

Syria in a joint attack on Israel in October 1973. The attack, which came on the Jewish holiday of Yom Kippur, caught the Israelis by surprise. Although a truce was established by the joint efforts of the United States and the Soviet Union before any major strategic changes occurred, and although the Israeli army rallied quickly and effectively, Arab military prestige (which had suffered in the wars since 1948) was improved. It was hoped this would make peace possible.

Arab oil embargo

One result of the Yom Kippur War of 1973 was an energy crisis that affected the whole world. It began in a limited way with an embargo by Arab oil states on petroleum exports to the United States and the Netherlands because of their friendship with Israel.

Iraq was among the first to develop its petroleum reserves. Saudi Arabia, having the largest oil supply in the group, became a major producer after World War II. These nations, with a group of small Arab sheikdoms along the Red Sea and the Persian Gulf — Kuwait, the United Arab Emirates, Oman and Yemen — form the heart of the traditional Arab oil empire. Libya and Algeria are also major petroleum producers. Politically, the countries are divided. Saudi Arabia and most of the sheikdoms are conservative, and relations between the United States and Saudi Arabia remain good. Iraq, Libya and Algeria are socialist, with friendly ties to the Soviet Union.

Despite their political differences, the *Organization of Petroleum Exporting Countries* (OPEC) agreed on the 1973 embargo. Non-Arab producers of petroleum, including Iran (Moslem but not Arab), Indonesia, Venezuela and Nigeria, also belong to OPEC. This group rallied around the Arabs — not for political reasons to pressure the friends of Israel — but to raise their oil prices. As a result, crude oil prices rose fivefold in two years, causing inflation around the world.

The United States was hurt by the embargo. Although it is one of the world's major oil producers, it uses so much petroleum that it must import large amounts. The U.S. response to higher oil prices was to reduce its oil consumption. Plants, businesses and homeowners reduced fuel use through stringent conservation measures. In 1975, U.S. autos averaged about 16 miles per gallon of gas; by the mid-1980s, this figure was up to almost 30 miles per gallon.

OPEC flows into hard times

The price of oil, like that of other natural resources, fluctuates widely. Even international cartels such as OPEC are not always powerful enough to overcome world market forces. High prices encourage exploration and development of new oil fields. World oil prices rose sharply during the 1970s but began to fall in the 1980s as new reserves were found. From $3 a barrel in 1973, prices soared to $39 a barrel in 1981; then the trend reversed. A worldwide recession between 1981 and 1983 drove prices down to below $30 a barrel. Oil prices remained relatively low throughout the 1980s.

OPEC attempted to counter the oil surplus by lowering world prices with fundamental cartel measures. It set floor prices, but occasionally a member would break from the group and set its price even lower in order to capture new sales. OPEC also attempted to reduce crude-oil production in order to maintain or increase the market price. From 1977 to 1979, OPEC nations were producing over 30 million barrels of oil per day. By 1983, the cartel's daily output had fallen to below 20 million barrels.

The oil bonanza to Saudi Arabia, Iran, Iraq, Kuwait and other Mideastern countries, as well as

At a demonstration in Beirut, a Shiite Moslem boy points a toy pistol at dummy representing the United States. The protesters oppose U.S. support for Israel.

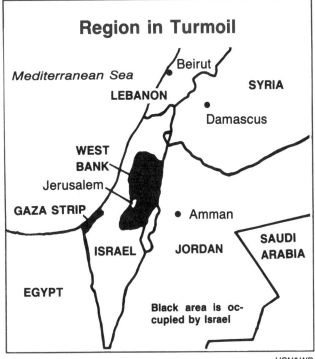

Region in Turmoil

Mediterranean Sea

Beirut
LEBANON
SYRIA
Damascus
WEST BANK
Jerusalem
GAZA STRIP
ISRAEL
JORDAN
Amman
SAUDI ARABIA
EGYPT

Black area is occupied by Israel

to Mexico, Venezuela, Libya and Nigeria, brought mixed results. Some of the energy-rich countries used the gush of oil revenues to finance industrial and public-works projects, acquiring huge loans from foreign banks on the strength of future oil income to help finance them. With the drop in oil revenues, some of the oil-rich nations were forced to reduce their development budgets, extend repayment schedules and reduce imports. They found themselves overwhelmingly in debt.

Egypt-Israeli peace efforts

In September 1975, Israel and its opponents reached an agreement to station their troops apart from each other, thereby reducing the threat of minor clashes. Israel agreed to withdraw from much of the Sinai; a buffer zone was set up between Israelis and Egyptians, and observation posts were staffed by civilian Americans. This was a definite step forward, but Egypt's President Sadat was to take an even longer stride.

Sadat moved sharply away from the Soviet Union, with whom Nasser had concluded a 50-year defense treaty in the year of his death. Sadat expelled Soviet technicians and military advisers from Egypt in 1972 and turned toward the West and the more moderate countries of the Arab League. It was important that Sadat achieve peace, because Egypt was suffering serious economic problems — despite aid from oil-rich Saudi Arabia and the United States.

In 1977, Sadat took the extraordinary step of going to Jerusalem to address the Israeli legislature, the *Knesset*. Since one of the major obstacles to

peace was the Arab states' refusal to recognize Israel, Sadat's move was an important one. It was soon reciprocated by a visit to Cairo from Menachem Begin, the Israeli prime minister.

Although the United States did its utmost to extract practical results for peace from these events, their outcome seemed to be another, even more intractable stalemate. The so-called "rejectionist" Arab states — Syria, Iraq, Libya and Algeria — joined together to pressure Egypt into ending negotiations with Israel. Begin, who led a conservative government into office in 1977, ending the Labor coalition that had governed Israel since its founding, refused to consider the occupied West Bank as a part of Palestine or Jordan. He referred to it, in historic terms, as Judea and Samaria (parts of Biblical Israel) and pursued a policy of establishing Israeli settlements in the occupied lands.

Israel regarded the Palestine Liberation Organization as a terrorist group without valid claim to sovereignty. Begin offered autonomy to the occupied lands but stipulated that Israeli military occupation had to continue for at least five years following the signing of a treaty. Sadat called for a complete Israeli withdrawal from all lands seized in 1967. The United States advocated Israeli withdrawal but suggested that some changes be made to provide a more secure boundary for Israel, as well as some kind of "homeland" for the displaced Palestinians.

The outlook for a separate treaty between Israel and Egypt seemed dim. The situation remained deadlocked — until Begin and Sadat met with President Carter, in September 1978, at Camp David, Maryland. At the conclusion of the Camp David "summit," these three men electrified the world by announcing their agreement on a "framework for peace" in the Middle East. Still, rising hopes were tempered by the certainty that the Begin-Sadat agreement would face stiff opposition in the Arab world.

In the *Camp David Accord*, Israel agreed to withdraw from the entire Sinai peninsula within three years. Palestinians living in the occupied West Bank and the Gaza Strip would gain self-rule after establishing a framework for elections, and Israeli troops would gradually withdraw from the area. Diplomatic, economic and cultural relations were established between Israel and Egypt, and the movement of goods and persons opened up between the two countries.

Israel was guaranteed free passage through the Suez Canal, the Gulf of Suez, the Strait of Tiran and the Gulf of Aqaba. The United States also guaranteed Israel a 15-year oil supply, and a road was planned across Israel's Negev Desert to connect the Sinai with Jordan.

Jimmy Carter brought together Israeli Prime Minister Menachem Begin and Egyptian President Anwar Sadat at Camp David (1978) in an effort to work out an agreement in the Middle East. The summit was a success because it initiated better relations between Egypt and Israel.

Israel's withdrawal from the Sinai proceeded. Most of the Sinai was demilitarized, with UN peace-keeping forces patrolling the strip that extended along the Israeli border. The truce between Israel and the other Arab countries remained on shaky ground.

In 1981, Sadat was assassinated by Islamic fundamentalists who resented his tilt toward Israel and the West. He was succeeded by his vice president, Hosni Mubarak, who has maintained close relations with the United States, but Egyptian relations with Israel have seriously declined. Mubarak restored diplomatic links with the Arab nations that condemned Egypt for recognizing Israel.

Lebanese war

Meanwhile, other problems plagued the Middle East. Lebanon, which was divided between Maronite Christians and Moslems, and had some 400,000 Palestinians within its borders as well, was hit by political violence in 1975. Part of the conflict sprang from Christian Rightist opposition to the Palestinian guerrillas who, by launching terrorist attacks on Israel, had brought reprisal attacks on Lebanon. Violence also stemmed from the old question of

balancing power between the Christians and the Moslems. Syria, which had long wanted to include Lebanon in a Greater Syria, assisted the Lebanese government in trying to work out a solution. The *Arab Deterrent Force*, a chiefly Syrian organization, went into Lebanon in 1976.

It seemed that a constitutional solution would be worked out, but border squabbles brought Israeli aid to the Christians and, later, an invasion of southern Lebanon. A United Nations peace-keeping force moved in and the Israelis withdrew, but battles broke out between Christian militiamen and the Syrians.

Driven from Jordan in 1970, Yassir Arafat had established PLO bases south of Beirut in Lebanon, forming, in effect, a state within a state. From there, the PLO launched attacks on Israel. The Israelis retaliated. Syria, which surrounds Lebanon on the north and west, periodically came to the aid of the PLO.

Terrorist attacks against Israel continued. In April 1982, Israel invaded Lebanon and quickly advanced northward along the Mediterranean coast and entered the Lebanese capital of Beirut, which was devastated. The PLO was in imminent danger of annihilation by Israeli forces and their Christian Phalange allies. The Beirut civilian population was caught in the crossfire and suffered heavy casualties. A truce was negotiated between the PLO and Israel, with U.S. assistance, which permitted PLO forces to vacate Beirut by sea to Libya, and by land to Syria. Once the PLO evacuated, Christian Philangists, supported by Israel and Syria, massacred hundreds in two Palestinian refugee camps. The

Kurdish child who died following a chemical weapons attack by Iraq's military on the town of Halabja, Iraq.

massacre was in retaliation for the assassination of Lebanese president-elect Bashir Gemayel.

American, French and Italian personnel were part of the multinational UN peace-keeping forces brought in to maintain the truce. In 1984, after months of terrorist attacks, the UN forces evacuated Lebanon.

Violence and disorder continued in Lebanon throughout the 1980s. Various opposing factions and nations prevented a peaceful solution to the end of the chaos. Two Christian armies fought each other for control of Lebanon's Christians. Fundamentalist Shiite Moslems, supported by Iran, hoped to establish an Islamic republic in Lebanon. Various opposing Moslem factions added to the violence. Syria, with a strong military presence, continued to encourage the chaos, hoping to ultimately annex Lebanon as part of their long term goal towards a ''Greater Syria.''

Terrorist groups, including many who held American and European hostages for years, operated out of Beirut. The hostage takers were members of the Iranian and Syrian-supported Party of God — Shiite Moslems whose aim is to establish traditional Islamic republics throughout the Middle East.

The overthrow of the Shah of Iran

For nearly four decades, Shah Mohammed Reza Pahlavi headed the military dictatorship that ruled Iran. Under the Shah, Iran became a major oil supplier to the United States and to other industrialized nations. In return, the Shah placed large orders for sophisticated aircraft, warships and other equipment manufactured in the United States. The Shah at-

tempted to modernize his country with American support, and a mutually supportive relationship developed between U.S. business, banking, and government interests and Iran.

The Shah's rule was unpopular with a large proportion of Iran's 35 million people — members of the Moslem Shiite religious sect. The royal family led an extravagant life, misappropriated funds and oppressed the Iranian people. The Shah's critics say that he embezzled billions of dollars during his reign and tortured, maimed or killed thousands of Iranians who opposed his leadership. In 1979, led by the exiled Ayatollah Khomeini, spiritual leader of the Shiite sect, the Shah was overthrown. Khomeini established a fundamentalist Islamic government.

In the wake of the Shah's downfall, and blaming the U.S. for his long reign, the new regime took 52 Americans hostage, mostly embassy employees. For 444 days, they were imprisoned in the capital city of Teheran until negotiations finally brought them home. Khomeini's government abolished the Shah's westernization programs and established traditional Islamic values. Many of those who opposed the new government were tortured and murdered.

Khomeini's death in 1989 brought Speaker of the Parliament Ali Akbar Hashemi Rafsanjani to power. As president, Rafsanjani infuriated Khomeini's followers when he used his influence to get Shiite Moslem terrorists in Lebanon to release American hostages in 1990. After 10 years of economic decline under Khomeini, Rafsanjani hoped to establish goodwill with the West as the collapsing economy, rather than Islamic purity, became the new Iranian ruler's priority.

Iran-Iraq War

In 1980, Iraq's President Saddem Hussein attacked Iran in an attempt to control the Shatt al Arab River and other disputed territory. Jordan's King Hussein rushed aid to Iraq; Saudi Arabia and the tiny Persian Gulf States gave Iraq their backing as well. Syria and Libya, however, threw their support to Iran, charging that Iraq and Jordan were weakening the Arab campaign against the Arabs' arch-enemy Israel. Egypt stood aloof from these issues.

In 1982, Iran turned the tables and attacked Iraq. The Ayatollah Khomeini, in a bold attempt, tried to oust the regime of President Saddem Hussein and spread Iran's brand of Islam throughout the Middle East. The Iranian government's stated goal was to march through Iraq and join forces with Syria to wage a holy war against Israel.

The war escalated in the mid-1980s, causing much damage to cities and oil installations in both countries. A cease-fire was declared in August 1988. More than 1 million people were killed in the eight-year war. Iraq spent over $50 billion on military equipment for the war — four times more than Iran — and, near the end of the war, developed long-range missiles. Iraq was also working toward the development of nuclear weapons as it sought military parity with Israel.

Iraqi President Saddam Hussein was ruthless in dealing with political opposition. In March 1988, Hussein ordered the use of poisonous gas against Kurds in the town of Halabja near the Iranian border. Over 5,000 Kurds, an Iraqi ethnic group opposed to Hussein's regime, were massacred. Chemical weapons were used against Kurds in other Iraqi towns, forcing over 100,000 Kurds to flee the country.

The *intifada*

In December 1987, a Palestinian uprising called the *intifada,* began a long period of violence in Israeli-occupied territory. A new generation of Palestinians battled Israeli soldiers and Jewish settlers in Gaza and the West Bank (annexed by Israel in 1967) where thousands of Palestinians live under Israeli rule. The outburst of violence was a renewal of Arab demands for the establishment of a Palestinian state within Israel's borders. The uprising consisted of mostly young Palestinians hurling rocks at armed Israeli soldiers and Jewish residents in the occupied territories. Palestinians strongly oppose new Jewish settlements in the occupied territories where Palestinians hope to establish their homeland.

The *intifada* brought new demands from the Arab nations for a peaceful settlement to the question of Palestinian statehood. The United States agreed to mediate a peace plan between the Palestine Liberation Organization and Israel. In 1990, peace negotiations were stalled with the Israeli government's two major political parties split over a plan for a peaceful settlement. A right-wing coalition government in Israel, led by Prime Minister Yitzhak Shamir, was formed in June 1990. The new government favored Jewish settlements in the occupied territories and opposed negotiations with the PLO. Tensions grew throughout the Middle East as the Arab nations denounced the new Israeli government.

Tensions escalate throughout the Middle East

An Arab summit meeting convened in Baghdad, Iraq, in 1990, to protest the influx of Soviet Jews to Israel. Many Middle Eastern nations were concerned that Arab-Israeli tensions would increase if Israel allowed Soviet Jews, emigrating in large numbers, to settle in the occupied territories.

The Arab nations are troubled by a lack of unity within the Arab world. President Hafez Assad of Syria, Hussein's arch-rival, refused to attend the summit. Syria's long-term ambitions in the Middle East — to expand its borders to include Lebanon, Israel and Jordon — conflict with the policies of other Middle Eastern nations.

Moderate Arabs, led by Egypt's President Hosni Mubarak — America's strongest ally in the region — appealed for a peaceful solution to the Arab-Israeli conflict. The hard-line Arab nations rallied around Iraq's Hussein and his anti-Israel, anti-American position. Iraq's growing military strength has given Hussein status as the Arab leader most willing to confront Israel.

An economic recession throughout the Middle East has forced many nations, including Syria and Iran, to tone down their anti-American position. Many Arab nations oppose the strong commitment of the United States to Israel. Yet, as economic problems increased in the Middle East, many nations sought Western support.

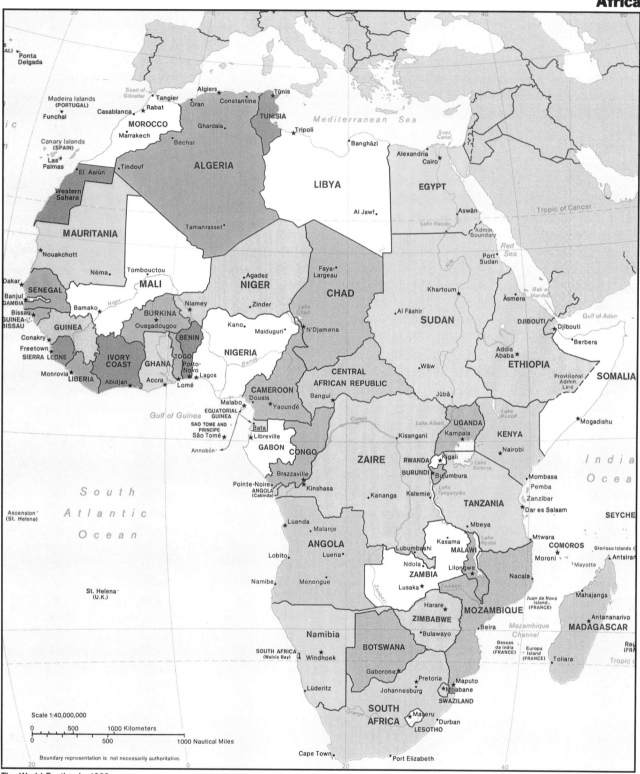

Scale 1:40,000,000

| 0 | 500 | 1000 Kilometers |
| 0 | 500 | 1000 Nautical Miles |

Boundary representation is not necessarily authoritative.

The World Factbook, 1989

134

Chapter 20

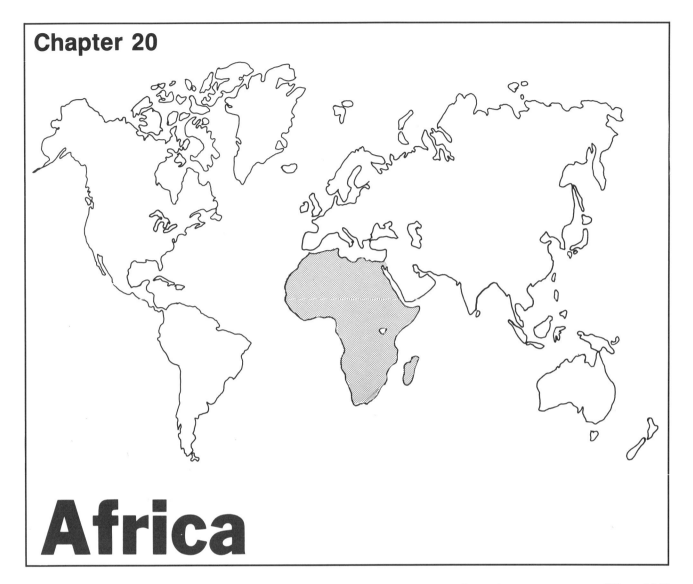

Africa

A continent rich in natural resources, Africa is home to many of the world's poorest people. Africa possesses the world's largest deposits of gold and diamonds but is plagued by famine, drought, illiteracy, political violence and pervasive poverty. Africa is made up of over a thousand ethnic groups — with as many religions and languages.

The late 19th century marked the beginning of a new age of European imperialism — expansion through the acquisition of new territory. From 1885-1900, the African continent, with the exception of Liberia and Ethiopia, was divided among the leading industrial nations of Europe. The African interior was attractive to European nations because of its abundance of resources. Many African tribal chiefs, not accustomed to the notion of land ownership, unwittingly signed away the rights to their land for a few trinkets. The people of the African interior possessed a rich cultural history but were unfamiliar with the ways of modern industrial societies.

Africans did not have the same concept of "wealth" as Europeans, so they did not think of gold and other resources as having a special value.

The colonial occupation of Africa lasted less than a century. The competition for economic and political control of Africa was a factor leading to World War I. When the power of the European nations was weakened following World War II, the colonial empires began to fall apart. In the two decades after World War II, most African colonies became independent nations with boundaries corresponding to the colonial divisions that were established by the former imperialist nations. A centuries-long tradition of tribal loyalties has inhibited the development of stable governments.

Economic development has also been hindered by inadequate transportation, communication and educational facilities. A high population growth rate and low per-capita income are other difficulties new African nations face.

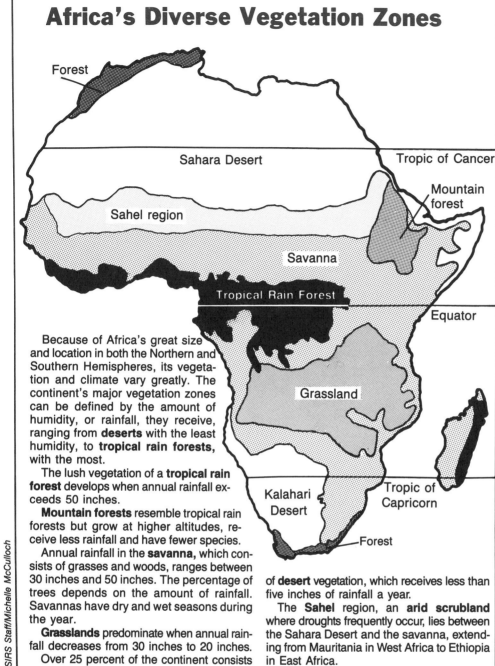

Africa's Diverse Vegetation Zones

Forest

Sahara Desert

Tropic of Cancer

Sahel region

Mountain forest

Savanna

Tropical Rain Forest

Equator

Grassland

Kalahari Desert

Tropic of Capricorn

Forest

Because of Africa's great size and location in both the Northern and Southern Hemispheres, its vegetation and climate vary greatly. The continent's major vegetation zones can be defined by the amount of humidity, or rainfall, they receive, ranging from **deserts** with the least humidity, to **tropical rain forests**, with the most.

The lush vegetation of a **tropical rain forest** develops when annual rainfall exceeds 50 inches.

Mountain forests resemble tropical rain forests but grow at higher altitudes, receive less rainfall and have fewer species.

Annual rainfall in the **savanna,** which consists of grasses and woods, ranges between 30 inches and 50 inches. The percentage of trees depends on the amount of rainfall. Savannas have dry and wet seasons during the year.

Grasslands predominate when annual rainfall decreases from 30 inches to 20 inches.

Over 25 percent of the continent consists

of **desert** vegetation, which receives less than five inches of rainfall a year.

The **Sahel** region, an **arid scrubland** where droughts frequently occur, lies between the Sahara Desert and the savanna, extending from Mauritania in West Africa to Ethiopia in East Africa.

SIRS Staff/Michelle McCulloch

Africa, the second largest continent, is an area of great diversity, with about 15 percent of the world's population. The Sahara, the largest desert in the world, covers the northern one-quarter of Africa. Most of the African population is engaged in subsistence farming. In the last 20 years, it has become a net importer of food.

The vast expanse of Africa, which straddles the equator, is covered by desert, savanna and tropical forest. A wide spectrum of wildlife, vegetation, climate, topography, culture and history exists on the continent.

Historical background

Anthropologists believe that the human species originated in Africa. From there, people fanned out to the Mediterranean coast and into Europe and Asia. It was relatively late, about 500 A.D., that people in the heartland of Africa emerged from a primitive, prehistoric state and began forming societies.

In the next thousand years, the Africans formed a number of rich and varied cultures. By the 1500s, tribal states flourished throughout south, central and western Africa. Often having a common language, individual tribes banded loosely together to form nations.

The Africans were largely agrarian or pastoral. They produced tools and weapons from iron and bronze. Artwork was created from metals, wood and ivory. Through contact with Arabian merchants, they learned to value gold and collected it to trade.

In the mid-15th century, a Portuguese fleet anchored off the coast of West Africa, and the continent entered a new period of its history. The Europeans had arrived. By the 17th century, the British, French and Dutch had joined the Portuguese in trading with African tribes.

Europeans came to the coasts of Africa in search of gold and ivory, but developments across the Atlantic produced a dramatic and radical change. The Caribbean islands and southern colonies in North America promised to become increasingly profitable producers of tropical crops — coffee, sugar, cotton, tobacco — while South and Central America were emerging as key mining areas. There was a demand for cheap, submissive labor to work the plantations and mines. Slave labor fit the bill, and human beings became the chief source of revenue for African traders.

For 300 years, until the early 1800s, the slave trade was the almost exclusive appeal of Africa to Westerners. Before slavery was abolished, some 10 million Africans were shipped to the New World. The slave trade was so lucrative that few other African goods were exported. Slave traders operated primarily along the coasts. Few forays were made into the interior. The heartland of Africa was considered mysterious, forbidding territory. Africa was called the "Dark Continent" because of its vast, unknown interior.

The advance of the imperialists

In the mid-19th century, courageous missionaries and a scattering of adventurers began exploring Africa's interior. Developments in transportation and breakthroughs in medicine to combat tropical disease were making Africa more accessible. Within decades, routes were charted to all parts of the continent. Increasingly, Africa was considered a source of raw materials and a marketplace for the commodities coming out of the industrial revolution then occurring in Europe.

In 1830, France invaded Algeria, beginning a long, costly occupation that lasted for 130 years. In the late 1830s, the Boers (Dutch farmers) established new colonies in South Africa. This was a prelude to the great wave of expansionism that swept over Africa half a century later.

By the late 19th century, imperialism and nationalism were dominant themes in European politics. Empires were needed to fuel industry. National pride depended on maintaining colonies. In 1882, England occupied Egypt. Fearing a British take-over in Africa, other Western powers rushed to establish colonies. In the ensuing scramble, almost the entire continent came under European control. Twenty years after the British arrival in Egypt, only the ancient state of Ethiopia and Liberia, a colony of freed slaves from the Americas, remained autonomous.

As a result of Germany's defeat in World War I, its colonies were divided between England and France. Ethiopia was conquered by Italy under Mussolini in the 1930s. Once established, the other colonies remained intact until the end of World War II.

Decolonization

Colonial empires began to disintegrate after World War II when the European powers became too weak to resist a rising tide of nationalism and clamors for independence. Decolonization became an important force in world politics. In some cases, the process was peaceful. Britain began a policy of gradually

divesting itself of its overseas possessions. Some African nations, notably Algeria, gained independence through warfare. By 1975, all the European nations had withdrawn from Africa. When the European governors left, a vacuum was created in Africa. In many nations, bitter struggles broke out to determine who would rule.

Nigeria achieved independence peacefully, but within a decade two military coups and a violent civil war rocked the country. The abrupt departure of the Belgians from the Congo threw that region into turmoil. A protracted guerrilla war raged between various factions in what is now Zaire.

Powerful and sometimes fanatic strong men gained power in some African nations. General Idi Amin seized control of the Ugandan government in 1972, deposing another military despot. Amin is reported to have executed as many as 300,000 of his enemies before he was overthrown in 1979 and exiled.

In the mid-1970s, communist governments became actively involved in African affairs. Cuban troops, backed by Soviet aid, helped install a Marxist regime in Angola. In 1978, the Soviets supported the Angolans in an attack on southeastern Zaire. French and Belgian paratroopers rushed to aid the Zaire government to discourage further communist advances.

Struggling to survive since their independence, many African nations assumed a nonaligned or "Third World" position. Banding together as a political bloc, Third World nations in Africa, Asia and Latin America have become a significant force in the United Nations.

Organization of African Unity

In May 1963, at a conference in Addis Ababa, Ethiopia, Emperor Haile Selassie called on his fellow African leaders to form "a single African organization through which Africa's single voice may be heard, within which Africa's problems may be studied and resolved." The resulting *Organization of African Unity* (OAU), a confederation of newly liberated countries, was designed to resolve conflicts among African nations and unify African power in the world arena. Virtually all African nations are represented in the OAU. Only Morocco and the Republic of South Africa are not members.

The OAU charter pledges members to "coordinate and harmonize general policies," promote African unity and progress, and eradicate all forms of colonialism in Africa. It further requires each member to refrain from interfering in the affairs of others and to respect one another's territorial integrity.

The OAU makes no provision for enforcing its decisions; it seeks unity through consensus. But almost 30 years after its inception, the OAU has only partially fulfilled its promise. Its major achievement was to end colonial rule. Other goals have proved more elusive: the settlement of intra-African disputes and keeping the continent free of superpower confrontation. South African apartheid has been the focus of OAU anger, but the organization has generally failed to condemn member countries for documented human rights abuses.

In 1988, the OAU sponsored an international conference on refugees and displaced persons in Southern Africa. Otherwise it has been unable to deal with the refugee issue. Another pressing problem is economic. Africa's external debt in 1987 was estimated in excess of $200 billion, and the OAU has called for restructuring that debt. Few member nations can feed themselves, much less pay their dues to the organization. The organization itself has a debt of many millions of dollars.

World Bank Photo by Ray Witlin
Aerial view of a typical African village in the Bobo-Dioulasso area.

Southern African Development Coordination Conference (SADCC)

In 1979, nine nations of Southern Africa formed SADCC. It was an attempt to reduce their economic dependence on South Africa for rail and air links, port facilities, raw material and manufactured goods, and the supply of electric power. By 1989, approximately half of the $6 billion in financing required for SADCC projects had been secured from sources including the World Bank. Rather than creating a central agency, the nine sector co-ordination agencies have been allocated to different nations.

Nations liberated from the British Empire

The British occupied Egypt in 1882, and their influence gradually spread down the east coast of Africa to include the lands of Sudan, Uganda and Kenya. The British Empire grew again following Germany's defeat in World War I. Germany's possessions in southwestern and eastern Africa were divided between England and France.

In southern and central Africa, Cecil Rhodes, an industrialist and statesman, provided the main impetus for British colonization. Amassing a fortune in diamonds from the lands that today comprise South Africa, Rhodes built railroads and public works in British South Africa and Rhodesia.

Exhausted by World War II, Britain began to divest itself of colonies. Most British colonies in Africa achieved their independence between 1956 and 1966, becoming part of the British Commonwealth, as nations like Canada, Australia and India had done before. One of the great legacies of British colonial policy was the practice of training indigenous peoples for service in the governmental bureaucracy. As nations gained independence, a cadre of trained individuals was available to carry on the essential functions of civil government.

Three former British colonies at the southern tip of the continent — South Africa, Zimbabwe and Namibia — have occupied a prominent place in world news during recent years due to their internal struggles to overthrow the last vestiges of white political domination. Further north, Kenya has remained a model of interracial harmony in the post-colonial era.

Republic of South Africa

The settlement of South Africa dates to 1652, when the Dutch East India Company established a port at the Cape of Good Hope to control the sea route to India and the East Indies. The company soon brought settlers from Holland, and the colony prospered. In the 19th century, the British moved in and took over the Cape Colony, and in 1836, the Boers (as the Dutch farmers were called) left for the interior in an extraordinary national migration known as the Great Trek. They formed two states: the Transvaal and the Orange Free State in the vast *veldt,* or tableland, which covers most of the region. The Vortrekkers went their own way, somewhat like American pioneers, a Bible in one hand and a rifle in the other, asserting their dominion over the black inhabitants, whom they called the Bantu.

Friction developed between the Boers and the British to the south, erupting in the Boer War in 1899. At first, the Boers held their own, but eventually they succumbed to superior British power and were absorbed into a new country called the Union of South Africa. In 1961, the South African government, dominated by fiercely nationalistic Afrikaners (the modern name for Boers), broke away from the British Commonwealth to form the Republic of South Africa. In 1990, the population was over 35 million: Fewer than 20 percent are white; the rest are blacks or people of mixed race called "coloreds." The Republic also has a large Asian population. Cape Town remains the legislative capital, but Pretoria is the seat of administrative government. Johannesburg is the nation's largest city and business center.

South Africa has a sophisticated economy, tradi-

UN Photo 155272/Allan Tannenbaum

Most black South Africans live in poor areas such as this shantytown in Capetown.

S.A. Tourism Board

The natural beauty of Africa surrounds the modern city.

AP/ WIDE WORLD PHOTOS

Historic meeting between South African President F.W. De Klerk and African National Congress (ANC) leader Nelson Mandela.

tionally based on gold and diamond mining. Recently it has diversified into other mineral production, as well as industrial manufacturing and agriculture. Its economy is on a par with those of the industrialized West, and its armed forces are by far the strongest and best-equipped in Africa. It is denounced by the black African states, yet their economies cannot survive without South African resources. Their railroad equipment, for example, is repaired in South African shops, and their exports and imports are shipped by South African companies. Thousands of blacks from other African countries work for South African employers, particularly in the mines.

In 1948, the National Party came to power. *Apartheid,* which guarantees complete separation of the races and white political and economic domination, was written into the constitution. Until recently this policy was sanctioned by the Dutch Reformed Church. (Sixty-five percent of the whites in South Africa are Afrikaans-speaking descendants of the Boers.) Racial incidents multiplied within the country, despite harsh government measures which attempt to keep black and white communities separate. By the 1960s, the government had banned numerous opposition organizations such as the *African National Congress* (ANC). Many black resistance leaders, including Nelson Mandela, were imprisoned.

In the 1970s, the government began to abandon ''petty apartheid'' regulations which separated the races in most social situations. A new constitution adopted in 1983 created a tricameral legislature with

one house for whites, one for ''coloreds,'' and another for Asians — but blacks continued to be excluded from South African political life. This sharing of power, even though limited, insured continued white control through veto power over the actions of the ''coloreds'' and Asians. A number of whites formed an opposition Conservative Party which challenged even limited change in racial policies.

Throughout the 1980s, people in many nations expressed outrage against South Africa's policy of apartheid. Opponents of apartheid appealed to governments, universities and businesses to apply economic sanctions by withdrawing investments from South Africa. Boycotts of companies with business interests in South Africa were organized. In many instances, white South African athletes were banned from international sports competitions.

Black South Africans demonstrated for their freedom. International pressure mounted for the release of Nelson Mandela — by now a legendary symbol of resistance to South African oppression. In 1990, with the support from a majority of white South Africans, South African President F.W. De Klerk agreed to release Mandela and repeal the ban against anti-apartheid groups, including the ANC. A long-imposed state of emergency was lifted, and proposals were made to include blacks in the political process.

Nelson Mandela embarked on a world tour in June 1990. Everywhere Mandela spoke, he was greeted with large, enthusiastic crowds. His commitment to human rights left a lasting impression on millions of people. Stating, ''I still have no vote,'' Mandela appealed for the continuation of economic sanctions against South Africa until all South Africans obtain equal rights. This will not be easy to accomplish, because many of the white minority feel that their property and lives will be threatened if the black majority gains control of the government.

Zimbabwe

Today, only South Africa remains under control of a white minority. South Africa and Rhodesia broke away from the Commonwealth in the 1960s after pressure from London to make concessions to blacks and abandon apartheid. Rhodesia later gave ground, but not enough to satisfy black aspirations. Guerrilla armies backed by the Soviet Union and China waged a war of national liberation between 1972 and 1979. Ultimately, Britain negotiated a peace settlement between white settlers and the black majority. The Lancaster House Conference in London drew up a constitution for a new nation, Zimbabwe, which reserved seats for the white minority in a new parliament, guaranteed citizenship rights and placed restrictions on major constitutional changes for a decade.

Zimbabwe was declared an independent state on April 18, 1980. Although the initial stance of the new government headed by Robert Mugabe was conciliatory toward whites and was hailed as a model of interracial cooperation, it has become increasingly repressive. Whites have lost their reserved seats in the legislative bodies, while the government has been rocked by corruption scandals. Those who question Mugabe's rule are branded dissidents, and factional strife has led to bloodshed. In the 1990 general election, Mugabe's party won an overwhelming victory but fell short of absolute control in the parliament which he needed to create a one-party state. Moreover, either as a form of political protest or through intimidation, only 54 percent of the people cast ballots. By contrast, in the 1980 and 1985 elections, over 90 percent of the electorate participated. Thus, the political stability of Zimbabwe remains precariously balanced.

Zimbabwe has an abundance of natural resources, a well-developed infrastructure and a diversified industrial sector. Its agriculture is highly productive — principal crops are tobacco, peanuts, corn, sugar and tea. In addition to chrome ore, mineral resources include gold, coal, asbestos and iron ore. Leading trading partners are South Africa and the United Kingdom. As with other newly-independent nations, Zimbabwe is preoccupied with land redistribution and restabilization of the economy.

Namibia

Namibia, originally the German colony of South-West Africa, remained a trust territory of South Africa for 75 years. In the 1960s, the United Nations voided the South African trusteeship and passed a resolution in the 1970s calling for Namibian independence. A nationalist movement, *South-West Africa People's Organization* (SWAPO), launched a war for independence. The territory became more famous in name than in substance, for it served as a rallying point for anticolonialist African opinion. Namibia is mostly desert and is inhabited by over 1 million people.

In 1979, South Africa allowed a UN mission to organize elections in the territory, and an interim government was formed which included blacks, whites and persons of mixed color. The election was boycotted by SWAPO, and the guerrilla activities intensified. In 1982, the South African government extended the interim regime for another year and announced its willingness to settle the political future of Namibia — but only after Angola removed the estimated 50,000 Cubans and Eastern Europeans whom it had harbored on the territory's border. The United States supported South Africa's position, but Angola and other African states rejected this or any other South African precondition to withdrawal, and the situation remained stalemated.

By 1989, political conditions in Africa were radically altered. The United States assisted in negotiating a settlement by which the Cuban troops in Angola would be phased out over several years, and South Africa would retain control over a strategic enclave at Walvis Bay on the Namibian coast. This cleared the way for UN-supervised elections in the territory. Following peaceful balloting in which SWAPO and other political parties participated, a constitution was written, and a parliament based on proportional representation was elected. Namibia became an independent nation on March 21, 1990.

Kenya

The East African republic of Kenya is regarded as the exemplar of a former British colony. Thousands of British farmers remained there and continued to prosper after Kenya's independence. The capital, Nairobi, has an elegant tourist atmosphere. Kenya has a good climate, big game animals and a stable government. This attracts tourists and investors from Western Europe and the United States.

Kenya was heavily colonized by British settlers in the decades following World War I because of the agreeable climate and living conditions in the so-called White Highlands, where coffee and tobacco were profitably grown. The eruption of Mau Mau terrorism in the early 1950s, as members of the Kikuyu tribe laid claim to the White Highlands, was speedily put down. With the restoration of order came the opening of negotiations with Kenyan nationalists. Jomo Kenyatta, who had been imprisoned as an alleged Mau Mau leader, was released. In December 1963, following a free election, Kenya became independent with Kenyatta as president. The British funded a "buying out" scheme to help resettle Africans on lands formerly farmed by whites.

A member of the British Commonwealth, the nation has received valuable development aid from the West, yet its people continue to face problems common to other African countries: a shortage of arable land and a limited base for export earnings. More recently, the rapid demise of the country's wildlife, particularly elephant herds due to ivory poaching, has focused world attention on Kenya.

Egypt

Egypt, a former British colony, is part of the continent of Africa but is more involved with the activities of the Middle East than with Africa, and politically is considered a Middle East nation. However, during the 1950s and '60s, Egypt provided sanctuary for the liberation movement leaders from many African states. Recently, Egyptian President Hosni Mubarek served as head of the OAU.

Nigeria

Nigeria is the most populous state on the African continent. It also ranks as a major petroleum producer. Although it has been independent since 1960, the country is an agglomeration of dozens of tribes, some of whom live uneasily together. In 1967, a major revolt took place among the Ibos of the east. Their objective was to set up a separate state of Biafra. A bloody and costly civil war ensued, which drew attention and sympathy throughout the world, much of it on the Biafran side. Nevertheless, the central government succeeded in holding the country together.

Ghana

Ghana, once known as the Gold Coast, was a source of turbulence during the early years of independence when its leader, the colorful but enigmatic Kwame Nkrumah, typified African leadership. After Ghana achieved its independence in 1957, Nkrumah set himself up as the head of a pan-African movement, fostering unity schemes among the countries of West Africa. Baffled by his lack of support from the West, he turned to Moscow and Beijing for sympathy, instituting totalitarian rule in his own country. While on a trip to these communist capitals in 1966, he was overthrown by a military coup and retired to exile in Guinea where he died several years later. Ghana has since been run by a series of military, or paramilitary, governments.

Malawi

Malawi is a long strip of a country that runs south between Lake Malawi, formerly Lake Nyasa, on the east and Zambia on the west. A former British protectorate (Nyasaland), it became independent in 1964 and has since been governed by its president for life, Dr. Hastings Banda. The Banda government has followed a moderate path internationally, but has aroused some animosity among other African states for continuing diplomatic relations with South Africa.

Sierra Leone

Sierra Leone lies on the west coast of Africa between Guinea to the north and Liberia to the south. It was originally founded in the 1700s as a home for liberated black slaves who were resettled in

---

Africa's Resources

AREA: 11.7 million square miles — more than three times as big as U.S.

DIAMONDS — almost all of world's reserves
CHROMIUM — much of the world's reserves
COBALT — 90 percent
COCOA — 65 percent of world production
GOLD — half of world reserves
PLATINUM — 40 percent of reserves
URANIUM — nearly a quarter of world reserves
BAUXITE — more than a fourth
COFFEE — 25 percent of output
COPPER — 20 percent of world reserves
NATURAL GAS — 12 percent
PETROLEUM — 8 percent of world reserves

Freetown, now the capital. Since independence in 1967, the government of Sierra Leone has experienced continual turbulence, and the country is now ruled by an authoritarian presidential regime. The chief export is diamonds

Sudan

Sudan is an immense country centered on the upper valley of the Nile River. In 1953, Britain and Egypt granted self-government to the Sudan; independence followed a year later. The Sudan has had a military leader for most of its history as an independent nation. It's economy revolves around high-grade cotton, which is cultivated in irrigated districts along the Nile.

Tanzania

Tanzania is the former East African colony of Tanganyika. German before the First World War and then British, Tanganyika merged with the island sultanate of Zanzibar to become Tanzania. It is one of Africa's biggest countries. The capital is Dar es Salaam. Tanzania's chief exports are coffee, sisal and spices. Zanzibar's principal product is cloves. Tanzania borders on the continent's three largest lakes: Victoria, Tanganyika and Malawi (Nyasa). Tanzania has a socialist economy. Since independence in 1961, it has been ruled by the Revolutionary Party.

Uganda

Uganda is best-remembered for the bizarre

behavior of its former ruler, General Idi Amin. This landlocked country of central Africa was a British protectorate until 1961. General Amin, a former sergeant in the British army, came to power in 1972 and shortly thereafter declared himself president for life. He earned the scorn of the world and the mortal fear of Ugandans, through a capricious and bloodthirsty dictatorship in which he persecuted resident Asians, Israelis, Christians and foreigners in general, as well as Ugandans who belonged to different tribal backgrounds. Entebbe Airport in Uganda was the scene of a spectacular raid by Israeli commandos who freed 103 hostages from an airliner hijacked by Palestinian terrorists in 1976. Amin's reckless handling of the Ugandan treasury impoverished a thriving economy, whose biggest export is high-grade coffee. In 1979, Amin was driven from power and fled to Libya. After many years of instability, the country is currently ruled by a military government.

Zambia

Zambia is a copper-mining state in south central Africa just north of Zimbabwe. Zambia was known as Northern Rhodesia until it achieved independence from Britain in 1964. It has had only one president, Kenneth Kaunda. Zambia produces other minerals including cobalt, manganese, lead and zinc. Its principal agricultural crops are tobacco, peanuts and corn. Zambia has not always been able to profit by its mineral resources in the world market because of fluctuating prices and the difficulty of shipping them out to East African ports. The country played a leading role in harboring guerrilla fighters during the civil war in Rhodesia. It has been a sanctuary for the African National Congress leadership in recent years.

Nations liberated from the French Empire

French influence in Africa began and ended in North Africa. In 1830, the French seized Algeria, taking it from the Ottoman Empire. For 50 years, it remained the sole French possession in Africa.

Following the British acquisition of Egypt, France expanded its interest in the Sahara, and into central and western Africa. After World War I, France controlled the German colony of Cameroon in West Africa. The French empire remained intact in Africa until the mid-1950s.

Algeria

The decolonization of Algeria was one of the bloodiest sagas in the history of modern Africa. A vast desert territory with a prosperous, fertile, coastal strip, it was colonized by the French in 1830. Over the years, the French settlers grew to number more than 1 million, ruling over many times that number of Moslem Algerians. France was Algeria's exclusive trading partner, Algeria was legally a part of France, and the two countries were closely knit.

Suddenly, in November 1954, the standard of Algerian independence was raised. In spite of French attempts to suppress it, the National Liberation Front rapidly gained adherents. Fighting increased steadily, and Algiers and other major cities became theaters of constant guerrilla battles. Whether "French Algeria" should be abandoned became a political issue that was to tear France apart.

So high were the passions generated by this bloody war that the French government, the Fourth Republic, was itself threatened. Die-hard colonialists, Algerian revolutionaries and their French supporters battled in the council chamber, in the press and even in the streets of Paris. In 1958, General Charles de Gaulle, a national hero for his leadership of the French resistance in World War II, returned from retirement to deal with the Algerian crisis.

Through a series of maneuvers, using both persuasion and force, de Gaulle was able to bring France and the Algerian nationalist leaders to the conference table. Finally, in 1962, the last ties between the two countries were severed, and the Democratic and Popular Republic of Algeria was born. De Gaulle still had to ride out a powerful backlash from the settlers and sections of the French army which felt he had betrayed them. Peace was inevitable, however, and hundreds of thousands of *pied noirs,* as the French residents of Algeria were called, resettled grudgingly in France.

Since then, Algeria has progressed steadily in the construction of a national economy to replace the colonial one. Algeria has remained on superficially friendly terms with France, maintaining many old economic links. Moreover, tens of thousands of Algerians regularly find jobs in French industry, providing an important source of income for their families.

Algeria's most important asset has been the reserves of oil and natural gas that were first discovered and developed by the French. Exports of oil and gas to the United States, among others, have helped raise the low standard of living of the 20 million Algerians. But the country is still poor and must struggle to maintain the sophisticated social infrastructure created by the French.

Morocco

Morocco is one of the oldest states in Africa. It

a separatist movement in the Western Sahara has been seeking independent status. Morocco left the OAU after the organization granted recognition to the rebels.

Morocco's people are among the most traditional in the Islamic world, and Moslem customs are strictly observed. Morocco has both Mediterranean and Atlantic coastlines. Cultivation of market crops, especially citrus fruit, is a lucrative industry on the coastal plains. The country also possesses rich phosphate deposits near the snow-capped Atlas mountains and some iron and coal resources as well. Morocco's old Moorish cities, its deserts, its beaches and its ski slopes attract great numbers of tourists.

Tunisia

Tunisia is the heir of ancient Carthage, whose ruins lie near the capital of Tunis. Its land mass juts out from the North African coast across the Mediterranean from Sicily. Tunisia became a protectorate of France in 1883 and gained its independence in 1956 without marked turmoil.

UN Photo/John Isaac

Dead cows litter drought-stricken areas of Africa.

enjoyed centuries of territorial and national integrity as the home of the Arabs and Berbers, heirs of the Moors who once conquered Spain.

Interestingly, Morocco is the oldest ally of the United States, having concluded a treaty of friendship with the infant republic at the end of the 18th century. In more recent times, Morocco came under the influence of France and Spain which, in 1912, divided the country between them. Spain took the smaller portion across the Straits of Gibraltar as a colony, and France established a protectorate over the larger part, including the cities of Casablanca; Rabat, the capital; and Marrakech, the ancient Moorish city on the edge of the Sahara. In 1956, the protectorate and colony were terminated. France and Spain relinquished their rights of rule. King Hassan II came to the throne in 1961. Since 1976,

Tunisia's people, mostly Arab, with a small Berber minority, has an old and established Moslem culture. Its Mediterranean regions are fertile and productive, and its desert oases in the south generally flourish. It does not have the oil riches of either of its neighbors, Algeria or Libya. Like them, it is a member of the Arab world.

Benin

Benin is a narrow strip of densely populated territory running north from the Gulf of Guinea. Named after a West African kingdom of the 17th century, it was formerly the French colony of Dahomey. Since it became independent in 1960, Benin has been governed by a succession of military regimes.

Burkina Faso

Burkina Faso, originally known as Upper Volta, is

a medium-sized republic located in the sub-Saharan interior of West Africa. Its territory is largely savanna and desert, and its people engage mainly in livestock raising and subsistence agriculture. The country has been governed under a one-party system since 1966, and it retains important economic ties with France.

Cameroon

Cameroon lies in the corner of the Gulf of Guinea, but its strategic position was ignored by European imperialists until the 1880s, when Germany organized a colony there. After the First World War, the territory was divided between French and British mandates. France received by far the larger share, which became part of French Equatorial Africa. When independence came in 1960, the two parts of the country were reunited within its present borders. Cocoa, coffee and hardwood timber are the chief exports. France is the chief trading partner.

The Central African Republic

This land-locked nation received its independence from France in 1960. Agriculture is the main occupation of 85 percent of a population of over 2 million. The prevalence of the tsetse fly restricts animal husbandry throughout most of the country. There are rich deposits of diamonds and uranium. The government is relatively stable.

Chad

Chad, in north central Africa, takes its name from a lake on its western frontier with Niger and Nigeria. It is part of the sub-Saharan region which was struck by a disastrous drought in the 1970s and 1980s, in which thousands died. The government of Chad has been marked by violence and disorder. Cotton is the principal crop and export. Most of the country is a desert that supports only a grazing culture.

Côte d'Ivoire

Côte d'Ivoire was originally known as Ivory Coast and is one of the most successful small states in Africa. The country, mainly rain forest, is well endowed with resources, exporting coffee, cocoa, timber and some petroleum products. It faces the Gulf of Guinea and has been a historical center for European trade. The seaside capital of Abidjan is a modern city with skyscrapers and comfortable hotels which appeal to tourists and business travelers.

Gabon

Gabon, a small country lying along the equator has uniformly high temperatures, humidity and rainfall. Most of the country is covered with equitorial forests. The major exports are wood and minerals, especially manganese, and petroleum. The country has a one-party government.

Equatorial Guinea

Equatorial Guinea was created from the former Spanish island of Fernando Poo plus holdings on the mainland. In 1983, the country joined the union of Francophone African nations, and French is mandatory in its schools. The country receives large budgetary credits from France, which is its major trading partner. Equitorial Guinea is an authoritarian, one-party state.

Guinea

Guinea became independent in 1958. The new government, led by Sekou Toure until his death in 1984, set a course of "positive neutrality." Initially, it received economic support from the Soviet Union but later opened contacts with the West. Guinea has extensive reserves of bauxite and is therefore better off economically than most West African states. It also exports coffee and pineapples.

Madagascar

Madagascar, formerly known as the Malagasy Republic, and one of the world's largest islands, lies in the Indian Ocean off the coast of Mozambique. It is generally considered part of Africa although Malayan and even Polynesian influences have been historically strong. It has had a turbulent political history and is currently controlled by a military regime which labels itself socialist. In 1990, a coup attempt against the government failed. The population lives predominantly off the land, producing coffee, vanilla and cloves for exports, as well as some petroleum products. The forested interior is the home of many rare species of fauna and flora owing to the island's isolated geographical and geological past.

Mali

Mali, the former French Sudan, is a large country in the West African interior, lying south of the Sahara in the region called the Sahel. It is mostly savanna and semiarid steppe, but its capital occupies a fertile strip along the upper Niger River. The legendary city of Timbuktu lies in northern Mali. The country's people, mostly cattle-raising nomads, suffered greatly in the Sahel droughts of the 1970s and 1980s.

Niger

Niger is a former dependency of France in the sub-Saharan Sahel. Like its neighbors, it suffered from the drought that afflicted the region in the early 1970s, when a third of its people were near starvation. Food sent from abroad, half of it from the United States, helped to alleviate Niger's sufferings. The southwestern portion of the country, where the capital is located, is watered by the Niger River. The rest of the country is given over to the raising of cattle and sheep on the arid plains. Since it gained independence in 1960, Niger has undergone a series of swings between military and civilian governments.

Senegal

Senegal is strategically located on the outermost curve of Africa's west coast and has historically been an important trading post for European commerce. It is a relatively poor country, with somewhat sandy soil, producing little more than peanuts and fish products. It has some mineral resources in the form of phosphates. In 1982, Senegal and Gambia (a small, former British colony which became independent in 1965) joined together in a confederation known as Senegambia. Although they will remain separate nations, they plan to develop common policies on defense, foreign affairs, economic policy and trade.

The Congo

The Congo, officially known as The People's Republic of the Congo, became independent in 1960. The country produces a great variety of agricultural products and timber. In addition, it has considerable phosphate deposits, while substantial deposits of petroleum have been found offshore. France is the major supplier of aid and imports to the Congo and is its major business partner in the extraction of petroleum. In recent years, the Congo government has assumed a leading role in African affairs. In 1987, it helped secure a cease-fire between Chad and Libya. The following year it mediated negotiations among Angola, Cuba, South Africa and the U.S. which culminated in the *Brazzaville Accord*, regarding withdrawal of Cuban troops from Angola and the question of Namibian independence.

Togo

Togo is a small nation, formerly called French Togoland. Its major agricultural exports are coffee and cocoa. Calcium phosphate is mined commercially. Since 1967, the country has been ruled by a military government.

Nations liberated from the Portuguese Empire

Portugal was the first European nation to have made contact with sub-Saharan Africa and the last to leave. In the 16th century, Portuguese explorers charted the western coast of Africa and established trade with the native inhabitants. The region of Africa that is now Angola supplied slaves for the Portuguese mines in Brazil. On the east coast of Africa, a Portuguese colony was established in Mozambique.

Portugal resisted the trend of decolonization throughout the 1950s and 1960s. During this period, guerrilla groups sought to gain independence for Angola and Mozambique. Finally, in 1974, following a political *coup d'etat* in the mother country, Portugal yielded to increasing guerrilla pressure and abandoned its territories in Africa.

Angola

Angola lies on the west coast of Africa, south of the Congo River basin and north of Namibia. It was discovered by Portuguese navigators in 1482 and remained under Portuguese control until it achieved independence in 1975.

The Portuguese method of colonizing Angola was to assimilate the natives, encouraging Portuguese settlers to marry with them and form a colonial caste. With independence, most Portuguese colonists left — or were expelled. Angolan statehood came about as the result of a bloody inter-tribal war intensified by Marxist ideology, a conflict in which Cuban troops helped carry the Marxist side to victory.

The National Union for the Total Independence of Angola (UNITA) continued to wage a guerrilla war against the central government. UNITA received weapons and supplies from South Africa, which sent its forces into southern Angola twice during 1982 to attack camps from which black nationalists were launching raids into Namibia. With the independence of Namibia in 1990, UNITA could no longer be supplied easily by South Africa. Recently, Angolan government forces and Cuban troops inflicted heavy losses on the rebels, and the UNITA leader Jonas Savimbi entered into negotiations for a settlement of the 15-year war.

Angola's people live in an agriculturally rich country which, before the revolution, exported coffee, cotton, rice and timber, as well as some light industrial goods. Gold, diamonds and iron were also exported. An American oil company has been producing oil near the city of Cabinda in the north, and this has proved an important source of revenue. Economic conditions remain uncertain.

Mozambique

Mozambique was the most avowedly Marxist country in Africa. A Portuguese colony for over 400 years, it became independent in 1974 after a 10-year effort by Portugal to block its independence movement.

Mozambique's people live in a poor but large country that stretches along the Indian Ocean for 1,500 miles. Development of the interior has been slow although the Zambezi River provides access to it. Tropical products such as sugar, cotton, cashew nuts and hardwood timber are the principal exports. The economy has nearly been destroyed as the result of a protracted war with the Mozambique National Resistance (Renamo). Originally an anti-Marxist rebel army supported by South Africa, it is now a bandit group which has killed over 100,000 people and ravaged the country. The government of Mozambique has renounced Marxism, and the United States sends millions of dollars in economic aid to avert starvation in the nation.

Guinea-Bissau

This small former Portuguese enclave in West Africa received its independence in 1974.

Nations liberated from the Italian Empire

Italy became a force in Africa when it established a colony in Libya in 1911. The Italians also established a colony in southern Somalia, a small region bordering Ethiopia.

Earlier, in 1896, the Italians had attempted to seize Ethiopia but were badly beaten in the battle of Adowa. In 1936, as a prelude to World War II, Italian troops under the Fascist dictator Benito Mussolini again invaded Ethiopia. Despite fierce resistance by the Africans under the leadership of Emperor Haile Selassie, the mechanized Italian army easily occupied the entire country. Following Italy's defeat in World War II, Ethiopia, Libya and Somalia secured their independence.

Ethiopia

Ethiopia is the oldest state in black Africa, dating back in recorded history 2,000 years. It is a mountainous country, occupying the center of the East African horn, consisting of a central plateau cut by gorges which extends down to heavily forested lowlands and arid grasslands.

Ethiopia was a feudal empire throughout its history. For much of this century it was ruled by Emperor Haile Selassie, the ''Lion of Judah,'' who first won international fame by fighting Mussolini's invasion. Restored to the throne after World War II, Haile Selassie attempted to introduce moderate reforms, particularly in landownership. In 1974, at the age of 82, after more than 50 years in power, he was deposed by the army. The next year, following a military coup, he died a prisoner in his palace at Addis Ababa.

A revolutionary military council announced that it was creating a socialist state in Ethiopia and began to receive Soviet aid. At the same time, the United States terminated military aid it had been giving to Ethiopia since the end of World War II. This amounted to a reversal of superpower alliances in East Africa. A rebel movement against the central government is centered in the northern provinces of Eritrea and Tigre.

Ethiopia's people are a mixture of races and tribes, many of which are still bound to a primitive economy conditioned by subsistence agriculture. Crops include coffee, sugar, maize, wheat and millet. The land is fertile but rugged and intersected by mountain chains and valleys so that it resists organization. Gold, platinum, copper and iron are among the principal mineral resources, but they have not been exploited on a large scale. Ethiopia suffered greatly from drought conditions during the 1980s and received world famine relief.

Libya

Libya was part of the Ottoman Empire until 1912 when Italy claimed the territory, which it held until the end of World War II. Libya then became independent under a royal dynasty headed by King

World Vision Photo
Ethiopians, displaced by war and famine, awaiting relief at a refugee camp.

147

Idriss, who reigned peacefully until he was overthrown in 1961 by a group of army officers led by Colonel Muammar el Qadhafi. Qadhafi nationalized the rich Libyan oil fields, which produce millions of barrels of oil a day. Qadhafi has become an outcast in most of the international community for his support of terrorist groups.

Somalia

Somalia lies at the tip of the horn of Africa, with coasts on both the Red Sea and the Indian Ocean. It is a fusion of the old colonies of Italian Somaliland and British Somaliland, which joined together after World War II and achieved independence in 1960 as the Republic of Somalia. The president was assassinated in 1969, and the army took over the government, renaming the country the Somali Democratic Republic.

Somalia is an arid country which has been decimated by the prolonged drought conditions of that region. Its inhabitants are almost exclusively employed in raising livestock. Such exports as it has are related to livestock.

Nations liberated from the Belgian Empire

In 1877, the Welsh-American explorer H.M. Stanley, who had contracted his services to the Belgian government, penetrated the previously uncharted region of the Congo, and the colony of the Belgian Congo was established.

Following World War II, undercurrents of unrest spread throughout the region. Belgium resisted granting independence until 1960 when, quite abruptly, the Belgians pulled out of Africa. This sudden departure led to a long and bloody civil war among rival black factions in the Congo.

Zaire

Zaire is one of the biggest and richest countries in Africa — only Algeria and the Sudan have greater land area — and has the largest French-speaking population. Formerly the Belgian Congo, its rain forests, network of tropical rivers and storehouse of mineral wealth cover the western half of equatorial Africa. Copper is the mainstay of the Zaire economy.

Zaire became independent in 1960. In 1965, Colonel Joseph Mobutu (now known as Mobutu Sese Seko) became president and remained in power, largely through the support of the United States and other Western countries. Despite the country's mineral riches, which are produced and exported

under the supervision of European mining operators, the Zaire government has suffered from chronic debt owing to its corruption and inefficiency.

In 1977 and 1978, a marauding force from Angloa invaded Zaire and was driven back by French and Belgian troops who were airlifted with American support. In the late 1980s, President Mobutu took a leading role in negotiating a resolution of many conflicts in Southern Africa, especially reopening relations with the Republic of South Africa. Nevertheless, the Mobutu regime is under constant internal pressure from discontented tribes and problems of economic unrest.

Rwanda and Burundi

Rwanda and Burundi are two small, densely-populated states lying in the high, remote watersheds of the Nile and Congo rivers in south central Africa. Both nations are divided into two hostile tribes. Warfare between the tribes has led to bloodshed and turmoil. The two countries just manage to feed themselves and have little commerce or communication with the outside world.

African microstates

A number of countries in Africa, all relatively new and most possessing seats in the United Nations, are designated *microstates*. In general, a microstate is a country with a population of less than 2.5 million, a low per-capita income and a small gross national product. Most are dependent on one or two raw materials. A microstate is dependent on a more powerful neighbor, or protector, or a group of friendly states. Over 20 microstates exist in Africa.

Mauritania

Mauritania on the northwest coast of the continent can be classed as a microstate even though its boundaries encompass a vast uninhabited desert one-and-a-half times the size of Texas.

São Tomé e Principe

At the other end of the territorial scale is São Tomé e Principe, a group of minuscule islands occupying a total of 375 square miles off the west coast of Africa. Both Mauritania and São Tomé e Principe have seats in the United Nations and are recognized by the world community. Both occupy strategic geographic positions.

Liberia

Liberia was colonized by the American Colonization Society as a home for freed slaves from America. Most migrated between 1820 and 1865.

The first settlement was named Monrovia after President James Monroe. In 1847 Liberia declared its independence. The government has been controlled by descendants of the original settlers even though they are a small minority of the population. In 1990 civil war broke out with tribal forces opposing the government of President Samuel Doe. The conflict is generally between the elitist descendants of American slaves and native Liberians.

Lesotho, Botswana and Swaziland

Lesotho is a mountainous country landlocked within the Republic of South Africa. It was already an independent kingdom early in the 19th century. However, it sought, and received, status as a British protectorate to avoid being absorbed by the Boers of South Africa as they settled the interior of the region. The nation became independent of Britain in the 1960s, as did Botswana and Swaziland. All three are members of the British Commonwealth. They also belong to the Southern African Customs Union with South Africa and are economically dependent on the Pretoria government. Transkei, Venda and Bophuthatswana are ''African homelands'' created by South Africa in pursuit of its apartheid policy. Although South Africa claims these ''homelands'' are independent nations, they are not widely recognized as such.

African island nations

Several island nations lie in the Indian Ocean off the African continent: **Seychelles, The Comoros,** and **Mauritius. Cape Verde,** a former Portuguese colony, is located in the Atlantic 325 miles west of Senegal. The most recently created microstate was **Djibouti** in 1977. The importance of the microstates is that they are easily penetrated by outside powers who vie for their economic and political allegiance.

The threat of wildlife extinction

Various species of African wildlife are endangered.

Asian demand for rhinoceros horns, believed to be a cure for many health problems, has led to the near extinction of rhinos in Africa. Asians are willing to pay high prices for the horns. The lucrative ivory trade has considerably diminished the African elephant population. The mutilation of these large mammals outrages conservationists throughout the world, but the rewards for those involved in the il-

legal trade of rhinoceros horns and elephant tusks encourages more killings. Low wages and few employment opportunities lead many people to poaching. The risks are minimal because many governments do not punish offenders.

Big-game hunting by wealthy European and American tourists also contributes to the vanishing African wildlife. In order to stimulate tourism, many African nations have few hunting restrictions. Modern weapons and hunting from motorized vehicles have depleted large animal herds.

Habitat destruction is a more serious threat to wildlife than hunting and poaching. The displacement of so many Africans due to famine and war has forced them to develop new farmland. Recent droughts brought cattle raising to areas susceptible to desertification through overgrazing. A growing population means less land that has traditionally been the habitat of Africa's wildlife.

Because many African economies are so poor, governments allow development in areas that are ecologically sensitive in order to develop the resources. The destruction of rain forests means the threat of extinction for many species of plants and animals.

The unstable political situation in much of Africa hinders the prospect of effective conservation measures. When people are desperate for food and have little or no education, conservation has a low priority.

The AIDS epidemic

In some areas of central and eastern Africa, as much as 30 percent of the population (about 3 million people) is infected with AIDS. AIDS afflicts both men and women as well as children born to AIDS-infected mothers.

Preventing the spread of AIDS in Africa is difficult. Treatment for AIDS patients is expensive and usually not practical because of Africa's lack of medical facilities. An AIDS test alone costs more than the average African pays for annual health care. There is no cure for AIDS.

The World Health Organization has established AIDS education programs in every African country. However, widespread programs are expensive, and educational materials developed in the West are not suited to the particular characteristics of AIDS in Africa. Monogamy is emphasized as the best means of prevention. Many tribes practice polygamy with one man allowed to have more than one wife.

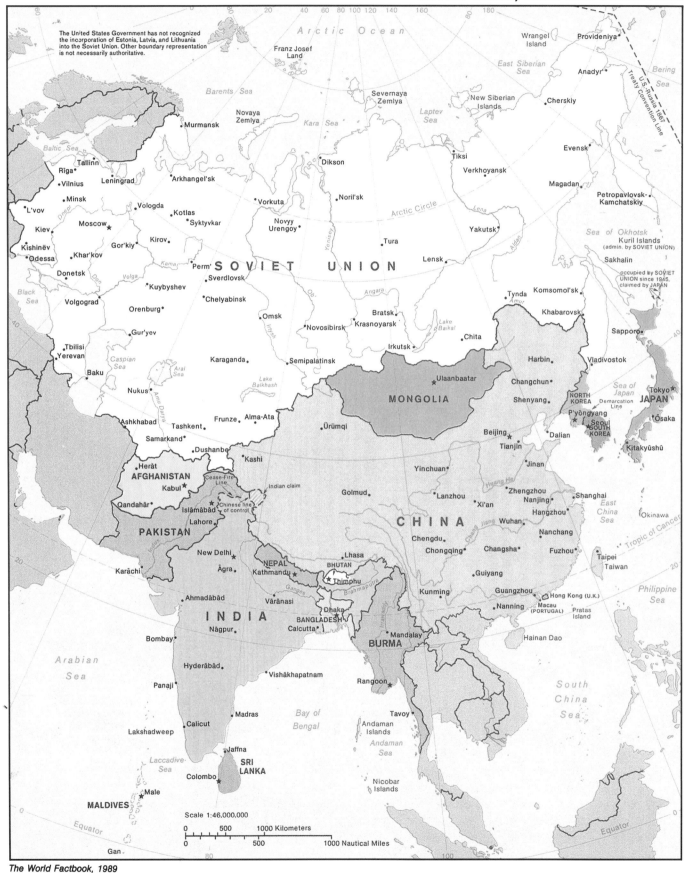

The United States Government has not recognized the incorporation of Estonia, Latvia, and Lithuania into the Soviet Union. Other boundary representation is not necessarily authoritative.

Arctic Ocean

Wrangel Island

Providéniya

Bering Sea

U.S.-Russia 1867 Treaty Convention Line

Anadyr

East Siberian Sea

Cherskiy

Franz Josef Land

Barents Sea

Severnaya Zemlya

New Siberian Islands

Novaya Zemlya

Laptev Sea

Evensk

Tiksi

Verkhoyansk

Magadan

Murmansk

Kara Sea

Dikson

Petropavlovsk-Kamchatskiy

Tallinn

Rīga

Vilnius

Leningrad

Arkhangel'sk

Vorkuta

Noril'sk

Arctic Circle

Yakutsk

Lena

Sea of Okhotsk

Kuril Islands (admin. by SOVIET UNION)

Sakhalin

occupied by SOVIET UNION since 1945, claimed by JAPAN

Minsk

Vologda

Kotlas

Syktyvkar

Novyy Urengoy

Tura

Lensk

Komsomol'sk

L'vov

Kiev

Moscow ★

Khar'kov

Gor'kiy

Kirov

Perm'

Sverdlovsk

S O V I E T   U N I O N

Angara

Tynda

Amur

Khabarovsk

Kishinëv

Odessa

Donetsk

Kuybyshev

Chelyabinsk

Ob'

Bratsk

Krasnoyarsk

Lake Baikal

Chita

Harbin

Sapporo

Vladivostok

Volgograd

Orenburg

Omsk

Novosibirsk

Irkutsk

Changchun

Sea of Japan

Tokyo ★

Gur'yev

Caspian Sea

Aral Sea

Lake Balkhash

Karaganda

Semipalatinsk

Ulaanbaatar ★

Shenyang

NORTH KOREA

Demarcation Line

JAPAN

Osaka

Tbilisi

Yerevan

Baku

MONGOLIA

P'yongyang

Seoul ★ SOUTH KOREA

Kitakyūshū

Nukus

Amu Darya

Frunze

Alma-Ata

Ürümqi

Beijing ★

Tianjin

Dalian

Ashkhabad

Tashkent

Samarkand

Dushanbe

Kashi

Yinchuan

Jinan

Herāt

AFGHANISTAN

Kabul ★

Cease-Fire Line

Indian claim

Golmud

Lanzhou

Xi'an

Zhengzhou

Nanjing

Shanghai

East China Sea

Okinawa

Qandahār

Islāmābād ★

Chinese line of control

Hangzhou

C H I N A

Nanchang

Fuzhou

Lahore

PAKISTAN

Chengdu

Chongqing

Changsha

Taipei

Taiwan

Tropic of Cancer

Karāchi

New Delhi ★

Āgra

NEPAL

Kathmandu ★

Lhasa

BHUTAN

★ Thimphu

Kunming

Guiyang

Guangzhou

Hong Kong (U.K.)

Nanning

Macau (PORTUGAL)

Pratas Island

Philippine Sea

Ahmadābād

I N D I A

Nāgpur

Vārānasi

Ganges

Dhaka

BANGLADESH

Calcutta

Brahmaputra

Mandalay

BURMA

Hainan Dao

Bombay

Hyderābād

Vishākhapatnam

Rangoon ★

South China Sea

Arabian Sea

Panaji

Madras

Bay of Bengal

Tavoy

Andaman Islands

Calicut

Lakshadweep

Andaman Sea

Jaffna

SRI LANKA

Colombo ★

Nicobar Islands

Laccadive Sea

Male ★

MALDIVES

Equator

Scale 1:46,000,000

0   500   1000 Kilometers

0   500   1000 Nautical Miles

Gan

Equator

The World Factbook, 1989

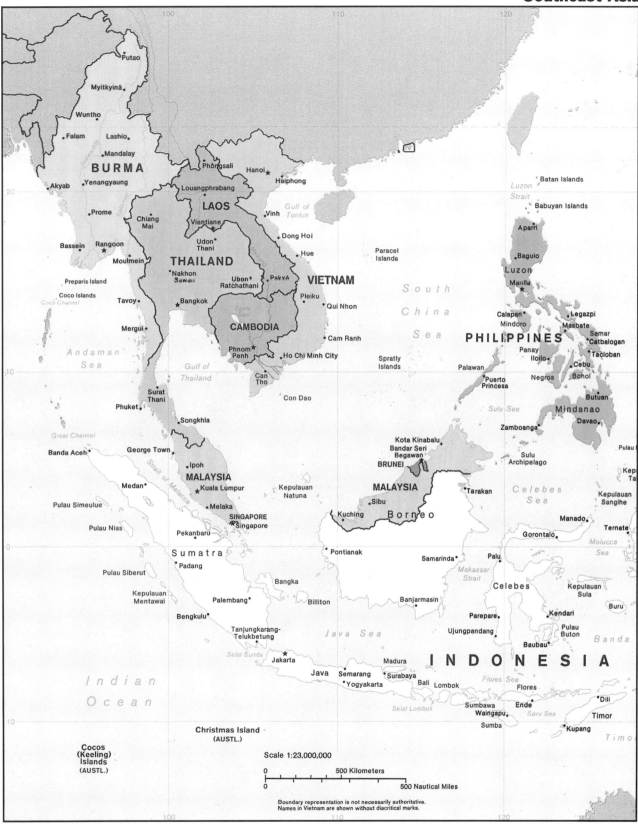

The World Factbook, 1989

The World Factbook, 1989

152

Chapter 21

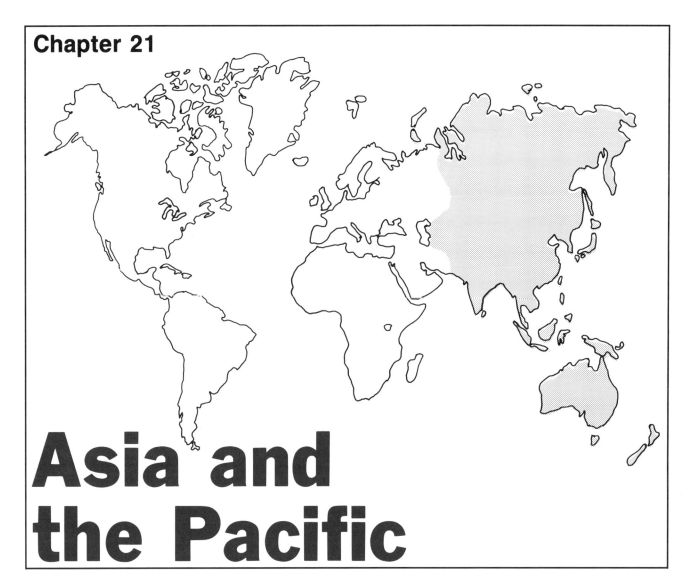

Asia and the Pacific

Great civilizations were developing in Asia at about the same time they developed in Europe. Little by little, over hundreds of years, Europeans became aware of Asia and developed interest in trading with that rich and exotic continent.

An Italian mechant, Marco Polo, traveled for 17 years throughout China in the 13th century. His wondrous tales aroused other Europeans to the delights of the Orient. There was silk and spices and other luxuries. Enormous profits could be made in trade between Europe and the Orient.

To reach Asia, European explorers sailed around the southern tip of Africa, a long and arduous trip, and established trading posts in the Far East. European nations competed for control of overseas colonies, as they did in the Americas and Africa.

By 1800, England had firmly established control of India — considered to be the jewel of the British Empire. Exploiting the military weakness of China, the major powers of Europe forced the Chinese to

open their ports to European ships. The European demand for Chinese luxuries created a unique problem for European merchants — there was almost no demand for European goods in China. The English offset this imbalance by supplying the Chinese with Indian-grown opium, prohibited in China but in high demand. This led to the Opium Wars between China and England. China's attempt to ban opium was met by British resistance and war ensued in 1840. The war resulted in the British acquisition of Hong Kong and the Kowloon peninsula.

Notorious "unequal treaties" of that period permitted several foreign powers, including the United States, to set up enclaves with their own courts and other attributes of sovereignty on Chinese soil. This humiliating arrangement lasted until after World War I. Preoccupations at home, where a vast hinterland remained to be developed, were probably a more important factor than any inherent virtue in inhibiting the United States from joining Japan and the Euro-

Courtesy U.S. Naval Academy

U.S. Navy Commodore Matthew Perry forces Japanese to open ports to foreign ships in 1854, thereby ending the island empire's two centuries of self-imposed isolation from the rest of the world.

pean nations in the scramble for additional territorial rights after the defeat of China in the Sino-Japanese War of 1895.

Japan ended its self-imposed isolation from the rest of the world in 1854 when the United States forced a reluctant *shogun* to open Japanese ports to foreign vessels.

The Japanese adopted Western industrial techniques, built a strong military and became a major power by 1900. During the 20th century, Japan competed with the United States and Europe in an attempt to control and profit from the resources of the Fear East.

American interest in Asia and the Pacific revived following the U.S. annexation of Hawaii in 1898 — the result of an American-led rebellion that overthrew the native monarchy and established a republic — and the acquisition of the Philippines and Guam during the Spanish-American War. Under the so-called *Open Door Policy,* Washington persuaded the other foreign powers in China to enter into an agree-

ment to respect each other's interests. Chinese resentment of the white intruders boiled over in 1900. A radical band calling itself the Righteous Harmonious Fists, a name that the foreigners translated into "Boxers," led a bloody uprising against the European colonialists.

Chinese nationhood

China entered a prolonged period of social and political reconstruction that encompassed two revolutions and is still going on today. The overthrow of the Manchu dynasty introduced the first republic under President Sun Yatsen in 1912. Educated in the West, Sun advocated China's adoption of a strong central government, Western political ideas and industrial development. He formed the Nationalist Party *(Kuomintang — KMT)* which, with Russian military help, eventually subdued the power of regional warlords seeking control of China. When Sun died in 1925, Chiang Kaishek succeeded him as leader of the Nationalist Party. Russian and Japanese incursions, the war against Japan, and the communist insurrection led by Mao Tsetung kept the country in turmoil for decades. The Nationalist government of President Chiang Kaishek was forced to retreat to Tawain in 1949. At that point, the intimate U.S. involvement in Chinese internal affairs, nurtured by military collaboration during World War II, abruptly ended on the mainland. The island of Taiwan, however, remained closely associated with the United States.

Antipathy toward foreigners, more than ideology, continued to be the principal bond uniting the Chinese people. The fraternal relationship established with the Soviet Union by the Chinese communists in the 1950s ran counter to the mainstream of history and survived for barely a decade before old antagonisms undercut this new and unnatural friendship. The departure of the Western powers left the Soviets as the only white colonialists on the Asian mainland.

World War II

The extension of American sovereignty over

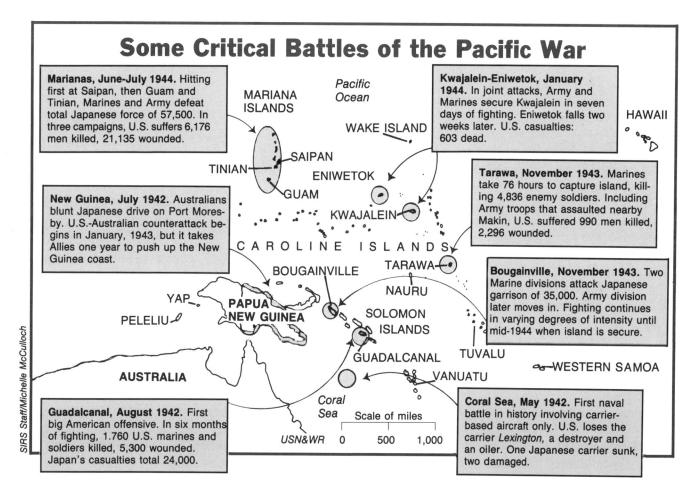

Some Critical Battles of the Pacific War

Marianas, June-July 1944. Hitting first at Saipan, then Guam and Tinian, Marines and Army defeat total Japanese force of 57,500. In three campaigns, U.S. suffers 6,176 men killed, 21,135 wounded.

Kwajalein-Eniwetok, January 1944. In joint attacks, Army and Marines secure Kwajalein in seven days of fighting. Eniwetok falls two weeks later. U.S. casualties: 603 dead.

New Guinea, July 1942. Australians blunt Japanese drive on Port Moresby. U.S.-Australian counterattack begins in January, 1943, but it takes Allies one year to push up the New Guinea coast.

Tarawa, November 1943. Marines take 76 hours to capture island, killing 4,836 enemy soldiers. Including Army troops that assaulted nearby Makin, U.S. suffered 990 men killed, 2,296 wounded.

Bougainville, November 1943. Two Marine divisions attack Japanese garrison of 35,000. Army division later moves in. Fighting continues in varying degrees of intensity until mid-1944 when island is secure.

Guadalcanal, August 1942. First big American offensive. In six months of fighting, 1.760 U.S. marines and soldiers killed, 5,300 wounded. Japan's casualties total 24,000.

Coral Sea, May 1942. First naval battle in history involving carrier-based aircraft only. U.S. loses the carrier *Lexington*, a destroyer and an oiler. One Japanese carrier sunk, two damaged.

Pacific Ocean — MARIANA ISLANDS — WAKE ISLAND — HAWAII — SAIPAN — TINIAN — ENIWETOK — GUAM — KWAJALEIN — CAROLINE ISLANDS — BOUGAINVILLE — YAP — PAPUA NEW GUINEA — PELELIU — TARAWA — NAURU — SOLOMON ISLANDS — GUADALCANAL — TUVALU — VANUATU — WESTERN SAMOA — AUSTRALIA — Coral Sea — Scale of miles — USN&WR 0 500 1,000

SIRS Staff/Michelle McCulloch

---

the Philippines between 1899 and July 4, 1946, when the islands became an independent republic, made the United States an Asian power. Air and naval bases on Luzon served as the westernmost line of American defense. American sailors and marines were familiar visitors in Chinese ports. The U.S. had a close relationship with China during the trying days of wholesale Japanese military intervention in China.

British, French and Dutch military positions fell to the Japanese soon after a crippling surprise attack on the American naval base of Pearl Harbor in Hawaii on December 7, 1941. As a result, the war in the Pacific became almost entirely an American responsibility. Troops from Australia and New Zealand came under the overall command of General Douglas A. MacArthur, while the naval war was run by Admiral Chester W. Nimitz, commander of the Pacific Fleet. The ultimate victory in 1945, which found U.S. forces occupying Japan and its outlying island dependencies halfway back to Hawaii, brought American power in Asia to its zenith. At that time, it could truthfully be said that the Pacific was an American "lake."

During the seven years of the occupation, Japan was virtually an American possession. A proposal from Moscow for Soviet forces to share in the occupation by taking over Hokkaido was disdained by General MacArthur, the Supreme Commander of Allied Forces. MacArthur's refusal doubtless spared Japan from becoming a divided country like Korea, Vietnam and Germany. But the Soviets did succeed in extending their borders by occupying a number of small Japanese islands north and east of Hokkaido and by occupying North Korea down to the 38th parallel. These World War II land divisions in Asia still existed in 1990.

The Korean War

Scarcely a decade later, the United States position in the western Pacific was strained by events in Korea, China and Southeast Asia. The defense of Taiwan had become a U.S. commitment when the Chinese communists defeated Chiang Kaishek on the Chinese mainland. The defense of South Korea, following an attack by the communist North on June 25, 1950, brought U.S. troops, under U.N. authorization, into a head-on confrontation with communist-Chinese forces. Despite 157,000 casualties, including 33,629 dead, the conflict ended inconclusively. The border between the two Koreas changed little from where it had been before the conflict — along the 38th parallel.

New nations

Meanwhile, a new political reality emerged in the

South Pacific, where the accelerating dissolution of white colonialism brought independence to Western Samoa, Fiji, Papua, New Guinea and several other island territories that had figured prominently as American battlefields or bases in World War II. These new island states, although frail economically and possessing scant political weight in international affairs, were strategically located and so became new voices in world politics. The Soviet Union, China, Japan and the United States rushed to establish embassies in the key island capitals, and the U.S. State Department added a Pacific Islands desk to its Bureau of East Asian and Pacific Affairs.

Regional cooperation

In Southeast Asia the new pattern of cooperation was blurred by the resurgence of old animosities between Vietnam and Cambodia (renamed Kampuchea by the communists), Vietnam and China, and Cambodia and Thailand. Longstanding territorial disputes resurfaced, as did an ancient distrust of the Chinese. Differences were exacerbated by the migration of refugees away from the new communist governments.

The inclination of small powers to band together for mutual support, exemplified by the organization of the *Association of Southeast Asian Nations,* commonly known by the acronym ASEAN, spilled over into the South Pacific. With encouragement from

New Zealand and Australia, the new island states formed a joint organization called the *South Pacific Forum* to serve as the political voice of the region.

Japan
Historical sketch

Japan is a very special kind of country, truly different from any other. Isolated from outside influences by the surrounding seas and by centuries of self-imposed seclusion, the Japanese have developed an extraordinary ethnic and cultural homogeneity that is the nation's most marked characteristic. With a few numerically insignificant exceptions, the approximately 125 million Japanese are descended from the founding Yamato race, a Mongoloid people of uncertain origin who arrived centuries ago from the Asian mainland and overran the indigenous Ainu. The Ainu, a Caucasoid people, were driven to the north, where some of their descendants still live. For centuries, under the feudal rule of the *shoguns,* or warlords, Japanese were forbidden to go abroad. Bans on foreign settlement survive to this day in stringent restrictions on immigration and naturalization. The only sizable community of outsiders are the Koreans: Imported during World War II as laborers, their descendants now number about 700,000. The mixed-blood offspring

The U.S. warship *Arizona* sinks during the Japanese surprise attack on Pearl Harbor on December 7, 1941, which brought the United States into World War II.

of Japanese and foreigners are looked down upon, as are ethnic Japanese born abroad who return to the ancestral land. Foreigners are called *gaijin,* a word meaning "outside person."

Japanese cultural unity

Cultural aspects of Japanese life, although largely derived from Chinese sources — with a frequent overlay of Korean influence acquired in their passage from China to Japan — have become uniquely Japanese over centuries in a closed society. The Japanese language is spoken throughout the islands, with some regional differences in dialect. It is written in Chinese ideograms, but the characters are given a distinctly Japanese pronunciation. Japanese religious practices encompass the precepts of Buddhism and Confucianism — Christians are a tiny minority — but the national faith is Shinto, "The Way of the Gods," a Japanese-created religion whose chief priest is the emperor. From one end of the country to the other, Japanese share essentially the same diet, wear the same type of clothes (generally Western for work and sports, Japanese for home wear and ceremonial occasions), watch the same national television programs and perform the same or similar songs, dances and theatricals — all, of course, with local mutations which originated in times when it was uncommon (because of restrictions on movement imposed by feudal lords) for ordinary Japanese citizens to travel even from one part of the country to another.

Cohesion and discipline distinguish the Japanese from other Asian peoples, not least of all from their more individualistic neighbors, the Chinese. Historically, the Chinese have tended to organize within narrow linguistic or regional interest groups. For example, in the bustling commercial seaport community of Hong Kong, which lies outside of the jurisdiction of the communist mainland government, one might encounter separate associations of entrepreneurs from Shanghai, Swatow, Guangzhou (Canton) and so on, all in the same business. For the homogeneous Japanese, on the other hand, there would be just one organization in each field, presenting a united front to the competition. Such Japanese togetherness, frequently characterized by coordination between private business interests and the official trading policies of the government in Tokyo, gives meaning in the West to the term "Japan Incorporated," implying a single-mindedness unachieved by other countries in the international marketplace.

Loyalty, unity and discipline are key characteristics in the collective Japanese personality. Loyalty to the feudal lord — to the point of death — is a classic theme of *kabuki* drama, one of the traditional Japanese theatrical arts. In the skeptical climate which has been fashionable in Japan since World War II, especially among the young, the former imperative of unquestioning fealty to the emperor may have less impact on the national consciousness than do the newer values of loyalty to one's company and obedience to the boss. Belonging to a group is very important.

In an earlier era, the heart of Japanese civilization was the *samurai,* a warrior mounted and dressed like a medieval knight, wearing two swords with which he was apt to strike off the head of a luckless peasant in order to test the steel. The martial arts of barehanded combat and fencing with sticks (*kendo*) were being refined by Japanese masters. Social graces like *chanoyu,* the elaborate ritual of pouring tea made from powdered green leaves, and *ikebana,* the art of flower arranging, were taught in temple anterooms. Gentlemen relaxed in the stimulating company of beautiful and talented courtesans known as *geisha,* a descriptive term meaning "art person." The emperor, accepted as a direct descendant of the Sun Goddess, was surrounded by reverence and ritual in his wood-and-paper palace in Kyoto, but the real ruler of the country came from successive lines of *shoguns.* Such was the structured life in which the Japanese temperament was molded, up until the era of westernization, introduced in 1868 under Emperor Meiji.

The Meiji reign, actually a kind of government by committee, has survived in various forms to this day.

The Meiji Constitution, proclaimed in the emperor's name in 1881, established a parliamentary government along the lines of Britain's. It even included a Japanese counterpart of the House of Lords, with a new peerage and titles, in English, ranking upward from baron to prince. A new legal code was modeled on that of France. A western system of banking was introduced, and education was modernized.

Japanese expansionism

The Japanese warrior tradition came to the fore following territorial disputes with China and Russia on the Asian mainland. Victory over China in 1895 gave Japan control of Korea, an independent kingdom that was converted into a Japanese colony. When war broke out in 1904 over conflicting claims in Manchuria, Japanese naval forces annihilated the Russian fleet. These achievements brought Japan to the attention of the world. Japanese arms extended the empire deep into the central Pacific with the seizure of the strategic Mariana, Caroline and Marshall islands from Germany at the outset of World

War I. Thus Japan became a major world power, less than 50 years after the abolition of feudalism.

In the 1930s, a militarist faction came to power in Tokyo and turned the country into a strict authoritarian state built around a mystical reverence for the emperor. Military incursions into China and French Indochina brought punitive economic measures by France, the Netherlands and the United States. An American embargo on petroleum shipments to Japan convinced the cabinet, then headed by General Hideki Tojo, that military action to assure access to vital raw materials was unavoidable. On December 7, 1941, the Japanese air force made a surprise attack on Pearl Harbor, Hawaii. The U.S. declared war at this time.

American occupation of Japan after World War II

In the early months of the war, Japanese forces advanced triumphantly through Southeast Asia, into northeastern India and threatened Australia. The tide turned with the destruction of major Japanese naval air units in the battle of Midway in June 1942. Although bitter fighting on land and sea would continue for three more years, the superior American industrial might made the outcome inevitable. The atomic bombing of Hiroshima and Nagasaki in August 1945 was the final blow. Emperor Hirohito, against the wishes of die-hard militarists, made the decision to surrender on Allied terms. The Hiroshima bombing ushered in the nuclear era that we live with today. Japanese have not forgotten that they are the only people on Earth to have suffered the terrible devastation of nuclear war.

The Japanese capitulation brought the United States to its historic height as a power in Asia. Although the occupation of Japan was nominally a joint responsibility of the Allied governments, Americans ran the occupation. Under the command of General Douglas MacArthur, the United States governed through the formal apparatus of the Japanese parliament, with the emperor retaining his ceremonial position. The entire social fabric of Japan was restructured between 1945 and the end of the American occupation in 1952.

Emperor Hirohito, in a personal broadcast to the nation on January 1, 1946, formally repudiated the ancient concept of the emperor's divine origin. Subsequently, a new constitution, approved by the occupation authorities, officially removed the emperor from direct participation in the government, reducing his status from head of state to "symbol of the unity of the state." The emperor's duties, which are purely ceremonial, include the signing of

U.S. Navy Dept., National Archives

Japanese military leaders sign surrender documents on board the *U.S.S. Missouri* on September 2, 1945, as General Douglas MacArthur (far left), later to be in charge of the American occupation of Japan, looks on.

legislation and the receiving of foreign envoys. The same constitution renounced the right of the state to make war and declared that Japan would never maintain an army, navy or air force.

Social reforms included land redistribution (abolishing large rural estates), equal rights for women, and many other freedoms that the Japanese now cherish as "basic human rights." With minor modifications — for example, the land laws were later changed to permit the grouping of separate small farms for more efficient cultivation — the sweeping reforms effected by the occupation are regarded as the keystones of the new Japanese democracy.

To an older generation which remembers Japan in the years preceding World War II, it is remarkable that Japan today is one of the most democratic countries in the world. There is an untrammeled press, complete freedom of association, and open expression of viewpoints and ideas. The exercise of these rights has been extraordinarliy effective. More than once, an outpouring of public opinion — often in noisy street demonstrations — has forced the government to change an unpopular position.

Postwar economic recovery

Japan's recovery from the virtually complete devastation of the country's economy during the war was astonishing. United States troops entering Japan immediately after its defeat found every major industrial center a wasteland of ash and rubble. City dwellers who had been evacuated to the countryside returned to find whole neighborhoods reduced to featureless deserts, in which they were unable to find where their homes once stood. Of the larger cities, only Kyoto had been spared because of its special character as a national repository of cultural treasures. Eighty percent of the nation's productive capacity had been destroyed. American submarines had sent the bulk of Japan's fleet to the bottom of the Pacific. Food was in extremely short supply — hunger stalked the land. The empire was deprived of nearly half of its territory, and the overcrowded main islands would soon be further burdened by the return of more than 4.4 million overseas Japanese, under an American-directed repatriation program.

But the Japanese spirit was intact and undaunted. As the American soldiers settled in for the occupation, legions of Japanese women, dressed in the shapeless jumpsuits that had become standard wartime wear, roamed the cities with wheelbarrows to clear the rubble for rebuilding. Reconstruction proceeded through several stages: First came makeshift huts of scrap lumber and then jerrybuilt structures of wood and stucco, which were gradually upgraded

until the redeemed cities took on the glossy appearance of urban Japan today.

Rapid industrialization

The recovery process was helped by an infusion of American economic aid, amounting to nearly $2 billion between 1945 and 1950. Food sent from the United States under the assistance program immediately after the end of the war averted a probable famine. In rebuilding, the Japanese replaced their obsolete machinery with modern equipment. The American commitment to defend an unarmed Japan enabled the nation to concentrate on restoring the economy, without the added burden of replacing the costly military forces lost in the war.

The expanding American military establishment in the Asia-Pacific region, with the occupation force as its core, provided a market for Japanese industry as well as employment for thousands of drivers, guards, clerks, maids, machinists and other workers. The former Japanese naval base at Yoskosuka became a major facility for the United States' Seventh Fleet, whose immediate task was to patrol the Taiwan Strait against any attempted crossing by communist Chinese forces. Okinawa became a huge American air base. U.S. tactical air power was deployed at fields all over Japan.

On June 25, 1950, North Korean forces invaded South Korea, and the United States found itself in another Asian war. The hard-working, systematic Japanese were prepared to provide all sorts of supplies to the American military, further rejuvenating industry. The same aircraft technicians who had developed the famous Zero fighter, used with devastating effect in the early days of World War II, had been quietly keeping abreast of developments in the art of manufacturing airplanes. The Japanese automotive industry, obliterated in the war, was beginning to struggle back through the efforts of men like Soichiro Honda, whose surname would soon become synonymous with fine Japanese motorcycles and small cars. The manufacturers of Canon and Nikon cameras and of Sony and Matsushita electronic wares were already preparing to enter international markets. The economic spin-off from the Korean War provided the capital structure which enabled Japan to launch its postwar recovery at top speed.

Return of the *zaibatsu*

Japan's economic takeoff gathered momentum toward the end of the 1950s. By then the controversial "purges" ordered by the occupation command, in which all Japanese deemed to have played an operative role in the war were removed from posi-

Japanese Emperor Hirohito appears in his ceremonial robes (left). Before Japan's defeat in World War II, he was considered divine. After the war, he renounced his divine origin, becoming a "symbol of the unity of the state" and an ordinary man (right).

tions of authority, had become an almost forgotten episode in history. The banished *zaibatsu,* as the prewar big-business combines were called, began to regroup under a new class of professional managers who replaced the old family control. In its zeal to mend the tattered economic fabric of the nation, the private sector achieved a high degree of integration with official policy. The government regulated the money market through the powerful Bank of Japan. Appropriate ministries, particularly the Ministry of International Trade and Industry — generally referred to in English and Japanese alike by the acronym MITI — periodically issued business advisory notices, called "administrative guidance," that almost had the force of law.

While Japanese business practice included lively competition both at home and abroad, it often seemed to foreign entrepreneurs that their competitors from Japan presented a united front. "You don't just compete with a Japanese company, but with all Japan," one American businessman complained. The accuracy of this image is denied in Japanese business circles, where official regulation is highly unpopular. In any case, such giant conglomerates as the Mitsubishi enterprise became formidable global competitors. So many Japanese businessmen were stationed abroad that the foreign office in Tokyo established a program to organize schools in other countries, so that their children would be educated in their native language and thus

qualify for admission to Japanese universities, a prerequisite for at-home success.

A generation after the war, Japan had become the world leader in shipping, stood second in automobile manufacturing and third in steel output. The total national industrial production was exceeded only by the United States and the Soviet Union. The wage level of Japanese workers surpassed the standard in many European countries. Armed with the yen's superior purchasing power, the ubiquitous Japanese tourist became the world's biggest spender among ordinary pleasure travelers. Owning the coveted "three C's" — car, color television and (air) conditioner — became an attainable goal for the average family. Unemployment was negligible under the traditional Japanese system of guaranteed lifetime work for the same company, once hired.

Japanese economic success was achieved in spite of an almost complete absence of natural resources. Virtually all of the raw material needed for manufacturing, as well as oil to fuel factories, run vehicles and heat buildings during Japan's raw winter, must be imported. There are extensive veins of low-grade coal, but the quality is so low and natural conditions make mining so costly, it is cheaper to import it. Once a largely agricultural nation, Japan has been forced to import much of its food since its own industrial revolution shifted the working population from field to factory. Today, the Japanese live on their manufacturing skill, to which they bring an extraordinary degree of competence, and on their zeal for selling. "Export or die," they are fond of saying. The validity of this aphorism is proved periodically, when various market factors produce a shortage of raw materials or a decline in demand, and the country sinks into one of its cyclical recessions.

Once known as a nation of copiers, turning out cheap gimcrackery and shoddy souvenirs, the Japanese have become outstanding innovators in high technology. Leaving simpler manufacturing to developing countries like South Korea, Taiwan and Singapore, Japan has become a leading purveyor of sophisticated machinery. It specializes in such fields as the construction of huge supertankers and in shipping entire factories abroad.

It has been said that Japan has only two abundant natural resources: rain and people. With the latter lies the secret of the country's amazing success. The answer to the puzzle of Japan is visible on the streets of a city like Tokyo at the beginning of any working day, as millions of neatly dressed, earnest-looking workers stride purposefully toward their assigned places in factories or offices. Quiet in demeanor and conservative in appearance even when modish, they personify an efficient, hard-working Japan.

The American occupation ended in 1952. Most U.S. military bases were put into Japanese custody as Washington began cutting back on its troop commitments abroad. The American military in Japan maintains a low profile except around its few remaining facilities, most of which lie far from the cities. Nevertheless, Japan and the United States remain linked in a *Treaty of Mutual Security,* concluded at the same time as the peace treaty and renewed since with modifications to suit the times.

Japan rearms

In recent years, Japan's own Self-Defense Forces have been far more conspicuous than the American military. Land, air and sea branches were established late in the occupation when the Americans had second thoughts about maintaining a totally unarmed Japan. The name — Self-Defense Forces — was carefully chosen to avoid the appearance of violating the constitutional injunction against reinstituting the old army, navy and air force. The new international prominence of Japan has raised doubts about how long Tokyo will be content to rely upon the American "nuclear umbrella" for the nation's security. Unquestionably, a deep-seated pacifism and what the Japanese call their "nuclear allergy," a legacy from Hiroshima, are strong factors.

Despite the self-imposed restrictions on military growth, the Japanese Self-Defense Forces are by no means insignificant. The giant Japanese arms industry, limited by law to the home market, is turning out highly sophisticated modern war planes under license from American companies and yearns to get into the lucrative international weapons trade. (China is the prospective major customer). With big business favoring rearmament and public opinion softening on the issue, Japanese military development promises to become a major international concern.

Japan's role in world affairs

After the war, Japan did not play a prominent role in world affairs. The government was conscious of lingering antagonism among the countries that were overrun by Japanese forces during the war. Apart from striving to improve relations with its two giant neighbors, China and the Soviet Union, Tokyo remained a passive participant in world events. Close ties with the United States, Tokyo kept repeating, was the keystone of Japanese foreign policy. As the decade of the 1990s began, however, Japan was beginning to play a major role in world affairs. It was exerting much more influence in Southeast Asia, especially in Thailand which did not suffer so much at Japanese hands during World War II. Also, Japan has become a major player in providing economic development aid to poor nations. Even so, it prefers a low profile in world politics.

Japan and China

In 1972, President Richard M. Nixon moved to establish diplomatic relations with the People's Republic of China. Although Japan was greatly offended at not being consulted in advance, it quickly followed suit. The Chinese had come to view the presence of the United States in Asia as a counterweight to the Soviet Union and were thus willing to accept the U.S. military presence in Japan. When full diplomatic relations between Tokyo and Beijing made it necessary for Japan to sever diplomatic links with the Nationalist Chinese government of Taiwan, an important customer, Tokyo managed to retain economic links with the island simply by changing the sign on the Japanese Embassy in Taipei, converting it overnight to a trade liaison office.

Japan had always felt uneasy about the artificial estrangement from mainland China, its cultural motherland and a natural economic partner. As a result of its protracted military adventure in China and its occupation of Manchuria, Japan had accumulated an immense background knowledge of China's affairs. Personal exchanges had continued after World War II, and the Japanese had an advantage over other foreign visitors in being able to read the Chinese language, whether or not they spoke it. More than any other outside observers, the Japanese were able to follow and understand the turbulent events in China.

The opening of diplomatic relations with Beijing drew Japan into the maelstrom of the deepening Sino-Soviet conflict. Tokyo wanted a peace treaty with both powers to supplement the agreements that had ended the formal state of war in 1945. China insisted that the document contain a clause denouncing "foreign hegemony" in Asia. This was a shot at the Soviets, and it brought immediate protests from Moscow to the discomfited Japanese. Tokyo's efforts to come to a full accord with Moscow had been stalled meanwhile by the Soviet's adamant refusal to return Japan's northern Kurile islands seized at the end of the war.

Trade policies

After much prodding by Washington, Japan finally moved beyond the buy-and-sell stage of its economic diplomacy into dealing with other industrialized countries of the non-communist world on broader problems of common concern. The three major trading units — the United Kingdom and Western Europe, the United States and Canada, and Japan — faced the following problems: persistent inflation; high unemployment in some of the countries; monetary problems and trade imbalances associated with the abrupt escalation of the price of Middle East oil; and the troubling disparity between the industrialized countries and developing lands, known as the North-South conflict. The United States attributed some problems to restrictive Japanese trade practices which kept foreign manufactured items from entering the Japanese market at competitive prices.

These common economic interests led to the founding of the *Group of Seven* (G-7), consisting of the seven major democratic economies in the world: Canada, United Kingdom, West Germany, France, Japan, Italy and the United States. Japan has been a major player among the G-7 nations who meet annually to discuss world economics and politics.

In comparative terms, Japan has not been in political contact with the outside world for very long. Its response to new situations has tended to be influenced by past practices, and it has been extremely difficult for the Japanese to accept the idea of cutting back on export earnings. The United States' contribution to international economic problems has been a huge deficit in foreign trade. Japan has had the opposite difficulty: high profits in overseas accounts. Although it was difficult to convince the Japanese

citizenry that it would be better to make less money, the forces managing the economy recognized that an increasingly expensive yen would eventually make Japanese products less desirable to foreign buyers. This in turn would reduce foreign sales, inviting a new round of cyclical recessions.

Japanese officials, industrialists and financiers are haunted by the specter of protectionism arising in western nations. "Imports No, Jobs Yes" has become the slogan of some American labor unions which equate imports of manufactured goods with high unemployment rates. In 1981, Japan began to respond to the complaints of its major trading partners, agreeing to limit the export of automobiles to the United States, West Germany and Canada; at the same time it lowered restrictions on imports such as food products. The yen soon dropped in relation to western currencies, making Japanese goods more affordable. Japanese auto firms are manufacturing cars and trucks in the United States in their own plants and in joint ventures with U.S. corporations.

Another concern for Japan is an increase in competition from other Asian countries where wages are lower and modern technology is being developed. The quality radio that would inevitably have come from Japan a few years ago may now bear the stamp, "Made in Singapore." Japan has been getting out of some businesses in which its plants are no longer competitive. For example, the Japanese government is offering low-interest loans to textile companies willing to go into a more rewarding line and has set up centers for the retraining of thousands of displaced textile workers. In some instances, companies that once flooded foreign markets with cheap clothing have moved into the manufacture of high-fashion garments. The major makers of electronic devices have gone beyond the familiar television sets and tape recorders and are turning out more complex equipment, like video cassette recorders, improved photocopying and facsimile (fax) machines. Advanced research is subsidized by the government through interest-free loans to innovative companies developing new products.

China

China has the world's oldest continuous history (4,000 years) and was once the most powerful empire on Earth. The brilliance of Chinese culture dazzled visitors from Europe like Marco Polo, the Italian traveler who, after discovering Chinese noodles, gave spaghetti to the Western world. A major Chinese invention was gunpowder. The ancient Chinese, insulated from much contact abroad by natural barriers, considered their country the home of civilization —

the Middle Kingdom. When emissaries from afar came to the imperial court in Beijing bearing gifts, the proud Chinese rulers accepted the offerings as tribute to a superior power.

Sino-American alliance in World War II

American involvement in China goes back to the middle of the 19th century and has been generally agreeable, especially in contrast to the behavior of other western powers. During the era of Japanese expansionism in China in the 1930s, the sympathy of the United States for the Chinese victims of aggression led to a militant anti-Japanese alliance. President Franklin D. Roosevelt slowed the flow of oil, metals and machinery to Japan; slipped weapons to the Chinese through Burma, which was then a British territory; and permitted U.S. Navy, Marine Corps and Army Air Force pilots to volunteer for the Flying Tigers, an expatriate air force organized by American General Claire Chennault to fight for the Chinese Nationalists. These moves culminated in the Japanese attack on Pearl Harbor, which brought the United States directly into World War II.

At the time, China was a shattered and divided country. Besides their puppet empire of Manchukuo in Manchuria, the Japanese held the main ports and nearly all the major cities. The Nationalist government of President Chiang Kaishek also had to contend with communist insurgents, who held large areas of territory. When Japanese launched a full scale invasion in 1937, using as an excuse a minor clash between Chinese and Japanese troops near Beijing, the Communists joined forces with the Nationalists in a common front against the enemy.

After Pearl Harbor, an American, General Joseph Stillwell, became the commander of Chinese troops fighting the Japanese in northern Burma. American supplies flowed into China from India "over the Hump" — the snowcapped Himalayas, which form a huge natural rampart between China and the Indian subcontinent. The carrier-based U.S. bombers that made a surprise attack on Tokyo early in the war under the leadership of General James Doolittle flew to Chinese airfields after dropping their bombs. Chiang Kaishek became one of the "Big Four" in Allied councils, along with U.S. President Franklin Roosevelt, British Prime Minister Winston Churchill and the Soviet leader, Joseph Stalin. In a conference in Cairo in 1943, it was agreed that Taiwan, with its associated islands, and Manchuria would be reclaimed from Japan and returned to China when the war was won.

The "two Chinas"

The alliance between the Nationalist and communist Chinese was an uneasy one. Chiang, who prevented American arms from reaching the communist Chinese forces, was accused of paying more attention to the internal enemy than to the defeat of the Japanese. After the Japanese surrender, an American peacemaking mission under General George C. Marshall went to China in an unsuccessful attempt to bring the two Chinese sides together. Meanwhile, the Soviet forces had taken Manchuria from the Japanese, along with huge stocks of weapons from the United States which the Japanese had captured from the Nationalists. The Soviets turned the territory and the arms over to the Chinese communists, who regrouped and attacked the Nationalists. By 1948, the communists had established themselves in the imperial capital of Beijing. The next year, Chiang and his Nationalists fled to Taiwan, a large island 100 miles off the mainland. Thus began the era of the "two Chinas."

The arrival of 2 million Nationalists on Taiwan was accompanied by a bloody purge. Thousands of intellectuals and others among the 9 million residents were killed by the Nationalists, an episode that left a lasting animosity among the Taiwanese toward the newcomers.

The government that Chiang brought with him from the mainland claimed to be the only legal government of all China. The United States and more than 100 other countries accepted the legitimacy of Chiang's position, on the theory that the Nationalist regime had been chased from the mainland but had not been conquered, thus remaining a nation under international law.

In the years since 1949, one country after another has accepted the reality of the People's Republic of China and recognized it as the official government of China. In the interim, however, with U.S. aid and the discipline of an authoritarian government, Taiwan built one of the most prosperous economies in Asia.

The complex American stand on the China issue included a mutual defense treaty, whereby the United States supplied Taiwan with arms and advisers. The U.S. State Department sent its China specialists to an institute in Taichung to learn the Chinese language. When it appeared that the communists might attack across the Taiwan Strait in the late 1950s, the United States backed up the formidable Nationalist land and air forces with the naval power of the Seventh Fleet and seemed prepared to go to war if the communists attempted an invasion. China backed down, and the crisis dwindled to an exchange of airborne propaganda material, fired in shells and carried by balloons across the narrow waters between the mainland and Nationalist-held offshore islands like Quemoy.

Under the fiction that Taiwan was the seat of

government for all China, the island was treated as a province with a separate provincial legislature and executive staffed by native-born Taiwanese. The number of Taiwanese in the government of the Republic of China, as the Nationalists continue to call their country, was increased after Chiang's death.

U.S. recognition of the People's Republic of China

While the United States continued to treat Taiwan as a sovereign state, Washington's attitude toward the communist regime changed. In a dramatic secret flight to Beijing, arranged with the help of Pakistan, Secretary of State Henry Kissinger negotiated the details of President Nixon's official visit to China in 1971. The outcome was a statement, known as the *Shanghai Communique,* issued jointly (but not signed) by Nixon and the late Prime Minister Chou Enlai. It served as a position paper setting forth the crucial points of disagreement and accord. The Chinese, calling the Taiwan issue "the crucial question," declared that the People's Republic was "the sole legitimate government of China;" that "the liberation of Taiwan is China's internal affair in which no other country has the right to interfere;" and that "all U.S. forces and military installations must be removed" from the island. The United States, in its section of the communique, acknowledged "that all Chinese on either side of the Taiwan Strait maintain there is but one China and that Taiwan is a part of China." The U.S. statement continued: "The United States government ... reaffirms its interest in a peaceful settlement of the Taiwan question by the Chinese themselves (and) affirms the ultimate objective of the withdrawal of all U.S. forces and military installations from Taiwan."

American insistence on a guarantee that the communists would not use force to reclaim Taiwan stymied efforts to normalize relations between the two countries. China rejected the stand on the ground that it was a clear interference in its internal affairs. "We don't want to see the Taiwanese people punished or attacked," President Jimmy Carter later explained. Some Americans contended that the Taiwanese forces, numbering nearly half a million with more than a million in reserve, were strong enough to deter a Chinese attack or to turn one back if it came. But U.S. officials, for internal and external reasons, were unwilling to abandon the Nationalists. The issue involved not only a volatile public opinion at home, but also the credibility of the U.S. defense commitment to other allies around the world.

While the two governments remained at odds on the Taiwan problem, contact continued on both official and unofficial levels. President Carter and Hua Kuofeng, who had become chairman of the Chinese Communist Party and head of the government following the death of Mao Tsetung, exchanged views through American emissaries periodically dispatched from Washington. A two-way traffic expanded in economic missions, scientific groups, and cultural and sporting delegations. China opened its

USN&WR

President Richard Nixon and Chinese Premier Chou Enlai toast each other during Nixon's historic visit to Beijing in 1972, which ended 22 years of hostility between the two nations.

door to tourists. Western business persons attended the annual trade fair in Guangzhou (Canton), the commercial center of South China, a short train ride from British Hong Kong. Despite an undercurrent of hostility on the government level, the vestigial friendship between the two peoples prospered. Full diplomatic relations between China and the United States were finally established in 1981.

In the United States, there were practical as well as political reasons for continuing the close collaboration with Taiwan. More than 200 American companies were established on the island. Besides, under the strong government of the Nationalists, Taiwan had become something of a showcase of Western-style capitalism — if not Western democracy. Its 20.3 million people enjoy one of the highest standards of living in the Asian-Pacific region. It is one of the four Asian "tigers," noted for rapid economic development.

China modernizes

When well-meaning foreign visitors sought to flatter the late Prime Minister Chou Enlai by praising the greatness of China among modern nations, the urbane and well-traveled Chou would laugh and assure them that they were mistaken. The country, he said, clearly had a long way to go before it would reach the front rank of industrial powers — a goal set by the communist policy-makers for the year 2000. Under the leadership of Deng Xiaoping, China embarked on a national plan to modernize by the year 2000. The "four modernizations" were: science and technology, defense, industry, and agriculture.

The real attributes of power were still lacking. China, with more than 3 million men under arms, could field one of the largest land armies in the world, but its equipment was inferior and outdated. Its aircraft were obsolete, and its navy consisted mainly of a few dozen old submarines and a few surface units. One of the major nuclear powers, China was believed to have several hundred atomic weapons in storage, but long-range missiles to deliver them to distant targets were few. Self-sufficient in petroleum and rich in many other raw materials, China was developing industries rapidly but was far behind many smaller nations in technology. It remained basically a peasant society with 80 percent of its people living in the countryside.

However, no recital of China's shortcomings can omit mention of the country's enormous industrial potential. Labor is plentiful: China has the largest population of any country (over 1 billion). And the Chinese are fully as capable and hard working as the Japanese, if not so homogeneous. (The Chinese nation is made up of numerous linguistic groups though they share the same writing system.) Isolation from other civilizations gave the Chinese a degree of unity over the centuries, but it remained for the communists to introduce a sense of common purpose. The vastness of the modernization problem has caused doubt that it will be achieved within the projected time frame, but the gains have already been impressive.

At the end of World War II, China presented a scene of startling social disorder in the areas still under Nationalist control. Crowded cities like Shanghai teemed with prostitutes, beggars and thieves. The depressed masses huddled in colonies of makeshift huts constructed of cast-off or stolen boards, burlap and tarpaper. Shiploads of relief goods sent from the United States under a United Nations program flowed more or less directly into the black market. Any vice could be pursued for a price, and if it was drugs, the price was cheap. The currency depreciated so wildly that paper bank notes were counted not singly but in bundles stitched together with thread. The supply of money needed for a trip to the market or a meal in a restaurant would fill a hand basket. In upper circles, corruption was a way of life. Highly placed or clever individuals amassed huge fortunes, while the poor went hungry.

China under communism

The communist victory brought wholesale changes, stringently enforced, to the Chinese social order. It will probably never be known how many "class enemies," wrongdoers or capitalists, as opponents of the regime were called without distinction, were put to death by communist executioners, but the figure is generally believed to total millions. Landlords were wiped out and their properties redistributed among their tenants. Beggars and prostitutes disappeared. With the *Little Red Book* of Mao's writings as their Bible, party cadres turned the chairman's aphorisms into the law of the land, promulgating strict rules for every aspect of personal as well as political life.

Work was delegated by the authorities, and assignments often separated husbands and wives, parents and children. Members of a family were sent to different sites, sometimes in distant provinces, to help build the new China. Youngsters, upon finishing middle school at about the age of 15, were sent away to work on the land. It would be decided later when and how they would continue their education, if they were fortunate enough to be chosen. In an effort to bring down the high rate of population growth, young women were forbidden to marry until they were 23 years old, young men, 27, or an approximation of those ages.

Communist doctrine also dictated what the populace should think. Loudspeakers in public places dinned accepted thoughts into Chinese ears from morning until night. All Western influences were banned from the cultural life of the nation. Lively Chinese theatricals were rewritten to purvey propaganda masked as entertainment, as in the popular ballets *Red Brigade of Women* and *The White Haired Girl,* the story of a wicked landlord's ruin, both presented on tours in the West. Everyone wore the unisex outfit of somber trousers and high-buttoned tunic known as the ''Mao suit.''

Long, rigidly scheduled workdays were followed by hours of study and political lectures on the glories of communism and the works of Mao. The nation was instructed to shun the polluting doctrine of Confucianism that had shaped Chinese personal relationships, ethics and thought for more than 2,000 years. Veneration of ancestors disappeared; so did subordination of the individual to the family. Buddhism and other religions were repudiated — the only faith permitted was communism. People were instructed to turn their backs on the ancient arts that had been the glory of Chinese civilization.

With the outbreak of the Korean War, especially after the Chinese entered the conflict with ''volunteer'' forces, the government made ''Hate America'' a national slogan. The ''foreign-devil'' Americans, especially in the caricature of Uncle Sam, became the villains in new theatricals performed throughout the country. Grade-school children of nine and 10 were instructed in the use of bayonets, using dummies dressed as Americans for their targets.

Cultural Revolution

Thought regimentation reached its peak in 1966 when Mao launched a new ideological campaign known as the ''Great Proletarian Cultural Revolution.'' This followed the failures of the ''Great Leap Forward'' campaign in which Mao had sought a massive economic advance by using simple methods such as primitive backyard factories, and the abortive experiment in free criticism known as the ''Hundred Flowers'' period. ''Let a hundred flowers bloom, let many schools of thought contend,'' Mao had said in announcing the policy; but it quickly got out of hand and was abruptly terminated as eager critics of Mao's policies came forward. Shocked by what he conceived to be an insidious resurgence of capitalist values among the leaders and the intelligentsia, Mao took extreme steps.

Soon the streets were filled with yelling, chanting Maoist youth groups called Red Guards, who brandished the *Little Red Book* as they marched on government offices, demanding recantation of presumed heresies against Maoism. High personages accused of backsliding from Mao's rigid Marxist-Leninist principles were denounced in mock trials and paraded through the streets in dunce caps. The names of suspected foes of radicalism appeared on huge paper posters that plastered the walls of the cities and campuses. Screaming mobs of Red Guards carried the message from town to town. Education came to a virtual standstill as millions of students returned to farms and factories, along with their professors and legions of bureaucrats, for reindoctrination in the work ethic proclaimed by Mao.

Education in China during this period of unbridled fanaticism suffered a blow that would set back the nation's material and intellectual progress by years. Study from textbooks was discouraged, all foreign sources of knowledge were expunged from the system, school enrollments were reduced, examinations were abolished, and teachers were denounced as foes of the ''class struggle.'' In those chaotic months, it seemed that the only stabilizing influence in an anarchic society was the People's Liberation Army, although the military also complied with Maoist orthodoxy by eliminating rank and insignia in the armed forces.

Wide World
During China's Cultural Revolution, the performing arts became a method of purveying Communist propaganda. A ballet troupe performs the dance *Red Detachment of Women*, glorifying the Chinese Communist state.

China was largely a mystery to the outside world during the days of the Cultural Revolution.

Purge of the radicals

Relative quiet returned after Mao was satisfied that the revolution had been steered back to proper channels in the "continuing class struggle." With the death of Mao in 1976, official policy changed again. Pragmatists like Deng Xiaoping, who had survived two purges to come back as the powerful vice premier, regained the reins, and it was the radicals who became the villains. The new leadership began purging the best-known radicals. Chief among these was Mao's widow, Jiang Quing (known by her maiden name, according to Chinese custom), a former film actress who had used her position as the chairman's wife to head a campaign for the extermination of Western influences on the arts. Among the many crimes attributed to Jiang Quing was the forgery of Mao's last testament in a scheme to enhance her powers and those of three extremist associates; they were denounced ceaselessly from one end of the land to the other as the "Gang of Four," responsible for all evil. The elimination of the "Gang of Four," who were imprisoned, enabled the more conservative leadership to forge a new unity at the top level of government.

Mao's policies reversed

The new government reversed Mao's course in education. As a result of the Cultural Revolution, teaching standards had deteriorated to the point where many students in graduate schools were unable to meet high school standards. Foreign textbooks in science and technology, banned during the upheaval, were restored. Remedial courses were instituted in high schools and universities for students who, while devoting their time to the Red Guards, had missed basic studies in science, mathematics, history and foreign languages. Restoring a sense of discipline among rebellious youth who had been encouraged to regard their teachers as "class enemies" was another problem faced by school administrators. As part of the "new course," educators rejected the Maoist doctrine that candidates for entrance to universities should be chosen for revolutionary zeal instead of grades. Also abolished was the old system of giving preference for advancement in education and jobs to young people from lower-class economic backgrounds, regardless of their accomplishments in the classroom. The scientists and intellectuals who had been reviled and forced to work in the fields during the Cultural Revolution again became honored members of the community.

The new regime abandoned the Maoist idea that the virtues to be derived from work with the hands were preferable to benefits from modern technology, and set out to learn from the West as rapidly as possible. The government began to send bright students to universities in Britain, Western Europe, North America and Australia and planned to expand the number into the thousands in future years.

"The Path of Steady Growth"

Industry, too, was given a new direction, with the accent on production instead of ideology. The old "revolutionary councils" that had taken authority away from plant managers and stressed right political thinking over good work were disbanded. With their penchant for slogans, the new regime formulated a new program called "The Path of Steady Growth," presumably more practical than a "Great Leap Forward." The government set targets for 1985 of 120 major projects, including 10 new iron and steel manufacturing complexes, 30 power stations, 6 new trunk railways, 5 new harbors, and 10 new oil and natural gas developments. An overall expansion of 10 percent a year in industrial output was projected.

More than 80 percent of the Chinese are engaged in agriculture (as opposed to less than 3 percent of Americans). The nation is self-sufficient in food, and no one goes hungry, yet the country imports millions of tons of grain every year, including wheat from the United States. At the same time, China sells farm products in order to obtain foreign exchange to pay for technology and equipment that Chinese industry cannot yet provide. The government developed a cautious policy toward foreign monetary aid, trying to avoid the debt problem that has plagued many developing nations.

After the Cultural Revolution, the government launched an attempt to develop chemical fertilizers, urgently needed for significant increases in food production. Complete plants were purchased from Japanese, Dutch, British, German and Italian companies, and an American firm was engaged to build a system of eight factories. A new official target was set to increase farm output by 4 percent to 5 percent a year.

Another significant departure from orthodox Maoism, and one of particular importance to the United States, was as new interest in foreign trade, an issue that the Maoists had scorned as a "national betrayal." American and other potential customers were encouraged to inspect Chinese wares at trade fairs. For their part, the Chinese began purchasing heavy goods: A $25 million oil rig bought from an American-owned company for offshore exploration is one example. Chinese department stores and art emporiums have now appeared in places as distant as Montreal.

The Sino-Soviet rift

Viewed from a historical perspective, the alliance between the two communist giants was an unnatural one. Czarist Russia, and afterward the Soviets, occupied vast areas of the old Chinese empire. Moreover, Moscow had sponsored the independence of Mongolia, a communist state formerly called Outer Mongolia and still regarded by Beijing and Taiwan as belonging to China.

A deepening ideological split in the late 1950s grew upon these historic animosities. China's leaders and the controlled press criticized the Soviet Union for taking "revisionist" paths that betrayed the principles of pure Marxist-Leninist philosophy. The Soviet Union retaliated by withdrawing all technical help from China and marshaled Eastern European allies to rebut the Chinese interpretation of proper communism. Soon only Albania remained on the Chinese side; eventually that country too would turn against China. In 1966, the Sino-Soviet rift escalated into brief border fighting. The Soviets stationed a quarter of their army along the frontier, raising the possibility of full-scale war.

Fully aware that they would be no match for the Soviet Union, the Chinese switched policies. The U.S. military presence in South Korea, Japan, Okinawa and the Philippines, which Beijing had protested for 20 years, now became an essential counterweight to the Soviet divisions on China's borders. The Chinese made it clear, moreover, that they were no longer interested in supporting a North Korean thrust into South Korea, which might embroil them in another military confrontation with the United States.

United States recognition of China represented a realistic adjustment to shifting political currents in the Asia-Pacific region. Hostility between China and the Soviet Union, growing out of ideological differences and a festering border dispute, had altered the strategic balance in Europe by tying down legions of Soviet troops along the Chinese frontier. This eased pressure upon the United States and its allies in the *North Atlantic Treaty Organization*. Both China and the United States reacted to the new situation in the spirit of the philosophy that "the enemy of my enemy is my friend."

A new constitution

There were major revisions in the structure of Chinese political life during 1982. A new National Constitution was adopted which, among other things, reestablished the office of President and restored the right of individuals to inherit property, but eliminated the right to strike and freedom of political expression. The Chinese Communist Party also adopted a new constitution which moved it further away from the tradition of one-man rule established by Mao Tsetung. The position of party Chairman was abolished and replaced by that of General Secretary, bringing China more in line with the party structure in other communist nations. The major policy-making body became the Politburo's six-member standing committee headed by Deng Xiaoping, China's top political figure of the 1980s.

The 1989 democracy movement

The new economic freedoms in China had created new opportunities for growth, and China's economy boomed along during the 1980s. But along with the new prosperity came new opportunities for corruption and economic inequality. Inflation was very high. By the end of the '80s, China was at another turning point.

Young people, mainly college students, became impatient with the pace of reform and began to speak out against the government in the spring of 1989. The immediate cause of the protest was the death in April of Hu Yaobang, former general secretary and chairman of the Chinese Communist Party. The conservatives had forced him from his leadership position in 1987 and criticized his reformist policies. Students swarmed to Tiananmen Square, the central plaza in Beijing where most official functions are held and where Mao Tsetung's body is on permanent display. Soon, more than 100,000 students and supporters of reform crowded into the Square and refused to leave. When Soviet leader Mikhail Gorbachev arrived in mid-May, 150,000 people had gathered in the Square, and his itinerary was changed. The protest overshadowed his historic visit. Two days later, 1 million people crowded into the Square, and the Chinese leaders knew they had a major problem on their hands. By late May, the fervor and number of the protestors had waned. Some of the student leaders were urging a return to the campuses. At that critical moment, the government decided to end restraint, and the People's Liberation Army (PLA) opened fire on the demonstrators. An estimated 500 to 7,000 people died in the crackdown, including members of the PLA. As many as 10,000 were injured. The citizens of Beijing were stunned, as were the people of the world who had followed the events transfixed.

Despite the crumbling of the communist governments in Eastern Europe and the economic *perestroika* and political *glasnost* advocated by Mikhail Gorbachev, the leaders in China took a hard line and refused to grant any concessions to the democracy movement. China, after appearing to open up to the world and to change, once more found itself isolated in the international community, and its effort to modernize by the year 2000 had run into a serious setback.

Many Chinese remember the chaotic and anxious days before the revolution in 1949; this memory places a brake on rapid change. The security of the present system in comparison to the dreadful past serves as a strong argument against the uncertainties of a more democratic, capitalistic future. As the revolutionary generation dies, leadership will pass to a younger group who may be more willing to risk change.

Even though many Americans were disturbed by events in China, the U.S. continues to maintain close ties. In 1990, President Bush signed a five-year renewal of a most-favored-nation trade agreement with China.

AP/ WIDE WORLD PHOTOS

A lone Chinese student halts tanks in Beijing's Tianamen Square to protest government policies. This picture was seen by television viewers around the world.

Hong Kong

Hong Kong, a British Crown Colony with a population of 5.7 million people, is an island lying 90 miles south of Guangzhou (Canton), China. In 1997, its 99-year lease will expire, and Hong Kong will again become part of China. According to an agreement signed by the United Kingdom and the People's Republic of China in 1985, Hong Kong is to be permitted to retain its capitalistic economy for 50 years following its return to China. Many of the citizens of Hong Kong, however, are very concerned about the transition, and some are immigrating to other nations. As members of the British Commonwealth, many wish to go to England, but the British government has refused to admit them.

The Indian subcontinent

Since time immemorial, the vast South Asian peninsula known as the Indian subcontinent has been a battleground of conquerors. Blackened silver coins left by Alexander's hordes from Greece still turn up in the dusty bazaars. Later invaders from the Moslem lands of central Asia influenced art, language and religion. The governments of India, Pakistan and Bangladesh, which now occupy most of the subcontinent, reflect the political heritage of the British, who came last. Although the days of the empire are long gone, rival powers continue to contend in South Asian capitals. Playing out what the 19th century British writer Rudyard Kipling called the "Great Game," they seek by persuasion, gifts and intrigue to induce a tilt

to one side or the other in the contest of ideologies that divides the world.

On a map, the subcontinent resembles an elephant's head viewed from the front, with the trunk extending into the Indian Ocean, one ear lapped by the Bay of Bengal and the other by the Arabian Sea. It is a land of stark contrasts. Burning plains, with vast desert areas where the only movement to be seen from an airplane window may be a wandering nomad and his camel, are bordered by sodden tropical forests. The wild northern region is separated from China by the snowy natural rampart of the Himalayas, the highest mountains on Earth. More than 700 languages and dialects are spoken, many by aboriginal tribes, including dwellers in caves and trees who hunt and fight with bows and arrows, spears and poisoned darts. The bulk of the people are descended from light-skinned Aryan invaders from central Asia who settled in the north and the dark-skinned Dravidians whom the Aryans drove south. The majority in both groups are followers of the Hindu religion. Their lives are governed by a rigid social structure founded on four hereditary castes — *Brahmans* (priests and scholars), *Kshatriyas* (princes and warriors), *Vaisya* (merchants) and *Sudras* (laborers) — and below all others, the casteless pariah class known as Untouchables, to whom are consigned the meanest occupations and whose touch is considered polluting by "caste Hindus." The lower classes — mostly Sudra Untouchable, but also Moslems, Christians and Buddhists — include millions of the world's poorest people living in hovels or mud huts in the rural villages, dressed in rags, hungry, illiterate and prey to disease. At the opposite end of the social scale are families of enormous wealth, including hundreds of former princes, now bereft of

169

power and absorbed into the ordinary citizenry, and an elite group of intellectuals.

Indian independence

Religious animosities in India pitted Hindu against Moslem. Intermittent violence eventually split the Indian independence movement led by Mohandas K. Gandhi, a Hindu. A Moslem faction headed by Mohammad Ali Hinnah, a wealthy Bombay lawyer and implacable foe of Gandhi's predominantly Hindu Indian National Congress, insisted that the largely Moslem provinces of British India be granted independence as a separate nation to be called Pakistan (Land of the Pure). Lord Mountbatten, the last British viceroy and architect of the British withdrawal, was unable to reconcile the two sides; British rule formally ended on August 15, 1947, with the subcontinent divided between two hostile sovereign states.

The immense and intricate job of dividing the assets of the British Raj between India and Pakistan was accompanied by bloody religious riots. At least 1 million people died in these clashes and in the simultaneous wholesale exchange of minorities. Some 6 million terrified Moslems living in India fled to Pakistan, and about 5 million Hindus left Pakistan for India during the first few weeks of independence.

They traveled mostly on foot and had only the possessions they could carry. The long caravans winding for miles across the hot north Indian plain were frequently attacked by members of the opposing religion.

Indian-Pakistani disputes

Scarcely two months after the British left, India and Pakistan became embroiled in a shooting war over the northern princely state of Jammu and Kashmir, which had a Hindu maharajah and an overwhelmingly Moslem population. A truce arranged under United Nations auspices left Pakistan in possession of the western part of the state while India held the rest, including the fabled Vale of Kashmir, and the capital, Srinagar. Other quarrels over the disposition of former princely states, whose rulers had been advised by the British to join one or the other of the two new Dominions, further poisoned relations.

The enmity between India and Pakistan created difficulties for the United States, which tried to be friendly to both. India, with a population of more than 600 million, the second biggest in the world after China, was the world's largest democracy. Pakistan was strategically situated with the borders

A passenger train near Bombay, India.

UN Photo 152,011/Oddbjorn Monsen

170

of China, the Soviet Union and Afghanistan meeting at the northwestern tip of Pakistani territory. Jawaharlal Nehru, prime minister of India after Gandhi was assassinated by a Hindu fanatic resentful of the leader's tolerant attitude toward Moslems, was a powerful voice among the nonaligned nations.

Formation of Bangladesh

When Pakistan was divided from India in 1947, it consisted of two non-contiguous parts: the West Pakistan, inhabited by Punjabis with language and cultural ties to the Arab Middle East; and the smaller, but more populous and resource-poor East Pakistan, inhabited by Bengalis with close tribal ties to India. Pakistan's government was controlled by the Punjabis until the election of 1970 when Bengalis won a legislative majority and sought autonomy from West Pakistan. When negotiations failed, the West Pakistan army invaded East Pakistan. India took East Pakistan's side in the dispute. Over 9 million Bengali refugees streamed into India. In late 1971, Indian military forces crossed the border and defeated the West Pakistan army. The new Bengali nation of Bangladesh was formed in 1972.

Destruction and animosities left by the war created economic and political problems for the new nation. Plagued by a series of devastating weather conditions, its agricultural population suffers extremely low health and living standards. It relies on India for food and other aid.

America between two fires

Since the United States had supported the struggle for freedom from British rule, it stood high in the regard of many Indians. India became the largest single recipient of U.S economic aid. Pakistan, besides receiving economic assistance, also obtained U.S. military equipment as an ally in Southeast Asian and Middle Eastern mutual defense arrangements.

American economic assistance to India incensed Pakistan, which felt that the food and other items furnished by the United States enabled the New Delhi government to divert its own resources into a military buildup aimed at Pakistan. Indians, on the other hand, were angered by America's supply of arms to Pakistan. Thus Washington, hoping to bolster the stability of the subcontinent by sponsoring a rough military balance between the two contending powers, incurred resentment on both sides.

Soviet-Indian relations

History favored the Soviet Union in the contest for the friendship of India and Pakistan. As the world's richest and most powerful country, the United States inherited much of the discredit as well

as the prestige that was attached to imperial Britain. The history of racial discrimination in the United States was well known and deeply offensive to Asians to whom, in any case, white skin connoted colonialism. The Russians escaped these stigmata despite their Caucasian race and colonialist history. The Indians, it appeared, equated colonialism with their experience of invasion by white people from across the sea.

The Soviets also profited politically from an inclination among Asians to equate capitalism with colonialism. Most Indians leaned toward socialism or the Nehru formula for a "mixed economy."

Moscow gained India's favor with economic aid and favorable terms in commercial exchanges. During the prime ministership of Nehru's daughter, Mrs. Indira Gandhi, New Dehli and Moscow entered into military agreement stressing mutual defense interests.

Indian-Chinese friendship

India was one of the first countries to recognize the People's Republic of China. There ensued a period of India-China friendship, in which the slogan *"Hindi-Chini Bhai-Bhai"* — roughly translatable as "Indians and Chinese Are Brothers" — appeared on banners all over India. The popular impression spread by New Delhi that the new relationship restored an old friendship was faulty history. There had been little contact between the two great Asian cultures over the centuries other than a few visits to India by Chinese travelers.

Indian-Chinese border war

The myth of Indian-Chinese brotherhood underwent a severe strain when China invaded Tibet in 1959. India, which wanted Tibet to remain an autonomous buffer state, strongly protested the invasion and gave sanctuary to the Dalai Lama, the Tibetan spiritual and temporal ruler. Shortly afterward, China forcibly occupied a disputed area along India's wild northwest frontier. A short, sharp border war ensued in which the Chinese swiftly demonstrated their superiority over the poorly equipped and badly led Indian defenders. After advancing deeply into northeastern India in a convincing show of strength, the Chinese withdrew to the boundary of the territory they claimed. India recalled its ambassador from Beijing but did not dismantle its embassy. Relations remained strained for many years.

The Gandhi regime

Vigorous efforts by the Indian government to improve the economy were hampered by inefficiency, corruption and poor harvests caused by alternate droughts and floods — standard hazards of the capricious Indian climate. Failures on the economic front have bred political unrest. The ruling Congress Party, which began as a broadly-based independence movement embracing many diverse groups, was torn by factionalism after the death of Nehru in 1964. Two years later, his daughter, Indira Gandhi, took over the prime ministership. She was the third prime minister since India gained its independence.

Mrs. Gandhi achieved a towering popularity after India defeated Pakistan in the 1971 war that severed East Pakistan which became the People's Republic of Bangladesh. Indians were delighted with Mrs. Gandhi's part in the victory, which deprived Pakistan of more than half its population and a major source of revenue from fields of jute and rice. Mrs. Gandhi's prestige reached a new peak with the first explosion of an Indian nuclear device in the Rajasthan desert in 1974, an event that disturbed Pakistan and other countries.

However, domestic dissatisfactions soon reasserted themselves. Mrs. Gandhi found herself confronting a powerful opposition movement which cut across political lines. United against her were disaffected members of her own Congress Party, the right-wing parties, socialists and others. The streets of New Delhi and other cities reverberated to the chants of anti-government marchers. In June 1975, Mrs. Gandhi declared a state of emergency, asserting that the country was endangered by a violent, irresponsible opposition. She ordered the arrest of thousands of dissidents, who were held without trials or hearings. She placed the normally outspoken Indian press under censorship, prohibiting the publication of critical material even when voiced in open Parliament. After Mrs. Gandhi was convicted on charges of minor election irregularities, she used her control of the parliamentary majority to change the constitution, weaken the judiciary and make the courts subordinate to the Parliament. With decrees and a ruthless use of the police, she brought India under authoritarian rule.

Mrs. Gandhi's methods, though denounced at home and abroad, were credited with administering a needed overhaul to India's chaotic economic and social environment that had long impeded progress. Under Gandhi's stern direction, punishment of wrongdoing was swift and harsh. Honesty and efficiency became part of Indian official life for the first time in memory. On the other hand, her suppression of virtually all civil rights outraged many

Outside Calcutta, Indians bathe in river alongside sacred cattle.

of the educated elite, among others, and resentment seethed beneath an outward calm.

Mrs. Gandhi's inexperienced son Sanjay, whom she had made her chief adviser and lieutenant, unwisely permitted the faltering national population-control program to be carried to an untenable extreme: Countless village males were forced to undergo sterilization by irreversible vasectomy, on pain of losing job promotions and other vested rights. Sanjay Gandhi was also accused of corruption — charges he and his mother would later face in court. Stung by the criticism emanating from many parts of the democratic world, as well as in her own country, and confident that her reforms had gained the affection of the Indian masses, Mrs. Gandhi called a national election in 1977, believing it would vindicate her policies. This proved to be her undoing. The fragmented Congress Party was overwhelmingly voted out of power, Mrs. Gandhi was soundly defeated in her home constituency, and Sanjay lost his first try for elective office. The reign of Indira Gandhi was over for the time being, but she would soon return to the political arena.

Closer relations with U.S.

The revolt at the polls elected a government founded on the new Janata (People's) Party, a coalition of opposition groups headed by Morarji Desai, a veteran of the anti-British agitation. Taking over as prime minister, Desai dismantled the authoritarian structure created by Mrs. Gandhi, restored constitutional rights, reversed the preceding government's drift toward the Soviet orbit and resumed what he called "true nonalignment." In practice, the shift in foreign policy meant closer relations with the United States.

One of Desai's early official acts as prime minister was to visit Washington. He assured President Carter that India had no intention of pursuing Mrs. Gandhi's nuclear experimentation with further atmospheric explosions. He declined, however, to commit India to the *Nuclear Non-Proliferation Treaty* sponsored by the United States, the Soviet Union and many other countries, on the ground that the pact discriminated against the smaller countries. The real need in India's view was universal nuclear disarmament.

The Desai government was divided by personal animosities and the inherent divisiveness of the Janata Party, an artificial union of clashing political interests brought together by common antipathy to Mrs. Gandhi. Unpopular policies in New Delhi alienated some provinces. One example was the determination of the new prime minister, a devout Hindu, to reimpose the total prohibition of alcoholic beverages — which had been tried and repudiated before — despite widespread opposition to the measure. Another was his insistence that Hindi, an Aryan vernacular spoken in the north, serve as the national language. The southern provinces have proud Dravidian linguistic traditions of their own.

Mrs. Gandhi, who by then was facing a series of legal charges growing out of the excesses of her administration, sensed a swing against the Desai government and attempted a political comeback. As she traveled around the country addressing rallies and denouncing the new regime's failures, it became apparent that she still had a substantial following of admirers. It seemed clear that Mrs. Gandhi remained an important political factor in India and on the international scene. The prospect that she might be sent to prison was less threatening to her comeback try than might be supposed: Going to jail for political offenses has long been considered an accolade in India — a result of the revolutionary experience in British times.

By 1979, the Janata Party coalition began to disintegrate, and Prime Minister Desai, at age 83, resigned. The following year, Indira Ghandi's Congress Party won a sweeping victory, and she was returned to office. This vindication by the electorate was marred, however, by the death in a plane crash of Sanjay, her son and political heir. Mrs. Gandhi was assassinated in October 1984 by two of her Sikh bodyguards. Rioting followed, thousands of Sikhs were killed, and 50,000 were left homeless. Her son Rajiv replaced her as prime minister. By the end of the decade, India's population had passed 800 million, second only to China.

Sri Lanka

In 1977, in the neighboring island state of Sri Lanka, formerly Ceylon, off India's southeastern shore, another strong-willed woman, Prime Minister Sirimavo Bandaranaike, was voted out at the polls by an economically-depressed electorate. Her successor, Junius Jayewardene, conservative and pro-Western, changed the island nation from a dominion into a republic and established himself as president. Like India, Sri Lanka suffered from strife between the Sinhalese majority, who were mostly Buddhists, and the Hindu descendants of Indian immigrants. In 1982, the nation held its first popular election for president, and Jayewardene won a new six-year term. The 1980s were plagued by civil strife between the Sinhalese and Tamils. Since 1983, over 10,000 people have perished.

Afghanistan

Afghanistan is a landlocked country located in central Asia. It is bordered by the U.S.S.R. on the north, Iran on the west, Pakistan on the south and China on its eastern tip. Few of its natural resources have been developed. Ninety percent of its population is illiterate. Most people live in rural areas. The average life expectancy is 40 years.

In 1978, the government was overthrown and replaced by a pro-Marxist government. The government signed a treaty of "friendship and cooperation" with the Soviet Union which supplied military and economic aid to Afghanistan.

Most of Afghanistan's people are Moslems. Opposition developed to Soviet influence in the country, and the government appeared on the verge of collapse. A coup occurred and a new president, Babrak Karmal, was installed. Tribal guerrillas opposed Karmal's government, and the Soviets sent around 50,000 troops to quell the rebellion. The Soviets claimed that they were responding to a request from the Afghan government to supply military aid. The Soviet Union has always considered Afghan mountain passes to be strategic routes to the Indian subcontinent.

The use of Soviet troops, tanks and helicopters — the latter used to bombard rebel villages with explosives as well as lethal gases — initially turned the tide in favor of the Karmal regime. However, Afghanistan is a wild, mountainous country better suited to guerrilla warfare than sophisticated battlefield technology. The Afghan *Mujahedeen* (fighters for the faith), operating from bases in Pakistan and supplied by non-communist nations, regained control of the countryside, and the fighting was stalemated. The Soviet losses mounted, and in 1982, the Russians entered negotiations to end the war. All Soviet troops were withdrawn in early 1989. Fighting continued between the government troops and the Mujahedeen with no conclusive outcome at the end of a decade of war.

Nepal

The shifting political tides of the late 1970s which swept the subcontinent reached even the remote Himalayan kingdom of Nepal, where the Chinese and Indian spheres of influence meet in the valley of Katmandu. China and the Soviet Union have given Nepal aid, as have India and the United States; but India's control of Nepal's access to the sea gives New Delhi the most powerful influence on the kingdom. Nepal may be the only country in the world whose constitution describes the government as "partyless;" All power resides with King Birendra, who is considered to be a reincarnation of the Hindu god Vishnu. In recent years, the young monarch has faced a demand for democratization.

Pakistan

Pakistan has remained in a state of marshall law since 1977, when the autocratic President Ali Bhutto was ousted in a military coup. He was convicted of responsibility for political murders and sentenced to death. Although political parties and activities are outlawed, President Mohammed Zia-ul-Haq, administrator of the marshall law regime, convened a national advisory council in 1982 to discuss a return to elected government within a few years. Zia was killed when his plane exploded in August 1988. Benizar Bhutto, daughter of former President Ali Bhutto was named prime minister, following elections in November 1988. She is the first woman to head a Moslem state.

Zia's government had been the target of attacks by terrorist groups which he claimed were backed by the Soviet Union. Relations between the two nations had been strained since 2.7 million refugees fled to Pakistan following the Soviet invasion of Afghanistan. Even though the Soviets have withdrawn from Afghanistan, the war continues, and Pakistan still has several million Afghani refugees.

Relations between the United States and Pakistan have had ups and downs. In 1979, a mob of Islamic fundamentalists destroyed the $21 million U.S. Embassy in Islamabad. Lives were lost, and the Pakistani authorities were slow to respond to the situation. The U.S. cut off aid for a time in 1980 when it was learned that Pakistan was secretly developing a nuclear device.

Southeast Asia and the South Pacific

Defenders of the American role in Vietnam used to cite the "domino theory," which held that the loss of one country to the communists would inevitably be followed by the loss of others in the region, like the fall of a whole row of dominoes after the first is tipped over, each in turn knocking down the one next to it. The theory was at least partially vindicated in Southeast Asia since the communist victory in Vietnam was followed quickly by the conquests of neighboring Cambodia and Laos. Proponents of the theory erred, however, in their assumption that a bloc of communist states in Southeast Asia would prove to be a united force, backed by their huge Chinese neighbor. Instead, the communist nations soon began quarreling among themselves. Ancient animosities began to surface that prevented a common communist front from developing.

The end of European colonialism in Southeast Asia

When Japan attacked Pearl Harbor on December 7, 1941, the only independent country in Southeast Asia was the kingdom of Thailand, known at that time as Siam. The sprawling welter of islands now called Indonesia was a Dutch colony known as the Netherlands East Indies. The other great Southeast Asian archipelago, the Philippines, belonged to the United States, a trophy of the Spanish-American War. The territory now comprising the sovereign state of Malaysia was a group of British colonies or British-protected sultanates. Britain also ruled Burma. Cambodia and Laos were vassal kingdoms under the French, as were the provinces of Cochin China, Annam and Tonkin, in what is now the Socialist Republic of Vietnam.

The Japanese expelled the European rulers from all these territories. The loss of Southeast Asia's vast wealth in tin, rubber, oil and other strategic materials was a serious detriment to the Allied war effort. The area evolved into revolutionary governments. Such was the genesis of the Republic of Indonesia, headed by President Sukarno, and the Republic of Vietnam, under President Ho Chi Minh. Unlike Indonesia and Vietnam, the British territories were freed peacefully in successive steps, as were the Philippines. Communist insurgencies quickly materialized in all the Southeast Asian countries and still smolder in Myanmar, Thailand, Malaysia and the Philippines. The Philippines, where an earlier agrarian guerrilla revolt was put down after years of fighting, have also been plagued by an armed uprising of Moslems in the southern islands.

The Golden Triangle

The opium poppy, a source of illicit heroin and morphine, has been grown in the rugged hills of Mayanmar (formerly Burma), Thailand and Laos for hundreds of years. The 70,000-square-mile region, called the *Golden Triangle,* produces more than half the world's heroin supply. Opium production in Maynmar, which is the world's largest producer, doubled between 1988 and 1990, mainly due to the end of a drought but also due to increasing world demand for heroin. Both Laos and Thailand assist in processing and smuggling the drug.

Growing opium poppies is an ancient tradition in southern Asia. The poor peasants in this region have no other way to make a living than to grow poppies. Though they are unaware of its importance,

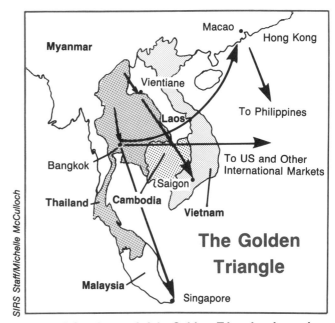

Map of Southeast Asia's Golden Triangle shows how opium grown from poppies in Myanmar, processed into heroin and smuggled through Laos and Thailand is distributed around the world.

their poppies contribute to the billion-dollar business of drug trafficking worldwide. During the Vietnam War, it was discovered that opium production could be turned into massive profits by selling heroin to American troops. From this start, the traffickers spread their market, first to Europe and then to the United States.

The Vietnam War

The conflict in Vietnam has gone down in history as the first war that the United States lost. The ill-fated U.S. involvement had come about slowly. After the defeat of the French in 1954, Vietnam was partitioned, pending free elections, into a communist north and a non-communist south. The United States supported the anti-communist regime of President Ngo Dinh Diem in Saigon. The projected elections never took place because the two sides were unable to agree on conditions. Guerrilla operations in the south escalated, with support from Hanoi, the northern capital. President Diem called upon the United States for military assistance. Washington moved from an advisory role and supplying large amounts of equipment and economic aid to an open combat role, eventually fielding hundreds of thousands of men from a network of expensive bases. Meanwhile, the Vietcong, as the insurgents in South Vietnam were called, were augmented by organized units from the north.

In South Vietnam, the guerrillas and their supporters had widespread local support. Americans, as white foreigners fighting Asians, inherited the odium that had been attached to the French. The

U.S. intervention, which extended into operations against rebels in Cambodia and Laos, was widely opposed in the United States, and by other countries around the world. U.S. military commanders complained that they were fatally handicapped by being forbidden, for political reasons both at home and abroad, from invading the North. Finally, as the southern capital, Saigon, was about to fall to the victorious communist forces in April 1975, the U.S. forces retreated by air; the war in Vietnam was over. Resistance to the communists also collapsed in Cambodia and Laos, ending 30 years of struggle to retain a Western foothold in Indochina.

More than 300,000 U.S. soldiers were wounded and 46,000 killed. The war cost about $140 billion. Several million Vietnamese lost their lives, and the country was devastated from bombings. More tonnage was dropped on Vietnam than in all of World War II.

Communist take-over of Indochina

The next years saw a consolidation of communist rule in the three countries. Refugees fled Vietnam by the tens of thousands in boats, many of them to perish at sea. Others slipped through the tropical rainforest into Thailand from Cambodia, or furtively crossed the Mekong River into Thailand from Laos. They brought with them stories of repression, including the evacuation of city dwellers to the country, where they were forced to labor in rice paddies. Despite these accounts, some foreign observers reported that the Vietnamese transition to communist rule appeared benign. Cambodia, which was renamed Kampuchea, became a closed country under the government of the Khmer Rouge, as the communists called themselves. Refugees described the execution of thousands of non-communists. A few neutral journalists and diplomats permitted into the country gave vivid accounts of deserted cities, whose inhabitants had been driven into the countryside, and the disappearance of any form of communication except hand-delivered messages carried from one village to another on foot. Over 1 million people were killed in a nation of 7 million.

Vietnam and Kampuchea quickly became enmeshed in large-scale border fighting over territorial claims and counterclaims dating from centuries-old wars. Long-standing animosities erupted between Vietnam and Thailand, where a large Vietnamese expatriate colony had long been the object of Thai suspicion and dislike. Complaints of official mistreatment by the sizable minority of ethnic Chinese in Vietnam brought Hanoi into conflict with Beijing. The incident recalled an ancient Vietnamese hatred of China, derived from more than a thousand years of oppressive Chinese occupation, a period still remembered in Vietnam although it ended in the 10th century.

The Vietnamese army invaded Cambodia in 1978 in support of a guerrilla movement opposed to the Khmer Rouge regime. It is estimated that during the next year, over half of the Cambodian population was killed in the fighting. By 1979, the Vietnamese and their allies had captured the capital, Phnom Phen, overthrowing the government of Pol Pot. The Vietnamese-supported government controlled virtually all of the nation, although various guerrilla elements continued to operate near the Thai border. In 1982, a coalition of exiled former leaders of Cambodia announced that they had formed a rival government called Democratic Kampuchea. It included such diverse elements as Prince Norodom Sihanouk, for 15 years Cambodia's king, as well as representatives of the Khmer Rouge and the right-wing Khmer People's National Liberation Front.

Eastfoto China

China's Chairman Mao Tsetung (left) and North Vietnam President Ho Chi Minh were allies during the war in Vietnam.

In 1989, the Vietnamese withdrew from Cambodia, leaving it in the hands of their handpicked government.

Whatever the outcome of this political power struggle, the fighting in Cambodia and neighboring Laos marked the emergence of Vietnam as the strongest military power in Southeast Asia. Its large and experienced army was equipped with enormous caches of arms left behind by the retreating Americans, including sophisticated war planes. Although replacing parts could become a problem, western military experts believe that the talented Vietnamese can keep the machines functioning indefinitely.

U.S. military presence in Southeast Asia

Nearly all of the non-communist governments of Southeast Asia improved relations with China, the Soviet Union and Eastern Europe following the breakdown of the American-sponsored *Southeast Asia Treaty Organization* (SEATO), an eight-nation group that originally included the United Kingdom, France and Pakistan as well as regional powers, but which ceased to have meaning after the loss of Indochina. At the same time, individual states retained traditional military ties with their Western allies: Malaysia and Singapore with Britain, Australia and New Zealand under a treaty known as the *Five-Power Defense Agreement;* Thailand and the Philippines with the United States.

Thailand remains a military ally of the United States under a mutual security agreement and receives U.S. equipment for its armed forces. But the huge United States defense presence, maintained during the Vietnam War with more than 40,000 American service personnel stationed at air bases and other installations, proved to be an irritant and has been withdrawn. The only American bases remaining in Southeast Asia are Clark Air Base and the Subic Navy Base, both near Manila in the Philippines, both maintained under a 1947 agreement. As in Thailand, the deployment of foreign troops on Asian soil has offended nationalist sensibilities in the Philippines and causes continual friction.

The Philippines

Relations between the Philippines and the United States have evolved from outright colonialism through a kind of "big-brother" period to equality. The United States supplanted Spain as the Philippines' colonial masters following the Spanish-American War of 1898. After the islands became an independent republic on July 4, 1946, the

AP/ WIDE WORLD PHOTOS

Corazon Aquino was democratically elected as President of the Philippines in 1986.

United States retained a privileged economic position until 1975, when a treaty guaranteeing U.S. businesses equal treatment with Filipino businesses expired. By then, American private investment in the islands had reached more than $1 billion. The Philippine government continues to welcome foreign investment as an aid to development.

Land ownership is vested largely with a few wealthy proprietors, and there has been political unrest among the peasantry. The dispersal of a communist insurgency led by the Hukbalahaps, or "Huks," a former anti-Japanese guerrilla organization, was followed in 1966 by the rise of the New People's Army, a Maoist group with a following among intellectuals, students, peasants and unionists. Frustrated by the government's inability either to put down insurrection or enact land reforms against the opposition of powerful interests, President Ferdinand E. Marcos suspended constitutional processes in 1972 and placed the country under martial law. By 1982, with his wife Imelda as his chief deputy, Marcos was still in the process of developing what he vaguely called a new form of "semiparliamentary" democracy. While many deplored his methods, which he candidly described as "authoritarian," many Filipinos admired his progress in bringing stability to an unruly society.

The Marcos' government took a tentative step toward restoring democracy in 1982, holding the first local elections in a decade. Marcos' visit to the United States for talks with President Reagan, however, drew protests from the Filipinos in this country, and was accompanied by condemnations of his alleged human rights violations by international organizations such as *Amnesty International.*

Following a rigged election in 1986, Marcos was declared a winner over Corazon Aquino. In the turmoil that followed, Marcos was persuaded to leave the country. He and his wife went to Hawaii under the protection of the U.S. government, and Mrs. Aquino became the President. She has survived several serious threats to overthrow her government. The next major challenge is to determine the fate of the two remaining U.S. air force and naval bases in the Philippines.

Australia and New Zealand

Australia and New Zealand, with a combined population of about 20 million people, are important players in Asian-Pacific affairs. Increasingly, their dynamic economies are becoming more interdependent with other Asian nations. Australia is rich in natural resources, especially coal which is exported to many East Asian nations. Both New Zealand and Australia fought on the side of the Allied powers during World Wars I and II. In 1951, Australia, New Zealand and the United States signed a pact of mutual security assistance (ANZUS). However, New Zealand's refusal to permit U.S. ships with nuclear weapons to enter its harbors ended the alliance in 1986.

Pacific islands

The only U.S. territory in the South Pacific is the tiny dependency of American Samoa, a group of seven small islands whose 30,000 or so Polynesian inhabitants are American nationals — but not citizens; they elect their own governor and legislature. Other territories with historic ties to the U.S. participate in South Pacific regional activities although they lie north of the equator. They include: the island of Guam, taken from Spain in 1898 along with the Philippines; the nearby Commonwealth of the Northern Marianas, former Japanese dependencies that voluntarily joined the United States; and the Trust territory of the Pacific Islands, or Micronesia, a United Nations Trusteeship administered by the United States.

In this group, the 29 atolls and five coral islands of the Marshall Islands represent a special legacy of the nuclear age. The questions of U.S. reparations for the population removed from the Bikini Atoll atomic test sight in 1946, and continuing use of Kwajalein as a missile test sight, are unresolved. A permanent political relationship between Micronesia and the United States, with local autonomy, is being formed. By 1982, the U.S. had granted limited independence to the New Federated States of Micronesia. Guam is an important military base. A strategic defense potential also exists in the Northern Marianas. Titian, one of the islands, was where the B-29 bombers took off from with the atomic bombs that were dropped on Hiroshima and Nagasaki. The heart of American defenses in the Pacific remains at Pearl Harbor and other major bases near Honolulu, Hawaii.

From Hawaii, the American defense lines extend south to Australia and New Zealand, with whom the United States is linked by a treaty of mutual security known as ANZUS. Despite local pressures for a more neutral stance in world affairs, ANZUS remains the keystone of foreign policy in both Australia and New Zealand. The wartime animosity against Japan in the Pacific has all but disappeared with that country's emergence as a major economic power. It is a common saying in the area that the Japanese have gained through trade what they failed to achieve by war.

Emerging island nations

Since the end of World War II, many of the South Pacific islands which figured prominently in that conflict as battlegrounds or bases have become independent. These include Fiji, Western Samoa, the Solomon Islands, Papua New Guinea, Tonga, Vanuatu, Kiribati, Nauru and Tuvalu (formerly called the Ellice Islands). Mostly small, and in some cases overpopulated, many of these new countries face endemic economic strains. For some, the main prospect for economic growth lies in the uncertain field of tourism. Island governments look to outside powers and international organizations for technical assistance in such areas as fisheries development. Financial help has been limited, but so is the capacity of most islands to absorb large amounts of aid.

The United States, the Soviet Union, the People's Republic of China and Japan were among the first powers outside the region to establish embassies in the new Island states. All of the new nations adopted constitutions modeled on the British parliamentary form of government, with modifications adapted to local traditions. They also became either members or associate members of the Commonwealth, a result of the former colonial connections with either Britain, Australia or New Zealand.

With the encouragement and participation of Australia and New Zealand, the independent and self-governing territories — those which have not yet gained their nationhood, like New Zealand's Cook Islands — formed an effective intergovernmental organization called the *South Pacific Forum.* It meets periodically to formulate common positions of mutual concern, such as international fisheries policy. Fiji, Western Samoa and Papua New Guinea joined the United Nations as full members.

France maintains the strongest western presence in the South Pacific, ruling a far-flung colonial domain including the mineral-rich island of New Caledonia, the vast collection of islands and atolls known as French Polynesia, and the small Polynesian territory of Wallis and Futuna. The French use the Mururoa atoll, in the Tuamotu group southeast of Tahiti, for nuclear tests. Under pressure by local independence movements, Paris has allowed varying degrees of autonomy in New Caledonia and French Polynesia, but has shown no willingness to dissolve the French empire in the South Pacific.

The Pacific Rim

Nations which border the Pacific Ocean in both Asia and the Americas are called the Pacific Rim. Economic growth on the Asian side of the rim was so rapid during the 1980s that some analysts predict the 21st century will be called the Pacific Century.

Japan is clearly the leading participant in this economic growth. The world's top 10 banks are located in Japan, and it has the world's largest stock market. Japan provides investment capital for growth in other Asian nations. Investments in U.S. and Canadian assets by buyers from Japan and Hong Kong have increased by leaps and bounds.

Japan and the four Asian "tigers" — South Korea, Taiwan, Hong Kong and Singapore — have led the world in economic growth rates during the 1980s and are increasingly looked to as role models by other developing nations such as Thailand and Mexico.

Mainly due to trade competition with these Asian centers, the U.S. trade deficit quadrupled in the 1980s from $40 billion to over $170 billion. In the 1990s, the Asian nations of the Pacific Rim will be as big a market as North America or Europe.

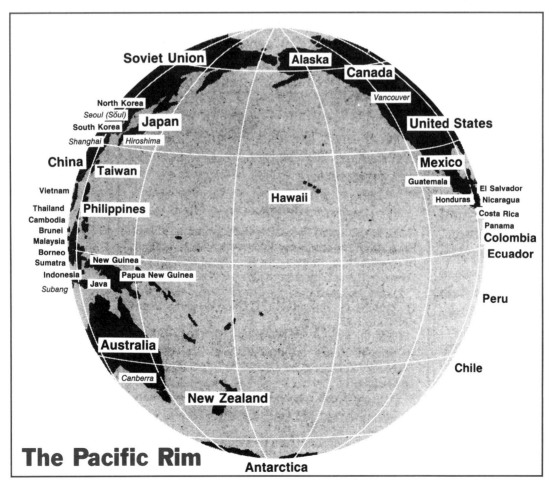

The Pacific Rim

Courtesy, University of Kansas Map Associates, Dr. George F. McCleary, Jr., Director

Scale 1:38,700,000

0 |—|—|—|—|—| 500 Kilometers

0 |—|—|—|—|—| 500 Nautical Miles

Boundary representation is
not necessarily authoritative.

The World Factbook, 1989

The World Factbook, 1989

The World Factbook, 1989

Chapter 22

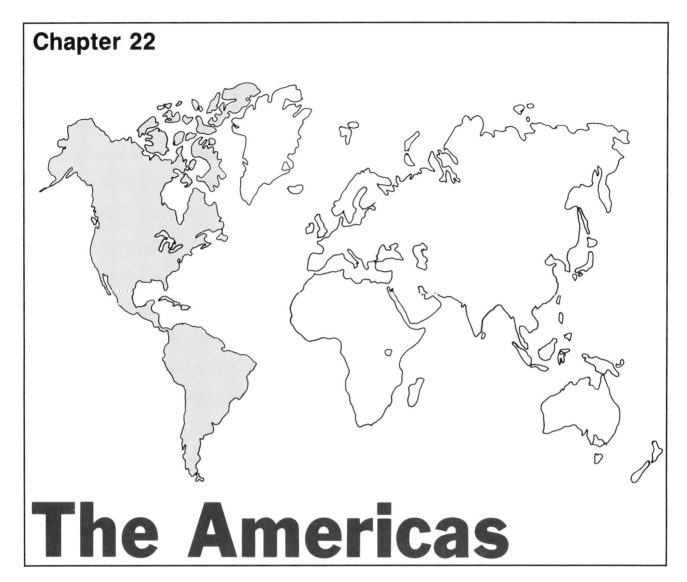

The Americas

In the 15th century, Europeans believed that a "new world" had been discovered. This New World, the Western Hemisphere of the globe, was called America.

Consisting of Canada, the United States, Mexico, Central America, South America and the Caribbean islands, the Americas is culturally divided into two regions — North America and Latin America. The beginning of European exploration and settlement of the Western Hemisphere goes back only 500 years. The predominant cultural influence in North America comes from the English; and in Latin America from the Spanish.

The Western Hemisphere was not a "new world." Thousands of years before the arrival of Europeans, the two continents had been populated by immigrants from Asia. These people, named Indians by Christopher Columbus, had come from Asia thousands of years before over a land bridge between Asia and North America.

Many Indian tribes were nomadic, and their beliefs concerning ownership of land differed from those of the Europeans. Most American Indians believed that no one could "own" the land. The Europeans, with more advanced weapons, conquered the Indian tribes and claimed the land. The Indians were treated as an obstacle to the European acquisition of wealth and land.

The "Age of Exploration" began when the techniques of long-distance sailing and navigation were greatly improved by the Portuguese during the 15th century. The search for gold and the luxury items of the East led to sailing expeditions around the southern tip of Africa to India and China. When Christopher Columbus, financed by the Spanish monarchy, sought a shorter, western route to China, he "discovered" the New World.

Many others followed Columbus' route, eventually circumnavigating the world. In this early modern period of European history, competition was fierce among nations in their quest for wealth and territory in the New World. In the 1500s, the three most powerful European nations were Spain, England and France. These three nations fought for control of the New World and its potential wealth.

Spain established settlements in Mexico, Central America and South America 100 years before the English settled on the east coast of North America. The French settled in Louisana and Quebec; Portugal controlled Brazil. Dutch, Swedes, Scots, Irish and Germans also settled in North America. African slaves accounted for a large portion of the colonial American population. The early European settlers created a new culture which mixed the prejudices and practices of their past with the economic and political promise of a new land. The traditions and customs, manners and fashions, languages and religions, social and political institutions brought from Europe are reflected in the present cultures of the Americas.

Canada

Canada is the second largest country, by area, in the world. Only the Soviet Union is larger. An enduring influence on Canada's history has been the fact that it was originally colonized by both England and France. In 1763, at the end of the Seven Year's War in Europe, France lost its colony of Quebec to England. Despite assimilation efforts by both the British and, later, Canadian governments, the culture and institutions established by the original French settlers remain to the present day.

Despite a common culture and history, the American Revolution fostered divisions between Canada and the U.S. Canada became a haven for British loyalists after the Revolution and was allied with Britain against the U.S. during the War of 1812. During the Civil War (1861-65), Britain was officially neutral but unofficially supported the separatist South. Fear of retaliation by Union forces against the nearest British entity, Canada, prompted many Canadians to favor a strong national government.

In 1867, the English Parliament passed the *British North America Act,* which laid the foundation for a Canadian nation. At that time there were only four political entities in Canada: West and East Canada, once known as Upper and Lower Canada (really British Ontario and French Quebec), New Brunswick and Nova Scotia. The Act was modeled on established British practice: A governor-general represented the Crown, and a Canadian House of Commons was to be elected and operated like its counterpart in London. In Canada there was also to be a Senate, with membership apportioned among

the provinces. The senators were chosen by the governor-general from names presented by the prime minister. Most important, any amendment to the 1867 Act had to be approved by the English Parliament.

Relations with the U.S.

Canada did not immediately develop its northern territories. Instead, Canada grew westward along the United States border. Travel was easier south of the border. The United States had built a transcontinental rail link in 1869. Canada did not do likewise until 1885, so much of the traffic between British Columbia and Eastern Canada went through United States territory. The same was true of many journeys to the plains areas west of the Great Lakes. This, plus the ease of crossing the unfortified border, created a considerable feeling of unity between Americans and Canadians.

Security. In the 20th century, security became a cornerstone of Canadian-American relations. Canada entered World War II in 1939 a British ally. The U.S. did not enter the war until 1941. Canada was an original member of the *North Atlantic Treaty Organization* (NATO), and special military ties between Canada and the U.S. were negotiated. As with many other aspects of NATO, the Canadian-American security connection has been muted in recent years. Canadian nationalists have not always been happy about their links with the United States. Some friction developed during the Vietnam War when many Americans crossed the Canadian border to avoid the draft and stayed. Nevertheless, in spite of some bitterness on both sides of the line, Canada and the United States continue to enjoy comfortable associations.

Trade. Perhaps the liveliest aspect of Canadian-American relations concerns trade between the two nations, and the domestic legislation that bears on it. Canada's wealth is derived in large part from its mineral holdings, particularly gas and oil. Other important resources include fish and lumber from Nova Scotia and New Brunswick, farm products from Prince Edward Island and Quebec, manufactured goods from Ontario, wheat from Manitoba and Saskatchewan, cattle from Alberta, timber and metals from British Columbia, and salmon from the Pacific coast.

In the early 1980s, the government of Prime Minister Pierre Trudeau began a policy of *Canadianization* in key sectors of the economy dominated by foreigners. The Ottawa government expressed concern that more than one-third of Canada's manufacturing was U.S.-controlled. It introduced a National Energy Program aimed at raising the federal government's share of gas and oil revenues,

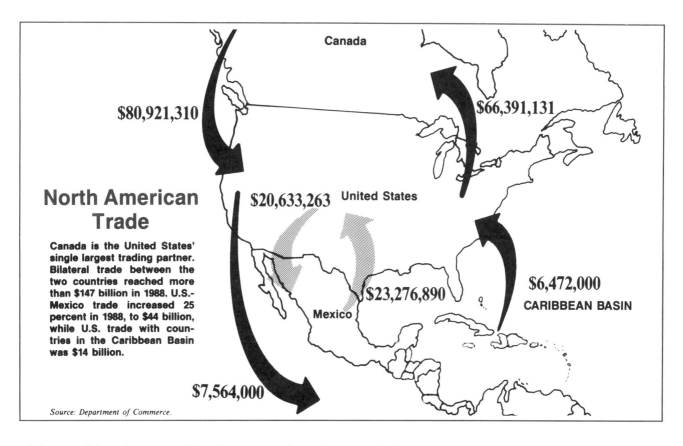

North American Trade

Canada is the United States' single largest trading partner. Bilateral trade between the two countries reached more than $147 billion in 1988. U.S.-Mexico trade increased 25 percent in 1988, to $44 billion, while U.S. trade with countries in the Caribbean Basin was $14 billion.

$80,921,310

$66,391,131

$20,633,263   United States

Canada

$23,276,890

Mexico

$6,472,000
CARIBBEAN BASIN

$7,564,000

Source: Department of Commerce.

giving special preference to Canadian companies and purchasing several large foreign firms. This "Canada First" policy, coming at a time of worldwide recession, had a high cost: unemployment, soaring inflation, a shrinking Canadian dollar and a flight of capital abroad.

A range of issues confronts the two nations. For many years boundary lines have been subject to negotiation, especially in the island-studded waters of Puget Sound and the Maine-New Brunswick coast. Most of these boundary disputes have been settled with little tension. This is not the case, however, when it comes to fixing boundaries at sea beyond the traditional three-mile limit, and establishing fishing rights.

Acid rain. Another thorny problem concerns industrial pollution of the atmosphere, which Canada claims is not taken seriously in the U.S. Thousands of lakes in Canada are now dead, a result of *acid rain* created by air pollution from northeast U.S. industry. In 1988, Prime Minister Mulroney and President Reagan agreed to a joint effort to combat the problem, although no final decision has been made on how the project will be funded. Nevertheless, Canada is committed to a 50-percent reduction by 1990 in domestic pollutants which cause acid rain.

Cultural imperialism. Canada is also troubled by America's *cultural imperialism.* Its cities are near the United States and can easily be overwhelmed by the flow of American television, movies, books and periodicals. Many talented Canadian artists and writers are lured to the more lucrative markets for their skills in the United States. Canada passed laws encouraging the use of Canadian talent within Canada (while discouraging Americans) and forbidding Canadian firms to take tax credit for money spent on advertising in the United States. Nevertheless, Canada continues to have close cultural ties to the U.S.

Provincial discontent

Until 1982, Canada was governed under the provisions of the 1867 British North America Act, which provided for a loose federation of four provinces, since grown to 10, plus the vast Yukon and Northwest Territories. Each of these political subunits claimed great political autonomy under the Act. Much of the insistence on provincial autonomy springs from the facts of geography and economics. The Maritime Provinces of Nova Scotia, Newfoundland, New Brunswick, and Prince Edward Island have known a good deal of economic distress and turn to the government in Ottawa for aid. Ontario is the major center of manufacturing and population and is particularly concerned with issues of tariffs and immigration. Manitoba and Saskatchewan are the Prairie Provinces, great producers of wheat: They are interested in good relations with China and the Soviet Union which buy much of their crop. Alberta is a semi-Prairie Province which raises cattle, but it is also rich in gas and oil and frequently is at odds with Ottawa over the pricing and distribution of these commodities. British Columbia, long cut off from the rest of Canada by the Rocky Mountains, does not care for federal regulations on production and pricing.

In 1931, the *Statute of Westminster* granted political independence to all of the Dominions of Great Britain. Canada had its own flag and effective political autonomy, although it still acknowledged the monarchy and ties to the mother country. Because Canada's 1867 constitution lacked an amendment procedure, only Britain had authority to approve constitutional changes. At Canada's request, Britain retained that right after Westminster. This unwieldly formula created a long-term dilemma for Canada. Often, when reform-minded leaders sought to modernize the government, conservative British leaders refused to approve implementing amendments. For another 51 years, Canada could not achieve a national consensus on the proper relationship of the provinces to the federal government in Ottawa. Following World War II, the reemergence of separatist movements, primarily in Quebec but also in other provinces, threatened the political and economic stability of the nation.

French separatism

Quebec has always presented a special case for cultural and linguistic *separatism*. When the French abandoned Canada, French-speaking enclaves were left behind in the Maritimes and Ontario. Quebec was the center of the French population and the heart of its cultural and political strength. The British moved in for business reasons; the French were primarily farmers and fishermen. Montreal, a major seaport in Quebec, developed a large *Anglophone* or English-speaking population. A number of French political revolts occurred, aimed at establishing the special rights of the French-speaking population. The Canadian Liberal Party depended heavily upon the French vote in Quebec, so the French-Canadian influence became considerable. Three prime ministers of Canada have come from the French-speaking community. It is a nation where 40 percent of the population is of British descent, 30 percent of French descent, and the remainder divided among a diversity of origins.

Some French-Canadians escalated their demands beyond an assurance of equal status for French as an official language. A separatist movement developed with the goal of having Quebec become a separate nation.

A new constitution

Although the question of Quebec's political separation was temporarily laid to rest, there is still strong sentiment for a French-speaking state among certain elements of the population. At the same time, the western provinces, particularly those with extensive gas and oil holdings, were grumbling about federal policies coming from Ottawa, and there were veiled threats of separatism from that region. The United States was becoming increasingly uneasy about the unstable nature of Canadian government. At this point, Prime Minister Trudeau made a strong move to achieve what had eluded his predecessors: the approval of a national constitution known as "bringing home the constitution." Actually, this entailed devising a formula for amending the existing 1867 Act to which all the provinces could agree. After intensive political maneuvering, the Canadian Parliament approved the amending formula, the Supreme Court found the action to be legal, and the formal petition was sent to London in December 1981. The English Parliament acted favorably on the bill, and Queen Elizabeth II gave royal assent to the measure. In April 1982, the Queen went to Ottawa where she read a proclamation ending the constitutional link between the two nations and signed the new constitution. The constitution and *Charter of Rights and Freedoms,* adopted in 1982, were meant to signal the beginning of a new era for Canadian unity.

A new government

Despite Trudeau's success in bringing home the new constitution, his party's popularity waned. In 1985, a general election brought the Conservative Party to power, led by Brian Mulroney, a Quebec lawyer, businessman and an eloquent bilingual speaker. Mulroney sought to re-establish Canada's traditional "special relationship" with the United States.

Approval of the new constitution remained a problem. Although it applied to Quebec, the province refused to endorse it and routinely exempted itself from the Charter when federal laws were passed. Quebec demanded constitutional recognition as a "distinct society" with the right to preserve its French culture, language and institutions; a greater share in federal decisions; and the right to veto future constitutional amendments.

In 1987, after exhaustive mediation by Mulroney, provincial leaders signed the *Meech Lake Accord,* which would recognize Quebec as a "distinct society" within the Canadian federation and give provinces veto rights over all future constitutional changes. The leaders gave themselves three years to win provincial ratification of this proposed constitutional amendment.

When the deadline approached in June 1990, ratification of the amendment did not occur. Newly-elected premiers in Newfoundland, Manitoba and New Brunswick objected to the amendment's wording, and Quebec's premier was unwilling to compromise. The long-standing controversy over Quebec's desire for maintaining the French language and customs is a difficult issue to settle.

Latin America

The Spanish settlement of Latin America began a century before the English settlement of North America. The discovery of the Western Hemisphere by Christopher Columbus in 1492 was swiftly followed by the establishment of Spanish colonies (in the Caribbean, Mexico and Peru) and a Portuguese colony in Brazil. By the time the first English settlers arrived in Jamestown in 1607, colonial empires were well established in South and Central America. The riches of the Indies had begun to flow toward Europe.

Spanish conquest

The Spanish colonization of the Western Hemisphere is one of the great adventures in human history. With a handful of men, a few horses and some cannon, Francisco Pizarro, Hernando Cortes and other conquistadors overwhelmed whole Indian empires such as the Aztecs in Mexico, the Mayans in Central America and the Incas in Peru. In part, a small number of Spaniards were able to achieve victory because the Indian populations had been greatly weakened and reduced in number by the spread of European diseases for which the natives had no immunity or cures. Great amounts of gold and silver were shipped back to Europe, enriching the coffers of merchants and aristocrats. Spain became the richest and most powerful empire the Western world had known since the Romans.

The Catholic church took an aggressive part in

SIRS Staff

A Mayan ruin in the Yucatan Peninsula illustrates the rich civilization that flourished in Central America for centuries before the Spanish conquest.

the Spanish colonial experience. The conquests were generally justified as holy crusades for the conversion of heathen savages. The church became rich and mighty, in step with Spanish military and civil power. The vast majority of Latin Americans remain nominally Catholic to this day. The church also played an important humanitarian role in the colonization. Priests complained about the treatment of the Indians by Spanish colonists who had reduced them to a state of slavery. As a result, the church pressured the Spanish crown to adopt a strict set of guidelines. This curbed some of the excesses committed by the Spanish masters against their subject populations, although it was difficult to enforce.

By the end of the 17th century, Iberian civilization stretched from Havana to Tierra del Fuego.

Independence movements

Gradually throughout the 18th century, the Spanish adventurers who had come to the New World settled down and gave rise to a city-dwelling middle class which began to absorb ideas from leaders of political movements in Western Europe. By the end of the century, small but important groups of Spanish colonists began agitating for independence from Spain. Meanwhile, the mother country, corrupted by the easy wealth of its New World possessions, had suffered a severe decline in power and prestige. When Napoleon's troops of the French Revolution invaded Spain, the spark was set to the revolutionary movement in the Spanish colonies. Charismatic leaders like Simón Bolívar in Colom-

bia and Venezuela, and José de San Martín in Argentina and Peru, assembled groups of patriots and initiated military action against the Spanish crown.

By 1830 most of the population centers of the old Spanish empire had thrown off the colonial yoke. Ten new republics were formed in South America, including the territory of Brazil, liberated from Portugal. Another 10 gained their independence in Central America and the Caribbean. Only Cuba and Puerto Rico remained under Spanish rule. On the South American continent, only three small colonies comprising Guyana were still controlled by other European powers.

For the new Latin American republics, the central economic and political fact was their relationship with the United States, the most powerful country in the hemisphere. Although many of the Latin governments and constitutions were influenced by the American revolutionary experience of 1776, their spiritual ties to Europe were much stronger. Latin Americans, moreover, had not shared the heritage of British political and parliamentary philosophy that influenced North America so strongly. Nor had they experienced the struggle for religious freedom and plurality of worship which was so important in North American society.

The Monroe Doctrine

The proclamation of the *Monroe Doctrine* in 1823, was an American response by President James Monroe to moves by European powers to reestablish their hold on former colonies in South

---

U.S. Involvement in Latin America since the Monroe Doctrine

1912 — NICARAGUA: U.S. troops were sent to silence opposition to American control of Nicaragua's economy. Military advisers remained in the country for 21 years to train military personnel to help support the Somoza dictatorship. The United States is still involved in Nicaraguan affairs.

1914 — MEXICO: The U.S. took control of the city of Veracruz in an effort to halt arms shipments to the rebels during the Mexican Revolution.

1915 — HAITI: American forces were sent to restore order after a number of political skirmishes threatened the government's stability. The forces remained in Haiti for 19 years.

1954 — GUATEMALA: CIA-backed forces rebelled against Guatemalan President Col. Jacobo Arbenz Guzman after he initiated a land-reform policy that would have split up tracts of land owned by the United Fruit Company, a U.S. corporation.

1961 — CUBA: In what became known as the "Bay of Pigs Invasion," an army of Cuban exiles, trained by the CIA, executed an unsuccessful coup against Castro's communist government.

1965 — DOMINICAN REPUBLIC: U.S. troops were sent to halt an attempted overthrow of the ruling military government.

1983 — GRENADA: After a reported coup attempt by the nation's pro-Castro government, U.S. troops invaded Grenada to protect American military bases on the island.

1989 — PANAMA: U.S. troops were ordered into Panama to avenge the killing of an American soldier, to overthrow the Noriega regime and restore democracy to Panama, to protect the Panama Canal, and to capture the country's president, General Manuel Noriega, a former CIA informant, now under indictment in the U.S. for drug trafficking.

America. The Monroe Doctrine stated that any European attempt to encroach on the hemisphere would be seen as a direct threat to the peace and safety of the United States and could not be looked upon with indifference. The Monroe Doctrine might have proved unenforceable had it not been for the British desire to open Latin American markets to their rapidly expanding commerce and to exploit the continent's vast natural resources. The British gave financial and military support to the independence movements against Spain, and the presence of the Royal Navy discouraged any schemes by Spain to retake the lost colonies.

Political turmoil

Although Latin America was freed from colonialist adventurers, it did not prosper. The new republics remained economic prisoners of their own raw materials: copper in Peru and Chile; wheat and cattle in Argentina; coffee and bananas in Brazil and other tropical territories. Their earning power was at the mercy of industrial markets. The new governments paid lip service to democratic principles, but frequently degenerated into oligarchies or dictatorships supported by armies. The Indian peasants in the countryside and the semi-industrialized workers in the cities continued to lead lives of poverty. A new upper class of Spanish descent assumed the privileges of the departed colonial viceroys and captains-general. The bright hopes of the time of independence receded in most of the republics, and Latin America sank back into economic stagnation.

At the end of the 19th century, the United States freed Cuba from Spanish rule and assumed control of Puerto Rico. Spain had lost its last vestige of power in the New World. Early in the 20th century another country emerged, the Republic of Panama. It detached itself from Colombia at the instigation of the United States, which wanted to build a canal linking the Atlantic with the Pacific. The Panama Canal, protected by a zone 10-miles wide across the Isthmus, was governed exclusively by the United States until treaties signed in 1978 promised full Panamanian control over the canal zone by the year 2000.

The Good Neighbor Policy

The importance of Latin America in the modern world was recognized in the 1930s when President Franklin D. Roosevelt, conscious of the vast human, economic, and strategic potential of the region, inaugurated his *Good Neighbor Policy,* designed to create, or revive, friendly ties between the United States and the countries to the south. Apart from some mining, agricultural, and transportation tech-

nology, there was almost no American economic presence in Latin America. Europeans, notably Great Britain, had achieved control of the supply of both capital and consumer goods. FDR's Good Neighbor Policy directed attention toward Latin America as a potential market for American goods and investment, beginning a process of economic reattachment which the Second World War completed. Commerce between Europe and Latin America was totally interrupted during the war, and the United States became the primary source of industrial goods and technology.

Latin America remained essentially a producer of raw materials. Business investment remained a high risk because of unstable political conditions in many of the countries and anti-Yankee campaigns, such as one which swept Argentina under the regime of Juan Perón (off and on between 1946 and 1974). It was to combat this view of the United States as the "Colossus of the North" that President John F. Kennedy launched his *Alliance for Progress* in 1960. He called for a partnership between the United States and Latin American peoples within a framework of economic justice.

Organization of American States

The greater part of the Western Hemisphere is encompassed in the *Organization of American States* (OAS): essentially, a partnership between the United States and the Latin American republics, with a few recent additions of non-Latin countries which became independent of declining European empires.

The International Union of American Republics was established at a conference held in Washington in 1889-90. Its name was later changed several times until it took its present form — Organization of American States. Its seat was established in Washington, as the major capital of the hemisphere. From time to time, proposals are made that the headquarters be moved to a Latin American capital, or that it be rotated among different Latin American capitals.

The OAS serves as the central organization through which the American republics maintain arrangements for defense of the Western Hemisphere; settle differences between member states; improve trade; and cooperate in such fields as science, technology, medicine and education.

At a 1945 conference in Mexico, the American republics adopted the *Act of Chapultepec* which established a system of continental security. This was followed two years later by the *Inter-American Treaty of Reciprocal Assistance,* signed at Rio de Janeiro. It established a security pact for the defense of the Western Hemisphere against attack, including the activities of international communists. Members have invoked the treaty 16 times. In 1954, with communist activities increasing in the hemisphere, a conference at Caracas adopted the *Declaration of Solidarity for the Preservation of the Political Integrity of the American States Against the Intervention of International Communism*. In 1962, Cuba was suspended as a member of the OAS following charges that Fidel Castro had plotted to assassinate the president of Venezuela and was promoting communist uprisings in sister republics. By 1975, a majority of members, including Venezuela, voted to authorize signatories of the Rio Treaty to "normalize" relations with Cuba if they chose to do so. Some did. Others, among them the United States, have not done so. Thirty-one countries are currently members of the OAS.

A majority of Mexico's people are poorly housed and badly nourished.

Mexico

Three centuries of Spanish rule in Mexico followed Hernando Cortes' defeat of the Aztec emperor, Montezuma, in the early 1500s. Under Spanish rule, the Mexican land and its inhabitants were exploited through a system of rigid bureaucracy and feudal landownership. The Indians were reduced to the state of serfs and were devastated by European diseases such as smallpox and measles.

Mexico established its independence from Spain in 1824. The social and political structure of the colonial period influenced Mexican society throughout the 19th century. The great mass of Mexicans continued to live in servitude to powerful landowners.

In 1910, the dictator Porfirio Díaz was overthrown, and that date is now accepted as the beginning of Mexico's modern revolution. After a period of uncertainty and turbulence in 1927, *the Partido Revolucionario Institucional* emerged as the governing party of the country. The PRI has led Mexico for over 60 years.

Serious conflicts between Mexico and the United States have erupted from time to time. In 1938, Mexico nationalized its oil resources and threw out American operators and kept them out for more than 40 years, despite a low level of oil production which made it necessary for Mexico to import large quantities from the Middle East. Tremendous new oil strikes in the far south of Mexico have raised the prospect of immense riches, and some economists project Mexico's future reserves are second only to those of Saudi Arabia.

The administration of former President José Lopez Portillo, banking on future oil income, embarked upon massive internal development projects through large scale borrowing; inflation went unchecked and the economy "overheated." In 1981, came the collapse of oil prices accompanying a worldwide economic recession. The Mexican government was a major international debtor, and its economy was in chaos. By the early 1980s, much of the confidence generated by petroleum riches had waned, and the future was filled with uncertainty.

Potential dangers, even possible bankruptcy, are evident in the present Mexican economic situation. The United States has taken an active role in trying to find a solution to Mexico's economic problems by helping to restructure debt payments and arrange new financing through the International Monetary Fund. Stringent economic reforms to reduce inflation at home and reverse capital flight abroad were implemented during the presidency of Miguel de la Madrid. These have continued since 1988 under the government of Carlos Salinas.

Population explosion

The majority of Mexico's nearly 90 million people are illiterate, poorly housed and badly nourished, while a small upper class of businessmen, bureaucrats and landowners control most of the country's wealth. The problem is compounded by the fact that Mexico has one of the highest population growth rates in Latin America; over three-quarters of a million young people enter the labor market each year while only half that number can be absorbed. Unemployment and miserable social conditions for millions of landless peasants, who flock to the cities each year, have been the cause of violence during recent years. Much of the surplus labor finds seasonal employment across the border in the United States, either legally or illegally. Evidence shows that many Mexicans entering the United States are engaged as *mules* in the illegal drug trade. The issues of illegal entry and border control create friction and controversy between the two governments.

The Caribbean

The Caribbean archipelago, stretching from Florida to the northeastern shore of South America was colonized by a number of European countries and by African blacks originally imported as slaves. Calypso music, sugar-cane fields, rum, hidden coves, and old seaside fortresses, from which pirates once set sail to rob the treasures of the Spanish main, have long made these islands fascinating to adventurers and writers. But in recent years one phenomenon, Cuba, stands out from the rest of this island world: The revolutionary leader Fidel Castro transformed the largest island of the Caribbean, 90 miles from the United States, into a communist society. Today, Havana alone is resisting the winds of political change sweeping the communist world. In contrast, much of the Caribbean region remains highly capitalistic.

In colonial times, these islands were all possessions of the maritime powers of Europe: Spain, France, Britain and Holland. The bigger islands were important sources of sugar in the 18th century, and slaves were brought from Africa to work the cane fields. They intermingled with Europeans and Indians living in the islands to form the mixed population that is typical of the Caribbean today.

Most of these islands have become independent countries, some of them so small as to be microstates, with tiny populations and no real source of income other than tourism. Many have one- or two-crop economies, producing bananas, sisal, coffee, sugar and sugar products. Tourism is the mainstay, and the effort to attract tourists is for many the principal government activity. Many Caribbean governments seek to maintain their independent status and have declined, except in one or two cases, to form federations which geography would seem to dictate.

The Bahamas

The Bahamas, the United States' closest Caribbean neighbor, are economically dependent on tourism and serve as a tax haven for international banks. Its 700 islands extend from near the Florida coast to the north shore of Cuba.

The Domincan Republic

The largest island after Cuba is Hispaniola, the first seat of Spanish government in the New World. Hispaniola is divided into two unequal parts, the larger being occupied by the Dominican Republic, a Spanish-speaking area that was ruled by dictator General Rafael Trujillo for 31 years. He was assassinated in 1961. In 1965, believing that there was an imminent danger of a communist take-over in up-coming elections, President Johnson sent U.S. Marines to the Republic. In 1978, the Dominican army interrupted yet another round of elections, fearing a victory by a left-wing coalition. Under pressure from Washington, however, the military allowed the leftist candidate, Antonio Guzman, to assume the presidency after he promised that he would not confiscate private property, nationalize foreign firms, or establish relations with the Soviet Union.

Haiti

The smaller part of Hispaniola belongs to the Republic of Haiti, the poorest country in the Western Hemisphere. Originally a French colony, Haiti became the world's first black republic by throwing off the rule of Napoleon in 1804. Later, one of the leaders of the liberation, Henri Christophe, proclaimed himself emperor and built a formidable fortress in the Citadel of Port-au-Prince. In 1957, François Duvalier, known as Papa Doc, came to power as much by terrorizing his opposition through his army of henchmen, the *Tontons Macoute,* and by captivating the Haitian people through voodoo, a cultural religion practiced by Caribbean blacks. Brutal repression and economic stagnation continued as Papa Doc's son, Baby Doc (Jean Claude Duvalier), assumed the presidency for life following his father's death in 1971. Baby Doc was deposed by a coup in 1986, and since that time the nation has been in a constant state of political turmoil with a succession of military-run governments.

Jamaica

Jamaica is the fourth largest island, after Puerto Rico, and smallest of the Greater Antilles. Important deposits of bauxite make it the richest Caribbean territory in minerals after Cuba; however, the demand for bauxite fluctuates. Its coffee and rum are famous. The island's beautiful beaches and tropical climate make it a favorite tourist destination. Jamaica achieved independence from Britain in 1962.

The Lesser Antilles

The other islands are grouped under the heading

of the Lesser Antilles and are mostly limited in area to a few thousand square miles. An example of a Caribbean microstate is Grenada, which has an area of 133 square miles, a population of 96,000, and a per-capita income of about $300 a year. Yet Grenada is a full-fledged member of the United Nations and casts a vote in the General Assembly. In 1983 United States military forces, in conjunction with the *Organization of Eastern Caribbean States,* invaded Granada to prevent the island from falling under the political domination of Cuba. Political stability was restored, but Grenada remains impoverished.

Some of the larger islands of the Lesser Antilles have remained possessions of their original owners in Europe, notably Guadeloupe and Martinique, which are departments of France. Britain has retained the allegiance of some of the islands as ''associated British states,'' a somewhat nebulous term, but has for the most part withdrawn in favor of native regimes. The Dutch still govern the Netherlands Antilles off the coast of Venezuela: Curaçao, Aruba and Bonaire. Spain no longer has any possessions in the Caribbean.

Cuba

The first Spanish colony in Latin America and the first European enclave in the Western Hemisphere, Cuba is now the major opponent of the United States in the region. This island country, long befriended by the Americans and liberated by them in the Spanish-American War of 1898, has been a communist state, actively supported by the Soviet Union for 30 years.

Rise of Fidel Castro

Fidel Castro came from the academic world of the Cuban middle class to lead a guerrilla movement centered in Cuba's western Sierra Maestra. From its start in the late 1950s, the movement attracted outside support, espe-cially from liberal Americans reacting to the excesses of Cuban dictator Fulgencio Batista. Upon gaining power, Castro declared a socialist state as the means to revolutionize Cuban society. Initially the United States reaction was noncommittal, neither friendly nor antagonistic. It was more or less an attitude of apprehension while awaiting further developments. This period was short-lived. A series of events moved Castro into the Soviet sphere.

United States-Cuban relations

At the time of Batista's defeat by Castro, essentially all Cuban industry was foreign-owned, principally by U.S. corporations. This was true of the largest Cuban industry, sugar, which was also responsible for almost all Cuban foreign trade credits. The nickel mines, oil refineries and tourist industries were also largely American-owned. Castro knew what the attitude of the U.S. government would be if he expropriated these foreign-owned properties, so he offered to purchase them from the American owners. To arrive at a purchase price, Castro offered to pay the value carried on the tax rolls. Under Batista, the properties were grossly undervalued in order to reduce the amount of Cuban taxes paid by the corporations and thus to attract American investment. The American owners refused the price offered and the other terms of sale, so in 1961, Castro expropriated the properties. At this, the American government cut off diplomatic relations

Fidel Castro at a rally of his supporters in Havana.

192

with Cuba. The U.S. then embargoed all Cuban products and forbade American exports to Cuba, including manufactured products, food, fuel and medical supplies. Cuba had lost its largest trading partner. With their standard of living under siege, thousands of educated and wealthy Cubans fled to the United States, depriving the country of an important human resource. Many moved to Miami, Florida.

Castro reorganized the country along communist lines. Schools, the civil service, the army and cultural institutions were rapidly reorganized on the Soviet and Eastern European models. Controlled newspapers, radio and television as well as innumerable mass meetings throughout the country were used to re-educate the public. Austerity was the answer to the U.S. trade embargo: This included rationing of commodities such as sugar, rice and tobacco. Today, rationing is still in effect. The lucrative American tourist trade ceased overnight. It is now possible for tourists to visit Havana, but only in limited groups or under special auspices. The U.S. retains a naval base at Guantanamo in southeast Cuba.

Soviet involvement

The economic forecast for Cuba, with no exports and no credit with which to import, was ominous. No country could long survive faced with these economic facts. At this point, the Soviet Union stepped in and offered to purchase the entire Cuban sugar production over a many-year interval. The Soviets offered to trade the credits built up by these sugar exports for food, fuel, machinery and military supplies. The agreement also called for the provision of Soviet technicians to teach the Cubans how to manage these materials, particularly those of a military nature. Castro accepted the Soviet offer, which in turn led to an attempted invasion of Cuba by Cuban exiles.

Cuban exiles who fled to the U.S. were armed and trained by the United States and returned as an invading force under a thinly veiled American cover. Contrary to intelligence reports that the Cuban people were ready to revolt against Castro and that all that was needed to foment a counterrevolution was a display of force, an army of counter-revolutionaries, with American support, landed at Cuba's Bay of Pigs and was quickly defeated by Castro's forces.

It was hard to imagine that Cuban-American relations could get any worse than they were at this time, but they did. The further deterioration brought the U.S. and the Soviet Union to the brink of war.

Cuban Missile Crisis

In 1962, not long after the Bay of Pigs fiasco, American aerial photographs of Cuba revealed the preparation of missile sites in southwestern Cuba. Other aerial reconnaissance showed Soviet ships on the high seas carrying missiles toward Cuba. President Kennedy saw this as a direct threat to American security and demanded the withdrawal of the missiles already emplaced. He informed the Soviet Union that the American fleet had orders not to permit additional missiles to be landed in Cuba. Castro claimed that the missiles were strictly defensive and, in view of the Bay of Pigs aggression, his government was justified in placing them.

Soviet Premier Nikita Khrushchev, however, heeded the American ultimatum, and the Soviet ships turned around and headed back to Europe. The Soviet missiles and technicians already in Cuba were also returned home.

Mariel Boatlift

In 1980, responding to an apparent invitation by President Carter, Cuban refugees in south Florida organized a massive convoy to bring their families to the U.S. The major port of embarkation was Mariel on the north coast of Cuba. Within a few weeks, over 120,000 Cubans had been brought to this country. Castro took advantage of this opportunity to send thousands of people from prisons and mental hospitals as well. The Cuban-American community complained bitterly and the boatlift ended. Although, the vast majority of *Marielitos* were honest and hard working, the criminal element among them has given the name a negative connotation. Thousands of the newcomers were detained in camps until sponsors were found, and a small number suspected of being hard-core criminals were held in U.S. federal prisons.

U.S. recognition question

In recent years, Washington has re-examined the question of whether America ought to end its policy of hostility to Cuba and renew diplomatic and trade relations. Some Americans believe that the isolation of Cuba has lasted long enough and that a renewal of ties is the best way for the United States to exert influence on Cuban policy. The argument can just as easily be turned against the resumption of relations. Many American policy makers and important sections of public opinion, including over 600,000 Cuban refugees, are firmly opposed to aiding a communist government in Cuba.

The Cuban economy remains almost totally dependent on sugar exports in a highly volatile world commodities market. The manufacturing sector is still geared to American methods and technology and needs new and replacement equipment for its factories, transportation and communication systems

Soviet technical and industrial material has been available to the Cubans for years, but it is expensive and often unsuited to Cuban standards. Cuba might welcome a chance to earn hard currency dollars to pay off its huge debts to non-communist trading partners like Japan. Cuba owes the Soviet Union billions of dollars, but the Soviets charge no interest on this debt, and it is not considered a pressing obligation. However, since Premier Mikhail Gorbachev came to power in 1985, the Soviet-Cuban relationship has changed dramatically. No longer can Russia be relied upon to prop up Cuba's economy.

Central America

Seven nations, clustered along a narrow isthmus of tropical forest and volcanic mountains connecting the North and South American land masses, comprise Central America. The history of Central America has been closely linked to the protection of U.S. interests there. For example, the Panama Canal is an essential waterway for inter-American trade, and its defense has historically been guaranteed by the presence of U.S. forces. There are also long-standing economic ties between business interests in this country and Central America. Early in his administration, President Reagan drew the line against communism in the region by stepping up economic and military assistance to regimes friendly to the United States. The U.S. Congress approved a Caribbean Basin Initiative plan that will provide $350 million for that purpose.

There is cause for concern about the future peace and security of the isthmus. Fear, tension and bloodshed threaten virtually every country. Several revolutions are challenging dictatorial and often-repressive military regimes. Caught in the middle are the Roman Catholic Church and millions of impoverished peasants. The Church is split. Some priests support revolutionaries who promise a better way of life for the people. The Vatican, head of the Catholic Church, has ordered the clergy to refrain from taking sides in the political struggle.

Guatemala

Guatemala is the northernmost country of Central America, lying just south of Mexico. In 1954 the U.S. intervened and backed an uprising against the regime of President Jacobo Arbenz, a communist-supported politician who had nationalized foreign investment and expropriated large agricultural estates, including banana plantations owned by the United Fruit Company, a large American firm. His successor was assassinated three years later, and the country has since been governed by a series of uneasy regimes. In 1968 the American ambassador to Guatemala was murdered by terrorists.

Guatemala is the most "Indian" country of Central America; over 3.5 million Indians of Mayan descent — out of a total population of 9 million — live in the highlands, almost completely outside the Spanish-speaking social framework. Although most Indians live at or below the poverty level, they have until recently taken no active role in the internal political disputes of the nation.

Guatemala has been ruled by a succession of military figures since 1970, when the army reduced the activity of terrorist groups through an intense counterinsurgency campaign led by Colonel Carlos Arana, who decreed a state of siege. When Arana became president, he adopted Guatemala's first comprehensive development plan.

In 1976, 22,000 people were killed in a devastating earthquake, and a large section of the capital, Guatemala City, was destroyed. The foreign aid that poured into Guatemala following the earthquake contributed to the country's economic progress until the worldwide recession of the late 1970s. Although there was an increase in terrorist activity, the military maintained a firm grip on the country. This era saw wholesale violations of human rights, with thousands of assassinations and abductions by paramilitary *death squads* of the political right and left. In 1986, a new constitution was adopted. Guatemala returned to civilian government, but the country is still plagued by both guerrilla movements and right-wing pressure against liberal social or political reforms.

Belize

Formerly known as British Honduras, Belize borders the Caribbean, east of Guatemala and south of the Yucatan peninsula. Although self-governing since the 1960s, it remains a British dependency with a British governor. Its coast is fringed with islands which have tourist potential.

Guatemala had a longstanding dispute with Great Britain over the rightful ownership of the territory. When Guatemala won its independence from Spain in 1821, it claimed the colony of British Honduras. The British resisted and in 1859 a treaty apparently settled the border of the two countries, although Guatemala never abandoned its claim. After Great Britain approved a constitution and the name of the country was changed to Belize, Guatemala threatened an armed invasion during the 1970s. Elements of the British navy were dispatched to the area, and a clash was averted. During the 1980s, diplomatic relations were restored between the two nations.

Thousands of people have "disappeared" in El Salvador. Mothers march in protest — demanding to know where their loved ones are.

El Salvador

El Salvador is the smallest Central American country and one of the most densely populated in the hemisphere with over 500 persons per square mile. The government is controlled by a small number of powerful families. Although the *Central American Common Market* (CACM) of the 1960s expanded the middle class and raised per-capita income, the vast majority of El Salvadorians are peasant farmers.

El Salvador's policies toward its neighbors have been hostile, especially towards Honduras, with whom it has had frequent border quarrels. The most notable was the "soccer war" of 1969 which began as a disruption of a football match between the two countries. Within a week, the nations had reached a cease-fire, but Honduras later withdrew from the CACM, precipitating an economic decline which worsened throughout the 1970s.

In that same decade, El Salvador's internal political situation deteriorated to the point of open warfare between the government and guerrillas. It began in 1972 when a land reformer, José Napoleón Duarte, apparently won the presidency, but the government would not recognize his victory. This led to open conflict between revolutionaries and the government. Conservative elements of the El Salvadorian military overthrew the government and recalled Duarte from exile to become president. He proceeded with land reform programs aimed at undercutting the guerrillas, but he alienated the landed oligarchy. The right and left continued to battle each other, committing flagrant atrocities, civil rights violations and bringing the nation's economy to near destruction.

In the election of 1982, which was boycotted by the guerrilla groups, Duarte's Christian Democrats won the largest number of votes, but not enough for a majority of seats in the national assembly. A coalition of extreme right-wing parties formed the new government. Although Duarte won the presidential election of 1984, the fighting between government forces and guerrilla units never ceased. By 1988 it was estimated that between 65,000 and 70,000 El Salvadorian citizens had died in the civil conflict.

Honduras

Honduras is the prototypical Central American "banana republic," meaning that its economy rests in large part on the growing and exporting of bananas under the supervision of the United Fruit Company's successor corporations, among others. The extent to which these companies have influenced government policies and social legislation is — and has been for decades — a topic of debate. Today, the influence of such firms has been lessened in the face of indigenous revolutionary movements which, with their threat of violent overthrow, are forcing government reform.

The people of Honduras generally practice subsistence agriculture or work on coffee and banana plantations. With 42,300 square miles, Honduras, as compared to neighboring El Salvador, is underpopulated. Nevertheless, when landless El Salvadorian peasants migrated there in the 1960s, Honduras tightened its land reform laws and forced them out.

The resulting tensions led in part to the 1969 "soccer war."

In the 1980s, Honduras became a haven for refugees fleeing the Sandinista revolutionary government in neighboring Nicaragua. These included both military allies of the former Nicaraguan dictator Anastasio Somoza, as well as disillusioned former supporters of the revolution. There were also numbers of Miskito Indians who were early opponents of the Sandinista regime. From among these elements, a military force was recruited, trained and equipped (with United States support) to fight a war with Sandinista forces along the Nicaragua-Honduras border. The United States also poured millions of dollars into building up the Honduran military and sent U.S. forces there for joint training exercises. Despite a strong internal protest against such intrusions, as well as continuing differences between the two governments, Honduras remains a close ally of the United States.

Nicaragua

Nicaragua is the largest and most sparsely settled of the Central American republics. It has been of interest to the United States for almost a century because of the possibility of building a sea-level canal across the isthmus through the 100-mile-wide Lake Nicaragua. Such a canal would be longer than the Panama canal, but would be much easier to build. In fact, the United States had plans at the end of the 19th century to do so, but lobbyists for the Panama venture persuaded Congress that a Nicaraguan canal would be endangered by active volcanoes nearby.

Political instability in Nicaragua at the beginning of the century led to successive U.S. military interventions after 1912. In 1936 Anastasio Somoza Garcia, the commander of the Nicaraguan National Guard, assumed the presidency, thus launching the harsh dynasty of the Somoza family. In the 1970s, a national offensive to overthrow the Somozas was mounted by the Marxist guerrillas of the *Frente Sandinista de Liberacion Nacional* and other political forces. The Sandinistas, named for a rebel leader who fought the U.S. Marines occupying his country during the 1920s, grew steadily in numbers and support. In the cities, there was rioting and general strikes protesting the Somoza regime's repressive policies. The tide of Somoza's war with the guerrillas turned against him and, in July of 1979, President Anastasio Somoza fled the country taking much of the national treasury with him. He was assassinated in Paraguay the following year.

Faced with imminent bankruptcy, the new Sandinista government sought funds from the United States. The U.S. turned down requests for aid. As in Cuba, the new government launched a massive land redistribution program and a successful literacy campaign. But the economy was in shambles, and there was little prospect of assistance from noncommunist bloc nations.

The Reagan administration provided covert support to counter-revolutionaries (Contras) based on the Honduran and Costa Rican borders. Most Latin Americans were repelled by the excesses of the Sandinista regime, as well as American intervention in the region. The leaders of several Central and South American nations (the Contradora Group) sought to achieve a regional settlement of the conflict. Ultimately, the Sandinistas bowed to international pressure and agreed to set a national election for 1989 only to have it postponed a year due to a devastating hurricane. In February of 1990, the people of Nicaragua cast ballots in a free election that was closely monitored by outside observers, including former U.S. president Jimmy Carter. In a stunning upset, the Sandinista leader Daniel Ortega lost the presidency to political newcomer Violeta de Chamorro, whose National Opposition Union (UNO) party had received strong economic backing from the United States. A truce was soon signed between the Sandinista and Contra forces as a prelude to the peaceful transfer of governmental power, which took place in April 1990.

Costa Rica

Costa Rica lies across the Central American isthmus between Panama and Nicaragua. It has a temperate climate owing to its upland elevation. Its people enjoy the rule of what is generally considered to be a model of democratic government. It is sometimes called the Switzerland of Central America.

Costa Rica contrasts sharply with its Central American neighbors, not only in its staunchly democratic tradition — following a brief civil war in 1948, Costa Rica abolished its military as being inconsistent with democracy — but also in its prosperous economy. It has a fairly evenly distributed national income, and its per-capita income is one of the highest in Latin America.

For some 40 years, the dominant force in Costa Rican politics has been the National Liberation Party (PLN). The former president, Oscar Arias, was awarded the 1987 Nobel Peace Prize for his efforts to bring about a peaceful settlement of conflicts in the region.

Panama

Because of the Panama Canal, the Republic of

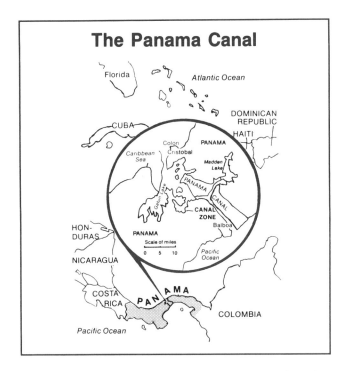

The Panama Canal

Panama has a far greater importance in the hemisphere, and in the world, than its size or resources would otherwise bestow. Only one quarter of its territory is inhabited, and its resources, apart from the canal, are few.

In the 1880s, a French engineer tried to build a canal in Panama. But financial woes and the ravages of tropical disease caused the attempt to founder. The United States took up the project. Negotiations with Colombia, of which Panama was then part, failed, so Washington encouraged the Panamanians to break away from Colombia and form their own republic.

A 1903 treaty between the United States and the new republic gave the U.S. the right to build and operate a canal across the Isthmus in exchange for $10 million. The project, which included the conquest of yellow fever and the design of complicated locks, was finished in 1914. To this day, it is an engineering masterpiece.

Since then, Panama has periodically asked for a greater share in canal revenue and, in recent times, for outright control of the canal and sovereignty over the ten-mile-wide Canal Zone. The Canal Zone borders the canal from coast to coast and has been administered as though it were United States territory. It was populated by thousands of American citizens and is dotted with military bases. The vulnerability of the canal has always been a prime consideration of American foreign policy.

Riots broke out in the zone in 1964 over the right to fly the Panamanian flag there. Following the riots, active negotiations were conducted in an effort to reorder the canal's future, with the assumption that Panama would have a greater voice in running the canal. In 1977, two treaties were drawn up. In 1978,

despite considerable opposition, they were ratified by the U.S. Congress. One treaty provides for the transfer to Panama the jurisdiction over and operation of the canal and its zone by the year 2000, thus nullifying the treaty of 1903. A second treaty guarantees the neutrality of the canal and implicitly gives the United States the power to defend it against foreign attack. American military bases in the Canal Zone will be phased out.

Supporters of the new treaties argued that they were necessary because without them the Panamians might seek to take the area by armed force. The United States would thus find itself involved in a prolonged war without any sure way of protecting the canal. Another argument was the decline in the canal's strategic value in the space and missile age. Despite the heated debate by many Americans, the treaties were hailed as a success for President Carter and for Panamanian President Omar Torrijos, who led the fight for Panamanian control of the canal.

In 1981, President Torrijos was killed in an airplane crash. As commander of Panama's National Guard, he had controlled the country since a military coup in 1968; when elections were held in 1978 he became president. Torrijos' death left Panama's political future clouded, with a group of National Guard officers holding power. Their American-trained forces appeared well prepared to defend the country.

One of the officers, General Manuel Noriega, seized power and became the despotic leader of the nation. Under his regime Panama became a haven for narcotics traffickers from South America and a staging point for moving their goods to the United States. In 1988, a federal grand jury indicted Noriega on drug charges; naturally, he refused to come to the United States to stand trial. Moreover, Noriega refused to recognize the result of a Panamanian national election which turned his party out of power. In January 1990, President George Bush ordered U.S. forces into Panama to depose the corrupt regime and bring Noriega to the United States for trial. After several days of intense fighting, the American forces gained control of the country; the legitimately elected government was seated; and Noriega was placed in a federal detention facility to await trial. This controversial intervention by the United States was condemned by many Latin American leaders and the Soviet Union, but appears to have been generally welcomed by the people of Panama.

South America
The Andean Group

The colossal Andes run along the entire length of

the South American continent, from Venezuela in the north to the tips of Chile and Argentina in the south. This mountain range, one of the outstanding ones of the world, inevitably placed its stamp on the character of the peoples and nations that it touched. Geographically, however, the mountains have been a barrier to closer relations between the Andean states, a barrier which is now being overcome by modern communications: the airplane, rail and auto transport, radio and television. These have made possible a trend toward economic unity among the Andean states of the north and the central part of the continent. Venezuela, Colombia, Ecuador, Peru, and Bolivia organized themselves into the "Andean Group" as a step toward creating a common market for the region.

Factors other than geography have prevented the unity of the Andean countries. Chile and Argentina have kept aloof from the others. Together with Uruguay, they comprise a unity of their own and are often referred to as "the Southern Cone" of South America. These three countries have a different cultural and racial character than those of the other countries in the Andean Group. The former are of predominantly white, European stock, with close European cultural ties. The latter are predominantly Indian, black and mestizo (of mixed Indian and European blood).

Chile joined the Andean Group for a brief period, and its withdrawal in 1977 illustrates another important difference and barrier between the two groups. With the exception of Colombia, the countries of the Andean Group were moving toward a socialist economic structure, with their governments exercising considerable control over the economy. Following the overthrow of the elected Marxist government of Salvador Allende, Chile returned in part to a free-enterprise economy. Looking to the United States and other industrialized powers to help develop its economy, Chile broke with the Andean Group over the group's restrictions on foreign investments.

Political differences among members of the Andean Group itself do not appear to have seriously interfered with their plans for economic integration.

Venezuela

Venezuela is one of the richest countries in South America. After the United States, it is the largest producer of oil in the hemisphere and one of the biggest in the world.

Oil was first discovered at Lake Maracaibo on the Caribbean in 1917; since then the Venezuelans have attained the highest income per capita in Latin America, with the highest living standard, the greatest

number of telephones, the greatest consumption of electricity, and one of the lowest rates of inflation. Oil profits have been poured into urban projects.

The capital, Caracas, is one of the hemisphere's most modern cities. Its skyline of tall buildings, built with oil profits, contrasts with its extensive slum areas. About one third of the people in Caracas live in poverty in hillside shantytowns. The city is badly polluted. It has some of the worst traffic problems of any major city.

The great liberator, Simón Bolívar, was born in Caracas in 1783, and Venezuela became one of the first Spanish colonies in Latin America to raise the standard of independence. But until recently, it has not been governed by democratic rule. A succession of dictators and strongmen ruled Venezuela during the 19th and early 20th centuries. In 1958 the last dictator was overthrown during a revolt supported by elements in the army. Romulo Betancourt served as president of Venezuela from 1959-1964. The Democratic Action party (AD) has been the dominant political force in Venezuela ever since.

Venezuela greatly benefited from the boom in oil prices in 1974, although it did not participate in the OPEC boycott. In 1976, the government nationalized 21 private oil companies, many of them U.S. subsidiaries. That year the country earned almost $10 billion from its oil. Venezuela possesses other mineral resources, notably iron. The mountain of iron ore, Cerro Bolivar, near the mouth of the Orinoco River, is one of the purest in the world. Cattle raising is another major occupation.

Throughout the 1980s, Venezuela experienced a deteriorating economic situation and social unrest.

Oil prices declined as more reserves were discovered around the world, and OPEC lost its power to keep prices high. The glut of oil on the world market had a serious effect on Venezuela's exports.

The inflation became so bad in the late 1980s that the money value changed almost on a daily basis, and the standard of living decreased rapidly. Crime increased in Caracas as the situation became worse for many poor people.

Carlos Andrés Peréz became the first former president re-elected to office; in 1989 he initiated economic measures to combat the inflation and a spiraling foreign debt. This led to rioting throughout the country, so a curfew was imposed, and civil liberties were temporarily suspended. The country enters the decade of the 1990s with many problems.

Colombia

Colombia, the South American country geographically closest to the United States, is the only one with both an Atlantic and a Pacific coastline. But Colombian life remains rooted in the past, still bearing the stamp of Spanish colonial culture.

Colombia is divided between three chains, or cordilleras, of the Andes and is a patchwork of valleys draining into the northward flowing Magdalena, one of the great rivers of South America. To the south and east of the Andean wall stretch the flat, seemingly endless prairies of the *llanos,* great grasslands drained by the headwaters of the Orinoco River. Here the main activities are cattle ranching and oil prospecting.

Colombia's people live for the most part at high altitudes — the capital, Bogotá, stands at 8,700 feet — where coffee is cultivated and gold, platinum and emeralds are mined. In the northern lowlands along the Atlantic coast, a tropical culture centers around the ports of Barranquilla, the second largest city, and Santa Marta. Ethnically, the population is mixed and always has been. More than 300 different Indian tribes occupied the territory when Spanish explorers pushed up the Magdalena in 1536.

The three mountain ranges break up the country so effectively that there is no rail connection between Bogotá and the sea. The roads, even when paved, wind so precipitously above mountain ravines that normal transportation schedules are difficult to keep. Therefore, flying is the accepted method of travel, and the air network covers every corner of the country.

Colombia's patchwork geography encourages local independence movements. In recent years, there has been guerrilla activity known generally as *La Violencia,* now considered to be under tentative control. Despite the violence, Colombia has a democratic tradition by Latin American standards. The military has seized power on only three occasions.

In 1982, Belisario Betancur became president of Colombia. Although there was violence during the campaign, the president promised to seek peace between the military and guerrilla groups, such as the Movement of April 19 (M-19), made up of radical labor and communist youth groups. A broad amnesty was offered, but only 2,000 guerrillas accepted. The internal pacification collapsed, and a national state of emergency was declared. The government also faced a problem in revamping the economy and lowering inflation — two causes of unrest in the nation.

In 1986, Virgilio Barco assumed the presidency with the twin goals of ending internal political violence and stopping drug traffickers who had gained virtual control of parts of Colombia. Most of the illegal drugs brought to the U.S., especially cocaine, originate in Colombia. Barco declared all-out war on the drug cartel centered in the city of Medellín, and leaders such as Carlos Lehder were extradited to the United States for trial and imprisonment. Violence between the drug traffickers and the government intensified. Early in 1990, President Bush attended a summit of South American leaders meeting in Cartagena, to show strong U.S. support for the drug war. Nevertheless, the violence has continued with frequent bombings and assassinations throughout the country.

The Colombian economy is essentially agricultural; high-quality, mountain-grown coffee is a leading export. Recently there has been considerable industrial development, especially in textiles. The Colombian balance of payments has been respectable in recent years, but inflation has kept the standard of living low. Some oil is produced, but not enough to meet the country's requirements. Oil prospecting is a major business not only in the *llanos* but also in the Magdalena valley.

Ecuador

Ecuador is one of the smallest South American republics and one of the poorest. Like all the west-coast countries, it is dominated by the north-south cordillera of the Andes and is split between a coastal plain and temperate highlands. In Ecuador the plain is centered around Guayaquil, the country's largest city and chief port. The bananas that constitute Ecuador's main export are grown in this area.

As its name indicates, Ecuador lies directly on the equator and is studded with spectacular volcanoes, some of which are active. The country lost a good portion of its forested lowlands east of the Andes, known as the Oriente, in a disastrous war with Peru in 1941. The remaining part of this territory has been successfully prospected for oil by American drillers, especially in the north near the Colombian border. American enterprise has played a part in Ecuadorian development from the beginning. The railroad from Guayaquil to the capital city of Quito was financed by American capital at the beginning of the century.

Pre-Columbian Ecuador constituted the northern reach of the Inca empire, and it is rich in archaeological treasure. It was conquered from Peru by one of Pizarro's lieutenants in the middle of the 16th century and was ruled by Spain until its liberation in 1822. Símon Bolívar persuaded the new state to join Colombia and Venezuela (also newly freed from Spanish rule) in the federation of Gran Colombia. The experiment did not last, however, and Ecuador broke away, reassuming its own name and forming its own government in 1830.

Ecuador controls the Galápagos Islands, 600

miles off the Pacific coast, where Charles Darwin formulated many of his theories of evolution and natural selection. The Galápagos are famous as the habitat of rare and unusual animal and bird species.

During its first 95 years of independence, Ecuador had 45 changes of government: presidents, dictators and military juntas rapidly succeeded one another. Between 1925 and 1948, no president completed his term of office. A new constitution was adopted in 1979, along with a return to civilian government. Even so, the country remained prone to unrest. In 1986 the president was abducted and held hostage for 11 hours by supporters of a military leader who had been arrested for plotting a coup. The president was returned only after the officer was granted amnesty. The country tends to remain politically isolated from other South American nations.

Peru

Peru, with its dramatic range of scenery, resources and climate, is the third largest country on the South American continent. The country's long Pacific coastline is lapped by frigid, northward-flowing waters that prevent the condensation of moisture from clouds passing eastward over the coast; hence the coastal plain is a virtual desert and a sun-obscur-

United Nations/Paul Almasy
Children fetching water from a community well in Peru.

ing pall hangs all summer long over Lima. From the coastal plain, the main spine of the Andes rises more than 20,000 feet in an almost unbroken barrier north and south. On the eastern slope of the Andes, the land falls away steeply to the lush forests of the Amazonian headwaters. This part of Peru is oriented to the Atlantic, thousands of miles away down the mighty river.

Peru's contemporary riches are mostly mineral, but its most important single export comes from the ocean: This is fishmeal, processed from the enormous schools of anchovies which thrive in the cold waters of the Humboldt current. A related product is the fertilizer processed from the guano of the great flocks of cormorants that feed voraciously on the fish. The sight of these glistening white rocks, or "guano islands," rising off the coast is striking.

Coastal Peru is the home of the country's modern cities and its industrialized middle class. High up in the Andes is another Peru, the country of the Quechua and Aymara Indians, many of whom do not speak Spanish and who constitute half of the nation's people. Descendants of the Incas, they cultivate highland terraces, growing potatoes and maize, crops native to Peru which the Spanish colonialists shared with the world.

The desolate mountain plains are stony and swept by cold winds all year long. Living at altitudes of between 11,000 and 15,000 feet, the Andean Indian has developed a barrel-chested physique to accommodate the great lungs needed to survive in the thin atmosphere. Most of these Indians have difficulty living at sea level; the increased air pressure makes them easy prey to respiratory disease. The social and political difficulties involved in improving the living conditions of these people is a problem in all the Andean countries, but especially in Peru. However, oil discoveries in the selva, or the eastern forest, and the construction of a pipeline to the Pacific raise hopes that Peru will not only be self-sufficient in petroleum but will have a surplus to sell abroad. Nationalization of the industry and worker participation in it have driven away some foreign investment. But the booming tourist trade, which brings outsiders to the Inca ruins in the hinterland, especially the mountain city of Macchu Pichu, is an alternative source of foreign exchange.

Peru was the last country to gain its independence, with the help of Bolívar in 1824, and its government has vacillated between military and civilian regimes. Most recently, from 1967 to 1980, the country was ruled by the military; then a new constitution was adopted and Peru returned to civilian government. Internal unrest and a declining economy have undermined the authority of subsequent governments. The greatest challenge has come from terrorist attacks by a Maoist group known as *Secundero Luminoso,* the ''shining path,'' and *Movimiento Revolucionario Tupac Amaru* (MRTA).

Bolivia

Bolivia straddles the center of the South American continent, its western third lodged in the high, desolate Andes and its eastern regions comprising tropical forests and savannas along a network of rivers flowing into the Atlantic. Seventy percent of its people are Indian, many of them so poor as to be wholly outside the economy.

Most of the Indians live on the altiplano, a high desert averaging 13,000 feet above sea sevel. Swept by cold winds and dust storms, it provides only the barest soil for the cultivation of potatoes and other tubers on which the Indians depend for survival. The severity of the landscape is relieved only by the huts of the inhabitants and by flocks of sheep, llama and alpacas. Llama and alpacas are used for transport and wool, respectively. Another wilder relative is the vicuña, highly prized for its wool but rarer than the alpaca. The Indian civilization of Bolivia originated in the pre-Incan culture of Tiahuanacu near the shores of Lake Titicaca which, at 11,000 feet, is the highest navigable body of water in the world.

Bolivia was colonized by the Spaniards in 1532. The lure was silver, mined around the town of Potosi.

Later, tin was discovered in large quantities and remains the mineral chiefly identified with Bolivia. Throughout the centuries of Spanish rule, and until recently, the mines were worked by thousands of Indians whose condition was close to slavery. The mines were nationalized in the 1950s, and conditions have since improved, although underground labor at altitudes above 11,000 feet can never be ideal.

Another geographic problem concerns Bolivia's capital, La Paz, which lies 12,000 feet above sea level and is easily reached only by air. Still another difficulty stems from the distribution of the population. Most Bolivians live in the inhospitable Andean region. Few inhabit the potentially rich eastern tropics, where food and cash crops can be produced in quantity. Distance and hostile geography remain the two great obstacles to the economic development of the nation.

Bolivia epitomizes Latin American political instability. Since its independence was established in 1825, scores of revolutions, coups and countercoups led by civilian politicians and military figures have rocked the country. Bolivia has had more changes of government than years of existence. Violence has been a constant of Bolivian political life.

The Bolivian economy was at a point of near collapse in the early 1980s. The nation was in default on its foreign debts, inflation was rampant, and the national currency was virtually worthless. The state-run mines, petroleum companies and other industries

Bolivian women selling their vegetables in a typical marketplace.

were all losing money, and there were threats of labor strikes for higher wages. In 1985 the new president, Victor Paz, instituted an economic austerity plan which triggered a general strike by the miners. At the same time, the world tin market collapsed with a catastrophic impact on the economy. The government also began a crackdown on cocoa production, a mainstay of the peasant farmers, and drug traffickers. The drug lords retaliated with a bomb attack on the U.S. Secretary of State's motorcade during a 1988 visit to La Paz.

The Southern Cone

Chile, Argentina, and Uruguay, the three southernmost countries of the Western Hemisphere, are in many ways the most European of Latin America. The native Indians of the region were nomadic warrior tribes and, as in the case of North American Indians, were pushed back and practically wiped out by the white settlers, although a considerable mixing of the races did take place during the process. The temperate climate of the region attracted a high influx of European immigrants (notably Germans, Italians, British and Irish) who easily intermingled and assimilated themselves with the original Spaniards, forming the most homogeneous societies in Latin America, with the highest literacy rate. These factors contributed to the development of a middle class with values and standards of living once comparable to those of the United States. But the region's record of relative political stability has recently suffered dramatically. Economic setbacks and political terrorism have destabilized these countries. Like other Latin American countries, all three have until recently been governed by authoritarian military regimes. Under continual pressure from civilian groups, the military has gradually returned the government to civilian hands through democratic elections.

Chile

Chile is the most remote of the Latin American nations, but it is among the best known because it is the first country to have adopted and then deposed a Marxist government.

In 1970, Chilean voters elected Salvador Allende, a Marxist-Leninist president. Chile's foreign earnings were, and are, largely dependent on its rich copper resources and subject to the fluctuation of world prices. Allende promised a socialist solution to Chile's economic difficulties through the nationalization of foreign enterprise, including management of the copper mines, and redistribution of farmlands.

But Allende's policies were bitterly opposed by the upper classes. They, and multinational corporations, withdrew millions of dollars from the country. In three years, the country suffered economic and political chaos. By refusing to compensate foreign companies for their expropriated copper mines, the Allende government alienated Chile's traditional friends abroad, including the United States. Foreign communist influence became pronounced. Attempts to socialize small businesses came up against stiff resistance from Chile's strong middle class. In 1973, a military junta led by General Augusto Pinochet and supported by the United States, seized the capital city of Santiago and overthrew Allende's government in a brief but bloody battle which cost the leader his life. Since that time, the government has eliminated the socialist reforms.

Most of the confiscated land was returned to private owners. Despite political tensions, and the collapse of world copper prices in 1981-82, the Chilean economy has made good progress. In 1988 it was able to renegotiate most of its foreign debt and expanded trade.

Politically, the Pinochet government had been repressive and stood accused of numerous documented human-rights violations. By 1988, the growing pressure for political reform from the U.S. and other nations, as well as a visit to Chile by Pope John Paul II, led Pinochet to hold a national plebiscite on continuing his regime. The nation overwhelmingly opted for a presidential election. There was broad participation by political parties, and the balloting was relatively incident-free. Pinochet was defeated and relinquished the presidential office early in 1990.

The chief problem facing Chile is something it cannot change: its geography. It consists of a ribbon of territory 3,000 miles long and less than 100 miles wide, stretching from mid-continent to the southernmost tip of South America. The ribbon runs from a waterless desert in the north, where it rains about once every 15 years; through a temperate zone of lakes and forests, inhabited by most of the population; to a barren and windswept south, hospitable only to grazing sheep and lumber camps. On one side of the long country are the jagged, snow-capped Andes, including the 23,000-foot Aconcagua, the continent's highest mountain. On the other side lies the Pacific Ocean.

Chilean independence from Spain came in 1810, when national hero Bernardo O'Higgins first raised the standard of revolt. Through the 19th century, the country was governed by a succession of authoritarian governments. In 1883, Chile was victorious in the War of the Pacific against Bolivia and Peru; it had conquered the port of Arica, gateway to the nitrate fields of the Atacama Desert, an important source of foreign exchange, until nitrates were replaced by synthetics.

Descendants of German, Swiss, Italian and English settlers have mixed with the original Spaniards to form Chile's present-day population. Most of the native Indians were absorbed, although about 150,000 pure-blooded Araucanians still live in the forests of central Chile. In contrast to the stagnation and poverty of rural life, the cities support a relatively high standard of living.

Argentina

Second only to its northern neighbor Brazil in land area and population, Argentina has one of the highest living standards in South America. Chiefly a producer of cattle and wheat, its vast *pampas* (or prairies) are occupied by gauchos, cowboys of Indian and Spanish descent, and their families. Its capital city, Buenos Aires, is one of the largest and most beautiful cities in the world.

Recent Argentine history centers around Colonel Juan Domingo Perón and his influential wife Evita. He first came to power in the 1940s, and their legacy continues to dominate Argentina. Perón founded his own political ideology, based on a populist appeal to the working classes. The ultranationalist policies he pursued brought him into conflict with the powerful Argentine oligarchy and with the United States. Perón came to power at a time when shortages of food in Europe, during and following World War II, created a huge demand for Argentine beef and wheat. Instead of building up Argentina's foreign reserves with the incoming revenue, or allowing private business to strengthen itself, Perón spent it on costly social programs and industrialization plans. The result was that when the foreign demand for Argentine goods decreased and prices dropped, the country's balance of payments suffered tremendously, and inflation got out of control. Perón was overthrown by the military in 1955 and sent into exile. He again became president in 1973 in response to the continued loyalty of his followers among the poor and the trade unions. He died in 1974, leaving the presidency to his second wife, Maria Estela Martinez de Perón. A former showgirl, she proved highly inept, and the government degenerated amidst corruption and widespread terrorism. Terrorists threatened the middle class and foreign business interests. As inflation hit 100 percent, Mrs. Perón was deposed by a right-wing military junta which imposed a strict program of economic austerity and took drastic measures to root out the terrorists.

In his efforts to industrialize Argentina, Perón neglected agricultural production. This is another cause of Argentina's current economic problems, since it still depends on agricultural exports for 80 percent of its foreign exchange. Argentina has been hit further by Britain's entry into the *European Community* which bans meat imports from nonmembers. Despite these setbacks, Argentina has the potential to become one of the few self-sufficient countries in the world.

Another bright spot in Argentina was the discovery and exploitation of large amounts of oil. In the past, oil had to be imported. Argentina suffered less than some Latin American countries from the energy crisis in 1974 caused by the enormous price increase in Middle Eastern oil. Argentina's greatest asset remains its well-educated and industrious population of 31 million, which continues to expand through immigration. New arrivals from Europe are constantly joining the already established populations of Italians, Germans and English who have mingled with the

President Juan Perón and his wife Evita at the peak of their power in Argentina.

original Spanish for many decades.

Despite its assets, the economy of Argentina in the 1980s was a disaster. Inflation rates of over 130 percent per year, constant devaluation of the currency and an overwhelming foreign debt were leading to civil unrest and uprisings against the ruling junta. The government of President Leopoldo Galtieri chose to gamble on a military venture which would divert attention away from the severe economic problems. On April 2, 1982, the Argentine military occupied the Falkland Islands — called *Islas Malvinas* by Argentina. Ownership of this group of islands in the South Atlantic had been disputed by Argentina and Britain for about 150 years. A ten-week air and sea war commenced between the two countries. The war ended on June 14 when Argentina surrendered.

The aftermath of the war brought instability to the government and further chaos to the Argentine economy. Shortly after the Falklands' defeat, President Galtieri was forced from office by the other members of the military junta. He was replaced by retired general Antonio Bignone in 1982. Soon there was a clamor for return to civilian government. The army was held responsible for both the worsening economy and the war. In 1983, Raul Alfonsín was elected president and set about reforming the military; One-half of the officer corps was forced to retire. Public opposition to the military was heightened by the discovery of 15,000 to 30,000 graves of citizens killed in the internal "dirty war" of 1976-83 between the regime and its opponents. A number of former junta members went on trial for abduction, torture and murder, but, to the public's dismay, few were convicted or imprisoned. A new government elected in 1989 faces the same economic and political problems which have plagued Argentina for decades.

Uruguay

Uruguay is one of the smallest countries in South America. Like Paraguay, it borders on Brazil and Argentina. With Argentina, its coast forms the Río de la Plata estuary. It consists largely of grazing land, centered around the capital city of Montevideo, whose people almost equal the number of the country's rural inhabitants.

Uruguay has enjoyed a reputation for social enlightenment. It established the 40-hour work week in the first decade of this century and has since inaugurated other "welfare state" benefits, including old age pensions, free medical care and paid vacations for workers. Uruguayan women can vote; divorce is legal; and illegitimate children have the right to inherit property. But these benefits are largely restricted to the urban classes. Most farmers and

ranchers are not covered. Taxes are high, and inflation is rising. Widespread unemployment caused strikes and a general state of civil unrest.

An intense terrorist campaign waged by a guerrilla group, the *Tupamaros,* provoked an internal security crisis in 1973, leading to the overthrow of the liberal regime by a military junta, and the establishment of a military-backed government. By 1980, in the face of worsening economic conditions and political protests, the citizens rejected a new constitution that would have continued military rule. A national election was held in 1984 without restrictions on the activities of political parties. A civilian president was elected, political prisoners released, and the military relinquished power. As in neighboring Argentina, there were investigations into human-rights violations committed by the military regime. Despite protests from left-wing parties, labor unions and students, a national amnesty law for the military was narrowly upheld in a 1988 plebiscite.

Paraguay

Southwest of Brazil and north of Argentina lies the landlocked country of Paraguay, one of the smallest and most backward republics of South America. Most of its people live east of the Paraguay River which divides the country on its way to the Río de la Plata estuary. To the west lies the scrub forest and range land of the Chaco, rolling desolately to the Bolivian border. The nearest metropolis to the Paraguayan capital of Asunción is Buenos Aires, 1,000 miles downstream.

In 1955, following a succession of failed governments, General Alfredo Stroessner seized control of the country in a coup and remained its president for 34 years. During his regime Paraguay gained notoriety as a temporary haven for accused Nazi war criminals who had fled Europe following World War II. A 1989 coup deposed Stroessner, and he was sent into exile in Brazil. A new military strongman, General Andrés Rodríguez, received 74 percent of the vote in the next election and was confirmed as president despite allegations of fraud.

Most Paraguayans are of Guarani Indian stock. Guarani is the language spoken in the rural areas; Spanish is reserved for the cities and the official class. Paraguay is basically an agricultural country, and income per capita is extremely low. The economy grew at a rate of only 1.1 percent per year between 1980 and 1986. The principal hope for the economy is the development of the hydroelectric potential of the Parana River which forms the border with Brazil. At present, the two governments are working on a million-kilowatt dam and generating plant at Itaipu at

The search for food takes many citizens of São Paulo to the garbage dump. In contrast modern skyscrapers rise in downtown.

a projected cost of over $6 billion. The plant will produce energy for Paraguay to satisfy its needs and have a surplus to sell back to Brazil. The first section of this project went into operation in 1982. When fully operational in the 1990s, it will be the largest hydroelectric power source in the world.

Brazil

Brazil is the largest country in Latin America and the fifth largest in the world. It possesses a multitude of natural resources within far-flung borders that stretch from the Atlantic to the Andes and encompass the vast basin of the Amazon River. Its fast-growing population is half that of the whole continent and is the original melting pot of the hemisphere. Descendants of Indians, Africans, Portuguese and other Europeans mix and marry without regard for racial differences.

It possesses one quarter of the world's iron ore and produces large quantities of steel. Its annual automobile production totals nearly a million units. Shipbuilding, petrochemicals, and electrical and mechanical equipment are other growth sectors. Its great rivers give Brazil enormous hydroelectric potential, but realization is slow because of the remoteness of dam sites and the difficulties of development.

Despite the country's industrial potential, about a third of all Brazilians till the land, and agriculture accounts for 40 percent of the country's exports. Everyone associates coffee with Brazil. During the early part of the 20th century, Brazil largely supplied the world coffee market. But overproduction brought about a disastrous glut. Brazil is still a major supplier of the world's coffee, but sugar, fruits, soybeans, cotton and meat share the export field. Minerals exported include copper, nickel, bauxite and manganese, as well as iron ore.

Brazil's growth is concentrated in its cities. The new (1960) capital city of Brasilia, for example, was created almost overnight in the Brazilian highlands and is a symbol of Brazil's faith in its own future. South of Rio de Janeiro lies the phenomenon of São Paulo, the largest city in South America, with over 15 million people. São Paulo is the heart of Brazil's industrial power. Rio de Janeiro remains the show place of the country. Far to the west, 1,000 miles up the Amazon, the old rubber boom town of Manaus is experiencing a vigorous expansion as skyscrapers rise above the riverside forest.

Chronic inflation has become a way of life. To Brazilians, money is something to be consumed, like bread — not invested: A loan today is sensible only if it can be repaid much more cheaply tomorrow. The inflation rate goes up and down. Recently, a regime of relative austerity has kept it manageable, without seriously undermining either growth or credit. But inflation appears to be a permanent economic condition.

Much of Brazil's potential for industrial development is tied into the international controversy concerning the rapid destruction of the Amazon rain forest. The Amazon rain forest, which covers nearly two-thirds of Brazil, is rich in iron ore, aluminum, copper and other metals. Thousands of acres of Amazon forest are destroyed each day — mostly to burn trees to provide charcoal for the processing of pig-iron.

Ranchers, timber companies, gold miners and land-hungry settlers, encouraged by government incentives to develop the land of the Amazon forest, also contribute to the destruction.

Farming and grazing quickly deplete the nutrients in the forest soil, rendering the land useless and forcing settlers and ranchers to move on to new areas. In the process of industrial development, Indian tribes who inhabit the rain forest may become extinct, along with thousands of animal and plant species.

International organizations concerned with the dangers of the disappearing rain forests have warned Brazilian officials that continued development without precautions might have serious ecological consequences.

From 1964 to 1985, Brazil was ruled by a military regime which presided over the country's spectacular economic expansion. José Sarney headed the first civilian government in 21 years and soon introduced direct voting in future elections, land reforms and a new economic policy. His anti-inflation program, known as the Cruzado Plan, was initially successful. However, government programs failed and the economy plunged into crisis by 1987. Brazil was forced to declare a moratorium on repayment of its foreign debts, and trade declined. A new constitution was adopted in 1988 which should bring greater long-term political stability, but Brazil is a country still beset by social and economic difficulties.

The Guyanas

The Guyanas are situated on the northeast coast of the South American continent. They were colonized by non-Latins. In language, customs and ethnic composition, they have more in common with the non-Latin part of the Caribbean than with the rest of Latin America.

The territory was divided into colonies by three northern European powers — Britain, France and Holland — and is cut off from Brazil and Venezuela, its two neighbors, by the natural barriers of highlands and rivers.

The most striking characteristic of the Guyanas is its population mixture. The people of the Guyanas, though numbering little more than a million, are primarily Asian: East Indian, Indonesian and Chinese. They are the descendants of laborers imported to work the sugar and rice plantations at the end of the 18th century. A black African minority is composed of former slaves and a sprinkling of indigenous Indians. Whites, or Creoles, are few in number. French, Dutch and English are the official languages. Virtually no Spanish or Portuguese is spoken.

Guyana

This country was formerly British Guyana. British troops intervened in the 1950s to prevent establishment of a left-wing government under Cheddi Jagan. In 1970 Guyana received its independence. Rice and sugar cane are the major crops, cultivated in the coastal plains around the capital, Georgetown. Some valuable mineral deposits exist in the interior, but they are remote and little exploited. Guyana condemned the U.S. military intervention in Grenada and became politically isolated within the hemisphere. Since 1988 relations between the two nations have improved.

Surinam

Dutch Guyana took the name of Surinam when it gained independence in 1975. It is considerably smaller in size than Guyana, which lies to the northeast, but it is important as one of the world's major producers of bauxite. Bauxite exports total about 2 million tons a year and account for virtually all of Surinam's foreign income. The United States is the largest customer for this ore, as well as for finished aluminum.

The Surinam economy has suffered greatly from a prolonged war between the government and guerrilla forces. Guerrillas have frequently attacked army posts and state-owned industries. Bauxite production has fallen dramatically in the last few years — about 60 percent since the early 1980s.

French Guiana

French Guiana has remained part of France, specifically a department of the Metropole, and is the only foreign territory remaining on the South American continent. Its famous penal colony, Devil's Island, was closed in the 1940s. The country depends on its exports of timber, shrimp and hides. The population resides almost exclusively in Cayenne. For some years the French government has been operating a rocket-launching site in French Guiana as part of its space program.

The influence of drugs in Latin America

With few exceptions, the nations of Central and South America have been greatly affected by the cultivation and export of illicit drugs. Drugs cultivated in Bolivia and Peru are sent to Colombia for processing and exported through extensive transportation networks to the United States and other nations where drug abuse is rampant. Money received through the sale of drugs passes through Panama, Nicaragua, Ecuador and other nations where it is transferred through so many bank accounts that it is impossible to trace. In many of these nations, the leaders and military are actively involved in drug-trafficking and money-laundering schemes, and many other officials have been paid to protect the traffickers' interests. Drug enforcement agents, journalists, politicians and others who openly oppose drug-trafficking are frequently hunted and killed.

The traffickers have banded together in groups, known as *cartels,* that have wielded tremendous power — a power that rivals or often exceeds the power of the ruling government. They have their own armies that terrorize anyone who opposes them. So-called narco-terrorism has invaded every aspect of life in these nations. Political candidates are murdered, elected officials corrupted and newspaper offices bombed. In an attempt to quash the powerful Medellín cartel, the government of Colombia has practically declared war on its own citizens.

Many of these nations are so poor that the drug trade is their biggest business. It is difficult for poor farmers and underpaid police to resist the cartels.

The drug trade is truly an international enterprise and undermines the economies of many nations. It is untaxed, unregulated and operating outside the confines of legitimate business. It is often described as the number-one problem of the Americas.

Latin American debt

In the early 1970s, OPEC nations raised the price of oil. Latin American economies were affected by this increase because it raised prices on energy and all oil-based products. In the 1980s, oil prices decreased, and a world-wide recession occurred. These nations had to borrow great amounts of money during the energy crisis of the '70s and had to pay high interest on the loans in the '80s. Prices for raw materials, which many developing countries export, fell an average of 40 percent. Some development investors panicked and withdrew capital. By 1988, capital flight from Latin America alone totaled $250 billion.

Some developing countries defaulted on their loans from international agencies and governments. Lenders retaliated by demanding that developing governments reduce spending in order to pay at least the interest on their loans.

With poverty already a way of life for many people in the poor countries, austerity measures, such as reducing food subsidies, led to declining living standards and rising political instability. By 1988, Third World debt had risen to $1.3 trillion. Eight of the world's 13 leading debtor nations were in Latin America. The payments of money from poor countries to rich countries far exceeded the money going from rich countries to poor countries, because interest and principal payments on debt were greater than development aid.

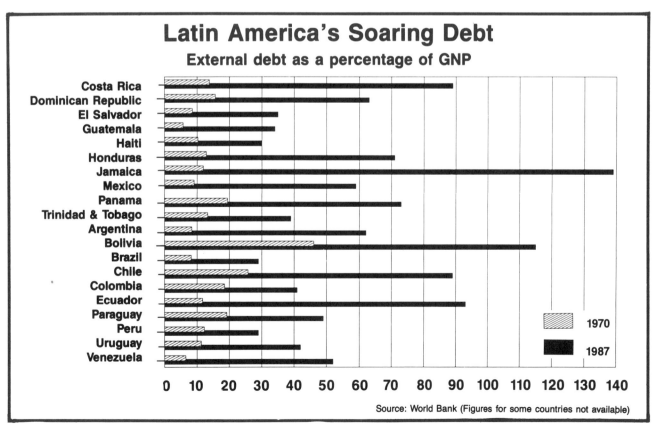

Latin America's Soaring Debt

External debt as a percentage of GNP

1970 · 1987

Source: World Bank (Figures for some countries not available)

INDEX

U.N. *See* United Nations

Unemployment, 34, 75, 104

UNESCO (United Nations Education, Scientific and Cultural Organization), 60

Union of Soviet Socialist Republics. *See* Soviet Union

UNITA. *See* National Union for the Total Independence of Angola

United Arab Emirates, 129

United Kingdom, 120. *See also* Great Britain

United Nations: Charter, 56-57; human rights declarations, 100, 104; organization chart, 58; peace-keeping by, 57, 128, 131, 132; refugee policy, 67; regulatory powers, 56; "Resolution 242," 128. *See also* agencies by name

United States: alliances, 51; armaments, 115; Asia relations, 177-78; Canada relations, 5; China relations, 154-55, 163-65; Congress, 49; Cuba relations, 192-94; Europe relations, 112; foreign aid, 53-54, 112, 147, 171; foreign policy, 49, 112; immigration, 65, 66; India relations, 171; Japan relations, 158-59, 161; Latin America relations, 188, 189; military intervention by, 192, 196, 197; Pakistan relations, 174; Panama Canal, 197; Revolution (1775-1783), 184, 188; Soviet relations, 111, 112, 116, 117, 118; space program, 115; World War II, 110. *See also* Marshall Plan; NATO; SALT; Truman Doctrine

Universal Declaration of Human Rights, 100, 104

Universe, 1, 4

Upper Volta. *See* Burkina Faso

Uranium, 77, 78

Urbanization, 44-45, 64

Uruguay, 204

U.S.S.R. *See* Soviet Union

V

Venezuela, 198

Viet Cong, 175

Vietnam, Republic of, 176-77. *See also* North Vietnam; South Vietnam

Vietnamese War (1957-1975), 175-76

Versailles, Treaty of (1919), 108-09, 111

Voyager, 1-3

W

Walesa, Lech, 119

War, 66, 93-98, 171. *See also* Cold War; specific wars

Warfare: conventional, 93; history, 108. *See also* Chemical warfare

Warsaw Pact (Treaty Organization), 24, 55, 115, 118

Wastes, toxic, 88, 92

Water: pollution, 47, 88-89; resources, 81-82

Weapons. *See* Nuclear weapons

West Germany, 118, 122: economy, 114, 120; politics and government, 114

Western civilization, 107-08

Western Europe, 5, 108, 110, 112, 113, 114, 115. *See also* European Economic Community; North Atlantic Treaty Organization

Wheat, 70

Wildlife conservation, 149

Wilson, Woodrow, 103

Women, status, 64

World Bank, 42, 52, 60

World Court (International Court of Justice), 60

World Food Program, 52, 53

World Health Organization (WHO), 47, 52, 60, 149

World opinion, 51

World War I, 23, 108, 111

World War II: Asian Theatre, 154-55; 158-59, 163; Canada, 184; casualties, 109; European Theatre, 23-24, 99, 107-10; Middle East, 127; Pacific Theatre, 155

Y

Yalta Conference, 111

Yemen, 126, 129

Yom Kippur War (1973), 129

Yugoslavia, 114

Z

Zaire, 137, 148

Zambia, 143

Zanzibar. *See* Tanzania

Zero population growth, 63

Zimbabwe, 140-41

Zionism, 125